Windows Vista™

The L Line,™
The Express Line to Learning

Windows Vista™

The L Line,™
The Express Line to Learning

Michael Meskers

Wiley Publishing, Inc.

Windows Vista™: The L Line,™ The Express Line to Learning

Published by
Wiley Publishing, Inc.
111 River Street
Hoboken, NJ 07030-5774
www.wiley.com

For general information on our other products and services, please contact our Customer Care Department within the U.S. at 800-762-2974, outside the U.S. at 317-572-3993, or fax 317-572-4002.

For technical support, please visit www.wiley.com/techsupport.

Wiley also publishes its books in a variety of electronic formats. Some content that appears in print may not be available in electronic books.

Library of Congress Control Number: 2006939462

ISBN: 978-0-470-04693-7

Manufactured in the United States of America

10 9 8 7 6 5 4 3 2 1

WILEY

About the Author

Michael Meskers, a native of New York City, is Professor of Technology at the city's New School University where he has taught for ten years. In the digital age, he is an onscreen instructor for the Microsoft Excel 2007 CD-ROM series produced by Learnkey, Inc. His eclectic background as teacher, lecturer, linguist, and well-traveled student (he has worked and studied for significant periods in four countries) brings a unique global sensibility to this tutorial on the latest in digital technology — which is itself global. His many years of experience as a professional producer of management seminars and as an Executive Coach help managers realize their potentials, giving this instructive volume a solid base.

Mr. Meskers has undergraduate and graduate degrees in Russian, French, linguistics, and psychology. His most recent literary work was the translation of Randy Gage's *How to Build a Multi-Level Money Machine* into Spanish. He holds certifications in Management and Seminar Facilitation and is a member of the National Speakers Association.

Publisher's Acknowledgments

Acquisitions, Editorial, and Media Development

Senior Project Editor
Paul Levesque

Senior Acquisitions Editor
Steve Hayes

Senior Copy Editor
Teresa Artman

Technical Editor
Lee Musick

Editorial Managers
Leah Cameron, Kevin Kirschner

Media Development Specialists
Angela Denny, Kate Jenkins,
Steven Kudirka, Kit Malone

Media Development Coordinator
Laura Atkinson

Media Project Supervisor
Laura Moss

Media Development Manager
Laura VanWinkle

Editorial Assistant
Amanda Foxworth

Senior Editorial Assistant
Cherie Case

Composition Services

Project Coordinator
Adrienne Martinez

Layout and Graphics
Elizabeth Brooks, Denny Hager,
Heather Ryan, Ron Terry, Erin Zeltner

Proofreaders
Laura Bowman, John Greenough,
Robert Springer, Brian H. Walls

Indexer
Lynzee Elze

Anniversary Logo Design
Richard Pacifico

Publishing and Editorial for General User Technology

Richard Swadley, *Vice President and Executive Group Publisher*

Andy Cummings, *Vice President and Publisher*

Mary Bednarek, *Executive Acquisitions Director*

Mary C. Corder, *Editorial Director*

Composition Services

Gerry Fahey, *Vice President of Production Services*

Debbie Stailey, *Director of Composition Services*

Author's Acknowledgments

I know that many books appear on the scene as the result of a sole author's hard work and perseverance. Some books require that and more, and are rather the result of a team of dedicated people involved in the process, from beginning to end.

In no special order, although they are all special people: Robert Blinken, Peter J. Brennan, Matthew Carnicelli, David Gonzalez, Marylou Long, John Moss, Anna Plitsas, and Olivia Whiteman.

The editorial staff — including Mary Bednarek, Steve Hayes, and Paul Levesque at Wiley — made this project a reality with an exceptional amount of focus and diligence. I also want to thank Lee Musick and Teresa Artman who labored intensively to keep the manuscript clean and on point.

Everything I learned about computers I DID NOT learn in kindergarten. For that matter, I learned nothing about them in school. It was at work, as an adult in the early 1980s, that I first laid my hands on a computer. It wasn't love at first sight. It was a challenge at first sight. And wouldn't you just guess it — I became a teacher of computer skills and have been one for some 20 years now. But I still call myself a non-geek geek.

Dedication

I want to thank my parents whose love and support gave me both life and a jump-start. I especially want to thank my grandfather, the late Hon. Louis Pagnucco, who served as the most powerful role model that a young person can have, and who lives on inside my heart as an example of true leadership, generosity of spirit, and love.

My heartfelt thanks.

—Michael Meskers
December 2006

Contents at a Glance

Contents

Preface

From the Publisher

Welcome to *Windows Vista: The L Line, The Express Line to Learning.*

This book is one in a new tutorial series from Wiley Publishing created for independent learners, students, and teachers. Whether you are learning (or teaching) in a classroom setting or gaining new skills while you explore Windows Vista for fun, this book is for you. As rigorous and replete as any college course or seminar, *Windows Vista: The L Line* offers instruction for developing your Windows skill set — specifically, the skills that everyone needs, from casual Windows users to company tech support gurus.

As do all titles in *The L Line: The Express Line to Learning* series, this book's design embraces the metaphor of learning as a journey — a trip on a railway system — with navigational tools and real-world stops along the way. The destination, of course, is mastery of Microsoft's new operating system, Windows Vista.

From the Author

A new look. A new feel. A new operating system — Windows Vista!

With Windows Vista, Microsoft makes a quantum jump from earlier versions of its graphical interface operating systems. Those, through Windows XP, featured a recognizable and utilitarian interface that was the boundary between the operator using mouse and keyboard or other device and the internal workings of the computer. The graphics were adequate; the security often less so. And the improvements from one version to the next were evolutionary rather than revolutionary.

Windows Vista represents a revolutionary change. For starters, it doesn't look like any previous version of Windows. Vista's graphics are highly interactive, offering the user many more ways to access, process, and keep track of information and processes. A fundamental change at the very core of the operating system (combined with an all-out effort to wall off security threats and even protect the system from its own users) makes this the most secure Windows operating system by far.

Vista is more flexible, more customizable and more secure than ever.

- If greater security and vibrant graphics are important to you, Windows Vista is made for you.

- If greater power and performance are what you are looking for (and who isn't?), Vista's new power plans and performance boosts give you more control and satisfaction than ever before in Windows.

- If you are familiar with previous versions of Windows, Vista allows you to use Classic modes that emulate features of earlier versions, thereby easing your transition to Vista, even as you learn to use its many new features and personalization options.

- If you are an Apple Macintosh user and want to run Windows Vista on your new, Intel-based machine, you will notice many similarities between the operating systems. These go beyond the colors of the dialog boxes and their transparent glass and rounded edges. You will especially note Vista's enhanced emphasis on security and customization and how much faster your programs and applications launch.

- Previous versions of Windows often needed an arsenal of third-party software to perform many tasks that Windows needed but could not handle itself. Many of those tasks are now built into Windows Vista. Some of these tools are also fun to use, being more entertainment than utility.

So welcome to the Windows Vista voyage of exploration!

Can Anyone Learn the Features of Windows Vista?

Of course! Mastering the ins and outs of a new operating system is an important journey — indeed, almost an essential one. Computer literacy is hardly an option in today's world where we rely more and more on our own computers for an ever-expanding range of tasks.

The Windows Vista learning curve is well marked with waypoints every step of the way. Microsoft has greatly enhanced its Help features to include links that immediately launch the tools you need as well as offering interactive demonstrations. Important pop-up alerts are now in standard language, avoiding much geek-speak.

This book takes you well beyond Vista's extensive help messages and intuitive cascading forms of option screens, windows, panes and pop-ups. Although styled as a classroom-in-a-book, this work was also prepared with a broader range of Windows users in mind. Whether you are in or outside a classroom, you can look up any topic or subtopic in the index, turn to the relevant section, and jump right into the steps to accomplish the needed task. The tips you'll find throughout the book will help you move forward even faster. And the practice exercises and exam questions will reinforce your learning. Several-hundred screen captures that plainly show what words cannot also help guide you all along the way.

How Do You Get Started in Windows Vista?

Start at the beginning!

- **Determine your hardware requirements.** The first chapter tells you what hardware and parameters you need at each level of Vista (five levels, each making increasingly heavy demands on your system) and tells you how to install Vista.

- **Get familiar with the brand new Windows Vista Desktop.** Learning all the visual options of Aero is just the beginning (assuming that your system's hardware will support the Aero Glass function). Then learn how you can tailor the desktop to your unique needs.

- **Master the new tools of Internet Explorer 7.** The World Wide Web is much more than simply about browsing. You'll learn how to use this new browser's built-in features to get where and what you want faster and more efficiently than was ever possible before. The browser, for example, is the key to Microsoft's new XML (eXtensible Markup Language) specification that allows you to generate unalterable documents and apply permissions to those documents.

- **Set up parental controls and other user controls that determine how other people access your computer.** Set levels of permissions for different users and even restrict what days and hours they may use the computer.

- **Make searching faster.** With metadata labels and other tools, classify everything on your computer to greatly speed up searches and retrieval of information stored in your machine.

- **Use conferencing.** Set up connections using the People Near Me tools so that you can hold conferences with other people in your office or beyond.

- **Run dual OSes.** Learn how to run two different operating systems on one computer in case you need time to get familiar with the newer system or have applications and data that are not compatible with the new system.

- **Use Gadgets.** Set up Windows Gadgets on your desktop that will tell you the time or how the stock market is faring; play slide shows; or monitor various programs running in the background.

- **Set up your home or office network.** This task, which could be a nightmare in earlier versions of Windows, is almost trivial in Windows Vista, provided you have the proper hardware.

What Do You Need to Know?

You don't need to know very much to run Windows Vista on your machine. The whole point of a graphical user interface (GUI) such as Windows Vista (or any other version of Windows, competing products such as Apple, and the various flavors of Linux) is to make the computer transparent to the user. To the extent that the user must become involved with the more arcane aspects of computer technology the GUI fails its primary purpose. The computer should be a tool that enables you to do more in less time and at lower cost than does any competing method, like using a typewriter to prepare documents or a calculator and paper spreadsheet to generate budgets. You don't agonize over your typewriter, nor do you expect to know exactly how it works. You just need to learn to type, and doing it with two fingers is perfectly acceptable. When the typewriter breaks, you take it to a repair shop.

Similarly with Windows Vista, you don't need to know what's going on inside your computer. You do need to know how to type (even if hunt and peck), how to use a mouse or other pointing device, how to insert and retrieve media (such as floppy disks and CDs from the appropriate drives), and how to send data to be printed to the printer. And, of course, you do need to know what all those things are on the desktop that Vista presents to you on your monitor and what happens when you click any of those items or type text and symbols into little boxes on the desktop. Teaching you that — not how fast the front-side bus is or how many RPMs your hard drive spins and why that matters — is what this book is about. Interfacing.

What Is This Book About?

It's about Windows. It's also about loads of how-to's, hot tips, and background information on why Vista is what it is and does what it does.

It's also about practice, experimenting, and having fun, even if you are only a modest gamer tempted by the occasional boredom-relieving game of Solitaire. Vista is also loaded with free tools to make work (and play) easier and more enjoyable. You learn how to use the most important features and how to get the most benefit from them.

Step into the Real World

Windows Vista is not just an incremental step but a developmental leap. Microsoft spent more time and resources developing Windows Vista than it has on any other project. Literally millions of beta testers are already familiar with it. Long before its official launch, Microsoft has provided more support than it ever did with any previous operating system version. Now that the train has already left the station and you've explored this new world of Vista, my guess is that you'll be happy to be aboard!

Some features, such as making your own DVD movies with the new Vista version of Windows Movie Maker or working with programming tools, are beyond the scope of this book. However, after mastering the lessons we cover in this classroom-in-a-book, you may want to check out the most comprehensive reference work, *Windows Vista Bible,* also a Wiley publication.

What Will You Learn?

After you finish this book, you should be able to depend on Vista as your sole operating system. It is that simple. That's the goal. Of course, you'll learn some other things along the way:

- **Desktop customization:** Colors, borders, sizes, gadgets, illustrations — set it up your way.

- **Mastering your browser's tools and tricks:** Open up tabs, cascade windows, develop secure documents, and find and retrieve information and applications worldwide.

- **Windows security:** Set permissions for users, monitor children's online activities, block unwanted content, and kill spam and phishing.

- **Searching:** You will learn about indexing so that your computer finds your documents as quickly as a search engine retrieves files from the World Wide Web.

- **Free tools and other bundled software:** You'll find Internet Explorer 7, games designed for Vista, spyware, and malware detection.

- **Connecting to the outside world:** Set up Internet connections, People Near Me, home and office networking, and e-mail.

- **Making your programs and devices work with Windows Vista:** Find drivers or updates to bring applications to Vista standards.

- **Enjoying your multimedia experience:** Enjoy interactive windows and panes, high-quality graphics, graphics, and memory power for gaming.

- **Maximizing your computer's power and performance:** Vista Update Advisor suggests updates and upgrades to existing hardware and program to meet Vista standards.

- **Keeping your system in top shape:** Available in Vista are automatic updates and system and disk management modules as well as defragmentation and disk cleaning utilities.

- **Finding that help you need:** Vita offers Help files galore, Internet searching, pop-up suggestions, intuitive activity, and option sequences.

What's in the Book?

This book has 12 chapters:

- **Installing Windows Vista:** Chapter 1 introduces you to what you need, where to begin, and what to look out for when installing Windows Vista.

- **Using the Windows Vista Desktop:** Chapter 2 covers the essentials of setting up the desktop, including the Aero Glass graphics (if supported) as well as the placement of shortcut icons, the taskbar, and Gadgets.

- **Welcome to Internet Explorer 7:** Chapter 3 discusses the new version 7 of Internet Explorer and how it can be modified, set up for security (including a phishing filter), and how to use tabbed browsing.

- **Security, Privacy, and Parental Controls in Windows Vista:** In some ways, Chapter 4 is the most important chapter, considering the escalating war of Internet security and the need to keep one's data and information private and protected from outside interference.

- **Working More Efficiently with Applications, Files, and Folders:** Chapter 5 gets to the heart of the computer's reason for being: creating shortcuts, efficient searching, indexing, file associations, and protecting documents with the new XPS file format.

- **Working with Vista's Free Tools:** Chapter 6 covers Voice Recognition, sound recording, creating notes and documents via Notepad and WordPad, the engagement calendar, image cropping, and more.

- **Connecting to the Outside World:** Chapter 7 covers e-mail, newsgroup discussions, faxing from the computer, People Near Me, the Windows Meeting Space, and setting up Vista networks.

- **Adding (And Removing) Programs and Devices with Vista:** Chapter 8 discusses installing other applications (Microsoft's and other vendors), installing peripheral devices, checking support via the Windows Vista Program Compatibility Wizard, and removing programs and devices you no longer need.

- **Working with Digital Media:** Chapter 9 covers Windows Media Player 11, managing media, creating CDs and DVDs, organizing photos in the Windows Photo Gallery, and playing games.

- **Maximizing Your Windows Power and Performance:** Chapter 10 discusses choosing performance options, using SuperFetch and ReadyBoost; setting power controls with Sleep; and scanning and defragmenting the hard drive.

Keeping Up, Backing Up, Disaster and Recovery: Chapter 11 talks about keeping up to date with Automatic Update, backing up files and system, using System Restore, and editing the Registry.

Getting Help and Support: Chapter 12 covers where to find Help (and get the most from it) as well as using online Help resources, Windows Vista Help demos, and Windows Remote assistance.

Additionally, each chapter begins with the "Stations Along the Way," which outlines at a glance the topics covered in the chapter. This element is followed by "Enter the Station," which is a list of study questions: a pretest designed to get you thinking about each chapter's content up front (and to help you study). The Express Line element directs you ahead if you're already up to speed on a particular chapter's subject.

At the end of each chapter are a couple of important elements:

Street Jargon: This glossary lists all the important terms introduced in the chapter.

Practice Exam: This is your last stop before exiting a chapter is the Practice Exam, which will test you on the concepts you learn in each chapter. All answers can be found at the back of this book.

Icons Used in the Book

You'll find several handy icons along the way:

Information Kiosk

These icons point out tips on efficient use of Windows features and functions or additional explanations of concepts discussed in the regular text.

Transfer

These icons refer you to other places in the book for more information on a particular subject.

Watch Your Step

These icons point out potential pitfalls you might encounter as you journey through Windows Vista — and advise caution when necessary.

Step into the Real World

These sidebars discuss problems or issues you might run into out in the real world — or additional considerations for you to mull over as you explore Windows Vista.

Using the Web Site

As a teacher for my entire adult life, my first wish is that you learn a lot from working with this book. But as much as learning is what it's all about, I want the experience to be truly enjoyable for you. If it is, you will not only learn and retain what you learn, but you will also be motivated to actually use your acquired knowledge. And there's more still. The companion Web site for this book — found at www.wiley.com/go/thelline — has even more ways of testing (and reinforcing) your newfound knowledge. With practice, plus some good old-fashioned trial and error, you can attain mastery of this new operating system. And you'll probably agree that it was worth the effort.

For Instructors and Students

Windows Vista: The L Line has a rich set of supplemental resources for students and instructors. **Instructors** can find a test bank, PowerPoint presentations with course and book outlines, and instructor's manual and sample syllabi online. Please visit http://he-cda.wiley.com/WileyCDA/Section/id-100213.html for access to these resources.

For students and independent learners, resources such as chapter outlines and sample test questions, can be found at www.wiley.com/go/thelline.

1

Installing Windows Vista

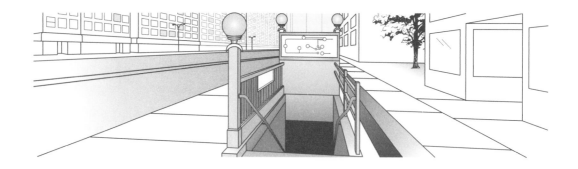

 # Enter the Station

Questions

1. What are the hardware requirements needed to install Vista?

2. What kind of guidance is there for installing a new operating system?

3. How do you get your machine ready to install Vista?

4. What are the five different versions of Windows Vista?

5. How do you choose the right version of Vista?

6. What if I have an older PC?

7. How much RAM do you need to run Vista?

8. Do you need a special video card to use Vista?

The Express Line

If Windows Vista has already been installed on your computer, move on to Chapter 2.

Windows Vista might well be the personal computer's first gigabyte application. Unlike other consumer-based applications that still arrive on a CD distribution (capacity about 650 megabytes [MB]), Vista arrives on a DVD (capacity about 4.7 gigabytes [GB], which is approximately seven times that of a CD). The reason Vista now arrives on a DVD instead of a CD is twofold. First, Vista's installation DVD includes all five versions of Microsoft's new operating system. The second, more significant, reason is that Vista's new visually enhanced applications require much more space to run and install than previous editions of Windows. In other words, Vista's new graphics features and computing capabilities take up more memory space, or RAM, to run properly.

The downside to this increase in system requirements is that older computers might not have enough free space on their hard drives to run Vista. If they do happen to contain enough memory to run Microsoft's new operating system, they might not have enough space left to run other third-party applications, or they might experience slower processing times when running Vista and additional third-party applications. Vista might also require that the drivers for some peripherals — including Web cameras and Internet network adapters that worked with earlier versions of Windows — be updated, or they might no longer be compatible with this version of Windows, in which case you must acquire (or download) new versions of these tools.

Vista requires an order of magnitude more of everything to run properly — RAM, CPU speed, graphics adapter, even network adapter. However, later I discuss the Vista Upgrade Advisor, which will tell you immediately whether your existing system can run Vista and if so at what level.

However, Microsoft is banking that the overall user experience of Windows Vista provides you with enough positive benefits to either purchase a new computer with Vista preinstalled or upgrade your current computer to include Vista. The new layout and functionality of Windows Vista is designed to let you find, organize, and view computer files in an easier, more intuitive, manner. This additional functionality is meant to streamline your overall computing experience. Vista's improved security, digital entertainment features, and productivity tools are all incentives meant to persuade you to invest your time (and money) into using Vista.

Windows Vista is by far the most complex and the most multifunctional version of Windows that Microsoft has ever produced. It needs lots of breathing room as well as a whole lot more sheer graphical and computing power in terms of CPU speed, main memory, and graphics adapter memory. However, after you are exposed to the bright and flashy colors of Vista, previous versions of Windows pale in comparison.

Evaluating Your System Requirements

Windows Vista has certain requirements that your computer must meet or exceed if the program is to run well — or even run at all. Microsoft has created two basic classifications for computers that are capable of running Windows Vista — Vista Capable PCs and Vista Premium PCs. The first grouping, Vista Capable, describes computers that offer only the bare minimum requirements for running Microsoft's new operating system. If you own or purchase a Vista Capable PC, you can run Vista successfully, but you might not get the full benefit of this new visually enhanced version of Windows. Vista Premium PCs, on the other hand, provide you with all the advanced Vista features. Which type of PC you use depends on the activities you are going to perform with your computer.

Choosing between a Vista Capable or Vista Premium PC

No matter what computer you decide on, Windows recommends a minimum size hard drive of 40GB with at least 15GB of free space, not only to accommodate the some 3,000 files that Vista installs but also to give the program breathing room as it writes temporary files and carries out housekeeping duties and other functions.

According to Microsoft, a Windows Vista Capable PC must have

- A fast processor, with a minimum of 800 megahertz (MHz)
- At least 512MB of system memory
- A DirectX 9-capable graphics adapter

Because Vista comes on a DVD, even the lowest level must have a drive that can at least read DVDs if not burn them. As for HD capacity, as noted, 40GB is considered minimum (it will run on less), but no optimum size is recommended. Vista is all about networking, so an Internet connection is also *de rigueur,* although it will run without one.

Transfer

To determine whether your computer meets these basic Vista requirements, skip ahead to the "Checking upgrade compatibility" section of this chapter.

If your computer is configured according to these standards, it should bear the Windows Vista Capable logo. A Windows Vista Capable PC runs the core functions of Windows Vista but does not support its more advanced features, such as enhanced

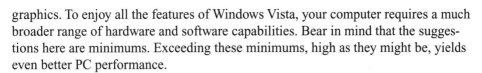

graphics. To enjoy all the features of Windows Vista, your computer requires a much broader range of hardware and software capabilities. Bear in mind that the suggestions here are minimums. Exceeding these minimums, high as they might be, yields even better PC performance.

The requirements for Vista Premium PCs are

- A 1 gigahertz (GHz) 32-bit (x86) or 64-bit (x64) processor
- 1GB of system memory
- Support for DirectX 9 graphics with a WDDM (Windows Vista Display Driver), at least 128MB of graphics memory, Pixel Shader 2.0, and 32 bits per pixel
- At least 40GB of hard drive capacity with 15GB of free space
- DVD-ROM drive (or a CD-ROM drive capable of reading DVDs)
- Audio capability
- Internet access

If your computer is configured as a Vista Premium PC, it should bear the Windows Vista Premium logo.

 Transfer

To determine whether your computer meets the Premium Vista requirements, skip ahead to the "Checking upgrade compatibility" section of this chapter.

Information Kiosk

Now that Windows Vista ships on a DVD, your computer must have at the very least a CD drive that can read DVDs, if not write (or burn) them.

Because downloading a 3GB file over a dialup telephone connection is not practical, you should only attempt to download Vista from Microsoft's Web site if you have a high-speed Internet connection, such as DSL or cable modem.

Checking your processor speed

Having a fast processor enables your PC to perform requested tasks quickly and efficiently. If you do not have a powerful processor, your computer can be sluggish during moments of activity. This is especially true with Vista.

Vista's highly visual nature requires a much quicker processor than most other operating systems. If your processor is not up to Vista's standards, you are going to experience prolonged moments of waiting while your computer loads images from selected menus and screens.

If you already have an earlier version of Windows installed on your computer and you want to determine the speed of your processor, you can find this data by accessing your PC's Control Panel:

1. **Click the Start button.**

The Start Menu appears onscreen.

2. **Select Control Panel.**

The Control Panel dialog box appears.

3. **Select System and Maintenance.**

The System and Maintenance dialog box replaces the Control Panel screen.

4. **Choose System.**

The System window appears, as shown in Figure 1-1. This window reveals the name and speed of your processor as well as its RAM limitations.

Information Kiosk

32-bit or 64-bit? Windows Vista ships in two data-path versions: 32-bit (x86) and 64-bit (x64). The numbers in parentheses refer to the CPU chip architecture. The x86 chip goes all the way back to 1978 when the original processor chips ran some of the earliest PCs. Subsequent chips up to the Pentium used similar architectures and were designated 80386, 80486, and so on — thus, the x86. (The Pentium was initially dubbed the 80586.) The x64 simply means 64 bits.

The 32- or 64-bits refers to the size of data chunks, or words, a computer can handle without splitting them into smaller chunks. Thus, all other factors being equal, a 64-bit machine may be faster than a 32-bit one, but not necessarily. The largest benefit flowing from 64-bit architecture is the chip's ability to address virtually unlimited system memory. A 32-bit machine is limited to 4GB (2^{32}) of RAM. At one point, that was more than enough memory. However, today's high-performance machines running enormous applications and databases are bumping against that ceiling. The 64-bit machine raises the ceiling to 2^{64} bytes, or about four billion times as much RAM as the 32-bit chips.

Average users, even high-intensity business users, have little need for the 64-bit version unless their data processing needs are such that they must have more than 4GB of system memory. In any case, much of the software and drivers that could benefit from the larger data chunk size have not yet been written.

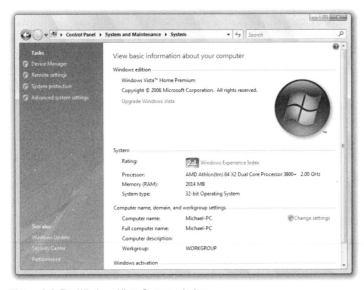

Figure 1-1: The Windows Vista System window.

Determining how much RAM is enough

The amount of random access memory *(RAM)* your Windows Vista PC has installed significantly affects the real-world performance of your computer. Therefore, if you plan to use your PC for *multitasking* (perhaps you want to listen to music online, check your e-mail, and view family photos all at the same time), you should consider adding more RAM to your computer. Installing additional RAM is also a good idea if you plan to access large documents or files for work-related projects. Memory-hungry applications, such as image editing software like Photoshop or AutoCAD, also slow your computer to a crawl when running on a PC with insufficient RAM. Therefore, you need to take the types of applications you plan to use on a regular basis into consideration when determining how much RAM to include on your Vista PC.

The following list outlines the suggested RAM requirements for basic PC usage:

 **256MB:** This is the bare minimum. With less than this amount, Windows Vista does not run. This is an acceptable amount of RAM if you plan to use your PC only for word processing, e-mail, or playing the occasional video clip — and even then, performance can suffer.

 **512MB:** A real-world bottom level for most general users. Power users, however, might not find this level of RAM sufficient for their purposes. For example, opening programs such as Photoshop, using e-mail, and running simultaneous downloads can cause your machine to run slowly at this level of RAM.

 **1GB RAM:** The recommended minimum level of RAM if you do a lot of multitasking and want to prevent application slowdowns or hang-ups.

 **1.5GB RAM or more:** Allows you to open and actively use a variety of programs simultaneously, without causing much RAM-related slowdown in your computer's performance. This is the optimal setting for multitasking PC users.

These factors (your hardware and how much RAM you have installed) are essential for the healthy operation of Windows Vista. These considerations carry a much higher significance than for any of Windows' predecessors.

To determine how much RAM your PC has, follow these steps:

1. **Click the Start button.**

2. **Select Control Panel.**

The Control Panel dialog box appears.

3. **Select Performance and Maintenance.**

The Performance and Maintenance dialog box replaces the Control Panel screen.

4. **Choose System.**

The System Properties pop-up box appears.

5. **Click the General tab.**

The Computer section of this tab reveals your PC's RAM limitations as well as the name and speed of your processor.

Locating your video card information

Ensuring that you have a video card capable of handling whatever chores Vista throws its way is also essential to making Vista run properly. Video cards that do not meet the minimum system requirements (usually the older video cards) do not support the glassy transparency effects of Vista Aero, nor can you see the 3-D tab flipping or the pop-up images of your Windows Vista tabs if you do not have an appropriate video card. In other words, not having a powerful video card limits the graphics capabilities of Windows Vista.

Information Kiosk

Few people are aware that the transparency effects did exist in Windows XP. It could be enabled, but again, with preconditions similar to those of Windows Vista; a latest card with the latest XP driver and 512MB on-board RAM.

To determine whether your video card is capable of displaying all the advanced features of Windows Vista, follow these steps:

1. **Click the Start button then select Control Panel from the menu that appears.**

2. **Select Appearance and Personalization.**

   The Appearance and Themes window replaces the Control Panel screen.

3. **Choose Personalization.**

   The Personalize Appearance and Sounds window appears.

4. **From this window, select the Display Settings option.**

   The Display Settings dialog box appears.

5. **Select the Advanced Settings tab from the Display Settings menu.**

   This tab contains information about your screen resolution and color quality.

6. **Click the Advanced button.**

   A window with several tabs all relating to your graphics card appears.

   This box contains several different tabs, including Adapter, Monitor, Troubleshoot, and Color Management. The last tab is most likely your graphics tab. This is where you can find information concerning your PCs current video card.

7. **Click the Properties button.**

   The Properties window for your card appears, as shown in Figure 1-2.

   If your system does not include a Graphics or Video tab, it might be listed according to the name of the third-party application. If need be, search through all remaining tabs to locate your current video card information. It should be listed under the System Information section of the appropriate tab. Here you can locate the name of your processor as well.

If your video card is less than the suggested minimum requirements, you might have difficulty running the power-saving mode know as "Sleep." In addition, you might encounter problems with Windows Media Player when viewing your video files, and you might not be able to play video games enhanced with intense, dynamic effects. Fortunately, updating your video card driver can solve most of these problems. You could also choose to invest in a brand-new video card; they typically cost less than $50 after rebates.

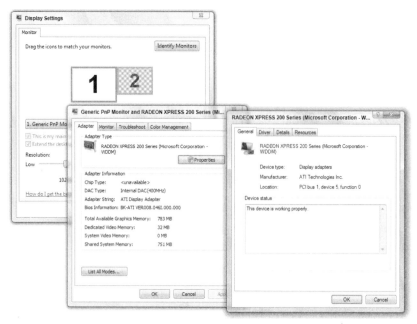

Figure 1-2: The Properties window for the graphics/video card installed on your machine.

Transfer

Refer to Chapter 8 for more information on how to update your existing video driver.

Choosing the right version of Vista

To create personalized Vista packages for several different types of customers, Microsoft offers five versions (or editions) of Vista. Each of these versions provides users with different features and capabilities:

- **Windows Vista Home Basic:** For those seeking better security and reliability, with basic computing needs — word processing and simple communications (e-mail), for example. The suggested retail price for the Home Basic version is $199 (or $99.95 if upgrading from a previous edition of Windows).

- **Windows Vista Home Premium:** Offers more versatility than the Basic edition, including entertainment functions (such as music and video, Web surfing, and some gaming) as well as basic financial accounting and communication capabilities. The suggested retail price for the Home Premium edition is $239 (or $159 if upgrading from a previous version of Windows).

- **Windows Vista Business:** Aimed primarily toward small or home-based business users. Features enhanced security, a better user interface, and robust communications capabilities. The suggested retail price for a full version of this edition is $299 (or $199 if you are upgrading from a previous version).

- **Windows Vista Enterprise:** For large global organizations with complex information technology (IT) requirements. Offers lower IT costs while providing several layers of security. The Vista Enterprise edition is available only to Microsoft Volume License customers.

- **Windows Vista Ultimate:** Combines all the best business features and security enhancements as well as top-level home entertainment capabilities, including the most demanding gaming scenarios. The suggested retail price for the Ultimate edition of Vista is $399 (or $259 if you are upgrading from a previous edition of Microsoft's operation system).

Information Kiosk

For an Information Technology manager with multiple machines to upgrade, the Vista upgrade can save a lot of time and thus money compared to installing previous versions. Properly done, a Vista installation is a set-it-and-forget-it operation that does not require constant human attendance and intervention.

It doesn't matter whether you are running XP Home or XP Pro, or Windows 3.1 for that matter; the installation process for Vista just moves the older OS out of the way into a temporary directory and then proceeds as if the old one did not exist. As stated elsewhere, every Vista installation is essentially a clean one.

Which edition of Vista you choose depends upon which activities you plan to use most often. If you only need the most basic computing features, you might want to choose Windows Vista Basic. If you plan to engage in a number of advanced gaming or other home entertainment activities, the Ultimate edition might be the better way to go. Or, to achieve a level somewhere in between the Basic and Ultimate extremes, perhaps the Home Premium edition best suits your needs.

Information Kiosk

A sixth version of Windows Vista — Window Starter 2007 — is scheduled to be released in countries with emerging PC markets. Available in multilingual editions, it features limited features and less-restricted hardware requirements. As of the printing of this book, the Starter edition is not slated to be marketed in the U.S. For more information, go to www.microsoft.com and type **"Vista Starter 2007"** into the Search box.

Installing Vista

When Vista becomes readily available as a preinstalled operating system on new computers, you might not need to concern yourself with the installation process for this operating system. You might, instead, be able to buy a computer with the appropriate level of Vista preinstalled by an *OEM* (Original Equipment Manufacturer). However, even if you do initially buy a computer with one of the lower levels of Vista already installed, you might decide to upgrade both machine and software at some future time. And, if the unthinkable should happen and a lightening strike utterly corrupts your operating system, you might need to know how to reinstall Vista from scratch even though you bought it as an OEM installation.

Information Kiosk

The installation DVD includes an unlock key that allows you to install the desired version of Vista on your computer. If you later wish to upgrade your operating system to another edition of Vista, you can buy an upgrade key and install the additional features, provided that your PC supports the higher levels of the new edition.

Determining your installation options

You have several different options to choose from when installing Vista. For example, you can upgrade your current desktop or laptop to Vista from a previous version of Windows, or you can choose to purchase a brand-new PC with Vista capabilities. You also have the option to install Vista on your current PC while keeping a version of your previous Windows system on your computer. A brief description of each of these scenarios is listed here:

- **Installing Vista on a brand-new laptop or desktop that bears the Windows Vista Capable or Windows Vista Premium logo:** (See the "Evaluating Your Systems Requirements" section earlier in this chapter to compare the Vista Capable and Premium requirements.) This computer most likely has an OEM version of Windows XP installed as well as other OEM programs such as Microsoft Office and Microsoft Word, among others. This computer comes with a stack of installation CDs corresponding to the operating system and other programs already installed. This computer probably does not have any data files on it yet.

- **Installing Vista on an existing computer running an earlier version of Windows:** This machine is probably a couple of years old and has obsolete drivers as well as some peripherals that are not quite Vista-ready. It also has your cherished settings for your operating system and every installed application as well as all the data files you have generated over the last few years.

Installing Windows Vista on an existing machine while also keeping the current operating system: This scenario is a *dual boot* option. When two operating systems are on the same machine, you are prompted when you start the computer to choose one. Setting up a dual boot machine can be complex and requires great care. A wrong step during installation, and your machine might become unusable. The benefit of using a dual boot system is that it allows you to run the two systems side by side. This capability allows you to become familiar with Windows Vista before you fully commit to it. It also permits you to continue using software and hardware that does not run or runs poorly under Vista. As you upgrade both hardware and software, you can migrate to Vista so that eventually you are running only Vista and can then remove the earlier version of Windows.

Watch Your Step

If you encounter problems during the Vista installation on a brand-new machine, nothing is lost. You just start over and do it right the next time. If you make an error with your old machine, though, you are in danger of losing all or much of the data you have painfully assembled over the years. To safeguard your existing files from this risk, be sure to make backups of all your data — correspondence, spreadsheets, movies, music, photos, and so on, as well as backups of installation copies or disks for all your programs currently on the computer. (See the "Preparing your computer for installation" section later in this chapter for instructions on how to back up your existing files.)

Checking upgrade compatibility

Assuming that you already have a computer running an earlier version of Windows and that you wish to upgrade to Windows Vista, the first thing you need to know before you even buy your copy of Vista is whether your computer can support Microsoft's new operating system. Fortunately, Microsoft has created a Web site dedicated to this purpose:

```
http://www.microsoft.com/windowsvista/getready/upgradeadvisor/default.mspx
```

This link leads you directly to the Windows Vista *Upgrade Advisor,* which is a small downloadable application that scans your computer and tells you to what degree your existing hardware and software meets or exceeds the minimum requirements to run Windows Vista. (See Figure 1-3.)

Information Kiosk

The Windows Vista Upgrade Advisor also gives you guidance with regard to steps you can take to ensure the smooth operation of your operating system. I highly recommended that you run the Upgrade Advisor before you install Windows Vista. In fact, you can and should run the Advisor before you even buy Windows Vista.

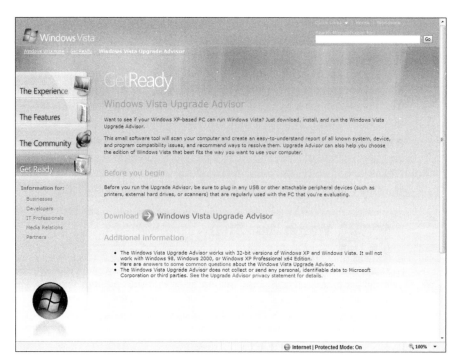

Figure 1-3: Download the Vista Upgrade Advisor application from Microsoft's Get Ready Web page.

The Upgrade Advisor scans your entire system, examining your processor, system memory, graphics adapter, printers, and all other peripherals such as Web cams, TV capture devices, network adapters, sound cards, and so on to determine whether each device meets Vista standards — and, if so, which edition of Vista will run best on your machine. If any part of your system does not meet the minimum standards, the Advisor tells you which devices are deficient and what you can do to remedy the deficiencies. The remedy might be as simple as replacing a driver with a newer Vista-tailored one or as complex (and potentially costly) as replacing your computer or various parts of your system including a graphics card, a sound card, or even your network adapter. The Advisor might also tell you that some of your installed software will not run properly after you install Vista. To remedy these situations, you might need to acquire upgraded software from the vendor or choose different software from another vendor.

To use Microsoft's Advisor evaluation tool

1. **Point your browser to the following Web page:**

www.microsoft.com/windowsvista/getready/upgradeadvisor/default.mspx

The Windows Vista Get Ready page appears. (Refer to Figure 1-3.)

2. Click the Windows Vista Upgrade Advisor download link.

A Security Warning box appears, asking whether you want to run or save this program.

3. Select Run.

You are prompted with an additional Internet Explorer Security Warning dialog box, asking whether you want to run this software.

4. Click Run.

The Advisor program is loaded to your computer.

5. If you are prompted with another Security Warning box, select Run again.

After this process is complete, the Windows Upgrade Advisor Setup Wizard appears onscreen.

6. Click Next.

A License Agreement page appears. Read through these terms.

7. Select I Agree.

A green dot appears in the I Agree radio button.

8. Click Next.

The Select Installation Folder appears. Choose where you would like to save the Advisor application on your computer.

The default folder setting is located in your PC's `C:\Program Files` drive. You can also type in the path route or use the Browse feature to change the default folder location.

9. Click Next.

The Confirmation Installation page appears.

10. Click Next.

The Upgrade Advisor software is installed on your computer. When this process is complete, you are prompted with an Installation Complete message.

11. Click Close.

This removes the Upgrade Advisor Installation page from your screen and brings up the Upgrade Advisor Welcome page, as shown in Figure 1-4.

12. Click the Start Scan link.

The Scanning System window opens, as shown in Figure 1-5.

While the program scans your system, you are invited to click the numbers at the bottom of the page to review information about several of Vista's new features. You can browse these screens while the scan continues.

Figure 1-4: The Vista Upgrade Advisor Welcome screen.

When the scan is complete, you are prompted with a Scan Complete message.

Figure 1-5: The Windows Vista Upgrade Advisor system scanner.

13. Click the See Details button.

The results of your scan are shown onscreen, as seen in Figure 1-6.

Figure 1-6: The Windows Vista Upgrade Advisor showing scanner results.

In this instance, this computer can run the Vista Ultimate edition. The machine has no obvious system problems, but you need to run further tests to determine whether your peripheral devices and installed software programs are Vista capable. If you click the right-arrow button (at the top left), you see the Device Details section of the Advisor Report, as shown in Figure 1-7.

Here are the four tabs underneath the heading Report Details: Windows Vista Ultimate. The first tab — System — describes which version of Vista you can run on your computer. The second tab — Devices — contains information about your PC's peripheral devices. The third tab — Programs — outlines any issues that Vista might encounter with regards to the software loaded on your computer. The fourth tab — Task List — provides you with a list of suggested remedies. Following the procedures included in this list can make it possible for you to install Vista on your PC.

Information Kiosk

You can check your PC against four different versions of Vista: Home Basic, Home Premium, Business, and Ultimate. To do so, simply click the name of the edition you wish to check (located to the left of the Upgrade Advisor results page), and then proceed through the various tabs to determine the Vista capabilities of your computer.

Figure 1-7: The Windows Vista Upgrade Advisor showing device details.

When reviewing these results, pay careful attention to the Caution icons, which bear a yellow triangle with a black exclamation point. These symbols let you know whether a potential problem exists between your system and Vista.

If you refer to Figure 1-7, you can see that in this example, one device (the Realtek audio device) needs a new driver and one device (the Epson Stylus printer) has no published information concerning its driver compatibility. In both cases, you are told to visit the manufacturer's Web site for more information or for a free download.

Clicking the next tab calls up the Program Details window, as shown in Figure 1-8.

In this example, you can see that no software program issues prevent the upgrade to Windows Vista. If the Windows Vista Upgrade Advisor finds any programs that would prevent your Vista installation, you would be provided with appropriate instructions. Under most circumstances, you would either have to disable or uninstall the offending program.

Clicking the Task List tab brings up a to-do list of issues that you must deal with both before and after you install Windows Vista. This list is a reiteration of the previous three windows. Print out the Task List before you start (just click the Print button at the upper right of the window); see Figure 1-9.

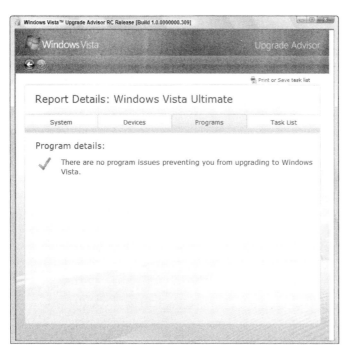

Figure 1-8: The Programs tab of the Windows Vista Upgrade Advisor Report Details window.

Figure 1-9: The Windows Vista Upgrade Advisor provides you with a list of suggested tasks to perform before and after installing Vista.

Information Kiosk

If you are technically inclined, visit the Microsoft Tech Net site at

`www.microsoft.com/technet/windowsvista/default.mspx/`

Here you can get information on up-to-date hardware requirements before you install Windows Vista.

Windows Vista, as with any new operating system, might not be compatible with every device or every program. As you can now see, though, you are not necessarily at a complete loss because of that. The Windows Vista Upgrade Advisor can spell out quite explicitly what you need to do *before* you install Windows Vista.

Preparing your computer for installation

If you are installing Windows Vista to a computer that already has another operating system installed on it — Windows XP, for example — you need to take a few precautions before beginning the Vista installation process. The following suggested tasks ensure that all your previous files and programs are not irrevocably lost should something go awry during the installation process.

First, you need to do some routine maintenance and housekeeping. This makes room for Vista on your hard drive and ensures that the software and files stored on your PC are not lost in case something goes wrong during installation. Begin with the following:

1. **Back up all your files offline.**

Your backup media can be CDs, DVDs (if you have a DVD burner), or another hard drive, preferably an external drive. Floppy disks are also a possibility, but their limited storage capacity and slow speed make them unfeasible — unless you don't mind endless disk swapping and tall stacks of floppies. Also be sure to back up programs for which you do not have original distribution disks. You might have downloaded these and saved the original file in a special directory on your internal hard drive.

2. **Clean up and clean out your drives.**

Use Windows' own Add or Remove Programs utility (Start → Settings → Control Panel → Add or Remove Programs) or a program's own uninstall facility to get rid of obsolete programs you no longer want. Then run Disk Cleanup (Start → Programs → Accessories → System Tools → Disk Cleanup), which gets rid of all sorts of temporary files, cache files, and other bits and pieces that Windows unfortunately scatters all over your drives. You can also use third-party utilities, of which there are many, to perform these tasks. These might or might not be more thorough than the built-in Windows utilities, especially in removing Registry entries and shortcuts left behind by departed software.

Watch Your Step

Although literally dozens of programs are out there that purport to remove all leftover bits when you uninstall a program — some free, some not — the more established programs out there are CClean (a free download from www.ccleaner.com), Macecraft Software's JV16, and Innovative Solution's Uninstaller PRO. Most do not do the job completely and it is usually necessary to use several in tandem.

3. **Defragment your hard drive.**

As you use your PC, files are added according to the space allotments located on your hard drive. When you install new software, you want to make sure your files are as close to each other as possible so that your system does not have to jump from one location to another to perform a desired task. This is especially important with a new operating system. Having all of Vista's components in one contiguous space requires less traveling time for the drive read/write heads. And the faster your system runs, the longer your drives will last.

The Disk Defragmenter is another Windows system tool. Choose Start ➜ Programs ➜ Accessories ➜ System Tools ➜ Disk Defragmenter to access it.

4. **Run the Check Disk utility.**

In My Computer, right-click the drive you wish to check, choose Properties from the contextual menu, choose Tools, then choose Check Now. Be sure to select the check boxes that force the utility to check the drive for physical errors and attempt to correct any that are found. This prevents existing errors from interrupting (or corrupting) Vista's files.

Transfer

For more on the Check Disk and Disk Defragmenter system utilities, see Chapter 11.

5. **Ensure that the partition in which you plan to install Windows Vista is large enough.**

Remember that the minimum drive size is 40GB and the minimum free space is 15GB. In My Computer, right-click the drive you wish to check and choose Properties from the contextual menu. An icon shows you the total capacity of the drive and the amount of free space. Bear in mind that even though you might have only one hard drive, it may be divided into several partitions, each of which has a drive letter. Normally, the C: drive is where the operating system resides. If C: is just one of several partitions on your single drive, you must ensure that the C: partition is both large enough and has enough free space for a Vista installation. You must also ensure that it is an *active* partition — the primary partition on a hard drive that contains and boots the operating system. A system may have several active partitions. The installation process itself provides you with the information and the means to make necessary changes.

Information Kiosk

In previous versions of Windows, when upgrading from an earlier version (say, Windows 98) to a newer (say, Windows XP) version, you could install the newer version on top of the older one, but the results could be disastrous. It was usually best to ignore the existing version, rename the directory in which it resided, and do a clean install from scratch of the newer version. Then you could move what you wanted from the old directory and reinstall all your other software and hardware. Windows XP provides a Files and Settings Transfer Wizard that brings the new installation up to the installed level of the old operating system. However, that utility is really intended to transfer information from an old computer to a new one, and not from one directory to another in the same computer. The older installation process also required significant input from the user during the installation. You cannot just set it and forget it, letting it install itself without further input from the operator.

Windows Vista greatly improves upon this process. It asks all its questions up front and then gets on with the installation, without bothering the user.

You still have the option of either installing on top of the old system, thus preserving your settings and configuration, or doing a clean install to which you then import your desired configuration. However, both these processes are quite different from those of earlier Windows versions.

Starting the installation process

To begin the installation process, turn on your computer and insert the Vista installation DVD into your PC's DVD (or CD) drive. Restart your computer — which automatically initiates the Install process — and then complete the following steps:

1. In the first screen that appears (see Figure 1-10), select the language you want to use to install Vista, the time and currency format, as well as the keyboard or input method you wish to use and then click Next.

Use the drop-down menus provided to make your selections.

Information Kiosk

When you first boot up the Windows Vista installation setup, the setup program actually installs a mini-operating system (Windows Preinstallation Environment, or *Windows PE*), which puts the computer into Windows mode so that the entire installation takes place in what looks like a Windows environment, not the DOS environment of previous version installations.

Figure 1-10: Installing Windows Vista.

Information Kiosk

The Install Windows welcome screen offers you two options: to check your computer's Vista compatibility online or to install Vista now. (See Figure 1-11.) If you haven't already checked whether your PC is capable of running Vista, do so now. After you are sure that your PC can handle the system requirements of Windows Vista, you can begin the installation process. Refer to the "Evaluating Your System Requirements" and "Checking upgrade compatibility" sections earlier in this chapter to determine whether your computer is compliant with Vista's minimum standards.

2. **Click the Install Now link in the Install dialog box, as shown in Figure 1-11.**

A new screen appears, asking you for the product key provided with your Vista installation software, as shown in Figure 1-12.

3. **Enter your product key.**

Type the alphanumeric key into the text box provided. (Dashes are added automatically; you do not need to enter these items.)

If you are not sure where to find your product key, check on the back of your installation DVD envelope case.

Information Kiosk

If you have an always-on Internet connection, choose the Automatically Activate Windows When I'm Online option. Clicking in the check box next to this option saves you from having to manually activate Vista later.

Figure 1-11: Installing Windows Vista.

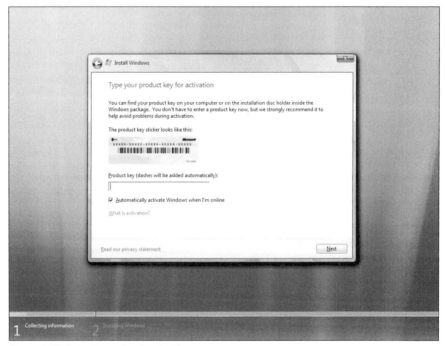

Figure 1-12: Enter the product key for Vista.

4. **Click Next.**

The EULA (End User License Agreement) appears.

5. **Read through the licensing agreement, place a check mark in the box to the left of the I Accept the License Terms option, and then click Next.**

Note: You must accept these terms if you wish to continue.

After you accept the licensing terms, two new boxes, Upgrade and Custom (as shown in Figure 1-13), appear.

- *Click Upgrade* if you want to install Vista on top of your present operating system.

  This preserves your existing settings and configuration.

  or

- *Click Custom* if you want to do a clean install from scratch.

If you choose Custom, you can hand-select where you would like to store the Vista operating system on your hard drive. If you select this option, the installer first shows you a list of available partitions. Click Drive Options (Advanced), and the program shows you the unformatted partitions or unallocated space.

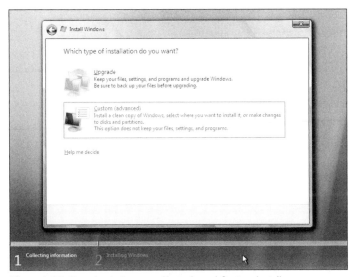

Figure 1-13: Choosing between an Upgrade and Custom install.

In actuality, these two options do not differ all that much because all new Vista installations are essentially clean installations. In the Upgrade mode, the program simply shoves the existing operating system aside in a renamed directory and proceeds to install Windows Vista in the Windows directory on drive C:. When the process is complete, it then copies your settings and configuration from the old system into the new one.

6. Choose the installation method (Upgrade or Custom) you wish to use.

The Installation Wizard shows you where on your hard drive you have enough space to save the Vista operating system.

Or you can also choose to hand select its location by using the Drive Options (Advanced) if you choose the Custom installation option.

7. Select the drive you wish to use for the installation and click Next.

Doing so opens a warning dialog box letting you know that if this partition contains files and folders from your previous version of Windows, they are going to be moved to a folder titled `Windows.old`.

8. To dismiss the warning dialog box, click OK.

The warning dialog box disappears and the installation process begins. The installer begins copying Vista to your hard drive. It installs Windows Vista in the partition of your choice without further input from you until the process is complete.

Note the green status bar located at the bottom of your screen. This tool provides you with a visual image of how far along in the process your PC is. This information is also provided in parentheses during each phase of the installation outline listed in the white box above.

Depending on how fast your PC is, this process could take a half hour to a full hour or more. After Vista has been installed, you might be prompted to select the operating system you wish to use at this time.

9. Select Windows Vista (not your previous version of Windows) and press Enter.

Your PC reboots automatically.

 Watch Your Step

Be sure to remove the installation disc before the reboot occurs; otherwise, you are taken back to the beginning of the installation process.

After your computer has rebooted with Vista, you are prompted with a number of setup windows. These boxes allow you to configure the system to your liking and include designating country or region; setting date, time, and time zone; entering a username, password, and user picture for your account; giving the computer a name and a desktop image; and telling Vista how it should handle updates. The instructions that follow walk you through this setup process.

1. The first setup window you see asks you to choose a username and password, as shown in Figure 1-14.

Type in the name and password you want to use for your user account.

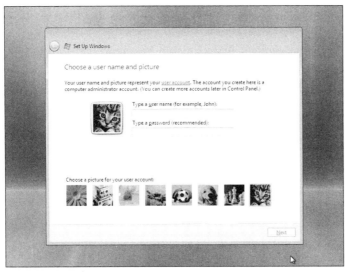

Figure 1-14: Choosing a username.

2. Click Next.

This opens the computer name and desktop page, as shown in Figure 1-15.

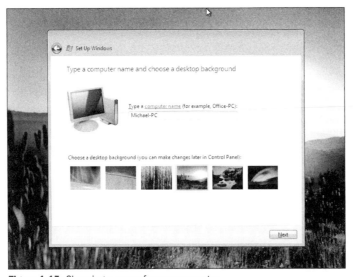

Figure 1-15: Choosing a name for your computer.

3. Choose a new name for your PC.

A default setting — usually *your name-PC* — is provided, but you can select any title you like.

4. Select the picture you would you like to use for your account's desktop background.

Clicking the thumbnail image of your preference gives you a full screen preview.

Note: You can always change this image later — you can even use a personal photo if you prefer — but you must first choose from one of the options provided.

 Transfer

See Chapter 2 for more information on how to personalize your desktop background.

5. Click Next.

Doing so opens up the Windows Updates page. From here you can choose how often you would like Windows to complete automatic update downloads for your PC.

6. Select an automatic update option and click Next.

You can choose to use the recommended settings, to install important Windows updates only, or to be asked later.

It is recommended that you select the first option because it helps protect you and your PC from unwanted harm or damage.

If you choose to only upgrade the important Windows updates, you might lower your chances of having your PC become damaged by possible viruses or security breaches, or you might simply miss out on new and improved functionality features of Vista. However, if you find that the upgrades are impeding your work-flow, you may want to choose this option instead of the recommended option.

If you choose the Ask Me Later option, you might be leaving your computer exposed to potential dangers lurking online. It is recommended that you select one of the other two options, preferably the first (recommended) settings.

After making your selection, you are prompted with the time and date settings page.

 Transfer

See Chapter 4 for more information on how to protect your PC from potential security risks and Chapter 11 for more on Windows Updates.

7. Select the correct time zone for your area.

Use the drop-down menu provided to select the correct time zone, as shown in Figure 1-16.

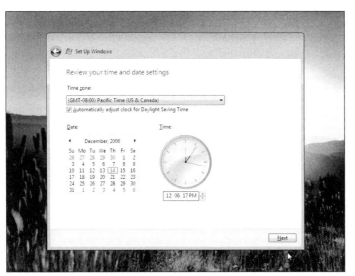

Figure 1-16: Setting the correct time zone, date, and time.

8. Choose the current date.

Today's date should already be selected; however, if you need to adjust the date setting, simply use your mouse to click on the correct date.

9. Set the time.

Use the time box (or arrow key buttons) provided to enter the correct local time for your PC, if it is not already selected. Simply type the correct time into the box provided or click the arrow buttons to the right to adjust your PC's time settings.

10. Click Next.

A new window appears, thanking you for selecting your PC settings.

11. Click Start.

This sets the wheels in motion for Vista to check your PC's performance levels. During this process Vista highlights some of its new and improved features.

Note the green status bar at the bottom of your screen. This line shows how far along in this stage your PC is.

After this process is complete, Vista automatically begins running on your PC.

Booting your computer with more than one version of Windows

There are several reasons why you might want to have two different versions of Windows running on the same machine. You might want a little time to get used to the strange new Vista before moving entirely away from a well-known and comfortable earlier version. Perhaps some of your existing software or hardware does not work very well or at all with Vista, and you do not want to upgrade or replace it at this time. Or, maybe you want to take your time transferring programs and data from the old operating system to the new one.

It is not difficult to set up a *dual boot* machine — a machine running two different operating systems — but doing it correctly is critical, or you can end up with no boot at all.

To install Vista as a dual boot, you need two active primary partitions, with one of them designated as drive C. You are going to install Windows Vista to this partition. The second partition may have any drive letter you like.

Do a clean install of the older operating system to the second directory. The earlier system **must** be installed first (before you install Windows Vista). Make sure that the earlier install is up and working properly. Because it is a clean install, you have to reinstall and set up all your settings, programs, and configurations. Make sure the new installation of the earlier operating system is working properly.

Then follow the directions earlier (see "Starting the Installation Process") for a custom installation of Windows Vista. Use the partition labeled drive C: for the Vista installation.

 ## Watch Your Step

Do not install Windows Vista on any other drive than C:. If you install it on drive G:, for example, it renames drive G: to drive C: and renames all your other partitions, too. Drive C:, for example, might become drive D:; this can wreak havoc with both systems because most of the data and programs you already have in the computer are identified to the operating system by their paths.

Even if you don't change the drive letters, programs that have to be installed won't run until they are reinstalled under Vista.

Programs that don't have to be reinstalled and reside on drive C: in your older system are now on drive D:, and get schizophrenic. They can't find themselves or their data. Programs that have to be reinstalled in Vista, be that a fresh installation or a settings and applications move, end up divorced from their data and perhaps essential parts of their operating code. So be safe: Always install Windows Vista on the real drive C:.

If all has gone well and the installations of both operating systems are successful, a black-and-white window automatically appears onscreen the next time you boot your computer, as shown in Figure 1-17. This new welcome page offers you two choices: to boot your PC with "Microsoft Windows" (Windows Vista, in other words) or "an earlier version of Windows" (whatever older system you had been running).

Select the operating system you wish to use at this time and press Enter. This instructs you computer to run the desired operating system. As mentioned earlier, this feature can be quite useful if you wish to prolong the process of completely upgrading your PC to Vista. This allows you to still run programs that are not yet compatible with Vista on your current PC and provides you with more time to accustom yourself to the new user interface and features of Microsoft's visually enhanced operating system.

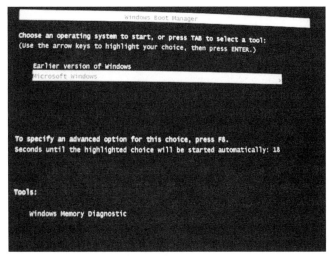

Figure 1-17: The Windows Boot Manager.

Transfer

In Chapter 11, you'll learn more about the technical aspects of customizing, enabling, and disabling different features of Windows Vista.

CPU (central processing unit) speed: Determines how quickly your computer's processor can decipher and perform specified tasks. CPU speed is measured in megahertz (MHz). The more MHz a machine has, the faster it runs.

continued

dual boot computer: A machine onto which are loaded two (or more) different operating systems (OSes), such as Windows XP and Windows Vista. The OSes do not run simultaneously. At bootup, a white-on-black screen offers the user the option of running, say, Windows Vista or an earlier version of Windows. To run a version other than the one currently in use, the user must first close that version and reboot. The benefit of using a dual boot system is that you can run different systems on the same machine. This option saves you from having to immediately re-install all your existing third-party software and reset your personalized settings on the new OS. Using a dual boot setup also allows you to familiarize yourself with the new system before committing to it completely.

EULA (End User License Agreement): A standardized contract imposed by software manufacturers on users. This agreement typically includes copyright, permitted usage, and limited warranty information. Most software products require that users read and consent to the terms outlined in the EULA before they can download or install the specified product.

gigabyte (GB): A unit of measurement used to calculate a computer's storage capacity. One GB of RAM stores one billion bytes of information.

megabyte (MB): A unit of measurement used to calculate a computer's storage capacity. One MB of RAM stores one million bytes of information.

megahertz (MHz): Measurement used to calculate frequency. One hertz (Hz) refers to one cycle per second. One MHz refers to one million cycles per second. The number of MHz a computer processor is capable of achieving is an indicator of how fast the machine can retrieve data and perform specific actions.

OEM (Original Equipment Manufacturer): A company that builds products or components used in products sold by another company. For example, a computer's operating system (such as Windows Vista) can be manufactured by a corporation separate from the company that markets and sells the computer.

operating system (OS): The software program responsible for managing the hardware and software resources of a computer, including controlling and allocating memory, prioritizing user requests, controlling input and output devices, facilitating networking, and managing files.

RAM (random access memory): The amount of memory your computer has to run all the files and programs, including the operating system, stored on its hard drive.

WDDM (Windows Vista Display Driver Model): A new driver from Microsoft, included as part of the Windows Vista Operating System to support video cards in use with Vista.

Windows Vista Upgrade Advisor: A downloadable application that tells you whether your computer can install and run Windows Vista properly. This automated tool can be found on the Microsoft Windows Vista Get Ready Web page.

Last Stop

Practice Exam

1. Name the five standard versions of Windows Vista.

_____

_____

2. What is the best version of Vista to install if you plan to do only word processing, check e-mail, and watch the occasional video clip?

_____

_____

3. What are the benefits of creating a dual boot installation of Vista with a previous version of Windows?

_____

_____

4. Why does Microsoft require 15GB of free disk space when installing Vista?

_____

_____

5. Is it possible to install Windows Vista with only 256MB of RAM?

_____

_____

6. If you want to install Windows Vista on a drive partition, which steps should you take to prepare the drive?

_____

_____

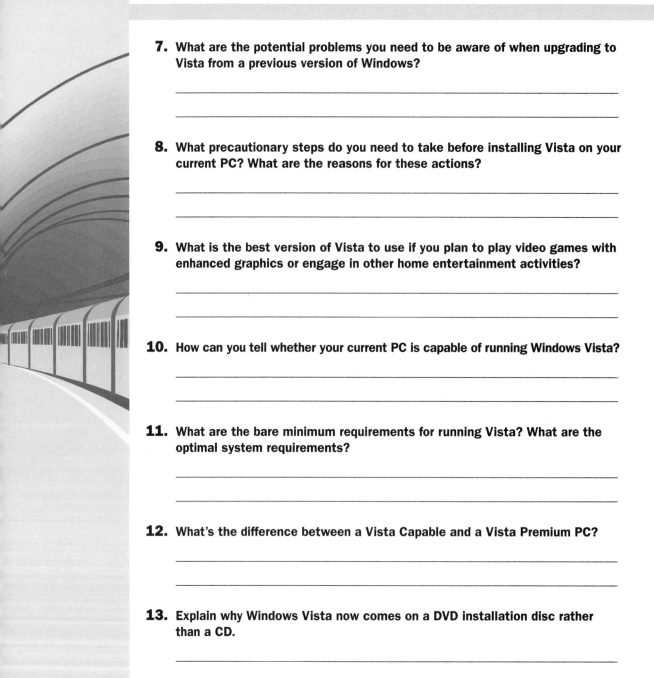

7. What are the potential problems you need to be aware of when upgrading to Vista from a previous version of Windows?

_____

_____

8. What precautionary steps do you need to take before installing Vista on your current PC? What are the reasons for these actions?

_____

_____

9. What is the best version of Vista to use if you plan to play video games with enhanced graphics or engage in other home entertainment activities?

_____

_____

10. How can you tell whether your current PC is capable of running Windows Vista?

_____

_____

11. What are the bare minimum requirements for running Vista? What are the optimal system requirements?

_____

_____

12. What's the difference between a Vista Capable and a Vista Premium PC?

_____

_____

13. Explain why Windows Vista now comes on a DVD installation disc rather than a CD.

_____

_____

EXIT

Using the Windows Vista Desktop

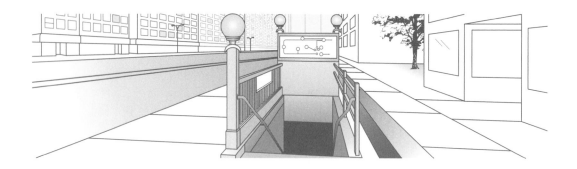

Enter the Station

Questions

1. How does the new appearance and organization of the Vista desktop help you work more efficiently?

2. What did the designers at Microsoft hope to achieve with Aero?

3. How can you use the icons, menus, and tools on the desktop to your advantage?

4. What's new on the Start menu?

5. How many different ways can you choose to launch your favorite files and applications?

6. What are the benefits of using the Windows taskbar?

Express Line

If you are already up on the basics of the Windows Vista desktop, skip ahead to the next chapter.

In the beginning, there was DOS (Disk Operating System). In those ancient days, there might not even have been a disk. In many early computers, programs, data, and the operating system were often loaded into memory from a cassette tape and similarly saved back to a cassette tape (all 64K of it) on the largest available personal computers of the day. If disks were used, they were five–eight inches in diameter and ran in expensive big external boxes, holding a maximum of a few hundred kilobytes (K). Hard drives were even more expensive, were external to the computer, and held a maximum of about 5 megabytes (MB) of data. With memory limited to about 32K for data and another 32K for programs and the operating system, one could accomplish a lot with an 8-bit machine running at 4 megahertz (MHz) — but it was complex.

One needed strings of arcane commands to make anything run, with nothing intuitive about running the various word processing and data management packages that soon appeared. Learning to use an early word processor program or database program was akin to learning a new language. Many early machines did not even offer lowercase fonts, which made everything look like Teletype. And indeed, the terminology of the time reflected the Teletype environment and the layout of the IBM standards for data input and output on 80-column punched cards. The best printers, though — the slowest at about 12 characters per second — were based on the IBM Selectric typewriter (a best-selling typewriter, first introduced in 1961), which was the standard for print quality.

As for the user interface (UI), there was nothing graphical about it. It came in one color — that of your computer monitor, which most likely was a standard black-and-white TV cathode ray tube with very low resolution. Otherwise, it was green or a rather unappealing amber. Those were your only options.

Any graphics consisted of large blocks that left much to the imagination. User interaction began with a cryptic >C:\ and a blinking block of a cursor. To find a program you wanted to run, you had to open a directory and use a command line to run the program — if you had a disk drive, that is. Otherwise, you loaded the program from a cassette tape and saved your work to a cassette tape. Graphics in the programs were not much better, but now at least you had a field into which you could type characters; name files; and save, retrieve, and correct this information. For all its primitive shortcomings, the early personal computers (PCs) were light-years ahead of pencil and paper spreadsheets and databases. They just were not very easy or intuitive to use.

Introducing the Graphical User Interface (GUI)

Microsoft did not invent the graphical user interface (GUI) that we know today as Microsoft Windows. The idea itself long predates digital computers, going back to prophetic writings by physicist Vannevar Bush in the early 1930s. Most people credit the Xerox research facility at Palo Alto, California (XeroxPARC), with the GUI's earliest useful implementation on a PC. And for some years, almost all personal computer makers developed and promoted their own versions of the GUI. Some, those by Apple and various versions of Linux, are still in existence with Apple remaining a strong, even dominant, contender in its market. But the millions of copies of Microsoft Windows in use worldwide dwarf the number of other GUIs.

All GUIs, however, have the same purpose — to make the computer and its intricacies transparent to the user. In other words, the purpose of a PC's GUI is to make it as simple as possible to use your PC to get work done. Windows Vista goes a long way to realizing that goal. It's all about running your applications, maintaining your folders and the files within them, and easily finding the information you need when you need it.

Your desktop is really the window into your computer. It is the first thing you see when you turn on your computer. It is also your point of departure. From the desktop, you decide what direction you want to take. In the old days of DOS, many people looked at a black (or green) screen. Based on its lack of visual appeal, those who weren't already predisposed to technology simply remained uninterested in going anywhere with it at all.

Windows made its grand entrance with Windows 3.1, which presented icons and a screen that — if you were lucky enough to have a color monitor — was a bright blue (although you could change it). It seemed that the developers of Windows were finally sensing the importance of the GUI to users (and potential users). With this new interface, which sported a much more effective design and layout, you had a sense of what you could do and where you could go — but you could only go so far.

August 24, 1995, saw the auspicious birth of Windows 95, which was promoted as a revolutionary concept in computing because it added something new to the mix: the ability to make personalized choices concerning the look and organization of your desktop. You could use your favorite color or mix your own. You could even have a photo or image that was meaningful to you greet you every time you turned on your machine. Now instead of a cold anonymous box, the PC was a companionable tool.

Coupled with the ability to personalize your desktop were more processing speed and the possibility of multitasking. This innovation in the PC market seemed so exciting that thousands of people actually lined up at stores all across the country the night before its release to be among the first to purchase this new operating system.

Since Microsoft's emersion into the PC market, each of its operating systems (Windows 98, Me, 2000, and XP) have presented more choices and gotten more powerful and stable as well. The desktop has definitely undergone some major changes, but it has been a gradual movement toward more colors, backgrounds, icons, and menus.

It is in this arena that Vista has broken through with the largest degree of innovative change and the most customization possibilities for its GUI.

If you choose to make the desktop background and its organization reflect your own interests and choices, which you can do through Vista's extensive options, the journey becomes one that is unique to your own personality.

Exploring the Windows Vista Desktop

The desktop devoid of icons, gadgets, windows, panes, and other visual elements is merely a blank sheet. Add an image, and the desktop becomes a picture. Attractive, but useless. As you begin to add elements to the desktop and as Windows Vista loads and runs, you begin to see its functionality. All those items that begin to appear, each with its distinctive format — the Gadgets to the right, the taskbar along the bottom, the Start menu and its cascading hierarchy to ever more levels of functionality lying beneath the desktop — are windows and doors to what is actually inside your computer. Without those windows and doors — and without the desktop and without your monitor — you cannot access the contents of your computer unless you run it remotely from another computer or plug in another monitor. In other words, Vista's GUI truly is *the* interface to your PC.

Using the Welcome Center

When Windows Vista boots up for the first time, you are greeted by the Welcome Center window (see Figure 2-1).

Figure 2-1: The Windows Vista Welcome Center.

The Welcome Center is your first point of entry for Windows Vista. It includes a small sampling of what is hidden beneath Vista's GUI. The Welcome Center page includes icon links to help you navigate your new operating system. The tools and applications located on this page allow you to personalize your desktop (and operating system; OS), locate information, and perform specific tasks.

You'll find two separate sections to the Welcome Center. The first section is the Getting Started section, which includes information on what is new in Vista and how to personalize your PC. The second section — the Microsoft Offers section — includes information on other products and services available from Microsoft.

Each of these sections provides information regarding critical (and interesting) features of Windows Vista. To determine what a feature does, simply click the icon representing that feature. This brings up a brief explanation for your selection at the top of the Welcome Center screen. Double-clicking an icon takes you to that particular feature's start screen. For example, double-clicking the View Computer Details icon shows basic information about your computer's operating system, processor, and memory. Double-clicking the What's New in Windows Vista link takes you to a Help window where you can explore articles on the new features of Vista.

Other links, such as the Connect to the Internet and Transfer Files and Settings options, are more narrowly focused. These selections open a whole new set of action items in which you must provide input in order to attain the desired results. For example, with the Internet connection option, you must decide which type of connection you would like to establish for your PC. The Easy Transfer Wizard requires that you specify which files and data you want transferred from your old PC to your new computer. Follow the steps provided for each of these tools in order to complete the requested tasks.

Information Kiosk

The Windows Easy Transfer Wizard enables you to transfer files and settings between two different computers. When you invoke the Transfer Wizard tool on your Vista machine, it transfers a copy of your old machine into the directory of your choice on your new machine. Obviously, the two machines have to be connected in some manner, usually through a local network. By following the instructions provided in the Easy Transfer Wizard, you can specify what items you want transferred to the new machine. Then all you have to do is sit back and wait while Vista copies the old information to the new system.

Transfer

See Chapter 5 to learn how to use Windows Easy Transfer. See Chapter 7 for details on how to establish an Internet connection for your PC.

Choosing a desktop background

Vista includes a built-in gallery of choices that you can select and change as often as you like, one of which is the desktop background. Your background choices run the gamut from solid colors to designer patterns, from photos to various works of art.

To select a background

1. **Right-click your desktop.**

   A pop-up menu appears onscreen (see Figure 2-2).

Figure 2-2: Right-click the desktop to bring up this pop-up menu.

2. **From the pop-up menu, choose Personalize.**

   The Personalize Appearance and Sounds window is revealed (see Figure 2-3).

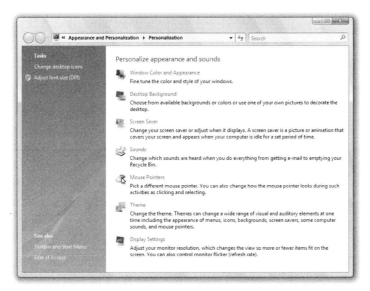

Figure 2-3: The Personalize Appearance and Sounds window.

3. **From within this window, select Desktop Background.**

   The Desktop Background dialog box appears. (See Figure 2-4.)

4. **Choose the background type you want from the drop-down list.**

   You can choose solid colors, textures, pictures, and more.

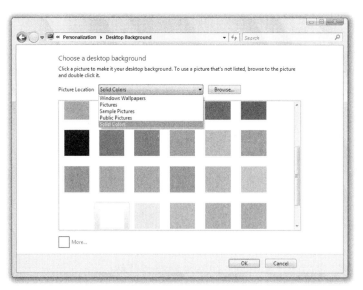

Figure 2-4: Choosing your desktop background.

5. Click the picture or color you want for your background.

This image or color automatically appears onscreen. Minimize the Desktop Background page to preview your selection.

6. (Optional) To select another image, return to the Desktop Background dialog box and click another color or picture.

7. Click OK.

The Desktop Background page disappears.

8. Close the Personalization page.

9. Click the X in the upper right of this box to reveal your new desktop background.

If you prefer more solid color options for your background, click More from the Solid Colors page. You then see the Color dialog box (see Figure 2-5).

Here you can pick any color you want from the palette that appears. Use either your mouse or the custom color entry boxes to create your own unique background color. Click OK after you make your selection. Click OK again in the Desktop Background dialog box to make this new color the official backdrop for your desktop.

If you would rather use an image from your personal files for your desktop background, click the Browse button to navigate to a graphic file stored on your hard drive.

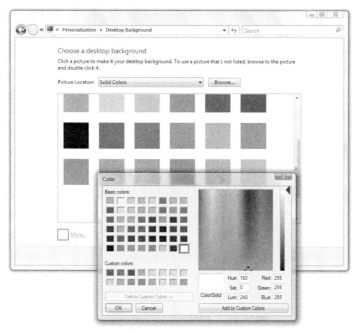

Figure 2-5: Choose your desktop background: more colors.

Information Kiosk

In previous versions of Windows, you might have wanted to have an image or photo as the background for your desktop, but when you loaded it, your beloved image sometimes looked awful. Either it was fuzzy, or the image was too small and was surrounded by a lot of blank space. To get rid of the blank space, you could choose the option to make the image appear in a tiled effect on your entire screen. However, choosing that option meant that your screen would be literally filled with a seemingly limitless number of copies of your image, just like mosaic tiles on a wall. For some images, that was okay. For many, it was annoying to look at — and for most photos, it was visually awful. (The tiling option has been dropped in Windows Vista.)

With Vista, if your image has a low resolution to begin with, you are still going to end up with a certain graininess to the image. Even with a high-end graphics card, Windows Vista can't produce a miraculous transformation, but it can provide you with an overall improvement in the contrast and sharpness of that image.

If your image is small (*small* being a relative term), it might still appear small on your screen. The solution lies in acquiring photo imaging software with which you can adjust the resolution and size of the photo you wish to use on your desktop.

Except under the two circumstances described here, Windows Vista does a fine job in allowing you to display your photo as your desktop background.

Selecting a Screen Saver

When your computer is idle, you might want to have a *screen saver* — a moving image or blank screen traditionally used to conserve the image quality of computer displays when they are not in use.

Information Kiosk

Is using a screen saver necessary? Not really. Because most laptops have LCD (liquid crystal display) screens, they are not really susceptible to image burn-in like the old tube monitors were way back when. Still, many desktop screens are CRTs (cathode ray tubes) and are very minimally susceptible. Using a screen saver is usually a good idea to greatly reduce any burn-in (no matter how unlikely this occurrence might be). Screen savers can also help prevent your screen displays from fading over time. The truth is, if you really want to extend the life of your monitor and keep it nice and bright, turn it off when you are finished.

Windows Vista gives you an extensive selection of built-in screen savers. Enabling one is very easy; here's how:

1. **Right-click your desktop.**

A pop-up menu appears screen. (Refer to Figure 2-2.)

2. **Choose Personalize.**

The Personalize Appearance and Sounds window shows up on your desktop.

3. **Select Screen Saver.**

The Screen Saver Settings dialog box appears. (See Figure 2-6.)

4. **Use the drop-down list to preview Vista's screen saver options.**

The default setting is the Windows Logo screen saver; however, you can select whichever screen saver you like best.

5. **Click OK.**

The Screen Saver Settings dialog box disappears.

6. **Close the Personalization page.**

Clicking the X in the upper right of the Personalize page removes this box from your screen.

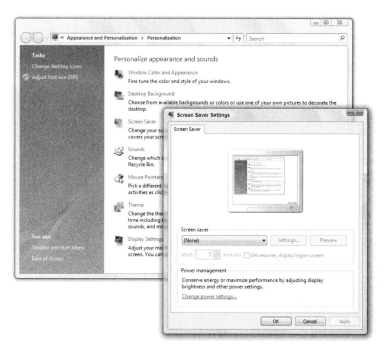

Figure 2-6: Choosing your screen saver settings.

![Information Kiosk icon] **Information Kiosk**

You can also specify how much time passes before your screen saver is activated. To do so, open the Screen Saver Settings dialog box and enter in the Wait box the number of minutes you want to elapse before the screen saver begins. Click OK when you are done. Selecting the On Resume, Display Welcome Screen check box sets it up so that you have to log back in to the computer to gain access. This can be useful if you work in a semipublic environment where you sometimes leave your computer unattended and you'd prefer that no wandering stranger gain access to your files.

Some of the Windows Vista screen savers offer specialized settings. If you select one that does offer these settings, you can customize quite a bit. For example, if you choose 3D text from the Screen Saver drop-down list, the Settings button becomes active.

To adjust the settings for your 3-D screen saver

1. Click Settings from the Screen Saver Settings dialog box.

The Settings dialog box appears (see Figure 2-7). In this example, you see the 3D Text Settings dialog box.

This screen allows you to make adjustments to the screen saver's size and time fluctuations.

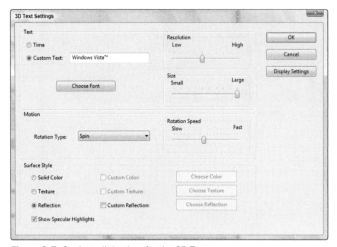

Figure 2-7: Settings dialog box for the 3D Text screen saver.

2. Select either Time or Custom Text.

By choosing Time, the 3D text displays the current time on your computer clock. Selecting Custom Text allows you to specify any text string that will appear in 3D animation. Use the Resolution and Size sliders to adjust the appearance of whatever you choose to display.

3. From the Rotation Type drop-down list, choose the text animation to be performed.

The slider to the right of the drop-down menu allows you to regulate the animation speed.

4. Further define the appearance of the text using the Solid Color, Texture, or Reflection option in the lower section of the dialog box, then click OK.

Each selection has its own settings, which you can access by checking the custom check box and clicking the button to the right.

5. Back in the Screen Saver Settings dialog box, click Preview to see how your screen saver will appear. (See Figure 2-8.)

Move the mouse to return to the Screen Saver Settings dialog box.

6. Click OK to close the Screen Saver Settings dialog box.

7. **Click the Close button to close the Personalize window.**

Your screen saver goes immediately into action.

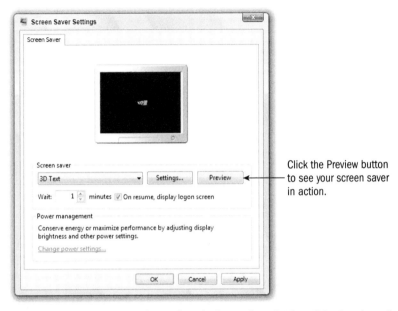

Click the Preview button to see your screen saver in action.

Figure 2-8: Clicking the Preview button from the Screen Saver Settings dialog box shows the selected screen saver in action.

You can also design your own customized screen saver. That is, you can use images or photos of your own to create a slide show to use as your desktop screen saver. Here's how:

1. **Begin by saving copies of the images or photos you wish to include in your screen saver slide show to a new folder.**

After you select all the images you wish to include, close this folder.

i **Information Kiosk**

It's easy to create a new folder in Windows Vista. The fastest way is to right-click on a selected folder in Windows Explorer (or right-click the Windows Vista desktop) and choose New ➔ Folder, as shown in Figure 2-9.

2. **Right-click the desktop.**

A pop-up menu appears onscreen.

3. **Choose Personalize.**

The Personalize Appearance and Sounds window is revealed.

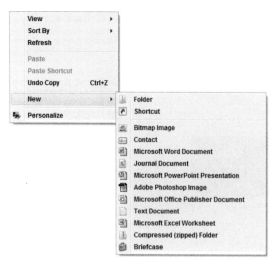

Figure 2-9: From the shortcut menu, choose New and then Folder.

4. **Select Screen Saver.**

The Screen Saver Settings dialog box appears. (Refer to Figure 2-6.)

5. **Choose Photos from the Screen Saver drop-down list.**

6. **Click Settings.**

The Photos Screen Saver Setting dialog box appears onscreen. (See Figure 2-10.)

Figure 2-10: The Photos Screen Saver Settings dialog box.

7. Choose the Use Pictures and Videos From option.

A green dot appears in the radio button for this selection.

8. Click the Browse button.

Use the pop-up window that appears to locate the folder you created in Step 1.

9. Click the name of the folder you created earlier.

A pale blue box surrounds the title of your folder.

10. Click OK.

The Browse For Folder dialog box disappears, and you are once again confronted with the Photos Screen Saver Settings dialog box.

11. Use the drop-down menu to select the speed for your slide show.

You can choose from Slow, Medium, or Fast.

12. Click Save.

The Photos Screen Saver Settings dialog box disappears, revealing the Screen Saver Settings dialog box.

If you wait a moment, your slide show is previewed on the small computer screen example. If this does not happen automatically, click the Preview button to see your slide show in full effect on your desktop screen.

13. Click OK.

The Screen Saver Settings dialog box closes, and you are returned to your desktop.

Information Kiosk

You might have already noticed that many Windows Vista dialog boxes present buttons that read Apply, Cancel, and OK. How are these commands different, and how should they be used?

Apply instructs Vista to immediately implement any changes you make in any specific tab within a dialog box encompassing multiple tabs. After you click Apply, you should be able to see that change implemented onscreen.

Clicking **OK** causes Vista to implement multiple changes across multiple tabs where the Apply button is not present. It will also close the dialog box.

Cancel instructs Vista to discard any changes across tabs that you might have made in any tab or dialog box. This option also closes the dialog box.

Watch Your Step

Here are two common pitfalls when enabling a custom screen saver:

1. Using a video as a screen saver uses a lot of system resources. Having at least 1 gigabyte (GB) of RAM and a fast processing chip on your machine is essential. Otherwise, your machine can slow down or even freeze.

2. If you decide to download a screen saver from the Internet, remember that many screen savers are small applications *(applets)*, which can contain viruses. Therefore, be sure to screen these files by using your antivirus program first before installing one. Vista warns you if you install one that may be suspicious.

Transfer

To see more on how to maximize your RAM resources, see Chapter 10.

Enjoying the Visual Advantages of Aero

Why Windows Aero? It is a development that one could say was a long time coming. In its 20-plus-year history, the user interface has truly developed according to a number of clearly identifiable stages.

When Windows first appeared, it was clearly seen as a step up from DOS. It had a few different colored backgrounds and fonts, and the documents were framed in what was an intuitively understood window frame. Within that frame, you were able to view and work with your documents.

The subsequent editions of Windows (Windows 95, 98, Me, and XP) continued to add more desktop options. Because additional functionality was continuously being introduced, you also saw the Windows frame itself becoming more and more crowded with various menus, buttons, and icons. It all looked utilitarian in nature.

Why then did Microsoft spend so much time (years actually) developing a visual look *(Aero)* in Windows Vista? How does Aero represent a departure from the previous versions of Windows?

Undoubtedly, a number of factors played a key role in Microsoft's decision to develop this new visual theme.

 If you've read any studies on how people take in information, you find that most studies indicate that approximately two out of three people are predominantly visual learners. They understand and retain mostly what they see.

In other words, they look, they learn. When exposed to information through any of the five senses, they picture that information in their heads. When they go to movies or the theater, they are most affected by visual images.

(ONE PANE) Studies also show that the amount of time people spend at a computer for both work and personal activities has become considerable and has more than doubled over the last five years. That being the case, if you can more readily understand what you are looking at — and, if that experience is visually pleasant, the overall experience tends to be both more enjoyable, and you are also likely to be more productive as an end result.

(ONE PANE) Through usability studies, Microsoft has determined that computer users experience too much frustration because they tend to get lost in the ever-increasing number of toolbars, icons, and buttons. Add to that the wide array of choices that users demand, and the number of possibilities become nearly insurmountable. Aero is, therefore, meant to be more than pretty. Microsoft also wants to make it task-oriented. By looking at any element, you should immediately be able to understand what it is and what it does.

(ONE PANE) There is also the market factor. Independent studies have shown that Macintosh enjoys a (some would say well-earned) reputation for its GUI. Overall, computer users in general regard the Macintosh interface as the most appealing. In comparison studies, most users consider the Windows desktop to be more utilitarian.

Windows Vista Aero (which, according to Microsoft, stands for *Authentic, Energetic, Reflective,* and *Open*) is the new visual theme that Vista uses. Aero is what gives the Vista desktop its enjoyable high-end visual effects. More importantly, perhaps, is that it makes it much clearer (through enhanced visual effects) what a feature, item, or icon actually does, stands for, or means.

Vista's new Aero theme includes a variety of effects that you can turn on, turn off, or modify at will. One example of Aero's special effects is the animated effect applied when windows are opened in Vista. When this feature is enabled, windows seem to progress onto the screen; then, when you close them, they seem to simply fall away. Aero also includes the ability to turn on a glassy look so that windows gleam. You can even add transparency levels to windows so that if you have several windows on top of each other, you can easily tell what is underneath without having to move another window out of the way. The overall effect is a desktop that gleams and glistens, looking clean, bright, modern, and cool. And these are all characteristics that you, the user, can adjust, customize, heighten, diminish, or personalize with just a few clicks.

Maximizing Aero performance

Aero is automatically enabled if your video card supports it. You might still need to adjust your settings to maximize Aero's visual effects, however.

To adjust your display settings for Aero

1. **Right-click your desktop.**

   A pop-up menu appears onscreen.

2. **Choose Personalize.**

   The Personalize Appearance and Sounds window is opened.

3. **Click Display Settings.**

   The Display Settings dialog box appears onscreen, as shown in Figure 2-11.

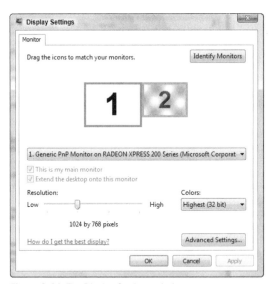

Figure 2-11: The Display Settings window.

4. **Move the Resolution slider to its highest level.**

   Click and drag the slider to adjust your computer's settings.

   Your PC's resolution must be at least 1024 x 768. This resolution is necessary for Aero's 3-D and transparency effects to work properly.

5. **Select the Highest (32 bit) Colors option.**

   Use the Colors drop-drop down menu to make your selection.

   The 32 bit color setting is required for the depth and saturation of color in many of Aero's backgrounds.

6. **Click OK.**

   The Display Settings dialog box disappears.

7. **Close the Personalize Appearance and Sounds window.**

   Click the X in the upper right of the Personalize Appearance and Sounds window to remove it from your screen.

Take a look at your desktop and try opening any window of your choice — the Start menu, the Control Panel, and so on. There should now be a glasslike effect on the surface and around the frame of this window. (See Figure 2-12.) If you move your window over any icon, you should be able to see the icon through the window. If you can't view these (glassy and transparency) visual effects, Aero is likely not enabled.

Indicates Aero is enabled.

Figure 2-12: The Appearance Settings dialog box in Windows Classic style; Aero is enabled.

Watch Your Step

If your video card does not support Aero, do not waste your time looking for the transparency or glass schemes; you won't be able to see them.

Transfer

See Chapter 1 for more on the hardware requirements that support the Aero effects of Windows Vista.

Here is another way to determine whether Aero is enabled on your PC:

1. Right-click your desktop.

A pop-up menu appears onscreen.

2. Choose Personalize.

The Personalize Appearance and Sounds window appears.

3. Select **Window Color and Appearance.**

The Window Color and Appearance dialog box pops up.

4. Select the **Open Classic Appearance Properties for More Color Options link.**

5. Check which color scheme is activated.

The current color scheme is highlighted in blue.

If the Windows Classic style is set up as your default color scheme and you see Windows Vista Basic included in the list of Color Scheme options (see Figure 2-13), Aero is not enabled.

To enable Aero, you must first upgrade your current graphics card to meet the minimum requirements for Windows Vista.

Figure 2-13: If Aero is not enabled, the first (highlighted) entry in the Color Scheme drop-down list reads Windows Vista Basic. No reference to Aero appears.

Transfer

See Chapter 1 to find out what the minimum requirements are for a Windows Vista graphics card.

Then see Chapter 8 to learn how to install drivers for a graphics card on your PC.

Customizing the Aero Glass interface

Within Aero, you have the Glass interface and an optional transparency effect. The Glass interface creates a visual depth, a 3-D simulation. It is also *translucent,* which means that light comes through it, making it seem as if it is gleaming. The transparency effect is what allows you to see through your open windows to view what is located behind your active screen.

The transparency effect is visually appealing to many people. It also has a practical effect, allowing you to see the windows or other screen elements you have open underneath so that you do not have to move windows around to reveal what is below. However, some people find the transparency effect distracting and prefer to make it opaque instead.

To adjust your Aero Glass and transparency effects

1. **Right-click your desktop.**

A pop-up menu appears onscreen.

2. **Choose Personalize.**

The Personalize Appearance and Sounds window is revealed.

3. **Select Window Color and Appearance.**

This brings up the Window Color and Appearance dialog box (see Figure 2-14), which offers you the following choices:

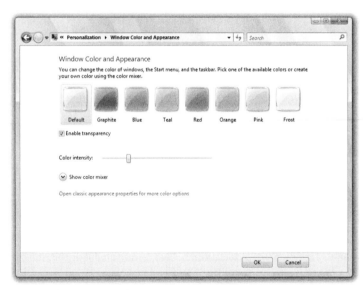

Figure 2-14: The Windows Color and Appearance dialog box.

- **Pick a Color:** Choose a color for the glassy effects in your windows.
- **Enable Transparency:** Enable it or turn it off.

- **Color Intensity:** This slider controls the intensity of the transparency. Click and drag the slider to the right, and it becomes more opaque. Click and drag it to the left, and it becomes more transparent.

- **Show Color Mixer:** Clicking this last option expands the dialog box to display a color mixer, which provides you with a means to create your own blended color for your window glass. Click and drag the sliders to adjust the color, saturation, and brightness of your window glass. (See Figure 2-15.)

4. **After making your adjustments, click OK to save your settings and close the Window Color and Appearance dialog box.**

Figure 2-15: The Window Color and Appearance window — showing the color mixer.

Information Kiosk

If you click the Open Classic Appearance Properties for More Color Options link, you can see your appearance settings in the Windows Classic style (a dialog box designed as in previous versions of Windows). In the Color Scheme drop-down list, the first entry (highlighted) reads Windows Vista Aero. When Aero is not enabled, this dialog box, in the "classic" style, is the one that you'll see.

Exploring the Windows Taskbar

The taskbar is an important feature of the Windows operating system. It is the tool responsible for launching and managing your computer's programs. In this section, you learn how to take advantage of the taskbar's built-in application management functions.

The taskbar is located at the bottom horizontal part of the window frame, as shown in Figure 2-16. From left to right, the taskbar is divided into four parts:

- **Start button:** Launches a menu containing your most important programs and documents
- **Quick Launch area:** Allows you to quickly launch a program or file by clicking icons located in this section of the taskbar
- **Windows tabs:** Displays what windows you have open
- **Notification area (formerly called the *system tray*):** Displays icons for the system functions currently running on your computer

The Start button   The windows tabs

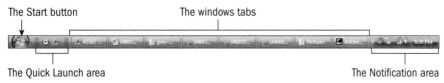

The Quick Launch area   The Notification area

Figure 2-16: The Windows taskbar. Note the four different parts.

The taskbar gives you a play-by-play status of the open windows on your system. As you open and close windows, the taskbar updates itself with new buttons to show you what is happening at all times. For example, if you start more than one program, you see an icon for each item you have opened in the taskbar, and you can easily switch between these programs by clicking the buttons located in the tabs section of the taskbar.

Repositioning the Windows taskbar

By default, the Windows taskbar is set up to display in the same place (the bottom of your screen) each time you launch Windows. To unlock the taskbar, simply right-click any open space within the toolbar and uncheck (or toggle off) the Lock the Taskbar option from the pop-up menu that appears (see Figure 2-17). This allows you to move or add icons within the taskbar, as well as move the taskbar itself around.

Figure 2-17: Right-click the taskbar to lock or unlock the options for this feature.

For example, the taskbar can be positioned at the bottom, right, top, or left edge of your screen. To move the taskbar to a new location on your desktop

1. **Right-click your mouse on a blank area in the taskbar.**

A pop-up menu appears.

2. **Select Lock the Taskbar.**

The check mark next to it disappears.

3. **Place your cursor on a blank area in the taskbar; then click and drag your mouse to the right.**

Your taskbar is now located at the right edge of your screen.

4. **Place your cursor on a blank area in the taskbar; click and drag your mouse to the top of your screen.**

Your taskbar is now placed at the top of your screen. By clicking and dragging it, you can move it to the left and bottom of the screen as well.

5. **Move the taskbar once again to the bottom of the screen.**

To ensure that the taskbar stays in its current location, lock it into place by right-clicking in an open space on the taskbar and choosing Lock the Taskbar.

Hiding and unhiding the taskbar

You can also easily hide and unhide the taskbar if you want to give yourself more screen real estate.

Here's how you hide/unhide the taskbar:

1. **Right-click a blank area in the taskbar.**

2. **Select Properties from the contextual menu that appears.**

The Taskbar and Start Menu Properties dialog box appears, as shown in Figure 2-18.

3. **Select Auto-Hide the Taskbar and then click OK.**

A check mark appears in the check box; the taskbar is no longer visible.

The auto-hide feature

Figure 2-18: Taskbar and Start Menu Properties with Auto-Hide the Taskbar enabled.

4. **Move your mouse to the very bottom of your screen.**

The taskbar is now visible. The taskbar is now set up to stay hidden until you call it up by moving the mouse to the bottom of the screen.

5. **Right-click a blank area in the taskbar.**

6. **Select Properties from the contextual menu that appears.**

7. **Select Auto-Hide the Taskbar and then click OK.**

The check mark disappears from the option box; the taskbar is now once again visible at all times.

Information Kiosk

As you explore the brave new world of Windows Vista, you may wonder at times where an option is to be found, or perhaps you think, "How do I do this?" Remember that there has always been an option since the earliest days of Windows. Select (or merely point at) the item you have a question about and then right-click. This always brings up a pop-up menu with entries relevant to what you are pointing at or selecting. Therefore, remember this mantra: "When you're not sure what to do, right-click."

Starting with the Start button

The Start button is the little orb sporting the brightly colored Microsoft logo in the bottom left of your screen. (See Figure 2-19.)

Figure 2-19: The Start button.

Users of previous versions of Windows might be used to seeing the word *Start* on this button. However, in accordance with Vista's new sleeker, cleaner design, the word *Start* has been removed. The new, seemingly anonymous icon is now known as the *Pearl*.

When you click the Pearl, a two-column menu, as shown in Figure 2-20, is launched.

Figure 2-20: The Vista Start menu.

The dual-column menu is one of the easiest ways to launch a list of your most recently used programs. You can also access the Welcome Center, Control Panel, Windows Search, and many other features by clicking this button.

Information Kiosk

You can also bring up the Start menu by pressing the Windows key on your keyboard.

The left side of the Start menu is divided horizontally into two sections. The top section contains fixed entries, which Windows automatically selects for you. The bottom section contains a constantly updated list of your most recently used programs. To open one of these applications, click the icon provided. At the very bottom of the left column is the All Programs button. Clicking this link opens a new menu that allows you to view every program you have stored on your computer. To open an item from this menu, click the appropriate icon.

The right side of the Start menu includes links to your personal documents (files, pictures, and music), computer settings, network connections, and games. You can also find the Search, Control Panel, and Help features in this part of the Start menu. And, of course, the Recent Items menu — which has an arrow to the right that when selected, shows you a list of your most recently opened files and documents — is located in this area as well. (See Figure 2-21 to see the Recent Items menu in action.) Another important button found in the right column of the Start menu is the icon used to turn off your computer. This button (which is red and shaped like a circle with a short line inside it) is how you shut down your computer. All the entries on the right side of the Start menu are fixed in their locations.

Figure 2-21: Accessing Recent Items.

Transfer

Just below the other items in the left column of the Start menu is the Instant Search box. If you like the idea of instant searching, power searching, and deep-level searching, Vista makes it possible. See Chapter 5 to learn more about searching with Vista.

Enabling the Start Menu Classic mode

If you prefer to view the Start menu as it appears in previous editions of Windows, you can. Here's how:

1. **Right-click the Start button.**

A pop-up menu appears.

2. **Choose Properties.**

The Taskbar and Start Menu Properties dialog box pops up.

3. **Select the Start Menu tab (if it is not already selected).**

You are offered two options: Start Menu and Classic Start Menu, as shown in Figure 2-22.

Figure 2-22: Choose your Start menu.

4. **Select the Classic Start Menu radio button.**

A green dot appears in the radio button to the left of this selection after you make your choice.

5. **Click OK.**

The Taskbar and Start Menu Properties dialog box disappears.

Using the Start menu in Classic mode gives this tool a completely different look. For example, the two-column design disappears. You are instead presented with a single list of options. Individual icons are replaced with topical headings. If you want to locate a particular program, you must access it through the Programs menu by clicking the arrow to the right of this selection, as shown in Figure 2-23.

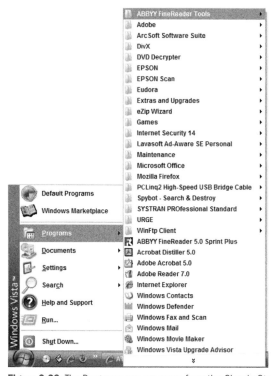

Figure 2-23: The Programs pop-up menu from the Classic Start Menu style.

Enabling this feature can save you some time in the beginning (while you are getting accustomed to Vista's new features). However, in the long run, it can be quite cumbersome because it forces you to take additional steps to achieve the same results. For many, it is much easier (and faster) to use the new Start menu for Vista, but it really is a matter of personal preference. Each menu contains the same information; just the method of locating items is different.

You can easily switch back and forth between the Vista and the Classic views as often as you like by repeating the preceding steps. To return to Vista's new Start menu, be sure to choose the Start Menu option and not the Classic Start Menu option in Step 4.

Personalizing your Start menu

Assuming that you have reactivated the Vista Start menu, you can perform certain actions to personalize this tool. For example, you can choose which icons appear in the right column of your Start menu, or you can decide exactly how many items are displayed within the Recent Items list.

To select the items included in the right column of your Start menu

1. Open the Start menu.

The Start menu appears in the bottom left of your screen.

2. Right-click in an empty space on the Start menu.

A pop-up menu appears.

3. Select Properties.

The Taskbar and Start Menu Properties dialog box pops up.

4. Select the Start Menu tab (if it is not already selected).

Make sure that the Start Menu option is selected. (A green dot should appear in the radio button to the left of this choice.)

5. Click the Customize button for the Start Menu option. (Refer to Figure 2-22.)

Note: If the Start Menu option is not selected, you can't click the Customize button. Select the radio button to the left of this option to enable it before proceeding.

The Customize Start Menu dialog box appears after you successfully click the Customize button.

6. Select (or deselect) the items you wish to include/exclude in the right column of your Start menu, as shown in Figure 2-24. (Be sure to use the scrollbar to reach all possible options.)

Figure 2-24: Selecting (or deselecting) items.

Selecting the check box to the left of an icon element adds it to or removes it from your Start menu list.

If a check mark is present, this particular item shows up in the Start menu. If no check mark is present, this item does not appear in the Start menu.

7. Click OK.

The Customize Start Menu dialog box disappears.

8. Click OK again.

The Taskbar and Start Menu Properties dialog box is closed.

Information Kiosk

You can also change the icons displayed in the Start menu if you use Classic mode. However, the process is slightly more complicated. To make personalized selections, follow Steps 1–5 in the preceding step list but be sure to select the Classic Start Menu and not the Start Menu option in Step 4. Then use the Add or Remove buttons to search for the items you wish to include on your Start menu.

To adjust the number of items displayed in your Start Menu's Recent Items list, follow these steps:

1. Open the Start menu.

The Start menu appears in the bottom left of your screen.

2. Right-click in an empty space on the Start menu.

A pop-up menu appears.

3. Choose Properties.

The Taskbar and Start Menu Properties dialog box pops up.

4. Select the Start Menu tab (if it is not already selected).

Make sure that the Start Menu option is selected. (A green dot should appear in the radio button to the left of this choice.)

5. Click the Customize button for the Start Menu option.

If the Start Menu option is not selected, you can't click this button. Select the radio button to the left of this option to enable it before proceeding.

The Customize Start Menu dialog box appears after you successfully click the Customize button.

6. Enter the number of items you would like displayed in your Recent Items list in the Start Menu Size section of this page.

You can enter any number from 0 to 30. (Refer to Figure 2-24.)

7. Click OK.

The Customize Start Menu dialog box disappears.

8. Click OK again.

The Taskbar and Start Menu Properties dialog box is closed.

Working with the Quick Launch area

To the right of the Start menu is the Quick Launch area, the second area of the Windows taskbar. (See Figure 2-25.) This convenient feature offers you another way to easily launch files and programs from your desktop, in addition to being able to select them from the Start menu or do an instant search. Being able to open these files directly from the taskbar is much more convenient than having to search through various menus to activate your files.

Figure 2-25: The Quick Launch area of the taskbar.

Adding icons to the Quick Launch area provides you with easy access to your favorite programs and files. These items can be any application, document, or folder you wish to keep at your fingertips. Follow these steps to add a new icon to the Windows Quick Launch area:

1. Open the Start menu.

The Start menu appears at the bottom left of your screen.

2. Select a program (or file) you wish to add to the Quick Launch area.

You can choose an item from your Recent Items list or use the All Programs link to locate the item you wish to add.

3. Right-click the desired program (or file).

A pop-up menu appears.

4. Select the Add to Quick Launch option.

The icon for this particular program now appears in the Windows taskbar Quick Launch area.

To open a program (or file) located in the Quick Launch area, simply click the appropriate icon. Your selection is automatically launched.

Information Kiosk

You can also click and drag icons from the desktop to the Quick Launch area of the Windows taskbar.

Watch Your Step

You can add an unlimited number of icons to the Quick Launch area of the taskbar. However, if you add more than three icons to this area, they become hidden behind the double-arrow << section of this tool. Therefore, choose only those applications or programs that you consider to be the most important or most useful to your daily activities.

To remove an item from your Quick Launch area

1. Right-click the desired program (or file).

A pop-up menu appears.

2. Choose Delete.

The Delete File dialog box (as shown in Figure 2-26) appears, asking whether you want to move this file to the Recycle Bin.

Figure 2-26: Deleting an icon from the Quick Launch area.

3. Click Yes.

The icon for this particular program disappears from within the Windows taskbar Quick Launch area.

Viewing Windows tabs

To the right of the Quick Launch area, you can find the Windows Tabs section, which is the third area of the Windows taskbar. You use Windows tabs to switch between open windows (programs, folders, documents, and so on). In Figure 2-27, you can see three open Windows tabs. Switching between windows is done by simply clicking the corresponding Windows tab. Clicking a second time on the same tab returns the window to its location on the taskbar — *minimizing* a window.

Figure 2-27: The Windows Tabs area of the taskbar.

> # **i** Information Kiosk
>
> When you have a number of windows open, you can minimize them all at once and return to your desktop by pressing Windows+D (think *D* for *desktop*). Because this action is a toggle, pressing it again brings back all your open windows.

Consolidating groups on a single Windows tab

Depending on how many programs or files you have open, the Windows taskbar can fill up fairly quickly. In Vista, when the taskbar fills up with Windows tabs, it consolidates all the files/windows within a single program into just one Windows tab. In other words, if you have two documents open in Microsoft Word, you see only one Word tab on the taskbar instead of two. You can access each of these documents by clicking that tab and selecting the file/window you want from the pop-up menu that appears. (See Figure 2-28.)

Figure 2-28: Similar documents are grouped together when the Windows Tabs area of the taskbar is full.

To turn off this feature, right-click the taskbar and choose Properties from the pop-up menu that appears. Then clear the Group Similar Taskbar check box. Each individual file now has its own Windows tab.

Flipping through Windows tabs using 3-D effects

With Aero enabled, you can flip through your windows in 3-D! Just press Windows+ Tab repeatedly to cycle through all open tabs, as shown in Figure 2-29.

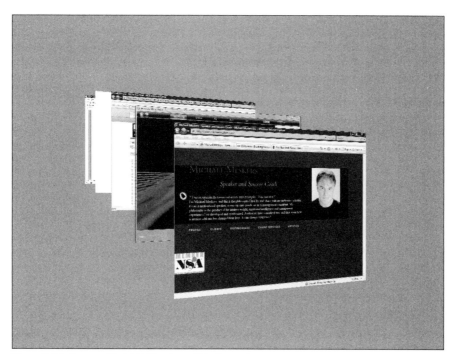

Figure 2-29: Aero-enabled 3-D Flip view of Windows tabs.

Another way of flipping through your open Windows tabs — a method available to both Aero-enabled and non-Aero-enabled machines — is to press Alt+Tab. Doing so displays thumbnail versions of your open screens, which cycle through for as long as you continue to press Alt+Tab. When you find the window you want to open, simply let go of the Alt+Tab key combination to automatically bring the selected window into view. (Figure 2-30 shows you a screen display with an Aero-enabled PC, and Figure 2-31 shows the non-Aero version.)

Figure 2-30: Aero-enabled Windows tabs.

Figure 2-31: Non-Aero-enabled Windows tabs.

Information Kiosk

You may want to use Windows+Tab and Alt+Tab whenever you have hidden the taskbar in order to enjoy more screen space. However, note that these shortcut keys display only the Windows tabs; they do not reveal the other areas of your taskbar.

Understanding the Notification area

To the right of the Windows Tabs area is the fourth area of the Windows taskbar, or the *Notification area* (formerly known as the *system tray*). (See Figure 2-32.) This section of the taskbar acts much like a Quick Launch area for your peripheral devices, some third-party software (usually security related), and your system settings, including volume control, update notifications, and the time.

Figure 2-32: The Notification area.

The Notification area displays select icons for programs that have been loaded to your PC's memory; however, not all programs place an icon in this tray. The icons that do appear typically relate to the settings found on your computer.

Several of the icons located in this area — including the system clock, volume indicator, network connections, and security updates — represent built-in programs for the Windows system.

Here is a brief explanation for each of the Notification area's standard icons:

- **System clock:** Shows the time. To change the time (or date) saved to your PC, left-click in an empty space around the system clock. A pop-up window appears, allowing you to make adjustments.

- **Volume indicator:** Allows you to raise, lower, or mute the sound from your system's audio device.

- **Network connections:** Shows what network devices you have installed on your PC and whether they are active.

- **Security updates:** Notifies you when new security updates are available for download from the Microsoft Web site.

- **Hardware devices:** Shows icons for added hardware devices (such as a printer or modem card) to your computer. These icons vary from one machine to another, depending on the hardware (or software) installed on the PC.

Transfer

In Windows Vista, you no longer see icons for Windows Firewall or for Windows Defender in the Notification area. See Chapter 9 to learn about the Windows Firewall and Windows Defender tools.

Information Kiosk

As you install new programs, the Notification area automatically contracts in order to make room for any icons associated with those programs. You can expand the Notification area icon display by clicking the Expand button to the left of this area.

Over time, you might begin to see what simply looks like too many icons in the Notification area. Chances are that you don't need them there. However, these icons loaded into the Notification area are actually programs, or parts of programs, taking up valuable memory space in the computer's RAM. To delete these items

1. Open the Start menu.

The Start menu appears in the bottom left of your screen.

2. Choose All Programs.

The All Programs menu appears in the left column of the Start menu.

3. Choose Accessories.

A list of items included in this folder appears, as shown in Figure 2-33.

4. Click Run.

The Run dialog box opens. (See Figure 2-34.)

5. In the empty field, type msconfig **and then click OK.**

The System Configuration dialog box appears. (See Figure 2-35.)

6. Select the Startup tab.

A long list of items that are currently running on your computer is produced.

7. Choose the programs you want to delete, using the check boxes to the left of the active programs to disable these items.

If no check mark appears in the program's box, it is disabled. If a check mark does appear, it is enabled.

You can also choose to enable or disable all programs by using the buttons provided at the bottom of the dialog box.

8. Click OK.

The System Configuration dialog box disappears.

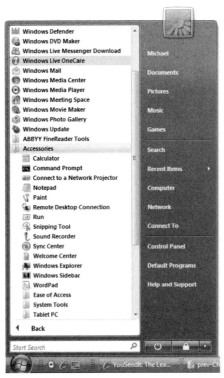

Figure 2-33: Choosing Run from the Accessories folder helps clean up your Notification area icons.

Figure 2-34: The Run dialog box.

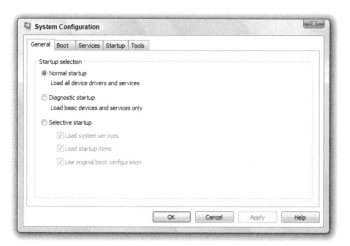

Figure 2-35: The System Configuration dialog box.

Customizing the taskbar

Many users find that customizing the taskbar saves them from having to play "Windows archeologist" — that is, not having to dig through menus and sometimes submenus simply to launch important programs and files. Understanding how to customize the taskbar can save you a considerable amount of time.

One way to customize your taskbar is to add frequently used toolbars to the Windows Tabs section. This allows you to access various documents and menu items quickly and easily. However, use this feature sparingly, or you won't have any room left on the taskbar for your Windows tabs.

To add a new toolbar to your taskbar

1. **Place your cursor on a blank space in the Quick Launch area and right-click.**

A pop-up menu appears.

2. **Choose Toolbars from the pop-up menu.**

The Toolbars submenu appears, as shown in Figure 2-36.

3. **Choose New Toolbar.**

The New Toolbar dialog box appears. (See Figure 2-37.)

4. **Click the folder or menu you wish to add to your taskbar.**

The name of the item you have selected now appears in the Folder text box.

5. **Click the Select Folder button.**

The New Toolbar dialog box disappears, and the folder you selected is automatically placed to the right of the Windows taskbar, as shown in Figure 2-38.

Figure 2-36: Start your taskbar customization here.

Figure 2-37: The New Toolbar dialog box.

Figure 2-38: Documents added to the taskbar.

The folder you chose has two double arrows next to it. Clicking these arrows makes all the items in this folder appear in a pop-up menu. Selecting a file or document from this menu automatically launches it from the taskbar.

To remove a toolbar from the taskbar

1. **Right-click the toolbar you want to remove.**

A pop-up menu appears.

2. **Choose Toolbars.**

The Toolbars submenu appears.

Your active toolbars are indicated by a green check mark.

3. **Click the name of the item you want to remove.**

The Toolbar submenu disappears, as does the designated toolbar.

Using the Windows Sidebar

The Sidebar is a newly added feature of the Windows desktop. This application allows you easy access to various *Gadgets* (or tools). Some of these Gadgets are reminiscent of the informational screen savers that provide continuously updated information, like real-time weather reports, stock quotes, and foreign exchange rates. Other items — such as the Calculator and Notes features — are just handy tools to have around. These items can be particularly useful when you do not have access to real-world materials (such as a calculator or pen and paper).

Activating the Sidebar

The Sidebar usually appears by default as a column against the right side of your desktop. If the Sidebar does not automatically appear onscreen, you can add it to your desktop by following these instructions:

1. **Open the Start menu.**

The Start menu appears in the lower left of your screen.

2. **Choose Control Panel from the right side of the Start menu.**

The Control Panel window appears. (See Figure 2-39.)

3. **Select Appearance and Personalization.**

The Appearance and Personalization dialog box appears, as shown in Figure 2-40.

Figure 2-39: Opening the Control Panel.

Figure 2-40: The Appearance and Personalization page.

4. Choose Windows Sidebar Properties.

The Windows Sidebar Properties dialog box opens. (See Figure 2-41.)

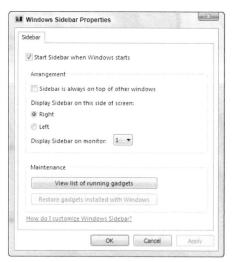

Figure 2-41: The Windows Sidebar Properties dialog box.

5. In order to have the Sidebar automatically open when Windows starts, select the check box to the left of the Start Sidebar When Windows Starts option at the top of the page.

A green check mark shows up in the box when your selection is made.

Note there are two options for positioning the sidebar: On the right or left side of the screen.

6. Click OK.

The Windows Sidebar Properties dialog box closes.

7. Close the Appearance and Personalization dialog box.

Clicking the X in the upper right of this page closes the Appearance and Personalization dialog box.

8. Restart your computer.

This automatically brings up the Sidebar when Windows opens.

When the Sidebar is open, you can close it by right-clicking in an empty space in the Sidebar and then choosing Close Sidebar from the drop-down menu that appears, as shown in Figure 2-42. To reopen this tool, simply click on the Sidebar icon located in the Notification area of the taskbar.

If you decide that you do not want to open the Sidebar tool each time Windows is launched (perhaps you find it to be too bulky, or maybe you just don't use it enough to afford it consistent screen space), simply repeat the preceding steps but clear the check box in Step 5.

Figure 2-42: The Windows Sidebar. Right-click to see its pop-up menu.

Information Kiosk

You can choose to move the Sidebar to the left side of your screen if you prefer. Just open the Windows Sidebar Properties dialog box and click the Left radio button in the Arrangement section. This moves your Sidebar from the right side of your screen to the left.

Choosing your Gadgets

Gadgets are the individual tools located within the Windows Sidebar. These items, despite the fact that they look somewhat toy-like, are actually mini-applications that perform some highly practical functions. Having a large clock, for example, or a calendar, notes, or contact list can help you stay organized. Having immediate access to weather information, stock tickers, and foreign exchange can be very useful to the business traveler.

Three applications are automatically included in the Sidebar when you first open it: the Clock, Slide Show (if you have created one), and Feed Viewer. However, you can add and remove Gadgets from the Sidebar at any time.

Here is a list of the Gadgets offered by Windows.

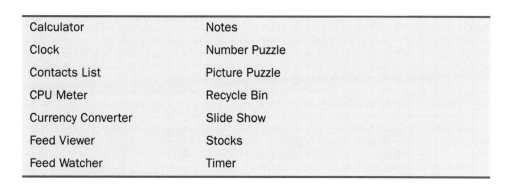

Calculator	Notes
Clock	Number Puzzle
Contacts List	Picture Puzzle
CPU Meter	Recycle Bin
Currency Converter	Slide Show
Feed Viewer	Stocks
Feed Watcher	Timer

Transfer

The Feed Viewer and Feed Watcher refer to RSS feeds, which you can read more about in Chapter 3.

Information Kiosk

The Recycle Bin, which has been on the Windows desktop for years, is also considered a Gadget even though it doesn't reside in the Sidebar.

To add a Gadget to the Sidebar

1. Open the Windows Sidebar.

Refer to the instructions in the earlier "Activating the Sidebar" section if necessary.

2. Click the Add Gadgets button at the top of the Sidebar.

This button, as shown in Figure 2-43, is a plus sign.

Figure 2-43: The Add Gadgets button.

The Gadgets Gallery opens (see Figure 2-44), which includes a list of available gadgets. If you are connected to the Internet, you can also choose to browse the Web for downloadable Gadgets.

3. Click and drag the desired tools from the Gadgets Gallery to the Sidebar.

The items you select appear in your list of existing Sidebar items.

4. Close the Gadgets Gallery page when you finish choosing your Gadgets.

Clicking the X in the upper right of this page removes it from your screen.

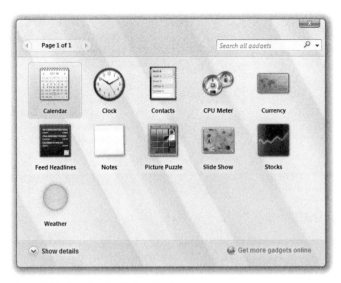

Figure 2-44: Opening the Gadgets Gallery.

Information Kiosk

You can rearrange the order of your Gadgets by clicking and dragging these icons to a new location within the Sidebar. You can even drag them onto your desktop.

If you decide that you no longer have a need for a particular Gadget, you can remove it from the Sidebar by clicking its individual Close button (located to the right of the gadget icon) or by right-clicking the Gadget itself and choosing Close Gadget from the drop-down menu that appears.

Information Kiosk

If you have more than four or five Gadgets in your Sidebar, Windows automatically creates a new page for these extra tools. Use the navigation arrows (located to the right of the Add Gadgets button) to move between the pages in your Sidebar.

Aero: The name of Vista's new user interface. This acronym stands for *Authentic, Energetic, Reflective,* and *Open*. It includes all sorts of desktop visuals. With a high-end video card (see Chapter 1 for hardware requirements), you can view a number of 3-D and special effects on your desktop.

Classic mode: The styles, layouts, formats, and forms from previous versions of Windows.

DOS (Disk Operating System): The name of one of the first UIs ever created for a personal computer.

Gadgets: Small applications (or applets) located within the Sidebar. These items can range anywhere from simple utilities meant to help you perform specific tasks to continuous feeds that provide you with up-to-the-minute information — all of which can be customized to reflect your own personal needs and tastes.

GUI (graphical user interface): A specific kind of UI; one that is highly visual in nature. GUIs typically include various types of images and other graphics to attract the user's attention.

opaque: In Windows, the visual effect of Vista that allows you to control the transparency of your windows.

Pearl: Microsoft's nickname for the new Vista Start button.

screen saver: The software application used to preserve your PC monitor's vitality. By applying a blank screen (or one with a constantly moving object) during periods of prolonged inactivity, you can help prevent long-term wear and tear on your computer's monitor.

Sidebar: The new Windows Vista feature that stores a number of handy Gadgets (or tools) for you to use whenever you need them.

taskbar: The toolbar located (traditionally) at the bottom of the Windows page. This feature consists of four main parts: the Start button, Quick Launch area, Windows tabs, and Notification area. This tool is the primary navigation tool for many Windows users.

toolbar: Bars of menus or buttons, usually docked at the top or the bottom of a Windows screen. Some have three by default; others can be added as needed. Each of these menus or buttons has functionality assigned to them.

transparency: Describes a glassy, see-through, luminescent effect added to the edges of the windows as part of the Windows Aero set of features.

continued

user interface (UI): The experience that a computer user encounters when interacting with his/her PC.

wallpaper: The background for your desktop screen. It can be an image, a photo, a color, or an individually created design. This feature lets you personalize your PC so that it reflects your own personality and tastes.

Last Stop

Practice Exam

1. What are the four main areas of the Windows taskbar?

_____

_____

_____

2. Which option enables you to keep the taskbar off the screen until you're ready to use it again?

_____

_____

_____

3. What are the benefits of using the Aero interface in Vista?

_____

_____

_____

4. What are some of the advantages associated with using the taskbar?

_____

_____

_____

5. How do you ungroup Windows tabs?

_____

_____

_____

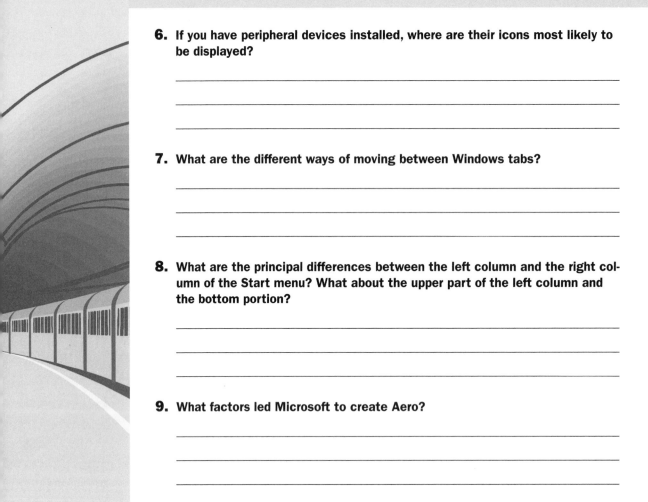

6. If you have peripheral devices installed, where are their icons most likely to be displayed?

_____

_____

_____

7. What are the different ways of moving between Windows tabs?

_____

_____

_____

8. What are the principal differences between the left column and the right column of the Start menu? What about the upper part of the left column and the bottom portion?

_____

_____

_____

9. What factors led Microsoft to create Aero?

_____

_____

_____

EXIT

Welcome to Internet Explorer 7

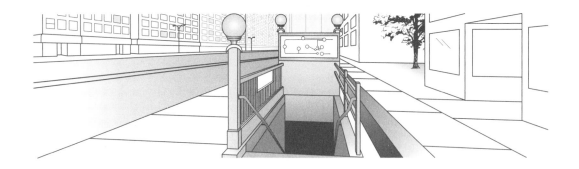

 # Enter the Station

Questions

1. What's new in the IE7 interface?

2. What is the Phishing filter and when should it be turned on?

3. How is exploring the Web faster and easier with IE7?

4. How can tabbed browsing help you manage your Web pages?

5. What's in the Favorites Center?

6. What can you do to personalize your browser?

7. How can IE7 help you locate files stored on your computer?

Express Line

If you are already up to speed on Internet Explorer 7, skip ahead to the next chapter.

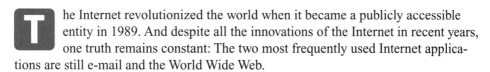

The Internet revolutionized the world when it became a publicly accessible entity in 1989. And despite all the innovations of the Internet in recent years, one truth remains constant: The two most frequently used Internet applications are still e-mail and the World Wide Web.

Starting in the early 1990s, various Internet service providers (ISPs) came into being. These ISPs, including companies like America Online (AOL), began offering public access to the Internet during this time. As people began to establish solid Internet connections, they began to use the Web more frequently. To many, the Internet has become such an ingrained part of their lives that they use it nearly every day, whether for work-related purposes, keeping in touch with family and friends, or exploring the abundant amount of information stored on the Web.

Nowadays, one can choose to engage in many different types of activities online. In addition to using e-mail or surfing the Web, Internet users can read news articles, view local weather data, listen to music, and watch video clips. The tool that permits users to access the information located on the Web is a *browser*. The browser included with Windows Vista is Internet Explorer 7 (IE7).

Microsoft's Internet Explorer has evolved a great deal since the first version was released in 1995. Microsoft's intent when drafting the original Internet Explorer was to create competition for Netscape, which until that point had held the leading Internet browser position. Since the introduction of Netscape and Internet Explorer, other browsers have come into being, including Opera and Firefox. However, Microsoft's browser continues to dominate the browsing market.

With the release of IE7, Microsoft manages to build upon its market-leading browsing tool. Microsoft has added new safety features, more accessible search capabilities, and a cleaner look that is consistent with Windows Vista's new desktop design.

This chapter reveals what's new in IE7 and how to use Microsoft's browser to explore the Internet. Exploring IE7's new interface, activating the Phishing filter and Pop-up Blocker, and using tabbed browsing are some examples of the IE7 features covered in this chapter.

Launching Internet Explorer

Launching, or opening, IE7 is the first step to exploring the Web. If Internet browsing is like a long distance road trip, launching IE7 is like starting the car before pulling out of the driveway. You must first start the vehicle before driving. In this instance, you must open IE7 before you can explore the Web.

Follow these steps to launch IE7:

1. **Click the Start button.**

A pop-up menu appears. (See Figure 3-1.)

Figure 3-1: The Windows Vista Start menu.

2. **Choose Internet Explorer.**

The IE7 page shown in Figure 3-2 appears onscreen.

The page seen at startup of IE7 is known as the *home page*. By default, it is set to open to the IE7 main page, but you can change your home page to any Web page you'd like. See the "Creating multiple home pages" section later in this chapter for more information.

Watch Your Step

You must first be connected to the Internet before you can use IE7 to browse the Web. If you are not connected to the Internet, you will see a `Cannot Find Server` or `Internet Explorer cannot display the webpage` error message when IE7 is launched.

If one of these messages appears on your screen, check your Internet connection. Make sure that your computer is plugged in to your telephone line (for dial-up access), connected to your cable/DSL modem, or that your wireless connection is set up properly on your computer. If everything seems to be in order, contact your Internet service provider for further assistance.

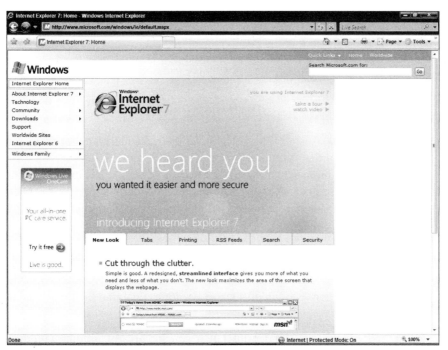

Figure 3-2: The IE7 home page automatically appears when the browser is first launched.

Introducing What's New in IE7

IE7 is the first major overhaul of Microsoft's Internet browser since version 4.0 was released in 1997. IE7 has a completely new look and several new features. This chapter discusses the new features and capabilities of IE7.

- **New user interface:** The new sleeker, cleaner-looking design of IE7 creates more room onscreen for Web browsing windows.

- **Phishing filter:** Activating this feature keeps you and your personal information safe from online predators.

- **Quick Search:** Use this tool to search the Web directly from the main page instead of having to seek out a separate search button.

- **Browser tabs:** IE7's new browser tabs feature lets you open several different windows within the same browser session rather than having to open up numerous IE screens.

Some of IE7's new features — like its new user interface, tabbed browsing, and Quick Search capabilities — provide you with an improved Web-browsing experience. Other features, such as the Phishing filter, offer added security.

Transfer

Many of the innovations of Internet Explorer 7 are about security. To learn about all the major security features of Windows Vista, skip to Chapter 4.

Looking at the new IE7 user interface

Much like Windows Vista itself, the IE7 user interface has undergone a major overhaul. If you are familiar with previous versions of Internet Explorer, you can see that IE7 now provides more screen space for browser windows. The extra screen space is available because many of the menus and buttons found in previous versions of Internet Explorer have been replaced with icons, relocated on the toolbar, or reorganized under a different menu.

Locating the menu bar

Activating the menu toolbar (the one with words, not icons) shows menu items as they appear in earlier versions of Internet Explorer. Enabling the traditional menu toolbar is a matter of personal preference.

The menu toolbar is a convenient feature if you are already familiar with the location of your favorite menu items. Using the menu toolbar also enables you to preview the items listed in a particular menu without having to click a menu button. (Moving your mouse over a title in the menu toolbar automatically pulls up the submenu for that particular category.)

To activate the menu toolbar

1. **Click Tools.**

   A drop-down menu appears. (See Figure 3-3.)

   If the menu toolbar is already enabled, a check mark shows up next to the Menu Bar option. If it is not yet enabled, no check mark is present.

2. **Choose Menu Bar.**

   The drop-down menu vanishes, and the menu toolbar appears in the upper left of the screen, as shown in Figure 3-4.

To remove the menu toolbar, repeat the preceding steps.

Information Kiosk

Right-clicking in the toolbar area also allows you to select or deselect the Menu Bar option. To activate the menu toolbar using shortcut keys, press Alt+F.

Figure 3-3: Use the Tools menu to add or remove the menu toolbar.

Adding the menu toolbar to your screen.

Figure 3-4: Activating the menu toolbar provides experienced Internet Explorer users with a sense of familiarity.

Diving deeper into the IE7 interface

The new sleeker look of IE7 is appealing because its use of icons and buttons creates more space for browser windows. Experienced Internet Explorer users might find that the switch to the new interface entails a slight learning curve, the most difficult aspect of which is learning what each button stands for and what it does. Discovering the names and functions of IE7's icons and buttons is also a task for users who are not familiar with previous editions of Internet Explorer.

Here's a brief explanation for each of the standard IE7 buttons and icons:

- **Back:** Clicking the left-pointing arrow takes you back to the previously viewed Web page.

- **Forward:** Clicking the right-pointing arrow takes you forward to the Web page viewed immediately after the page currently appearing onscreen.

- **Recent Pages:** This drop-down menu contains a list of recently viewed Web pages. Highlighting a site from this list redirects the browser to the selected page.

- **Address bar:** This is where you enter Internet addresses.

- **Refresh:** Clicking this circular-looking button *refreshes* (updates) the content of the active Web page.

- **Stop:** Clicking this red X button halts the transmission process, prohibiting IE7 from connecting to a requested site.

- **Live Search:** Entering a word or term in this toolbar commences an Internet search for related Web sites, articles, newsgroups, and so on.

- **Search Options:** Use this magnifying glass icon and drop-down menu to find and choose a default search engine.

- **Favorites Center:** This houses links to your favorite sites, RSS (Really Simple Syndication) feeds, and browser history.

- **Add to Favorites:** Clicking this star button saves an open page to your Favorites.

- **Browser tabs:** Clicking a browser tab brings the selected Web page up onscreen.

- **Home:** Clicking this house icon transfers the open Web page to your preferred home page(s). You can also add or change your home pages from this drop-down menu.

- **Feeds:** This indicates whether a Web site has RSS feed capabilities.

- **Print:** Use this to print Web pages with just one click. Previewing a print job and altering settings are also options found in this icon's drop-down menu.

- **Page:** This menu is a combination of the old File, Edit, and View menus. With it, you can open a new IE7 session, cut, copy, paste, save Web pages to your computer, e-mail links to friends, and adjust viewing preferences.

Tools: This menu contains a variety of viewing and browsing tools. Options here include deleting browsing history, accessing the Pop-Up Blocker and Phishing filter, managing add-ons, adding or removing toolbars, and adjusting your Internet options.

 Double arrow: Clicking this button reveals the Help and Windows Messenger features.

Figure 3-5 shows the placement of these features at the top of the new Internet Explorer 7 interface.

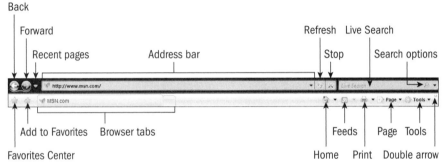

Figure 3-5: Getting to know the new IE7 user interface.

Information Kiosk

To see the name of an IE7 icon, hover your mouse over its button to bring up the icon or menu title.

Accessing Web sites quickly

The fastest way to access a Web site is to type its URL (Uniform Resource Locator), or Internet address, in the Address bar. Typing a site's URL into the Address bar ensures that the browser goes directly to the site you wish to see. Knowing a site's URL is more efficient than searching for a Web page. However, if you do not know a Web site's URL, the Search feature is an excellent way to locate this information.

 ## Transfer

To learn more about using IE7 search features, check out the "Quickly searching the Web" section, later in this chapter.

To access a specific Web site by using a URL

1. Left-click in the Address bar.

The current URL is highlighted.

2. Type the new URL into the Address bar.

You can use any URL you like. Some examples you might try include `www.amazon.com`, `www.microsoft.com`, or `www.wiley.com`.

3. Press Enter (on your keyboard).

The browser is directed to the specified Web site.

Watch Your Step

The first time you attempt to access a new Web page, the IE7 Phishing Filter dialog box appears. Check out the next section of this chapter to learn more about the Phishing filter.

Information Kiosk

Typing domain names (the part between the `www.` and `.com` portions of a URL) into the Address bar and pressing Ctrl+Enter generates the same results as typing a Web site's entire URL. Using this keyboard shortcut instructs IE7 to resolve the address on its own and then add the `http://www.` and `.com` sections of the URL for you, saving you both keystrokes and time. (This shortcut only works for URLs with a .com extension; however, if you are going to a site with another domain extension, simply use this shortcut and then — after the page loads — backspace over the extension part of the URL and type in `.org`, `.gov`, `.edu`, and so on.

Activating the Phishing filter

The Phishing filter is a new Internet Explorer security feature, which keeps you (and your personal information) safe from online predators.

Phishing (fishing) refers to a form of deception where Web users surfing the Net are unwittingly directed to a fraudulent Web site, where attempts are made to collect personal information about the user. This can be both dangerous and annoying for people surfing the Web unprotected.

Phishing is dangerous because some culprits who use this method of collecting data can attempt to steal personal information (like credit card, online banking, or Social Security numbers) to perform malicious acts. They might even try to use this information to assume your online identity and make outrageous purchases or obtain loans under your name.

Phishing can also be annoying. For example, you might click an advertisement for multivitamins and instead be directed to a site about male enhancement drugs. This can also be risky if you become a victim of phishing while at work. (Obviously, no one wants to lose their job because their browser inadvertently visits a pornographic site when they're actually trying to research a work-related topic on the Internet.) This is also something parents should be aware of if they have children who use the computer to surf the Web.

To help prevent someone from stealing your identity or sending your browser to an unwanted Web site, activate the IE7 built-in Phishing filter. However, keep in mind that this security feature is not foolproof because you are still free to ignore the warnings and proceed forward (perhaps to your detriment).

The first time you access a new Web site in IE7, the Microsoft Phishing Filter dialog box (see Figure 3-6) automatically appears onscreen.

The Microsoft Phishing Filter dialog box offers the following three options:

Turn On Automatic Phishing Filter (Recommended): Clearly, Microsoft strongly recommends activating the Phishing filter during your very first browsing session.

Figure 3-6: The Phishing Filter dialog box automatically appears the first time a Web site is accessed in IE7.

Turn Off Automatic Phishing Filter: If you decide to ignore Microsoft's advice, choose this option.

Ask Me Later: If you are unsure whether to turn the Phishing filter on during your first browsing session, the activation process can be postponed until the next time IE7 is opened. To take advantage of this option, select the Ask Me Later check box. The next time IE7 is launched, the Phishing Filter dialog box appears again as it did before. These same results can be achieved by closing the Phishing Filter dialog box before selecting a filter preference.

Click OK in the Microsoft Phishing Filter dialog box to confirm your decision.

Transfer

For a more in-depth understanding of how the Phishing filter feature is crucial to your browsing the Web securely, see the next chapter.

Whether you opt to activate, postpone, or disable the Phishing filter during your first visit, you can always choose to change your Phishing filter preference later. For example, if you originally elect to turn off the Phishing filter but decide you now want to enable this feature, you can. The same is true if you initially chose to activate the Phishing filter but later wish to disable this feature.

To change your Phishing filter preference

1. **Click the Tools button on the right side of the main menu.**

A drop-down list appears.

2. **Highlight Phishing Filter.**

The Phishing Filter submenu appears to the left of the Tools menu. (See Figure 3-7.)

3. **Select Turn On/Off Automatic Website Checking.**

The Phishing Filter dialog box appears onscreen. (Refer to Figure 3-6.)

4. **Select the radio button of your choice.**

Selecting Turn On Automatic Phishing Filter (Recommended) activates the Phishing filter security feature.

Selecting Turn Off Automatic Phishing Filter disables this security feature.

5. **Click OK.**

The Phishing Filter dialog box disappears.

Figure 3-7: Changing your Phishing filter status via the Tools menu.

Taking advantage of the Pop-Up Blocker

Although not new to IE7 — it actually dates from IE6 — the Pop-Up Blocker can make your online life a bit pleasanter. Although the Pop-Up Blocker doesn't necessarily protect you from unwanted invasions, it does protect you from unwanted annoyances.

The Pop-Up Blocker does exactly what its name suggests: It blocks pop-up windows. The Pop-Up Blocker is the tool that enables you to explore the Internet without being bombarded with advertisements that do not interest you while still affording you with the opportunity to view the pop-ups you do wish to see.

Although most users find unsolicited pop-up windows intrusive, some pop-ups should be seen — for example, a printer-friendly version of a Web page, or a link to a map providing directions to a place you are planning to visit, as shown in Figure 3-8.

Enabling (or disabling) the Pop-Up Blocker

Like with the Phishing filter feature, IE7 permits you to enable or disable the Pop-Up Blocker whenever you like. Whether you decide to enable the Pop-Up Blocker depends on how often you receive unwanted pop-up windows. If the Web sites you visit do not typically expose you to unwanted or unsolicited pop-ups, you might opt to leave the Pop-Up Blocker off. However, if you are constantly bombarded with information that you have no desire to receive, enabling the Pop-Up Blocker can be quite beneficial. (Keep in mind that there are some Web sites that actually request you to turn off Pop-Up Blocker in order to use their site.)

Figure 3-8: The IE7 Pop-Up Blocker restricts the amount of unwanted pop-ups but allows requested information to be viewed.

To enable the Pop-Up Blocker

1. Click the Tools button on the right side of the main menu.

A drop-down menu appears.

2. Highlight Pop-Up Blocker.

The Pop-Up Blocker submenu appears to the left of the Tools menu. (See Figure 3-9.)

3. Select Turn On Pop-Up Blocker.

The Pop-Up Blocker is enabled.

On the other hand, if IE7's Pop-Up Blocker is prohibiting pop-ups that you wish to see, you might prefer to turn this feature off. Simply repeat the preceding steps but select Turn Off Pop-Up Blocker in Step 3.

Figure 3-9: Use the Tools menu to enable or disable the Pop-Up Blocker feature.

The pop-ups information bar

When the Pop-Up Blocker is enabled and a pop-up window is blocked, a yellow information bar appears onscreen to notify you of this occurrence. The information bar, as shown in Figure 3-10, is located just below the IE7 toolbar.

Right-clicking the information toolbar produces a drop-down list, which offers you three options:

- Temporarily allow pop-ups.
- Always allow pop-ups from the current Web site.
- Adjust the Pop-Up Blocker settings.

Information Kiosk

If you don't want to view a pop-up but would like to remove the yellow bar from your screen, click the X on the right side of the toolbar. This closes the information toolbar — at least until the next pop-up window is blocked.

Information toolbar

Figure 3-10: A yellow information bar alerts you when a pop-up window is blocked.

The Temporarily Allow Pop-ups feature

Of the options available from the information toolbar drop-down list (refer to Figure 3-10), the Temporarily Allow Pop-Ups option is the most popular. This selection is used most often because it allows you to view pop-ups on a case-by-case basis. If, for example, you want to see a specific pop-up window but don't necessarily want to receive pop-ups from this Web site in the future, select the Temporarily Allow Pop-Ups feature. This lets you view the current pop-up at this particular instance without having to worry about receiving a bunch of unwanted pop-ups from this site later.

Watch Your Step

When choosing to temporarily allow pop-ups, you might not necessarily know beforehand whether the pop-up window is something you want to view.

Information Kiosk

Right-clicking a pop-up window produces a menu that allows you to save, copy, or create a shortcut directly to the window; add it to your Favorites; or make it a screen saver.

The Always Allow Pop-Ups from This Site feature

If you're familiar with the pop-up generating Web site and don't mind receiving pop-ups from this site on a regular basis, you can select Always Allow Pop-Ups from This Site from the information toolbar instead. This option prevents you from having to manually open every pop-up window generated by a trusted Web site. Always allowing pop-ups from trusted Web sites is convenient for sites that are visited frequently and that have links to information you wish access on a regular basis, say for online e-mail accounts. By always allowing pop-up windows from a selected e-mail site, you do not have to worry about giving IE7 permission to open each message you wish to read, saving you the hassle of having to open each message individually.

Amending your Pop-Up Blocker settings

Of course, you can add Web sites to the list of trusted pop-ups without having to wait until you receive a blocked pop-up from each site. Amending the browser's Pop-Up Blocker settings allows you to add (or remove) a Web site from your trusted pop-ups list.

To add Web sites to your trusted pop-ups list, follow these steps:

1. **Click the Tools button on the right side of the main menu.**

   A drop-down list appears.

2. **Highlight Pop-Up Blocker.**

   The Pop-Up Blocker submenu appears to the left of the Tools menu. (Refer to Figure 3-9.)

3. **Select Pop-Up Blocker Settings.**

   The Pop-Up Blocker Settings dialog box appears. (See Figure 3-11.)

Figure 3-11: Use the Pop-Up Blocker Settings dialog box to add or remove URLs from your list of trusted pop-up Web sites.

4. Enter the URL for a trusted Web site.

Type the Internet address, or *URL,* of the Web site you want to exempt from the Pop-Up Blocker filter into the Address of Website to Allow field. (Refer to Figure 3-11.)

5. Click Add.

The address for the trusted Web site appears in the Allowed Sites field. (Refer to Figure 3-11.)

Note: To add additional Web sites to this category, repeat Steps 4 and 5.

6. Click Close.

The Pop-Up Blocker Settings dialog box disappears.

If you decide to remove a Web site from your trusted sites list (perhaps you receive too many unwanted pop-ups from this site), you can use this same Pop-Up Blocker Settings dialog box to delete the site's URL as well.

Information Kiosk

In IE7, the entire URL of the pop-up window is displayed, allowing you to see the origin of the pop-up and determine whether it's an advertisement or information from the site itself.

If the URL indicates that the pop-up is from an unwanted source (such as an advertising site), you can block ads from that site by using the Pop-Up Blocker.

Exploring the World Wide Web

You can do many things while surfing the Web: Check local weather conditions, read today's news, shop online, listen to music, watch videos, and so on. The list is practically endless. However, all these activities have one factor in common: They all use IE7 to get you to the sites you want to visit.

Transfer

To learn more about how to listen to music or watch videos online, check out Chapter 9.

The fastest way to access a Web site is, of course, to enter its URL into the Address bar. (See the "Accessing Web sites quickly" section, earlier in this chapter.) However, you can locate Web pages other ways even if you don't know a site's URL. Fortunately, IE7 has built-in features to help you find these sites.

Finding recently viewed URLs

The Recent Pages drop-down list is useful when you can't remember the URL of a Web site you've visited lately. This tool keeps track of all the Web sites viewed during the past two weeks (unless you use the Internet Options dialog box — see Figure 3-14 — to change the default settings).

To find the URL for a Web site you visited recently

1. Click the drop-down arrow at the right of the Address bar.

A drop-down list of URLs appears. (See Figure 3-12.)

2. Click the URL you wish to view.

The browser redirects the open page to the new Web site.

If you can't recall the URL for a Web site, you might be in for a bit of trial and error when using the Recent Pages list. However, if you can remember at least the beginning of the URL (for example, you're sure it begins with an *e*), you can narrow down the list of URLs to choose from by using the AutoComplete feature.

The AutoComplete feature works very much like the Recent Pages list. Instead of using the drop-down icon, though, you type the first part of the unknown URL directly into the Address bar.

Figure 3-12: Viewing recently visited URLs.

To find a URL with the IE7 AutoComplete feature

1. **Left-click in the Address bar.**

   The current URL is highlighted.

2. **Begin typing the first part of the incomplete URL.**

   A drop-down list of Web sites matching the letters or words you are typing automatically appears. (See Figure 3-13.)

   This list continues to change as you type, narrowing the list down even further with each new letter that is entered.

3. **Click the URL you wish to view.**

   The browser redirects the open page to the new Web site.

Sometimes, after a lot of browsing activity, the AutoComplete list can become a bit too extensive, making using the AutoComplete feature more cumbersome than helpful. Deleting the AutoComplete history files remedies an overabundant amount of URLs. It will also delete AutoComplete entries in Web forms. And if you choose to clean up your AutoComplete items, it will also clear any mistyped entries that may have been saved. (Keep in mind, though, that you cannot selectively delete history files; your only choice is to delete all such files.)

Figure 3-13: AutoComplete saves typing and helps find recently viewed URLs.

To clean up the AutoComplete history list

1. **Click the Tools button on the right side of the main menu.**

A drop-down menu appears.

2. **Select Internet Options.**

The Internet Options dialog box (shown in Figure 3-14) appears.

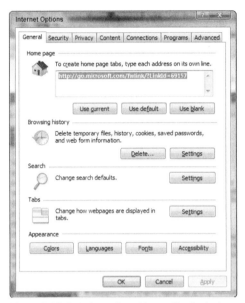

Figure 3-14: Deleting tedious history files in the Internet Options dialog box.

3. **Choose the General tab (if it's not already selected).**

The General tab is divided into five sections: Home Page, Browsing History, Search, Tabs, and Appearance. (Refer to Figure 3-14.)

4. **Click the Delete button in the Browsing History section.**

The Delete Browsing History dialog box appears, as shown in Figure 3-15.

5. **Click Delete History.**

A dialog box appears, confirming whether you want to delete your history of viewed Web sites.

6. **Click Yes.**

The confirmation dialog box disappears.

7. **Close the Delete Browsing History dialog box.**

The Delete Browsing History dialog box disappears.

8. **Close the Internet Options dialog box.**

The Internet Options dialog box disappears.

Figure 3-15: Delete temporary Internet files, cookies, browser history, form data, and saved passwords here.

Quickly searching the Web

IE7 has added a new Live Search feature to its main page. The new Live Search toolbar lets you search the Web directly from the IE7 home page without having to select a separate search button or menu. Having this Live Search feature on the IE7 main page saves you time and keystrokes (or rather, clicks). The Live Search box is located in the upper right of the screen. (See Figure 3-16.)

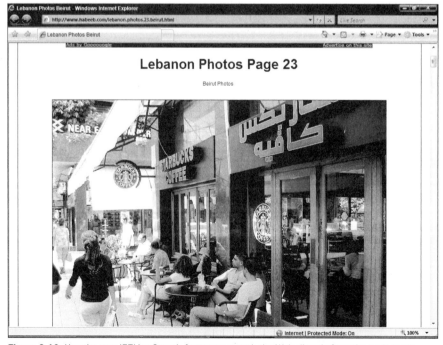

Figure 3-16: Use the new IE7 Live Search feature to search the Web directly from the main page.

To use the new IE7 Live Search feature

1. Click in the Live Search text box.

The words Live Search disappear, and you can type in whatever word or term you like.

2. Type a search word or term into the Live Search text box.

To find what's playing at a local theater, for example, enter **movie theaters**.

3. Press Enter.

A list of related Web sites, articles, news groups, and other links is generated and posted on your screen.

A Related Searches list also appears on the right side of the screen. This list offers suggestions for more specific search topics. To select one of these search terms, click the bolded word. Your browser automatically generates a new list of search material based on your selection.

Figure 3-17 shows what you might get if you searched for *movie theaters*.

4. Select a Web site.

Clicking a Web site link redirects the open page to the new location.

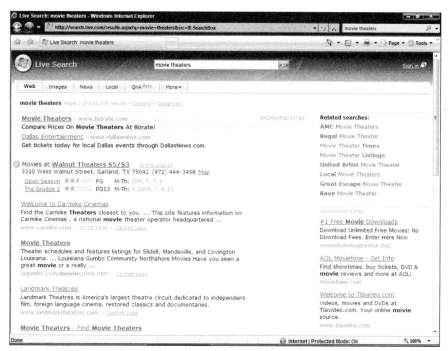

Figure 3-17: Searching for local movie theaters is a one-step process with the Live Search feature.

If you don't find the information you need on the first Web page, use the Back button to return to the search results page and then select a new link.

Information Kiosk

If you find that you're not quite satisfied with the results you get when using the Live Search feature, consider changing your default search engine. (The default search engine for IE7 is MSN.) To change your default, just click the Search Option pull-down arrow to the right of the Live Search box and choose a different search provider. (Google is a popular choice, but Yahoo! also has its advocates.)

Refreshing a Web page

When you refresh a Web page, you basically tell the browser to reconnect to the current Web site address. The refreshing feature comes in handy if your computer (or the Web site server) loses its connection. Refreshing Web pages is also recommended when viewing pages that are constantly updated with new information.

If you monitor stock market prices online, for example, you might encounter a continuously updated (or dynamic) Web site. Obviously, you need the most recent information before deciding to buy or sell a particular stock, and refreshing your Web page gives you the latest, most accurate pricing information. Or, you might use the Refresh feature with a dynamic Web site to track scores for several basketball games that are all taking place at the same time. With a little help from the Refresh button (and a site like ESPN.com), you can be kept abreast of changing scores by clicking the Refresh button to load the most recent scores.

To refresh a Web page, just click the green, circular arrow button to the immediate right of the Address bar. (See Figure 3-18.)

Refresh button

Figure 3-18: Refresh a Web page with the click of a button.

Information Kiosk

As with Windows Explorer, you can also refresh an IE7 Web page by pressing F5 or by pressing Ctrl+F5. The latter option is especially useful with Web pages loaded with dense, dynamically changing elements. However, it takes a little longer than doing a simple (F5) refresh.

Zooming in on Web pages

Most sites format their Web pages so that users can easily view (or read) their content. If you do happen to run across a site that isn't legible because the text is too small, you can easily zoom in for a better look.

Zooming in (or out) allows you to control the size of the content you are viewing. Using this feature can either bring the content closer to you or move it out so that you get a better look at it from a distance. This feature is particularly useful for people who have problems with their vision. If you are nearsighted, zoom-in; farsighted, zoom out. Practice using this feature so you don't end up straining your eyes when you're reading what's onscreen.

To access the IE7 zoom feature

1. **Click the Page button on the right side of the main toolbar.**

   A drop-down menu like the one shown in Figure 3-19 appears.

2. **Select Zoom.**

   The Zoom submenu appears to the left of the Page drop-down list. (See Figure 3-19.)

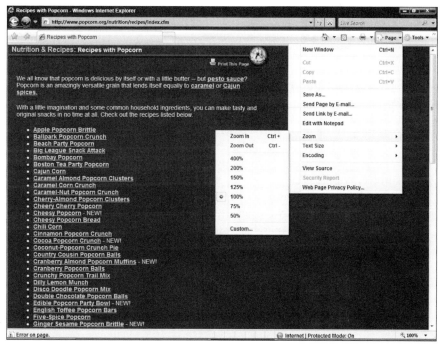

Figure 3-19: Use the Page menu to access IE7 zoom features.

3. **Click Zoom In.**

The Page and Zoom menus disappear, and the open Web page adjusts itself according to your selection. In this case, it gets bigger.

If the new Web page view is still too small for your taste, repeat Steps 1–3 until you get the size you like.

To zoom out on a Web page, follow Steps 1 and 2 but instead of selecting Zoom In during Step 3, select Zoom Out. The Web page content gets smaller, appearing as if it is moving farther away.

Information Kiosk

For a quick zoom in, use the keyboard shortcut Ctrl+. For a quick zoom out, use the keyboard shortcut Ctrl–. Or, use the Zoom submenu to select the precise zoom percentage you want. To view a Web page in full screen (without seeing any toolbars, buttons, and so on), press F11. Press F11 again to return to the normal view. You can also use the Zoom and Full Screen features together. First, zoom in to the desired amount and then press F11.

Watch Your Step

The Zooming feature affects only how you view Web pages onscreen. It has no affect on how Web pages print.

Printing Web pages

Web pages are designed in many different ways, and you see them differently depending on your monitor. In the past, you might have printed a Web page that appeared to fit on your screen but spilled over the sides when printed. This can be a frustrating and wasteful process. Fortunately, the new IE7 Shrink to Fit feature has made this a problem of the past by allowing you to print Web pages on a single printed page. The Shrink to Fit feature — the default setting in Vista — automatically adjusts the width of the current Web page to fit on one printed page rather than carrying information from the page's margins over to a second page.

Watch Your Step

The IE7 Shrink to Fit feature adjusts only the width of a Web page, not the length. If the Web site contains a lengthy amount of information, the printed version might still require more than one printed page. Use the Print Preview feature (shown in Figure 3-20) to determine whether the Web page printout will take more than one page.

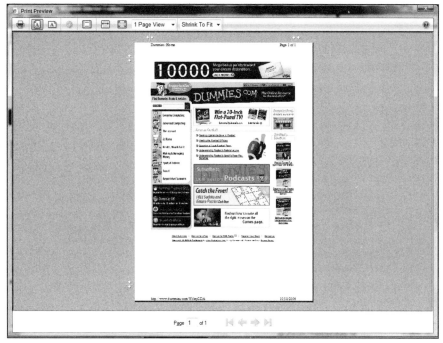

Figure 3-20: The Print Preview screen shows you what a Web page looks like when printed.

 Information Kiosk

If the Shrink to Fit feature makes it difficult to view (or read) the printed version of the Web page, you can manually select a more fitting size percentage from the Print Preview screen. Use the Shrink to Fit drop-down list to locate the percentage you want, then click the Print button.

Using tabbed browsing

Tabbed browsing allows you to preserve IE7's new cleaner, sleeker look by allowing several Web pages to be open within one window. In previous versions of Internet Explorer, if you wanted to open more than one Web page, you had to launch multiple versions of the browser. In IE7, you can now open several different Web pages within the same browser session by using separate tabs. (See Figure 3-21.)

Opening (or adding) new tabs

If you want to access a new Web site but don't necessarily want to close any pages you have open, you must open (or add) a new browser tab.

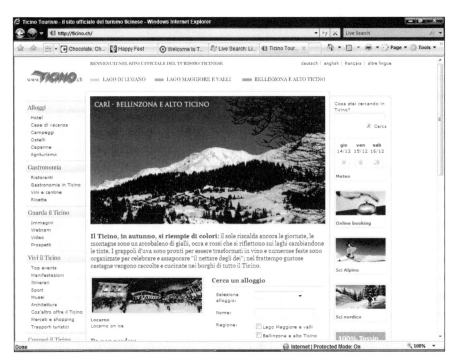

Figure 3-21: Browser tabs help keep your screen clutter-free.

You can open (or add) tabs in two different ways:

- Click the small empty tab to the right of your current tabs.
- Press Ctrl+T.

Whichever path you take, the new browser tab opens to the right of the last available tab.

You don't need to wait until the Web page from one tab loads before you move on to another tab. Just keep in mind that the more tabs you add, the longer it takes the browser to launch and close.

ℹ Information Kiosk

You can open more than 60 Web sites with browser tabs. However, you probably don't want to have more than ten tabs displayed at a time because the tabs become difficult to read.

Moving between tabs

The easiest method to navigate from one tab to another is to use your mouse to click on the desired tab. The Web page you wish to see automatically appears onscreen.

Information Kiosk

When you have multiple tabs open in IE7, you can also use Ctrl+Tab to move from one tab to the other. This keyboard shortcut moves your open Web page to the site being viewed in the tab to the right. To move to the left through your tabs (backward, in other words) use Ctrl+Shift+Tab. You can also rearrange the order of your tabs by clicking a single tab and dragging it to a new location. The ability to move your tabs allows you to place related tabs next to one another or to relocate tabs you use most frequently near the front of the list.

Closing and saving tabs

You have a couple of different ways to close browser tabs. You can close each tab individually by clicking its Close Tab button, or you can close all your open tabs at once by exiting the IE7 browser session. Which method you use depends upon where you are in the browsing process and whether you still want to view the contents of your other open Web pages.

If you no longer need a specific Web site but you want to be able to view the rest of your open pages, close only the window you are finished with by clicking its Close Tab button (it is the square with the red x) located in the right corner of the browser tab (as shown in Figure 3-22). This method of closing tabs allows you to keep open the tabs that you are still using.

Close Tab button

Figure 3-22: Closing unwanted browser tabs can be accomplished with a single mouse click.

Information Kiosk

Selecting a tab you wish to close and pressing Ctrl+W also removes the unwanted tab from your browser session.

If you're finished viewing all your open tabs, the fastest way to close your open Web pages is to exit the entire browser session. To close IE7, click the Close button in the upper right of your screen.

A dialog box appears asking whether you want to close all tabs (see Figure 3-23). If you are finished with this information and do not wish to be able to access it again the next time you open IE7, click Close Tabs.

Figure 3-23: Clicking the Close Tabs button deletes your open Web pages and exits the browser session.

However, if you plan to later open the exact same Web sites you have open, consider saving your tabs, which is convenient when you plan to revisit these Web sites. For example, if you visit certain Web sites on a regular (perhaps, daily) basis, save these tabs as a group so that you do not have to open each Web site the next time you launch IE7. This feature also comes in handy if you are interrupted in the middle of a complicated research project. If you have several different Web sites open and are suddenly called away from your computer, you can use this feature to save your current browsing session.

To save your open tabs

1. Click the IE7 Close button.

A dialog box appears onscreen, asking whether you want to close tabs. (Refer to Figure 3-23.)

2. Click Show Options.

Two new options appear in the dialog box. (See Figure 3-24.)

Figure 3-24: Clicking the Show Options button of the Close Tabs dialog box reveals an option for saving tabs.

3. Select the Open These the Next Time I Use Internet Explorer check box.

A green check mark appears in the box next to your selection. This saves your open tabs for future use.

4. Click Close Tabs.

IE7 closes.

Watch Your Step

You must choose the Open These the Next Time I Use Internet Explorer option each time you close your browser. If you do not select this option, your open tabs won't be saved, which means they won't automatically open the next time you launch IE7.

Information Kiosk

If you open more than one IE7 browser session and open several tabs within each browser and then choose the Open These the Next Time I Use Internet Explorer option when you close both open browser windows, all the tabs saved within all the open browsers open together in one browser the next time you launch IE7.

Opening multiple tabs faster

If you want to take advantage of the ability to save tabs but do not want to wait for each page to open before you can view your Web pages, you can adjust your Tabs settings so that the browser opens a little faster by opening only the first home page the next time the browser starts. Here's what you can do:

1. Click the Tools button on the right side of the main menu.

A drop-down menu appears.

2. Select Internet Options.

The Internet Options dialog box appears, and the Tools menu goes away.

3. Select the General tab (if it's not already showing).

The General tab has five different sections: Home Page, Browsing History, Search, Tabs, and Appearance.

4. Click Settings in the Tabs section.

The Tabbed Browsing Settings dialog box appears, as shown in Figure 3-25.

5. Select the Open Only the First Home Page When Internet Explorer Starts check box.

A green check mark appears in the box to the left of this option when your selection is made.

6. Click OK.

The Tabbed Browsing Settings dialog box disappears.

7. Click OK again.

The Internet Options dialog box closes.

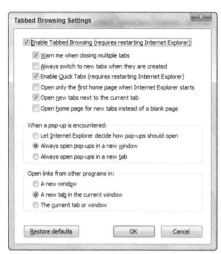

Figure 3-25: Customize tab settings by checking the designated check boxes.

8. **Close the browser, being sure to select the Open These the Next Time I Use Internet Explorer option.**

If you don't select this option, you lose your saved tabs.

Now launch the browser again and watch your (first) home page tab opening. You can then start to work while the other tabs are opening.

Using Quick Tabs

The IE7 Quick Tabs feature consists of small thumbnail images of all your open tabs. (See Figure 3-26.) This tabs preview page lets you see all your opened tabs in a single-screen format. Using the Quick Tabs feature is especially useful if you have a large number of tabs open. By accessing this bird's-eye view of your open tabs, you can more easily find and select the specific Web page you want.

To use this new Quick Tabs feature, click the Quick Tabs button located to the left of your first browser tab. Clicking this button displays all your open tabs at once. (If some of your pages are still loading at the time you click the Quick Tabs, you can see them come in progressively.)

To select the Web page you wish to view, click its thumbnail image. The requested Web page opens in its designated browser tab.

Quick Tabs button

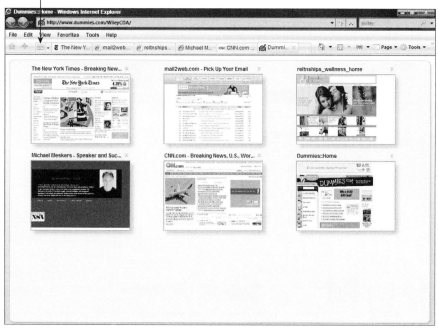

Figure 3-26: Using the Quick Tabs feature makes finding Web pages a snap.

Exploring the Favorites Center

The Favorites Center is IE7's centralized storage center for your favorite and recently viewed Web sites. Each category specializes in a different area of browser activity. The three main parts to the Favorites Center are

- **Favorites:** This section houses your favorite Web sites.

- **(RSS) Feeds:** This section contains a list of Web sites that offer RRS-enabled feeds.

- **History:** This section contains a list of all your recently viewed Web pages.

The Favorites Center is located on the far left side of the browser toolbar, tucked away out of sight behind the yellow star icon. Clicking the Favorites Center button brings forward the Favorites Center window. (See Figure 3-27.)

Figure 3-27: The Favorites Center window.

Choosing Favorites

When you visit a site that you want to be able to access again in the future but you don't necessarily want to rely on Recent Pages to find (or store) this information, you can add the Web page to your Favorites menu. Then, with a few clicks, you can revisit this site any time you want. As long as that Web page's location does not change, you can go back and visit the selected page by clicking on its entry in the Favorites menu.

The Favorites menu comprises a list of bookmarked Web sites. These bookmarked sites are places you visit that you would like to be able to refer to again. Bookmarking a Web page is very much like folding down the corner of a magazine so that you can find the article you are reading at a later time. Adding a site to you Favorites list works in much the same way except everything is done electronically.

Watch Your Step

Being able to have your favorite Web sites at your fingertips is certainly what makes the Favorites category a popular tool, but use this feature sparingly. If you add too many Web sites to your Favorites list, it starts to look like a lot like your Recent Pages or History list.

Web sites are added to your Favorites only when you want them to be. Hand-selecting the sites for this list allows you to personalize your browser features so that the pages you visit most frequently are readily accessible whenever you need them.

To add a Web site to your Favorites list

1. **Open the Web page you want to add to your Favorites.**

2. **Click the Add to Favorites button on the IE7 toolbar.**

   A drop-down menu appears.

3. **Choose Add to Favorites from the drop-down menu.**

   The Add a Favorite dialog box appears, as shown in Figure 3-28.

Figure 3-28: Add a Web site to your Favorites menu.

4. **(Optional) Type a name for this site.**

   IE7 automatically generates a name for your Favorites link. However, if you prefer a different name (perhaps one that's easier for you to remember), you can change it here. Short, concise titles work best.

5. **Click Add.**

   The Add a Favorite dialog box disappears, and the Web site is added to the Favorites menu.

 Information Kiosk

Pressing Ctrl+D also lets you add an open Web page to your Favorites list.

To find a Web site stored in your Favorites menu, do the following:

1. **Click the Favorites Center button.**

   The Favorites Center window appears.

2. **Select the Favorites tab.**

   A list of your Favorite Web sites is displayed.

3. Select the Web page you wish to see.

IE7 redirects the open Web page to your Favorites site.

Information Kiosk

When you add a new site to your Favorites list, IE7 automatically tacks the link onto the bottom of the list. However, you can rearrange your Favorites list by clicking and dragging entries up and down in the Favorites menu. This lets you place the Favorites you use most often near the top of the list.

It's also handy to note that when you add a file to your Favorites list, you will see an identifying icon displayed before the name in the list, such as the Windows Explorer icon before a Web page, an icon representing Adobe Acrobat before an Adobe Acrobat file, a folder file before a folder name, and so on.

To remove a site from your Favorites list

1. Click the Favorites Center button.

The Favorites Center window appears.

2. Select the Favorites tab.

A list of your favorite Web sites is displayed.

3. Right-click the link you wish to remove.

A pop-up menu appears.

4. Choose Delete from the contextual menu.

A confirmation dialog box appears, asking whether you are sure you want to send the selected site to the Recycle Bin.

5. Click Yes.

The Web site is removed from your Favorites list.

Subscribing to feeds

The Feeds portion of your Favorites Center refers specifically to RSS (Really Simple Syndication) feeds.

RSS feeds pertain to constantly updated, syndicated information that you subscribe to by using the new Feeds feature found in IE7. Using RSS feed subscriptions allows you to view only new content from a Web site. This saves you time by filtering the information that you have already seen. When you subscribe to a feed, sites that continuously update content deliver only updated content to your screen. This frees you from having to scour the entire page looking for new material.

When you access a Web page that offers RSS-enabled feeds, the Feeds button (located between the Home and Print buttons on the right side of the toolbar) turns red. This change of color indicates that this particular site offers RSS feeds. Many different kinds of sites offer RSS feeds, but what they have in common is updated content around other, perhaps static, elements. Most major new sites (CNN.com, NYTimes.com, as well many other content-rich sites) offer RSS feed capabilities.

To see the Feeds feature in action, visit one of the sites listed above (such as CNN.com) and follow these steps:

1. Click the red RSS button.

The Feeds button turns red only if the site offers RSS feed capabilities. If the Feeds button is not red, you cannot complete the rest of these steps. When you find a site that does provide RSS feed capabilities, move to Step 2.

Clicking a red Feeds button redirects the open Web page to the RSS Feeds page. On this page is a yellow box at the top of the screen. This information box includes the name of the open feed, a brief explanation of how to use feeds, and the option to subscribe to this feed.

2. Select the Subscribe To This Feed option.

Clicking this option brings up the dialog box shown in Figure 3-29.

Figure 3-29: Subscribing to feeds provides a direct link to only the new information posted by participating Web sites.

3. (Optional) Type in a name for this feed.

IE7 automatically generates a name for your Feeds link. However, if you prefer a different name (perhaps one that's easier for you to remember), you can change it here. Short, concise titles work best.

4. Click Subscribe.

You are subscribed to the RSS feed you've chosen, and the Subscribe To This Feed dialog box disappears.

To find your feeds

1. Click the Favorites Center button.

The Favorites Center window appears.

2. Select the Feeds tab.

A list of the feeds you subscribe to is displayed.

3. Click the feeds page you wish to see.

IE7 redirects the open Web page to the selected feeds page.

4. Choose a link to view newly posted information.

Clicking one of the provided links takes you to updated content recently posted by the feeds provider.

To remove a site from your Feeds list

1. Click the Favorites Center button.

The Favorites Center window appears.

2. Select the Feeds tab.

A list of your favorite RSS feeds is displayed.

3. Right-click the link you wish to remove.

A pop-up menu appears.

4. Choose Delete from the contextual menu.

A confirmation dialog box appears, asking whether you are sure you want to delete this feed.

5. Click Yes.

This site is removed from your Feeds list.

 Information Kiosk

You can rearrange the order of your feeds in the Favorites Center by clicking the name of the link you want to move and dragging it to a new location.

Making History

When you want to revisit a Web page you have been to recently (and perhaps you do not know the URL or have not added it to your Favorites), History can lend you a helping hand.

The IE7 History feature keeps an alphabetic list of the Web pages you've visited. This list — located in the Favorites Center — is organized by days of the week. For example, if you go to Amazon.com today, the link to this site shows up under Today's list. If you also visited Amazon.com on Monday, the link to the Web site shows up in Monday's list as well. In other words, History keeps track of each site you visit every day.

The tricky part of using your History files is knowing exactly which day of the week you viewed a Web page. Therefore, this feature is most useful when searching for recent browser activity. For example, you might use History if you decide to visit a Web page you looked at yesterday or the day before. Using History to search for a site you visited last week is much more difficult unless you happen to know exactly which day of the week you looked at the Web page in question.

To locate your browser's History information

1. **Click the Favorites Center button.**

The Favorites Center window appears.

2. **Select the History tab.**

A list arranged by the days of the week appears. (See Figure 3-30.)

Figure 3-30: Viewing the History list in the Favorites Center.

3. **Click the day you wish to view.**

An alphabetical drop-down list of the sites you visited that day appears.

4. Select the Web site you wish to view.

A list of Web pages related to that particular site appears beneath the selected link.

5. Click the page you wish to view.

Clicking the link provided redirects your browser to the new site.

If you want to store this entry for future reference, add it to your Favorites. (See the "Choosing Favorites" section, earlier in this chapter.) To delete an individual entry from History, right-click the entry and choose Delete from the pop-up menu that appears.

Information Kiosk

You can adjust the time limit that History stores entries. To do so, choose Internet Options from the Tools menu. Select the General tab, and then click the Settings button in the Browsing History section. Locate the Days to Keep Pages in History option at the bottom of the Temporary Files and History Setting dialog box and change the default value according to your own preference. (Any number between 0 and 999 is acceptable.) Click OK.

Transfer

Privacy concerns might prompt you to delete your entire browsing history. See Chapter 4 for more information.

Creating multiple home pages

IE7 now makes it possible to select and store more than 50 different home pages. The ability to store multiple home pages is a new feature of IE7. This new capability allows you to save numerous home pages to your browser, which can then be accessed with the click of a single button.

This feature can be quite a timesaver if you have a number of Web sites that you use on a regular basis. You can include all of your most frequently visited sites as home pages so that you can open them all quickly and easily at a later date.

Before you can take full advantage of this new feature, you must first choose which sites you want to include as your home pages. Then you can begin adding new home pages.

To create a new home page

1. Open the Web page you wish to add to your home page collection.

2. With the page open, click the down arrow to the immediate right of the Home Page icon.

Be sure to select the Home Page drop-down menu and not the Home Page icon. If you accidentally click the Home Page icon, all your currently open tabs are closed while your preselected home pages are loaded in new browser windows.

When the arrow button is selected, a drop-down menu appears onscreen, as shown in Figure 3-31.

Figure 3-31: Use the Home Page drop-down menu to add or change your home page selections.

3. **Select the Add or Change Home Page option.**

The Add or Change Home Page dialog box appears, as shown in Figure 3-32.

Figure 3-32: The Add or Change Home Page dialog box allows you to save home pages.

4. **Select the Add This Webpage to Your Home Page Tabs option.**

A green dot appears in the radio button to the left of your selection.

Watch Your Step

Choosing the Use This Webpage as Your Only Home Page option from the Add or Change Home Page dialog box replaces all your existing home pages with the one new home page you selected.

5. Click Yes.

The Add or Change Home Page dialog box disappears from your screen, and the selected Web site is added to your list of home pages.

After you complete your list of home pages, you can open each and every one of these Web sites by simply clicking the Home Page icon. Using the Home Page icon closes all your open browser tabs and replaces them with only your saved home pages.

Information Kiosk

You can also choose to open just one of your preferred home pages by clicking the Home Page icon's downward-pointing arrow and accessing its drop-down menu. Selecting a single Web site from this menu opens only the home page you've requested rather than all your saved home pages. Clicking an individual link in the Home Page menu opens the specified Web page in the current browser tab.

If you no longer want to include a particular Web site as one of your home pages, you can delete it by using the Home Page drop-down menu. Here's how:

1. Click the down arrow to the immediate right of the Home Page icon.

A drop-down menu appears. (Refer to Figure 3-31.)

2. Highlight Remove.

A drop-down menu appears to the right of the Home Page menu. (See Figure 3-33.)

3. Select the Web site you wish to delete.

The drop-down menu disappears, and the Delete Home Page dialog box appears onscreen, as shown in Figure 3-34.

4. Click Yes.

The selected Web site is removed from your list of home pages.

Figure 3-33: Choose Remove from the Home Page menu to delete existing home pages.

Figure 3-34: Clicking Yes in the Delete Home Page dialog box removes unwanted Web sites from your list of preferred home pages.

Managing add-ons

Add-ons are extra tools that you can attach to your browser in order to customize it in a practical way. These additional browser tools are called add-ons because they have to be added to your browser; they do not come as part of its standard features. In other words, add-ons are completely optional in nature. Some are free; others are for purchase.

Add-ons tend to influence the functionality of your browser rather than its appearance. These additional tools include various forms, controls, utilities, special browsers, and even entertainment applications. IE7 offers a variety of different add-ons. Its available add-ons have been organized into four categories: Security, Time Savers, Browsers, and Entertainment. Each of these categories contains a number of add-on tools.

To locate the IE7 add-ons

1. Click the Tools button on the right side of the main menu.

A drop-down menu appears.

2. Choose Manage Add-ons from the contextual menu.

A submenu appears to the left of the Tools menu, as shown in Figure 3-35.

Figure 3-35: Managing add-ons via the Tools menu.

3. Choose Find More Add-ons.

The IE7 Add-Ons Web page appears in the open browser tab. (See Figure 3-36.)

From this page, you can browse and select whichever add-ons you want. Notice that each add-on tool includes a brief description of what it does and how much it costs.

After you find an add-on that interests you, you can attach it to your browser by clicking the yellow download button to the right of the add-on description.

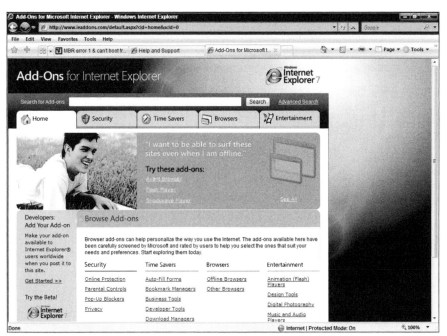

Figure 3-36: Choosing add-ons for IE7.

Watch Your Step

Not all IE7 available add-ons are free. Pay attention to the price of these tools, or you might incur some unexpected expenses.

Because each add-on is different, the steps to install these tools vary. However, most add-ons prompt you with a dialog box asking whether you want to save or run the add-on program. Selecting Save allows you to save the installation file on your hard drive before you run it. Choose Run and the installation will take place immediately — although you will not have saved a copy of the installation file, which may mean that you have to download the file again later if your copy of the add-on is somehow damaged.

Deleting an add-on is a bit more straightforward. Here's how it's done:

1. **Click the Tools button on the right side of the main menu.**

A drop-down menu appears.

2. **Choose Manage Add-ons.**

A submenu appears to the left of the Tools menu. (Refer to Figure 3-35.)

3. **Choose Enable or Disable Add-ons.**

The Manage Add-ons dialog box appears onscreen, as shown in Figure 3-37.

Figure 3-37: Managing add-ons in IE7.

4. **Click the name of the add-on you wish to remove.**

Your selection is highlighted in blue.

5. **Select the Disable radio button in the Settings section.**

A green dot appears in the radio button, and the selected add-on is moved to the Disabled section of the add-ons listed.

To remove additional add-ons, repeat Steps 4 and 5.

6. **Click OK.**

A new Manage Add-ons dialog box appears informing you that you must restart IE7 before these changes take effect.

7. **Click OK.**

The Manage Add-ons dialog boxes disappear.

Step into the Real World

Although IE7 is, by design, an Internet browser, it also possesses the power to search and open files stored on your computer. This added functionality allows you to use IE7 much like you would a traditional Windows search.

You can view and open files located on your hard drive by typing the file's pathname (starting with the drive letter, colon, and backslash) into the IE7 Address bar. For example, if you enter **C:** into the Address bar, a list of that drive's contents displays onscreen just like a list of recently visited Web pages would appear if you were typing an Internet address.

After you locate the file you want, press Enter, and the selected file is opened in the appropriate window. If IE7 cannot display the file and cannot find an application to launch in order to display the file, you are prompted with an `Open With` message. In that case, you must select the appropriate application to open the desired file. If no application on your computer can display the file, you receive an error message informing you that the page cannot be displayed, in which case you must install the appropriate application before viewing the file.

add-ons: Programs, templates, and other tools that are downloaded and plugged into a given application for the purpose of providing additional functionality.

AutoComplete: The feature that stores Web sites and other entries in your system's memory cache so that you do not have to manually retype this information each time you wish to use it.

browser: The application that Internet users use when accessing information stored on the World Wide Web. The standard browser for Windows Vista is Internet Explorer 7.

Favorites Center: The IE7 centralized storage center for all your favorite Web sites, RSS feeds, and historical browsing records.

phishing: A form of deception where browsers are unwittingly directed to a fraudulent Web site, where attempts are made to collect personal information about the user.

continued

 **continued**

pop-up: A new window that appears in your Web browser as the result of you taking some sort of action, most often when you click a link or simply when you visit a Web page. Most pop-ups serve as some form of advertising.

RSS (Really Simple Syndication) feeds: Constantly updated, syndicated information offered by participating Web sites. RSS feeds provide links to a site's newly posted content, saving subscribers time by automatically filtering out information that has already been viewed.

URL (Uniform Resource Locator): An abbreviation that represents the name given to a Web site's individual Internet address. An example of a URL is www.wiley.com.

Last
Stop

Practice Exam

1. How do you open additional browser tabs?

_____

_____

_____

2. How do you activate the Phishing filter?

_____

_____

_____

3. In IE7, the classic Menu toolbar is hidden by default. How do you enable this feature?

_____

_____

_____

4. What are RSS feeds and why would you want to subscribe to them?

_____

_____

_____

5. What are two different ways to zoom in/out on a Web page?

_____

_____

_____

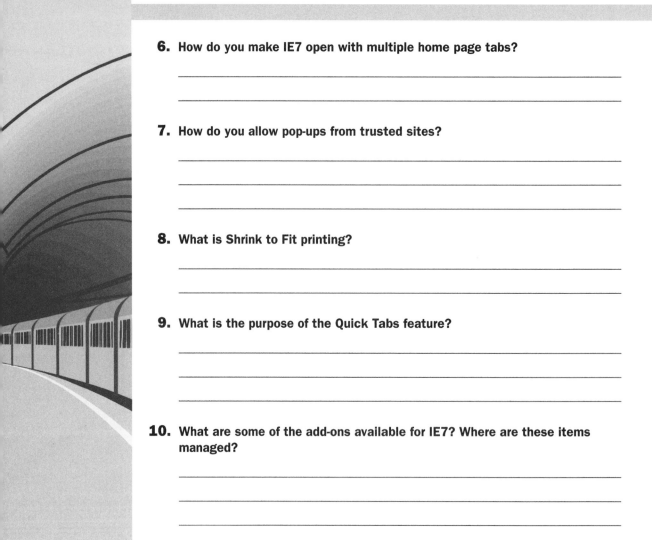

6. How do you make IE7 open with multiple home page tabs?

_____

_____

7. How do you allow pop-ups from trusted sites?

_____

_____

_____

8. What is Shrink to Fit printing?

_____

_____

9. What is the purpose of the Quick Tabs feature?

_____

_____

_____

10. What are some of the add-ons available for IE7? Where are these items managed?

_____

_____

_____

Security, Privacy, and Parental Controls in Windows Vista

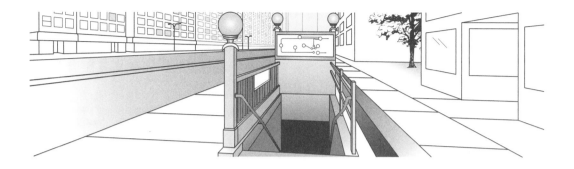

Enter the Station

Questions

1. What is the Windows Security Center?

2. How do you master the many security settings in Windows Vista and IE7?

3. What steps do you need to take to ensure safe Web browsing behavior?

4. How can you enjoy and maintain privacy while online?

5. Can you protect your data if your computer is lost or stolen?

6. What types of restrictions can you apply to your children's user accounts?

7. How do you set up customized Parental Controls?

Express Line

If you are already up on the security feature basics for Internet Explorer 7 (IE7) and the Windows Vista Security Center, skip ahead to the next chapter.

A s you learned in the previous chapter, you need to be aware of certain dangers while working online — phishing and identity theft being two of the most important. However, there is more to protecting your computer (and yourself) than just adjusting your IE7 settings. A number of security and privacy issues need to be addressed before your computer can be considered (predominantly) safe.

For example, your computer can be at risk if you elect to use an always-on Internet connection, such as DSL (digital subscriber line) or a cable modem. Although these services can be very convenient (because they provide you with instant access to the Internet any time you want), they can also be a danger because they also provide malicious online predators and hackers constant access to your computer. One way to prevent these nefarious folks from accessing your computer files and online information is to use the new and improved Vista Firewall to help keep unwanted eyes and applications out of your system.

Other ways to prevent unwarranted invasion include visiting only secure Web sites and using password-protected features that keep your personal information confidential. And, of course, you always want to use precautions when surfing the Web. For example, you never want to visit a site or open an e-mail that seems suspicious because it might contain a computer virus. You can also contract these unwelcome programs by downloading applets, videos, games, and so on that come from an unknown source.

Spyware is another tool that individuals and/or companies can use to obtain information about your computer use without your knowledge. These programs can be harmless if they are meant solely for marketing research purposes. However, some people still feel that the act of tracking their online behavior is an invasion of their privacy.

Other *malware* (or malicious software programs), such as viruses and worms, can cause damage to your PC. Although such damage might be somewhat minimal and create only a minor slowdown in your PC's performance, it might prove more severe and cause you to lose all your saved files, programs, pictures, and so on basically crashing your hard drive and leaving you with nothing but a blank screen and an operating system.

You want to protect yourself and your children from all these things while using your PC. Of course, bugs can always slip through the cracks, but you can take certain measures to prevent these negative events.

Vista provides you with added security features, such as its improved Firewall (a software application that filters the information that enters or leaves your PC), Windows Security Center, Windows Defender, Automatic Updates, and new Parental Controls capabilities. Each can help protect your PC from some of these security dangers.

This chapter provides you with a solid understanding of the dangers associated with using Vista and a better comprehension of the features available to help protect your PC.

Exploring the Windows Security Center

Windows Vista places the controls for the main security functions of your computer in one centralized area: the Windows Security Center, which is located in the Security area of the Control Panel. (See Figure 4-1.)

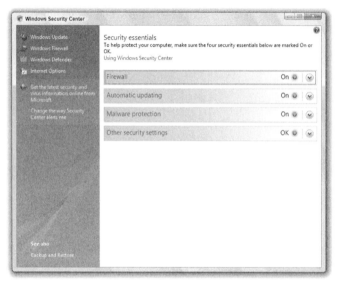

Figure 4-1: The Windows Security Center.

This page includes information on your firewall activation, automatic updating preferences, malware protection, and other security settings. Here is a brief description of each of these security features:

- **Firewall:** This built-in Windows Vista security program manages the content permitted to enter and exit your PC or internal network. If it detects any potentially dangerous materials, this feature prohibits them from interacting with your PC. Think of this tool as your first line of defense against unwanted software or malware.

- **Automatic Updating:** Turning on this feature tells your computer to automatically collect and install any new software — including security-related fixes — pertaining to Windows Vista. This feature saves you from having to manually collect and install these updates yourself, which is particularly useful if you do not frequently visit the Vista Updates site. That way, you do not accidentally overlook an important update and inadvertently become a victim of a security- or privacy-related error, especially one that could have been easily prevented had you downloaded the appropriate correction.

Note: Use this feature with some caution. If you are comfortable with Microsoft's updates, then go ahead and allow Vista to update automatically. But if you want more control over what Microsoft installs on your computer without bothering to ask you, then you might want to elect to examine the updates presented before you download and install them.

 Malware Protection: This section of the Windows Security Center includes two different features — the antivirus and spyware/malware protection information for your PC. Ensuring that both features are active helps protect your computer from malicious software attacks.

 Other Security Settings: This section of the Security Center also includes two distinct categories

- *Internet Security Settings,* which can also be accessed via Internet Explorer 7 (IE7)

Transfer

Read about IE7 in Chapter 3.

- *User Account Control,* which lets you restrict certain PC activities for various users

These controls are particularly useful if you want to limit the amount of time your children are allowed to spend online or if you want to be able to choose which sites they may visit. (Find more Parental Controls later in this chapter.)

Information Kiosk

Double-clicking the Windows Security Alert icon in the Notification area of the taskbar also brings up the Security Center page. Or, you can find it by doing an Instant Search from the Start menu. Type **security** in the Search box, and the Security Center appears in the left column of the Start menu as the search results are listed.

If you look at each listing in the main section of the Security Center window, notice that some of these categories are shown in different colors. These colors indicate each feature's current status:

 Green: On (or functional)

 Red: Off (or not found)

 Yellow: Not automatic (In other words, its settings need to be adjusted manually or via automatic updates.)

You want each Security Center feature to be green. If any item is not green, you can adjust its settings by clicking its name in the column to the left to open its Details page. Use the options on this page to turn on/off or adjust the current status of the selected feature.

If there is not a specific link for the feature that you need to correct to the left, click the title bar for the feature in question. A brief explanatory sentence appears below your selection as well as instructions for correcting (or activating) this feature. After you finish reading about the feature, you can hide the information by clicking the title bar once more.

Information Kiosk

In some instances, you might need to search for related software online. If this is the case, you are provided with a button instructing you to find the appropriate program. Clicking the proffered button takes you to a Web site that contains a list of Vista-compatible software selections from which you can choose.

Automating Windows Update

Microsoft continually issues updates for the Vista operating system as well as the applications bundled with it. Although keeping Vista updated with these software updates and patches is important for overall functionality, updates can often (and more importantly) be vital for the security of your PC and operating system.

The Windows Vista default setting for this feature should already be enabled. (Using Automatic Updates is the recommended setting, as I stated earlier.) If its setting is not enabled, the Automatic Updating section of the Security Center appears in red or yellow. To activate this feature

1. **Click the Windows Update link in the left column of the Security Center window.**

   The Windows Update page opens, as shown in Figure 4-2.

2. **Click the Change Settings link from the column on the left.**

   The Change Settings dialog box appears.

3. **Select the Install Updates Automatically (Recommended) option.**

   A green dot appears in the radio button next to your selection.

4. **(Optional) Select the time and how often you would like to perform the Automatic Update downloads.**

Figure 4-2: The Windows Update page.

Use the drop-down lists found below the Install Updates Automatically option to choose which day and at what time you would like for your PC to locate and install the available updates.

I recommend selecting a day and time when you are most likely not going to be using your computer. Otherwise, the update process might impede your PC's performance.

Also, the more often you choose to download available updates, the less likely you are to be caught in a vulnerable state. (Daily update scans are highly recommended.) This also makes each update session go quicker because there are not as many updates to install during each session.

5. **Click OK.**

The Change Settings page disappears.

6. **Close the Windows Update page by clicking the X in the upper-right corner.**

The Windows Update page disappears.

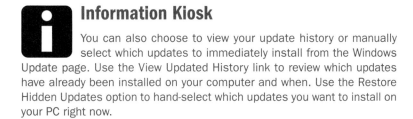

Information Kiosk

You can also choose to view your update history or manually select which updates to immediately install from the Windows Update page. Use the View Updated History link to review which updates have already been installed on your computer and when. Use the Restore Hidden Updates option to hand-select which updates you want to install on your PC right now.

Enabling the Windows Firewall

Firewalls are software programs created to act as a barrier between various computer systems or networks. Firewalls, like the one built in to Windows Vista, are meant to restrict the spreading of malicious programs and files. In other words, they prevent harmful communications from occurring between computer users that interact with one another.

Most firewalls focus on blocking harmful materials from getting to your PC; however, the Windows Firewall is *bidirectional,* meaning that it protects you from both incoming and outgoing dangers. It checks not only for malicious programs and viruses coming in, but it also scans documents and programs that are sent from your computer. This ensures that you do not infect your friends and colleagues with harmful viruses, worms, spyware, or other malware programs.

 Watch Your Step

Before connecting to the Internet, check to make sure that your Windows Firewall is turned on. This should be your PC's default setting. If it isn't, you'll want to make sure you activate it before connecting to the Internet because it is your first line of defense against harmful programs and software.

The Windows Firewall should automatically be turned on when you install Vista. If it is not, you can activate this feature by following these steps:

1. **Open the Security Center window.**

You can find this feature in the Security section of your computer's Control Panel.

2. **Click the Windows Firewall link in the left column. (Refer to Figure 4-1.)**

This opens the Windows Firewall page.

3. **Select the Turn the Windows Firewall On or Off option from the left column of this page.**

This opens the Windows Firewall Settings dialog box, as shown in Figure 4-3.

4. **Select the General tab (if it is not already selected).**

This tab allows you to turn on/off the Windows Firewall.

5. **Select the On (Recommended) option.**

A green dot appears in the radio button to the left of your selection.

6. **Click OK.**

This closes the Firewall Settings dialog box.

7. **Close the Windows Firewall and Security Center windows.**

Both of these pages are closed, and you are returned to your desktop.

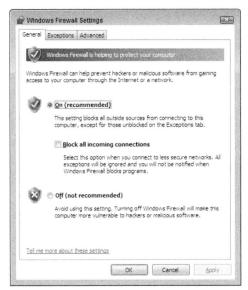

Figure 4-3: Turning on/off the Windows Firewall.

If you want to turn off the Windows Firewall, follow the preceding steps, but in Step 4, select the Off (Not Recommended) button.

Information Kiosk

You can also choose to allow a particular program through the Windows Firewall. To do so, enable the Allow a Program through Windows Firewall option from the main Windows Firewall page. Clicking this link brings up a list of programs you can choose to allow (or restrict) by using the check boxes provided. If a check mark appears in the box next to a particular program, it is allowed through the Windows Firewall. If no check mark is present, it is not permitted to pass through the Windows Firewall.

As for which programs to select, you may want to allow Microsoft access to your computer for updates and troubleshooting. Other vendors may also need your permission to check out a balky piece of hardware or software. Some interactive games require data sharing between your computer and others connected to the Internet. Webcam, chat rooms, and conferencing programs may need entry, as well as communications with your financial institutions. Just be sure you know who wants access and why before you permit it.

Note also that there are two types of firewalls: hardware and software. Both operate in much the same manner. They examine the headers on Internet traffic and allow or deny access based on criteria that either the user has defined or has been built in to the hardware. These days, hardware firewalls are often included in the routers that serve networks, thus providing security to several computers with one device. Software firewalls are loaded into each computer and give the user finer control over what is and is not allowed in or out. A well-protected system uses both types.

> ### Step into the Real World
>
> Microsoft, as of the writing of this book, has not yet provided an all-in-one security solution, but it is getting close. The missing element in Windows Vista is antivirus software, which has yet to be included with Microsoft's operating system. Thus, you still need third-party antivirus software.

Watch Your Step

Having the Windows Firewall built in to Vista saves you from having to install another firewall from a third party and also saves you the trouble of having to find a Vista-compatible firewall application. If you still decide that you do not want to use the Vista Firewall — perhaps because you prefer another firewall program — be aware that having more than one firewall enabled on your computer might create conflicts between these two programs. If a problem arises, the Windows Security Center icon appears, bearing a red X in the Notification area of your taskbar, in which case you need to decide which one to keep. If you voluntarily select the third-party firewall software, you may choose to use this program instead of the Vista Firewall. (Follow the earlier instructions to disable the Windows Firewall.) However, if you do not recognize the program and did not request that this software be installed on your PC, delete it immediately: It could be a malware program.

Information Kiosk

Because the firewall (Windows Firewall) and antimalware (Windows Defender) programs are default settings for Vista, you do not typically see icons for these items in the Notification area of your taskbar. These icons appear only when a problem arises.

Using the Windows Defender

Microsoft Windows Defender is the security feature used to fend off spyware and malware. *Spyware,* in its most basic format, is a program that watches what you do on your computer. Spyware can also collect data about which Web sites you visit as well as information that you transmit over the Internet (including personal passwords or credit card information). *Malware* — software that is meant to behave maliciously — comprises a variety of hostile, intrusive, and annoying programs. A program is considered malware when the intent of its creator is to do harm to the inflicted PC or computer user. Some examples of malware include computer viruses, worms, trojan horses, and other malicious or unwanted software.

Windows Defender is more than just free antispyware and antimalware software, though. Its principal functions also include

Detecting changes that might have been made to your system by spyware

Performing constant real-time surveillance of your system in the hunt for any spyware-type activity that needs to be removed from your computer

Allowing direct communication with Microsoft through an optional tool called *Microsoft SpyNet,* through which you can send spyware reports to Microsoft to aid in developing new definitions to help future updates protect you against any new threats

As with Windows Firewall, Windows Defender is automatically enabled when you install Vista. To verify its activation, visit the Security Center to ensure that Windows Defender is actively searching your computer for harmful spyware and malware. If Windows Defender is not activated when you install Vista, you can turn on this security feature by following these steps:

1. **Open the Security Center window.**

You can locate this feature within the Security section of your computer's Control Panel.

2. **Click the Windows Defender link in the left column. (Refer to Figure 4-1.)**

This opens the Windows Defender page.

3. **Click the Tools menu.**

This opens the Windows Defender Tools and Settings page, as shown in Figure 4-4.

4. **Select Options from the Settings section.**

Figure 4-4: Use the Windows Defender Tools menu to change this security feature's settings.

This opens the Windows Defender Options page. (See Figure 4-5.)

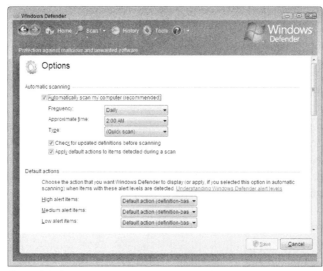

Figure 4-5: Select when to scan your computer for spyware and malware programs.

5. **Select the Automatically Scan My Computer (Recommended) check box located in the Automatic Scanning section of this page.**

A check mark appears in the box to the left of this option, indicating that your selection has been made. Using the drop-down menus, you can define how often the scan takes place, at what time and what type (full scan or quick scan), and what happens to detected items — fix, ignore, or remove.

6. **Click Save.**

The Options page is closed.

7. **Close the Tools and Settings and the Security Center windows.**

Both of these pages are closed, and you are returned to your desktop.

To review the findings of the Windows Defender (after it is enabled), visit the Windows Defender page of the Security Center. Here you can peruse the various programs detected by Vista's built-in antispyware and antimalware tool.

Step into the Real World

Many experts recommend that you use more than one spyware program: The theory is that what one misses, the other catches. And, if you have more than one antispyware program installed, you shouldn't have any conflicts whatsoever.

Watch Your Step

When you first connect to the Internet, glance at the Notification area of your taskbar to see whether the Windows Security Alert icon (the yellow shield bearing an X) is present. If this icon is present, you have a problem with your security settings. Click the Security Alert icon to open the Security Center. Here, you can review and correct any existing security errors.

Information Kiosk

As of this writing, Microsoft has not included antivirus software as part of Windows Vista although you can purchase Microsoft's new *One Care solution,* which does include antivirus software as well as firewall and antispyware, system, backup, and restore utilities. In addition, Microsoft does provide information on its Web site about antivirus software programs that are compatible with Windows Vista. This compatibility is critical because not all antivirus software runs under Windows Vista.

Unlike antispyware, if you have more than one antivirus program installed on your PC, you might encounter conflicts between these programs. If so, you see the Security Center icon warning in the Notification area of the taskbar, alerting you of this situation. Deleting one of these programs should correct this problem.

Ensuring Safe Web Surfing

Another way to keep your computer (and your personal information) safe is to practice precautionary behavior when surfing the Web. In this section of the chapter, you'll have a chance to examine in some detail additional security features built into Windows Vista that can help you use the Internet safely. First and foremost is the Vista security-enabled notification system, which is a feature that lets you know when you are visiting a site that is considered safe by Vista and IE7 standards. You'll also gain a more detailed understanding of how to identify potential phishing hazards.

Transfer

A general overview of phishing can be found in Chapter 3.

Finally, you'll find out how to remove stored passwords from your computer. All these items are especially useful when making purchases online or transmitting confidential information over the Internet.

Identifying security-enabled sites

When you visit a Web site that is *security-encrypted* — the site scrambles any electronic transmissions with a special encryption code that can be understood only with the correct key — you see a golden padlock to the right of the site's URL. This icon appears whenever you visit a site that IE7 believes is secure. (See Figure 4-6.)

Padlock icon

Figure 4-6: Identify a secure Web site from the padlock icon located to the right of the URL in the browser's Address bar.

This notification system is particularly helpful if you shop online or transfer confidential information (such as banking account data) via the Internet. When the golden padlock appears, you know that not only are Windows and IE7 trying to keep your information confidential, but so is the Web site you're using. This new Vista feature helps you make better decisions about when to divulge your personal information. If you do not see a padlock icon, you might want to think twice about whether you want to include any information you would prefer to keep confidential.

A Web site is identified as secure by Vista and IE7 after its URL and site Security Certificate have been verified. You can review a site's URL and Security Certificate by clicking the padlock icon. Doing so gives you access to detailed information about the site's URL which will then help you decide whether you should trust this particular Web page or not. When you see the golden padlock, though, chances are good that submitting sensitive information to this site is safe.

You might encounter the padlock icon if you order items from Amazon.com, eBay, or other online vendors. You might also see a padlock notice when viewing your checking account information online. All in all, this new Vista security feature is a visual reassurance that your data is going to remain safe and confidential.

Antiphishing in IE7

Elaborate scams based on phishing usually begin with an e-mail sent to you from what seems to be a reputable source (such as a financial institution, eBay, PayPal, or Network Solutions). These e-mails always contain a link that is supposed to take you to the affiliate's Web site — but don't be fooled! This link is your first indication that this message could be a potential phish. The most obvious giveaway comes from the link provided itself. Pass your cursor over the provided link; in the status bar, you can see the actual URL of the site you would go to if you do click this link. If this URL does not match the one for the genuine Web site, do not click the link or respond to any inquiries requesting personal user information! Doing so can expose you to the risk of becoming a phishing victim — in which case, you could lose control of your personal account information, which can be quite costly if you are entering sensitive banking or credit card information.

Transfer

Check out Chapter 3 for more information on what exactly phishing is and how to activate your browser's Phishing filter.

See Figure 4-7 to view an example of a phishing e-mail message. Note how the URL in the status bar (bottom of the page) does not match the URL in the message. Yet note how the originator of the e-mail craftily included the domain name in the link to confuse the user.

The URL does not match

Figure 4-7: A phishing e-mail. Note difference in URL.

Very often, when you click this type of malicious link, you are taken to the log-in page of a Web site that resembles the real Web site of the genuine institution. *Spoofers* — people who dishonestly copy a Web page for illicit purposes — can pull off this feat because they have copied much of the HTML (HyperText Markup Language) code of the genuine site. At first glance, you'd likely not notice much of a difference between this Web page and that of the original site.

When you attempt to log in to the spoofed site, though, the login seems to not work, and you might even find yourself trying to log in repeatedly in hopes of finally making it to your account. This is exactly what the spoofers are hoping for: After you enter your username and password, you have instantaneously given your personal information to these thieves. They can now access your account information by using the data you entered into the fields of this false Web site.

With this in mind, always be very careful when entering confidential information into a site provided via a link from an unsolicited e-mail message. If you do find yourself accidentally using a spoofed site, contact the actual company or your Internet service provider (ISP) immediately to alert them of any potential foul play. Also be sure to change your password right away so that the phishing culprits cannot access your account information.

Some other indications of a suspicious (phishing) e-mail include

- Messages that start with something like, *Dear PayPal account holder.* The give-away is that you're not being addressed by name.

- Ads for free ISP-hosting services. If the e-mail is from a legitimate institutional site, it should not carry this type of ad.

- URLs that do not match their links in the e-mail message. A non-matching URL is a sign that the site you are sent to when you click the provided link is not the one you think you are viewing. It might even be very different in appearance. (Refer to Figure 4-7.)

Deleting stored passwords

If you think that your computer is at risk of being accessed by unauthorized users, consider deleting any passwords you have saved to your computer. This ensures that all your account information is kept confidential from those people that have access to your PC.

This is particularly important if you share your computer with others. For example, if you have a colleague or roommate with whom you share a PC and you do not necessarily want the other person to be able to access your personal information (such as e-mail or online banking information), you should remove all traces of your saved passwords from the computer. This prohibits anybody else from being able to log into your accounts using the passwords already stored on the shared machine.

An example of when you might need to erase your passwords is if you notice charges or activity reports for your online e-mail account that you know you did not make. For example, if you notice that there are days or times of activity when you are positive you were not using your e-mail account, someone else might be accessing your Internet connection for free — or rather, at your expense. If you notice these types of situations, be sure to contact your ISP, and then make sure you change your e-mail account password as well.

The same goes for online banking activities. If you notice that transactions are being made on your account without your consent, chances are good that someone else has gotten your account information and is using it for his own expenses. (Admittedly, it could be a simple error on your bank's part, but it is more likely the former rather than the latter.) In this instance, be sure to contact your bank immediately and discuss the appropriate measures to correct this incident. You might need to set up a new account, or you might simply be able to change your existing password to prevent this type of situation from progressing.

In either scenario, be sure to remove saved passwords from your computer in case that is how the culprit gained access to your personal information in the first place. And you should probably elect not to save your e-mail or banking passwords to your computer in the future to prevent this type of occurrence from happening.

To delete saved passwords from your PC

1. **Open the Tools menu in IE7.**

A drop-down menu appears.

2. **Choose Internet Options.**

The Internet Options window appears, as shown in Figure 4-8.

Figure 4-8: Use your Internet Options settings to delete saved passwords.

3. **Select the General tab (if it is not already selected).**

This tab includes options for IE7's Home Page, Browsing History, Search, Tabs, and Appearance settings.

4. **Click the Delete button in the Browsing History section.**

The Delete Browsing History window opens. (See Figure 4-9.)

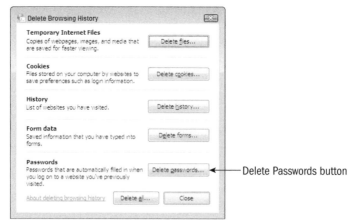

Figure 4-9: Deleting saved passwords from your PC helps keep your personal information confidential.

5. **Click the Delete Passwords button.**

A warning dialog box pops up, asking whether you're sure you want to delete all saved passwords.

6. **Confirm by clicking Yes.**

The confirmation dialog box disappears.

7. **Click the Close button in the Delete Browsing History window.**

This removes the Delete Browsing History window from your screen, revealing the Internet Options window.

8. **Click OK.**

This closes the Internet Options window.

Transfer

See the upcoming "Deleting browsing history in IE7" section for instructions on how to delete your browser history information so that others cannot view the Web sites you've visited during your most recent Internet sessions as well.

Fixing your IE7 security settings

IE7 includes a number of default security settings meant to protect you while you are connected to the Internet. (You can view the details for each of these settings by opening the Security tab in the Internet Options window.) These medium-to-high security levels restrict the activities that are permitted to run on your PC. In other words, these default settings prohibit potential malware from attaching itself to your PC.

I highly recommended that you leave the default IE7 settings as they appear when you first install Windows Vista. These settings have been established to ensure that you do not encounter any hazardous software or files while you surf the Web. Still, you might be tempted to adjust these settings because certain sites do not display properly without *active content* — certain visual or dynamic effects achieved by loading scripts from a Web site on to your PC. Just beware that if you do choose to manipulate your browser's security settings, you might inadvertently permit malicious software to run on your computer.

Although not recommended, if you do choose to adjust your security settings manually, here's how:

1. Open the Tools menu in IE7.

A drop-down menu appears.

2. Choose Internet Options.

The Internet Options window appears.

3. Select the Security tab.

The Security tab includes settings for your Internet, Local Intranet, Trusted Sites, and Restricted Sites. (See Figure 4-10.)

Figure 4-10: The Internet Options Security tab.

4. Click the icon for the zone you want to adjust.

Again, your choices are Internet, Local Intranet, Trusted Sites, or Restricted Sites.

Your selection is highlighted in blue after you make your decision, and a brief description of the zone you are working with appears below the zone selection bar.

5. In the Security Level for This Zone section, use the vertical slider to set the desired level for the chosen zone.

6. (Optional) For greater control of your security settings, click the Custom Level button.

The Security Settings page for the zone you selected opens, as shown in Figure 4-11.

Figure 4-11: Customize your IE7 security settings.

7. (Optional) Use the radio buttons provided to adjust how your computer handles specific content and/or applications.

From here, you can enable, disable, or elect to prompt the user before running any of the program types listed.

When you choose an option that might open the door to vulnerability, you immediately see `not secure`, in parentheses, to the right of that option. If you choose to enable one of the options, pink highlighting alerts you that this setting is considered unsecure.

8. (Optional) Click OK when you are finished.

This saves your new settings and closes the Security Settings window.

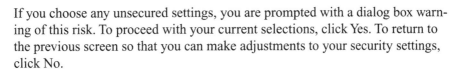

If you choose any unsecured settings, you are prompted with a dialog box warning of this risk. To proceed with your current selections, click Yes. To return to the previous screen so that you can make adjustments to your security settings, click No.

9. **Close the Internet Options windows.**

The Internet Options window disappears from your screen.

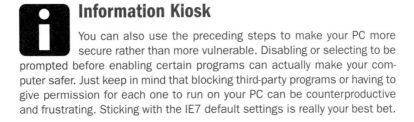

Information Kiosk

You can also use the preceding steps to make your PC more secure rather than more vulnerable. Disabling or selecting to be prompted before enabling certain programs can actually make your computer safer. Just keep in mind that blocking third-party programs or having to give permission for each one to run on your PC can be counterproductive and frustrating. Sticking with the IE7 default settings is really your best bet.

Here is where the next step in the IE7 built-in protection mechanism kicks in. If you enable an unsecured security setting and you happen to encounter one of these types of potentially dangerous programs, IE7 notifies you with a yellow information bar, as shown in Figure 4-12.

Information bar

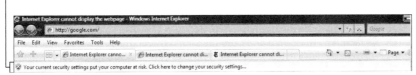

Figure 4-12: IE7 Security Settings warning.

By readjusting your security levels before you continue your browsing session, you greatly lessen the possibility of malicious software from gaining a foothold on your machine.

To return your security settings to their previous state

1. **Click the information bar.**

A pop-up menu appears, as shown in Figure 4-13.

2. **Choose the Fix Settings for Me option.**

A dialog box pops up asking whether you want to fix your security settings.

3. **Choose Fix Settings.**

Your browser's security settings are readjusted to the default safe level. The dialog box disappears, and you can proceed with your browsing session.

Figure 4-13: IE7 offers a simple solution: Fix Settings for Me.

Watch Your Step

Many Web sites require you to run active content so that you can fully enjoy the features of the site. If you want to be able to view such content, leave your browser's settings at a secure level (as described earlier). Then, when the information bar asks whether you want to run active content for an individual site, choose Yes. You should make your decision based upon whether you believe it to be a trusted site. If you are unsure at all, don't run the content.

Figure 4-14 shows an example of safe content you can allow to run on your PC.

If you choose to ignore the security warnings, the next time you launch your browser, you get the screen shown in Figure 4-15.

Although you could continue to browse in this unsecured state, it is suggested that you adjust your security settings before proceeding. If you ignore these warnings, you get either the information bar warning pop-up or the full screen warning each time you use your browser. The only way to get rid of these warning messages is to readjust your security settings to a safe level.

An add-on warning.

Figure 4-14: The browser warns you about downloading an add-on.

Figure 4-15: IE7 attempts to stop you from proceeding until you correct the vulnerability.

Transfer

For definitions of some of the most frequently encountered active content programs, see the "Street Jargon" section at the end of this chapter.

Using the Protected Mode in IE7

Protected Mode in IE7 was designed to cope with two particular situations:

- When a user (when logged in as a standard user and not as an Administrator) attempts to download software or applets onto your machine

- When a Web site attempts to run software on your computer

Transfer

Check out the "Setting up user accounts" section later in this chapter to learn more about administrator and standard user accounts.

You are protected in the sense that you (and other standard users) are prevented from installing software, changing settings, or deleting necessary system files that might affect other users.

This is a nice feature to have if you share your PC with others. Having the Protected Mode in place prevents others from being able to make important changes to your PC without your consent.

The Protected Mode is turned on by default in IE7. You can tell whether you are operating in this mode by looking at the status bar at the bottom of your screen. If the words Internet|Protected Mode: On appear, as shown in Figure 4-16, this protection measure is active.

Protected Mode is currently on.

Figure 4-16: Protected Mode on.

Information Kiosk

IE7 can operate in Protected Mode only if you use Windows Vista as your PC's operating system. If you use a dual-boot with another version of Windows or if you use IE7 on a non-Vista computer, you cannot take advantage of this new security feature.

When using IE7 in the Protected Mode, attempting to download or remove software that can affect another user's computing experience produces a warning message saying that you have to be logged on as an Administrator to continue. You must then log out and log back in as an Administrator before you can proceed.

If you are the only person using your computer and you do not necessarily want to log in as an Administrator each time you start your PC — or perhaps you want to be able to allow other users to download software without having to get your permission — turn off the Protected Mode in IE7.

To disable this feature

1. **Open the Tools menu in IE7.**

A drop-down menu appears.

2. **Choose Internet Options.**

The Internet Options window opens.

3. **Click the Security tab.**

This tab allows you to make adjustments to your PC's security settings. (Refer to Figure 4-10.)

4. **Select the Internet zone.**

Clicking the Internet icon assures that you are adjusting the correct security settings for you PC.

5. **Clear the Enable Protected Mode check box.**

This disables IE7's Protected Mode.

6. **Click OK.**

This closes the Internet Options window.

7. **Restart your browser.**

This reopens IE7 in the new unprotected mode.

Although disabling this feature does give other users the ability to download or alter your PC's programs and settings without having to check with you first, it is recommended that you leave this feature on and instead adjust the other users' permissions.

Transfer

See the upcoming section, "Setting Parental Controls," for more information on how to limit or monitor another user's account.

Protecting Your Privacy

In addition to keeping your PC safe from online threats and potential malware, you also want to make sure that the materials and activities you perform on your PC are kept confidential. In other words, you want to keep your computer files and online activities private from others.

Managing your PC privacy is just as important as keeping your machine virus and spyware free. Fortunately, you can take precautionary measures to keep your data away from prying eyes, the first of which is applying the Vista BitLocker encryption tool. (*Note:* This feature works only with the Ultimate and Enterprise editions.) The next two methods — deleting cookies and browser history — erase all traces of your online browsing activities.

Protecting your files and folders

Password-protecting files and folders is not possible on the level of the operating system. (Individual programs, such as those in Microsoft Office, are responsible for this capability.) However, in Vista, you can control access to various files and folders by granting permissions via user accounts and controls.

Setting up user accounts

Windows Vista (like many other operating systems) has basically two different kinds of users — and thus, two kinds of user accounts. The first user is an *administrator*, who is someone with the power to make changes to any setting or program stored on the PC. *Standard* users, however, can make only limited changes to a computer's settings and installed programs. By restricting user access via standard accounts or by setting up password-protected administrator accounts, you can protect your confidential files as well as your computer's settings and installed software and hardware.

I recommend setting up your computer so that most user accounts are standard accounts. However, you might want to create a few administrator accounts if you are sharing a computer with someone you trust. For example, if you and your spouse share the same PC, you might want to create two separate administrator accounts rather than having just one. That way, both users can make changes to the computer's settings as well as install software and hardware.

On the other hand, if you share your computer with someone whom you would rather not have access to your information — perhaps you share your PC with a co-worker — you want to be sure that the other person's account is set up as a standard user and not as an administrator. Otherwise, you might unexpectedly turn on your computer one day to find that all your favorite settings are changed, unwanted software was installed (or important programs uninstalled), or you suddenly have missing hardware connections — all of which can be frustrating and time-consuming to correct.

The account you create when you first install Vista is automatically an administrator account. Any account you create thereafter can be set up either as a standard or an administrator account.

Information Kiosk

A third user account type is a Guest setting. *Guest accounts* are used for short-term (or temporary) access. People working as Guests cannot install software or hardware, change settings, or create new passwords on your PC. This account can be turned on or off via the Manage Accounts screen. (For more on managing accounts, see the following steps list.)

To create a new user account

1. Open the Control Panel from the Start menu.

2. Choose User Accounts and Family Safety.

3. Click the Add or Remove User Accounts link.

The Manage Accounts window opens, as shown in Figure 4-17.

Figure 4-17: Managing user accounts.

4. **From the Manage Accounts screen, click the Create a New Account link just below the box containing your current user accounts.**

This opens a Create New Account window like the one shown in Figure 4-18. From this screen, you can name and select either the Standard user or Administrator option for the new account.

Figure 4-18: Choosing an account type.

5. **Enter a name for the new account.**

The account name is the title that appears onscreen when the user logs in. It can be anything you would like it to be: a name, a nickname, or some other defining characteristic such as an employee identification number.

6. **Select an account type (Standard User or Administrator) and then click the Create Account button.**

If you choose Standard User, the person using the account will be able to access most installed programs (excluding those that require passwords) as well as any settings that do not affect other users.

If you choose Administrator, the person using the account will be able to make changes to any aspect of the PC's settings and/or install software and hardware.

Clicking the Create Account button returns you to the Manage Accounts window. Notice that the new account you just created now appears in the box of existing user accounts.

After you create the new account, you can assign a password to this user so that others can't log in (especially as an administrator), preventing them from accessing information that is not their own.

To create a password for a user account

1. **While in the Manage Accounts window, double-click the account for which you wish to create a password.**

This opens the Change an Account screen, like the one shown in Figure 4-19.

Figure 4-19: Making changes to an existing user account.

2. **Click the Create a Password link.**

This opens the Create Password window, as shown in Figure 4-20.

Figure 4-20: Creating a password.

In this example, I'm creating a password for an administrator account.

3. **Enter a password for the user account. Then retype it into the confirmation box below.**

Entering the password twice ensures that the spelling and capitalization is exactly how you want it.

Note: User account passwords are case sensitive. Therefore, if you enter the password with Caps Locks on, you need to type your password in capital letters each time you log on.

4. **(Optional) Type a password hint.**

You can also choose to enter a simple question or reminder message to help you remember the password. However, keep in mind that anyone who has access to your machine will also see the hint. Therefore, make sure the password and hint are not something that someone will be able to figure out easily.

5. **Click the Create Password button.**

The user account password is created, and you are returned to the Change an Account window.

From here, you can either close the Change an Account window by clicking the red X in the upper-right corner, or you can click the Back arrow in the upper-left corner to return to the Manage Accounts page to create passwords for additional user accounts.

Enabling the User Control feature

The Vista *User Account Control* (UAC) feature is a new tool used to help prevent unauthorized users from making changes to your computer. User Account Control prompts users with a dialog box asking for permission — or an administrator password, if one has been created — before the user can proceed with certain activities. The operations that are affected by this application comprise pretty much anything that pertains to how your operating system functions as well as any computer settings that affect other users.

To determine whether the User Account Control feature is turned on

1. **Open the Control Panel and select Security.**

2. **Choose the Security Center option.**

This opens the Security Center window. (Refer to Figure 4-1.)

3. **Click the down arrow to the right of the Other Security Settings category.**

Two new subcategories appear below: Internet Security Settings and User Account Control.

If the User Account Control feature is turned on, a green dot and the word On appear to the right. (See Figure 4-21.)

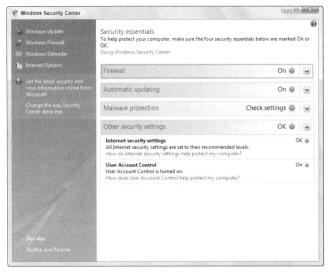

Figure 4-21: Viewing an enabled User Account Control computer.

If it is not turned on, you see a red dot, the word Off, and a button that allows you to turn on this feature with the click of a button. (See Figure 4-22.)

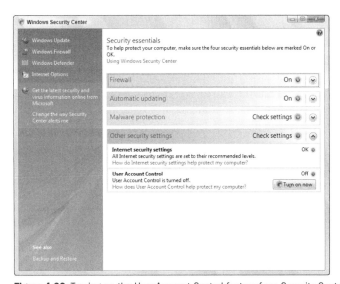

Figure 4-22: Turning on the User Account Control feature from Security Center.

Information Kiosk

You can also turn on/off User Account Control by opening the Control Panel and choosing User Accounts and Family Safety ➜ User Accounts. However, make sure that you are logged in as an administrator first, or you will be asked to provide an administrator password in order to continue.

From the User Accounts window that appears, you can turn User Account Control on or off. Clicking this link opens up a new window. Place a check mark in the box provided to enable this feature (or remove the check mark to disable it) and then click OK. You are informed that you must first restart your computer before this change goes into effect. Choose to Restart Now or Restart Later to finish.

BitLocker: The ultimate in offline security

I use the word *ultimate* deliberately here because the BitLocker Drive Encryption feature is available only in the Ultimate and Enterprise editions of Windows Vista.

Watch Your Step

If you plan to install BitLocker on your machine, you need to create another drive partition. This can be done most easily with a drive partition management program; the most well known is Partition Magic.

BitLocker is a whole-disk encryption scheme that automatically encrypts data while it is entered into the computer and then decrypts it while the data is read out. The data on the drive is unreadable at all times, but what appears on the monitor or printer is normal — in the clear. When the machine is shut down, all data remains encoded on the idle drive. If the BitLocker-protected computer and/or drive is lost or stolen, the data on it cannot be accessed by anyone lacking the decryption keys. Of course, the hardware itself continues to have value regardless of the information it contains, so BitLocker is no barrier to plain old-fashioned theft.

As many incidents have shown, data is far more valuable than hardware and its loss or theft, and transfer to the wrong hands can be catastrophic. The next section shows you how to install and use BitLocker to ensure that your PC's files remain confidential.

Installing Bitlocker

To install BitLocker, you must have two formatted partitions on your drive:

- A large primary (system volume) partition
- A second, smaller primary (system volume) partition, with this smaller partition made active

You also need a USB drive — also known as a *USB Flash drive* or a *thumb drive* — for storing your encryption keys, your passwords, or passphrases.

Watch Your Step

The safety and integrity of your encryption key (residing on a USB flash drive) or password is crucial. If you lose or corrupt these recovery items, your data and Windows Vista become inaccessible. You can no longer access any of the materials stored on your PC. You can, of course, reinstall Vista but not your files.

Transfer

Return to Chapter 1 to revisit how to create a separate partition on your PC's hard drive.

Install Windows Vista in the larger partition in the normal manner. This partition also contains all the data you wish to protect.

The second partition, which is not encrypted, houses the Vista boot loader and other files needed to access the encryption key and boot.

After Vista is installed

1. **Click the Start button.**

The Start menu appears in the bottom left of your screen.

2. **Choose Control Panel from the right-hand panel of the Start menu.**

The Control Panel window appears.

3. **Choose Security.**

The Security window appears.

4. **Select BitLocker Drive Encryption.**

The BitLocker Drive Encryption page appears.

If you can't use this device on your computer, you are notified on this page.

5. **Select the Secure Startup option.**

The Secure Startup window appears.

6. **If your machine has TPM (Trusted Platform Module), choose Turn on Secure Startup**

or

insert the USB device that contains your memory key and select Turn on Secure Startup.

The Secure Startup Wizard starts, as shown in Figure 4-23.

Figure 4-23: Saving your key.

Note: You'll know if your machine has TPM because a TPM Administration link appears at the bottom of the left panel in the BitLocker Drive Encryption window.

7. **Follow the remaining steps in the wizard, which saves your recovery key to a USB device and your password to a folder on another computer or a different non-encrypted hard drive.**

Watch Your Step

I cannot emphasize too much that the safety and integrity of your key/password is paramount. Lose it or corrupt it, and your data and Vista are gone. You can reinstall Vista — but not the data.

8. **Begin to encrypt the drive by clicking the Encrypt button.**

This process could take several hours, but you can use the machine while encryption is underway. The next time you boot your computer, you must first insert your USB key or enter the recovery password. Vista then runs and encrypts/decrypts with complete transparency.

Information Kiosk

It doesn't matter at what point you insert the key. The system will boot from the BIOS. But the drive with Vista will be inaccessible until the password (key) is entered.

Privacy and cookies in IE7

When speaking in computer terms, *cookies* do not represent sweet baked treats. Rather, they are small bits of information that are placed on your PC by a third-party server so that it can recognize you as a returning visitor in the future. Cookies can also be used to track and monitor specific user activity, such as site preferences and even the types of items you purchase when shopping online.

In essence, a cookie is a small text file placed on your hard drive. It is not an application or even an applet. Nor is it a virus. In and of itself, it represents no threat to the data or files on your computer. Under most circumstances, a cookie is but a convenient tool that stores personal information, saving you from having to reenter it. The most frequent example of a cookie is a saved username on a log-in page. This type of cookie can make for rapid log in and sometimes for quicker check out at e-retail sites.

The two types of cookies are

Session: *Session* (temporary) cookies exist and function during one browser session: They are removed when you close your browser. For example, if you select to not store a username or password or choose to not store address or credit card information on an e-retail site, these cookies are stored only until the end of the browser session. After you close the browser, they are gone. The next time you visit this Web site, you are prompted with the same options (to save your username, password, address, or credit card information).

Persistent: *Persistent* (saved) cookies are stored on your computer. These cookies can include usernames, passwords, or personal preferences having to do with a site's contents. (This is the technology used to greet you by name when you revisit a Web site.) For instance, if you refer to the examples given for session cookies (saving your username, password, address, or credit card information to an e-retail site), you would not be prompted to provide this information again the next time you visit. If this information were stored via persistent cookies, it would already appear onscreen when you accessed the appropriate Web page. There is obviously a convenience factor when evaluating the use of cookies. However, whether the convenience factor outweighs the privacy issue — that is, having other people be able to view and track your online activities — is what you need to decide when choosing whether to allow these items to be saved to your PC.

In general, cookies do not present a security threat in Internet browsing except under certain special circumstances, such as when cookies are intercepted by unauthorized users — in which case, the recipients could possibly access your user information. And although any shared personal information can represent a certain level of vulnerability, it is about the same level of vulnerability that exists when you carry membership cards to frequent buyer clubs or retail establishments. If someone were to peek into your wallet, he could easily identify which clubs you belong to and perhaps which stores you prefer to shop at, but that does not necessarily mean he will rob you and use your membership cards for his own personal benefit. It just means that someone discovered a little more about your current interests by referencing your past.

IE7 has two ways of managing these privacy issues:

- **Delete all your browser cookies.** This also removes the convenience factor associated with using cookies.
- **Restrict which sites you allow to place cookies on your PC.** This option lets you hand-select which Web sites you are comfortable having cookie capabilities and which sites you do not want to have access to your online activities.

If you choose to delete all cookies, you lose the positive functionality of cookies. As a consequence, you have to

- Enter all your usernames and passwords
- Re-enter contact information on retail sites you frequent
- Lose relevant user-oriented marketing information directed toward you
- Lose any user preferences you might otherwise have stored on Web sites

If you still wish to delete all cookies

1. **Open the Tools menu in IE7.**
2. **Choose Internet Options.**

   The Internet Options window opens.
3. **Select the General tab.**

   From this tab, you can make adjustments to your saved Home Pages, Browsing History, Search, Tabs, and Appearance settings.
4. **Click the Delete button in the Browsing history section.**

   The Delete Browsing History screen appears, as shown in Figure 4-24.

Figure 4-24: Deleting cookies.

5. **In the Cookie section, click the Delete Cookies button.**

A dialog box appears, asking whether you want to delete all cookies in the Temporary Internet Files folder.

6. **Click Yes.**

The dialog box disappears.

7. **Close both the Delete Browsing History and Internet Options windows.**

You are returned to your current browsing session.

Information Kiosk

One recent area of contention is that search engines use cookies to store keywords that you use to search the World Wide Web. The information that is retrieved and stored by the search engines using these cookies has been requisitioned by the U.S. government. AOL has complied with this request and provided the information, but Google has not (as of this writing) agreed to do so.

Your second privacy-protection option with IE7 involves identifying exactly which Web sites you do and do not want to store cookies on your machine, all in the name of preventing what could be construed as an invasion of privacy.

To decide which sites to permit to use cookies depends on whether you trust the site in question. If you frequent this site on a regular basis and have never encountered any problems there, feel free to add it to your acceptable sites list. You should also consider adding to your accepted sites list those Web sites you visit that do not necessarily contain sensitive information. This provides you with the convenience factor I mention earlier. Obviously, any suspicious sites or sites that contain confidential information (e-mail login sites, for example) should be included in the restricted Web sites list.

Here's how to selectively allow/restrict cookie placement:

1. **Open the Tools menu in IE7.**

A drop-down menu appears.

2. **Choose Internet Options.**

The Internet Options window opens.

3. **Select the Privacy tab.**

The Privacy tab, as shown in Figure 4-25, appears.

4. **Click the Sites button.**

This opens the Per Site Privacy Actions page. (See Figure 4-26.)

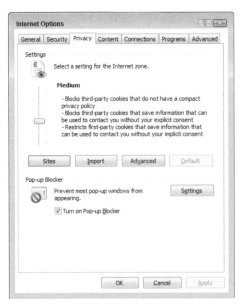

Figure 4-25: The Privacy tab.

Figure 4-26: Select which Web site can place cookies on your PC.

5. **Type the URL of the Web site you wish to permit/block into the Address of Website field.**

The address for the selected Web site appears in the text box provided.

Notice that the IE7 AutoComplete feature also works in this window.

6. **Click the appropriate permissions button.**

- *Block:* Click this to reject cookies from this Web site.

- *Allow:* Click this to accept cookies from this Web site.

After you make your selection, the Web site's URL is relocated to the Managed Websites box, along with a description of whether cookies are allowed from this site.

To add additional Web sites, repeats Steps 5 and 6.

To remove a Web site from the Managed Websites box, click its URL and then click the Remove button. You can also choose to remove all your entered Web sites and start over with a blank slate by clicking the Remove All button.

7. **Click OK when you are finished.**

This closes the Per Site Privacy Actions window.

8. **Close the Internet Options windows.**

You are returned to your current IE7 browsing session.

Information Kiosk

When you block a site from storing cookies, the blocking applies only to future cookies. You have no control over information that might have been collected from previously stored cookies.

Deleting browsing history in IE7

If you don't want others to know what Web sites you have visited — say, you're researching online for your spouse's upcoming birthday present, or you don't want your boss to know the non-work-related Web sites you visited via the office computer — IE7 provides you with a way to erase this information from your PC. In Windows Vista, you can delete your browser history in a matter of a few clicks:

1. **Open the Tools menu in IE7.**

A drop-down menu appears.

2. **Choose Internet Options.**

The Internet Options window opens.

3. **Select the General tab.**

From here, you can alter your Home Page, Browsing History, Search, Tab, and Appearance settings.

4. **Click the Delete button in the Browsing History section.**

This opens the Delete Browsing History window. (Refer to Figure 4-24.)

5. Click the Delete History button in the History section of this window.

You are prompted with a dialog box asking whether to delete your history of visited Web sites.

6. Confirm by clicking Yes.

This removes the dialog box from your screen.

You might also notice a status bar pop up while your records are deleted.

7. Close the Delete Browsing History and Internet Options windows.

You are returned to your IE7 browsing session.

Watch Your Step

You cannot undo the Delete History command, so don't do this if you want to keep a record of places you've been to on the Web.

Deleting your browsing history does not necessarily guarantee that the Web site entries you are trying to remove from your PC are not going to show up in the IE7 AutoComplete list when you start typing similar URLs into the Address bar.

Transfer

Glance back to Chapter 3 to find out more about your browser's AutoComplete feature.

If you want to make absolutely sure that these sites do not appear in your Address bar, delete this information from your saved AutoComplete records. Here's how:

1. Open the Tools menu in IE7.

2. Choose Internet Options.

3. Select the General tab (if it is not already selected).

4. Click the Delete button in the Browsing History section.

The Delete Browsing History dialog box opens.

5. Click the Delete Forms button in the Form Data section of this window. (Refer to Figure 4-24.)

A dialog box appears, asking whether you want to delete previously saved *form data* — information such as name, address, credit card number, password, and so on, you may have entered into a Web-based form.

6. Confirm by clicking Yes.

This removes the dialog box from your screen.

7. Close the Delete Browsing History window.

This page is also removed from your screen.

8. **In the Internet Options window, click Apply.**

   This saves the changes you made.

9. **Click OK.**

   This closes the Internet Options window.

Setting Parental Controls

When it comes to raising your children, you have established certain guidelines as a parent — ones you hope provide your children with a safe yet engaging environment in which to grow. For example, your children probably are not permitted to stay up late except on special occasions. You've also probably asked them to introduce you to their friends to make sure they don't associate with people who might lead them astray. You set rules for the types of movies and music they can watch or listen to. And you do your best to monitor their comings and goings to keep them out of harm's way.

The computers your children use, though, can bypass all your protective plans and policies.

As you are probably well aware, not all the universe that lies beyond that glowing monitor is pretty, and some of it can even be predatory. Today's Internet is a virtual real world, operating with real-time audio and video communication. People miles away in cyberspace are right there on the desktop chatting with and showing live video of themselves to your children. They are almost literally in the room with your child. Also, the Internet allows your child — as it allows anyone else — to find, see, and read all sorts of inappropriate (and even illegal) material.

In the past, you might have tried to monitor your children's online viewing habits, but until the advent of Vista, it has been difficult for parents to monitor — much less control — what their children (or any one else) can do on a computer. Fortunately, IE7 now offers you a variety of measures to control the activities your children are allowed to engage in while online. It also affords you with tools to monitor the Web sites your children visit as well as how much time they are permitted to spend online.

Virtual supervision

Although third-party software has been available to monitor and control computer access, such functions have not generally been part of the operating systems themselves.

Previous versions of Windows, notably XP, have allowed Administrators (typically parents) to set access permissions and to establish separate accounts for non-Administrators. Only the parent-Administrator had full access to the computer, its files, and the programs that could be run. Other users could be restricted albeit not much. Any computer-savvy child could quickly and easily bypass most limitations and gain access to prohibited areas, leaving no tracks.

Vista changes all that.

The Parental Controls that come with Vista allow you to set all access terms for subordinate — likely, your children's — accounts. It can even limit

- **When:** The hours during which a user may use the computer
- **What:** The types of information the user may access
- **Where:** The places the user can go on the Web and in chat rooms
- **How:** The use of any microphones or Webcams

Parental Controls records all activity in the selected account so that you may later examine that information and see exactly where (online) your child went, what programs they ran, which files were accessed, and when. A computer-savvy child could circumvent some controls and get into forbidden files and places, but the password-enabled and -protected User Account Protection function that pops up whenever anyone or anything attempts to access the computer should defeat any unauthorized user's attempt to alter the Parental Controls settings.

Information Kiosk

Parental Controls is not just for blocking children's access to the computer. It also keeps your private files and activities secure from the eyes of anyone else who might use your computer, with or without your permission — co-workers, roommates, baby sitters, houseguests, siblings. . . .

Setting Parental Controls

Before you can make selections concerning which activities your children can (or cannot) engage in online, you must first establish a separate account for each user. To create a new user account

1. **Click the Start button to open the Control Panel.**

2. **Select User Accounts and Family Safety.**

   This page allows you to create new user accounts and set Parental Controls. You can also remove accounts that are no longer needed from this screen.

3. **In the User Accounts section, click the Add or Remove User Accounts link.**

   This opens the Manage Accounts window. (Refer to Figure 4-17.)

4. **Click the Create a New Account link.**

   This option is located just below the box containing your existing user accounts.

   Clicking this link takes you to the Create New Account page. (Refer to Figure 4-18.)

5. **Type your child's name into the New Account Name text box.**

This is the name that appears onscreen when your child logs on to the computer.

Note: This does not have to be the same as the username he or she uses for other online activities, like e-mail. It can be a nickname or just her initials.

6. **Select Standard User.**

Be sure that you child's account is not set up as an Administrator. Having your child's account set up as an Administrator prevents you from being able to create Parental Controls for this account. This also provides your child with complete access to your PC's files and settings, which is one of the things you may be trying to limit with the IE7 Parental Controls tools.

7. **Click the Create Account button.**

This takes you back to the Manage Accounts page.

8. **Repeat Steps 4–7 until you create all the user accounts you need.**

After you create separate user accounts for all your children, you can start creating personalized controls for each of them. To access the Parental Controls window

1. **Return to the Manage Accounts window.**

This page should already be open. If it's not, repeat Steps 1–3 of the preceding example to locate this screen.

2. **Click the icon for the first child whose parameters you wish to set.**

This opens your child's Change an Account window. (See Figure 4-27.)

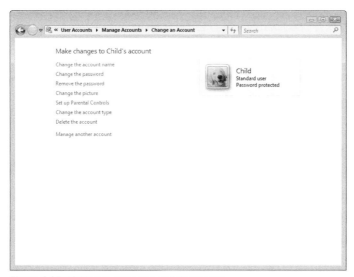

Figure 4-27: Making changes to a child's account.

3. **Click the Set Up Parental Controls link.**

This opens the Parental Controls home page, as shown in Figure 4-28.

Figure 4-28: Locating Parental Controls.

4. **Choose the user account you would like to create Parental Controls for.**

Clicking the icon for a user automatically opens his User Controls screen. (See Figure 4-29.)

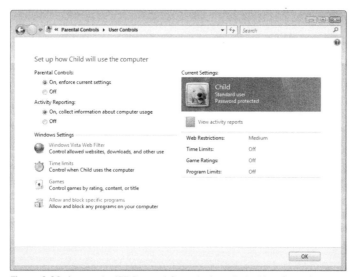

Figure 4-29: Access the IE7 Parental Controls through the User Controls screen.

5. Select the On, Enforce Current Settings radio button in the Parental Controls section of this window.

From here, you can make adjustments to your child's Parental Controls.

Information Kiosk

After you have established Parental Controls for your child's account, you can periodically review his or her computing activities by accessing a weekly Activity Report. These reports include information on the top 10 Web sites your child has visited, as well as the top 10 Web sites that he or she tried to visit but couldn't because they were blocked by Parental Control settings, any Web overrides, file downloads (including blocked download attempts), the times he or she was logged on to the computer, which applications he or she used, games played, as well as e-mail, instant messaging, and other media activities.

To take advantage of this feature, be sure to enable the Activity Reporting option in the child's User Controls window. Just click in the radio button to the left of the On, Collect Information about Computer Usage option to be able to access this data later.

Transfer

To learn more about how to set up and use Activity Reports, refer to the "Viewing activity reports" section, later in this chapter.

Using Parental Control Windows Settings

Four different Windows Settings sections are located on the User Controls page. These items refer to the areas where you can make changes to limit your children's online permissions. Here is a brief explanation of each of these categories:

- **Windows Vista Web Filter:** Controls the Web sites your child is allowed to view
- **Time Limits:** Determines when your child is permitted to use the computer
- **Games:** Outlines the types of games your child is allowed to play
- **Allow and Block Specific Programs:** Identifies the programs your child is able to use

Examples of when you might want to use these features, as well as instructions for how to make adjustments to these controls, follow.

Windows Vista Web Filter

If you worry about what types of Web sites your child views, use this feature to choose exactly which sites your child can see. To hand-select these sites, follow these steps:

1. **Open your child's User Controls window.**

   Use the earlier directions to locate this page if necessary.

2. **Select Windows Vista Web Filter.**

   This opens the Web Restrictions pages, as shown in Figure 4-30.

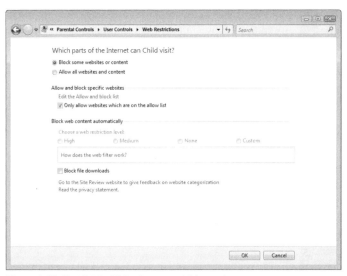

Figure 4-30: Restrict the Web sites your child can view.

3. **Select the Block Some Websites or Content radio button.**

   This option is located below the heading, Which Parts of the Internet Can *child's name* Visit?

4. **Select the Only Allow Websites Which Are on the Allow List check box.**

   This item can be found in the Allow and Block Specific Websites section of this window.

   A check mark appears after you make the selection.

5. **Click the Edit the Allow and Block List link.**

   This opens the Allow Block Webpages screen. (See Figure 4-31.)

   From here, you can enter exactly which sites are permitted for viewing.

6. **In the Website Address field, type the URL of the site you wish to allow/block.**

   Be sure to use the complete URL, including the www. and .com/.org parts, to ensure that the correct site is detected.

7. **Choose whether to allow or block.**

   Clicking the Allow or the Block button to the right of the Website Address box determines whether your child can view a particular site.

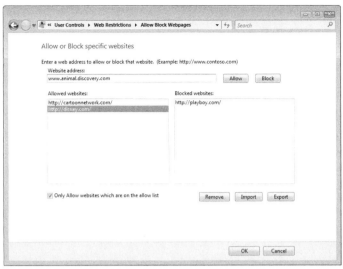

Figure 4-31: Choose which sites your child can view.

After you make your selection, the URL is moved to the appropriate list.

8. Repeat Steps 6 and 7 until you have a complete list of the sites you want to allow/prohibit.

9. Click OK.

This saves your list of permitted and restricted Web sites and returns you to the Web Restrictions window.

10. Click OK again.

This closes the Web Restrictions page and returns you to the User Controls window.

Information Kiosk

You can also allow additional Web sites to be viewed by your child if you clear the Only Allow Websites Which Are on the Allow List check box on the Web Restrictions page. This allows you to restrict certain sites without also having to identify every site you child is permitted to view.

As an alternative to creating separate lists of sites your child can visit, you can choose to set the IE7 filter device to weed out questionable materials. Obviously, choosing to identify the specific sites you want your child to view is safer than relying on IE7 to filter potentially inappropriate material. However, choosing only a handful of Web sites severely limits your child's ability to surf the Web. This might be a viable option if you have very small children that are allowed to visit only a few Web sites (like Disney.com, or other children-oriented pages). However, such tight travel restrictions can impede older children and teenagers. As a workaround, you can use the IE7 filter feature.

To activate Vista's built-in filter device

1. **Choose Windows Vista Web Filter from the User Controls page.**

Use the earlier instructions to locate this page if necessary.

This opens the Web Restrictions window.

2. **Select the Block Some Websites or Content option.**

3. **Ensure that the Only Allow Websites Which Are on the Allow List check box is clear.**

If a check mark is present, remove it to enable the Block Web Content Automatically options.

4. **Click the filter level you feel is most appropriate for your child.**

You can choose a high restriction, medium restriction, no restrictions, or a customized restriction level.

If you choose the custom option, a new menu box appears below this item, as shown in Figure 4-32. Enable the check boxes for the categories you wish to block.

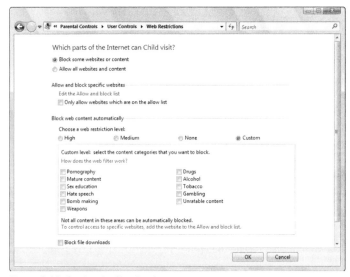

Figure 4-32: Setting the filter levels.

5. **Click OK.**

This closes the Web Restrictions window and returns you to the User Controls page.

Information Kiosk

You can also choose to block your child's ability to download files from the Web Restrictions page. Select the Block File Downloads check box at the bottom of this window to prohibit this kind of online activity and protect your PC from potential malware.

Time Limits

One way to limit your child's online behavior is to limit the amount of time he or she is permitted to use the computer. For example, maybe your child is allowed only a couple of hours each day to surf the Web. Set up a schedule (perhaps the first few hours after school) for your child's online activities. Selecting a time when you are going to be home can also deter children from visiting sites they know you would disapprove of, especially if you are sitting in the next room. This feature can also be used to help evenly distribute computer time amongst several users. If you, your spouse, and your children all share the same PC, setting up a schedule for each user can help limit conflicts about who gets to use this computer first; this is an especially handy feature for siblings.

To set up time restrictions for your child

1. **Choose Time Limits from the User Controls page.**

Use the preceding steps lists to locate this page if necessary.

This opens the Time Restrictions window, as shown in Figure 4-33.

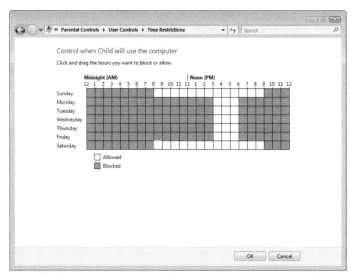

Figure 4-33: Restrict the amount of time your child is permitted to use the computer.

2. **Click (and/or drag) your mouse over the schedule boxes to indicate whether your child is permitted to use the computer during this time.**

You can change the color/permissions level for each box by simply clicking it with your mouse.

If a box is highlighted in blue, it is *blocked* — your child may not use the computer during this time. If a box is white, your child is allowed to use the PC at this time.

3. **Click OK.**

This saves your settings and closes the Time Restrictions windows, returning you to the User Controls page.

Games

The types of games your child plays can be just as important as the content they view online. Some games are rated M or A, indicating that they are meant to be played by mature audiences only. Many of these games are given this rating because of their high levels of violent content. By restricting your child's ability to play these types of games, you are also limiting his or her exposure to violence, foul language, and other potentially inappropriate behavior.

To specify which types of games your child is permitted to play

1. **Choose Games from the User Controls page.**

Use the preceding steps lists to locate this page if necessary.

This opens the Game Controls window, as shown in Figure 4-34.

From this page, you can choose whether your child is permitted to play games at all or to limit the types of games she plays by selecting the appropriate gaming level for his or her age.

2. **Select the Yes radio button in the Can *Child* Play Games? section.**

This allows your child to play the games you deem appropriate. However, you must complete the remaining items in this steps list to identify the types of games you want your child to be able to play. If you do not specify which games your child is allowed to play, choosing this option gives her the ability to play all types of games.

If you do not want your child to be able to play any games whatsoever, select the No radio button. Then click OK to close this window. This prohibits her from accessing any types of games stored on your PC.

Figure 4-34: Control the types of games your child is permitted to play.

3. **Click the Set Game Ratings link.**

This option is in the Block (or Allow) Games by Rating and Content Types section of this window.

Clicking this link opens the Game Restrictions page. (See Figure 4-35.)

Figure 4-35: Select age-appropriate games for your child.

4. **Select the appropriate gaming level for your child.**

Each gaming level provides a brief description and age recommendation.

After you make a selection, you can see that all the levels preceding your choice are highlighted as well. This indicates that they, too, are allowed to pass through to your child.

Note the option at the top of the page to either allow or block games without a rating. It is recommend that you block all unrated games. This ensures that no M- or A-rated games slip through the cracks, exposing your child to unwanted or inappropriate situations.

5. **Click OK.**

This saves the gaming preferences you have selected for your child and closes the Game Restrictions window.

6. **Click OK again.**

This closes the Game Controls window and returns you to the User Controls page.

Allow or Block Specific Programs

The final Windows Settings feature provides you with the option to hand-select which programs your child is permitted to access. You may choose to allow your child access to all the programs on your PC, or you can select a few choice items he can use. For example, if your child spends too much time listening to music online — say, instead of doing homework — you can use this feature to block Windows Media Player.

 Transfer

See Chapter 9 to learn more about Vista's built-in Media Player and working with other digital media.

To access this Parental Controls feature

1. **Select the Allow and Block Specific Programs option from the User Controls window.**

Use the preceding steps lists to locate this page if necessary.

This opens the Application Restrictions window. From this page, you can grant your child access to all the application programs on your PC, or you can choose to limit the items he can access.

If you choose to grant him access to all programs (which is the more common choice), select this option and then click OK. This closes the Application Restrictions window and returns you to the User Controls page.

If you decide to block certain programs from your child, complete the remaining steps listed.

2. **Select the *Child* Can Only Use the Programs I Allow radio button to restrict the items your child can access.**

This opens up a new menu box below (see Figure 4-36). This box contains a list of programs stored on your PC.

If you cannot locate the files you wish to block, you can search for them by using the Browse button provided at the bottom of the page.

3. **Choose which programs you want your child to be able to use.**

Selecting the check boxes to the left of the program's description allows your child access to that application.

Note the Check All and the Uncheck All buttons at the bottom of your screen. This feature comes in handy if you wish to block only a couple of items. Simply check all the available boxes, by using the button provided, and then deselect the items you wish to block.

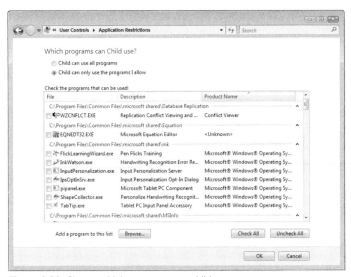

Figure 4-36: Choose which programs your child can use.

4. **Click OK.**

This saves your settings and closes the Application Restrictions page. You are then, once again, returned to the User Controls window.

Viewing activity reports

After you establish Parental Controls for your children, you probably want to know how to monitor this information. To keep track of your children's online activities as well as their general PC usage, you can create an activity report to outline exactly what they have done while using the computer. This summary generates information about which Web sites your children visit, the files they access or download, the games they play, and how much time they spend doing each of these things.

Watch Your Step

Be sure you turn on the Activity Reporting feature (located in the User Controls window) when you set up your child's Parental Controls. Otherwise, you cannot access this data.

Information Kiosk

If you wish to check what Web sites your child has visited but you have not yet set up Parental Controls, you can still access this information by checking your computer's browsing history. *Note:* This does not explicitly identify which user visited which sites. Or, you can go to the URL field in IE7 and type in a single letter of the alphabet to see what sites come up in the AutoComplete list.

To view your child's (or any other user's) activity report

1. Open the Control Panel window.

You can locate this menu by clicking the Start button.

2. Choose User Accounts and Family Safety.

This opens the User Accounts and Family Safety window, as shown in Figure 4-37.

3. Click the View Activity Reports link in the Parental Controls section of this window.

Clicking this link opens the Activity Viewer. (See Figure 4-38.)

This page includes specific information relating to your child's online and general PC activities. From this report, you can identify the top ten sites that your child visited as well as the top ten blocked Web sites he attempted to visit. You can also see what, if any, files your child downloaded, the applications he used, and any games he played. Also noted on this page are your child's log-in times, e-mail, instant messaging, and media activities.

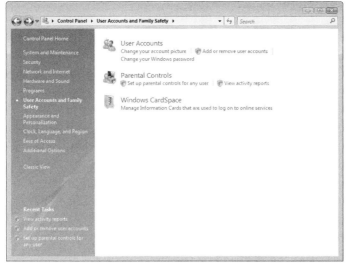

Figure 4-37: The User Accounts and Family Safety page.

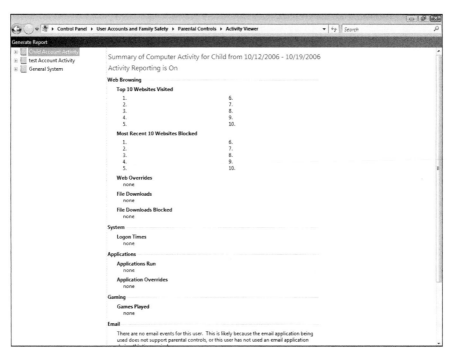

Figure 4-38: Reviewing activity reports.

active content: Scripts that run on your computer from a Web site you are visiting in order for you to experience certain visual or dynamic effects. If you are safely browsing the Web — meaning that you are using secure settings — you are prompted by IE7 to allow these scripts to run.

The three most common forms of Active Content are

> **ActiveX:** A scripting tool created by Microsoft; it describes programs run on Web pages for the purpose of adding extra functionality.

> **Java:** A distant cousin of JavaScript, this program can be downloaded onto your computer or run through your browser.

> **JavaScript:** IE7, as with all Web browsers, has a built-in JavaScript interpreter. JavaScript is not a program but rather a script usually embedded into HTML, which produces dynamic effects, such as buttons lighting up when you select them. JavaScript can be used maliciously, for example, when it redirects you from the site you selected to browse to an illegitimate one where obtaining personal information is attempted. Some of these illegitimate sites might even attempt to download malicious software onto your machine.

BitLocker: An encryption-on-the-fly feature in Vista that encrypts and decrypts information going to and from the hard drive in real time. The drive is always encrypted and can be read from and written to only when it is unlocked by a password or encryption key. The drive cannot be read without the encryption key, thus safeguarding the system's data if the computer is lost or stolen or attacked by unauthorized persons.

cookies: Small text files placed on your hard drive by a third-party server to identify, monitor, and track information about your Web site preferences and online activities. By themselves, cookies cannot be used to harm the computer or its user in any way. However, if the information contained within these files is intercepted by a malicious party, the user could be at risk.

firewall: A piece of hardware or software that filters the information coming to or from your computer. This security feature manages the content permitted to enter and exit a PC or its internal network. If the firewall detects any potentially dangerous materials, it prohibits them from interacting with your machine. This tool acts as your first line of defense against malware or other unwanted software.

malware: Malicious or harmful software designed by its creator with the intent to infiltrate or damage a computer system. Malware is typically added to a PC without the owner's knowledge or permission.

 *continued*

Parental Controls: A suite of Vista software settings that proscribe a user's access both to the computer and to the Internet. Named Parental Controls with children in mind, it can also be used to limit anyone's access to the computer or Internet.

Security Center: A Vista module through which the administrator can establish levels of permissions for other users as well as set various levels of security, including encryption, for the entire system.

security encryption: A protective measure used by Web sites to ensure that the information provided by the user remains confidential. This security method scrambles electronic transmissions by using a special encryption code that can be understood only with the correct deciphering key.

spoofing: Copying a Web site and redirecting a user to that copy to collect personal data to be used for fraudulent purposes.

spyware: A software program that monitors what users do with their computers. Spyware can be used for harmless purposes — such as collecting information for marketing research — or it can be used for more malicious acts, such as obtaining personal information (like passwords or credit card numbers) for illegal or unwarranted use of this data. In this sense, sypware can be considered a type of malware or simply a device used to invade one's privacy. Spyware is capable of tracking all types of (unsecure) information transmitted over the Internet.

USB Flash drive: A portable, lightweight memory-storage device used to back up or transport data from one computer to another. One of the most common uses for Flash drives is to store personal files, such as documents, pictures, and videos.

virus: Another example of malware. Computer viruses are self-replicating programs that alter how a computer operates. Whereas most computer viruses are destructive in nature — meaning they often destroy your computer's system files and programs — they can also simply be annoying as well, such as when a computer continually repeats the same message over and over again on your screen. Like with other forms of malware, viruses are usually downloaded to a PC without the user's prior knowledge or consent.

worm: A form of computer virus that uses network connections to send copies of itself to other systems, sometimes without any interaction from users. Unlike viruses, worms do not need to attach themselves to existing programs. Instead, they use the system's network to execute the commands contained within its own code. Worms are meant to wreak havoc on the afflicted network (if only by consuming large amounts of its bandwidth at one time), whereas viruses attack or corrupt files on individual computers.

Last Stop

Practice Exam

1. If you receive a phishing e-mail, what clues should you look for that you are being directed to a spoofing site?

_____

_____

_____

2. What warning indications do you encounter when you try to change your browser's security settings to ones that are less secure?

_____

_____

_____

3. If you don't remember where the Security Center is found within Vista, what is (are) the easiest way(s) to find it?

_____

_____

_____

4. Why don't icons for the Windows Firewall and Windows Defender display in the Notification area?

_____

_____

_____

5. How can you prevent search engines from storing your keyword searches in their databases?

_____

_____

_____

6. How much can you limit your children's online and general computing activities using Parental Controls?

_____

_____

_____

7. What are the benefits of using BitLocker? At what point can you decide to employ BitLocker?

_____

_____

_____

8. What are the main areas of the Windows Security Center?

_____

_____

_____

9. Is BitLocker available for all versions of Windows Vista?

_____

_____

_____

10. What signs indicate that you're visiting a secure site? Where are such signs displayed onscreen?

_____

_____

_____

11. When is it safe to run active content from a Web site on your machine?

_____

_____

_____

12. Is it good to have more than one spyware program? Why or why not?

_____

_____

_____

13. If Parental Controls are not turned on, how can you determine what Web sites have been visited?

_____

_____

_____

Working More Efficiently with Applications, Files, and Folders

STATIONS ALONG THE WAY

O Creating shortcuts for your applications, folders, and files

O Learning the ins and outs of searching in Windows Vista

O Making searching easier and faster

O Learning how to associate file types with applications

O Protecting your documents with Vista's new XPS file format

O Partitioning your hard drive

O Transferring your files from one computer to another using Windows Easy Transfer

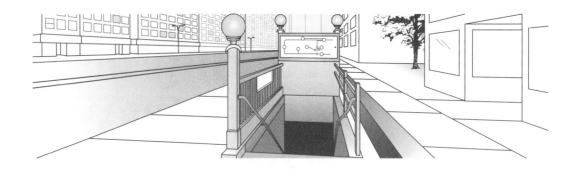

 # Enter the Station

Questions

1. How can desktop shortcuts make your computing experience more productive?

2. What choices do you have in locating your files?

3. What is metadata and how can it help you create a personalized classification system for your documents?

4. What do you really need to know about file associations?

5. How can you use Vista's new XPS format to create safer documents?

6. What can you accomplish by partitioning your hard drive?

7. How can you use the Windows Easy Transfer Wizard to access customized programs and settings from your old computer?

Express Line

If you are already up on applications, folders, files, and searching in Windows Vista, skip ahead to the next chapter.

I n this chapter, you gain a better understanding of your data, how to organize it, how to get to it, and how to search for it with ease. By better organizing and filing your data, you can increase your productivity.

Windows Vista offers a number of ways to achieve this level of efficiency — some tried and true, and some relatively new. One tried-and-true method involves creating shortcuts to the folders or documents you use most often. (Creating such desktop shortcuts enables you to significantly reduce the amount of time you spend hunting for the appropriate materials.) Vista's new search capabilities also aid in your search for files, documents, and application programs. The easy access of Vista's new search features makes finding the items you're looking for quick and convenient. Restructuring (or partitioning) your hard drive can also make your files easier to locate. Knowing how to save your files in a certain manner can also make them easier to identify and print.

Transferring files from another computer can be a confusing and troublesome task. However, Windows Vista includes a special transfer wizard to eliminate some of the tricky details that take place behind the scenes of this process. After you have these files converted over to the new machine, you can apply the methods mentioned earlier to classify, organize, find, and use some of your favorite files and folders from the existing computer.

Creating Shortcuts

A blank desktop — whether the old wooden or the new "virtual" computer kind — may look neat and gleaming, but with nothing ready in-hand, it is not particularly efficient. Files and folders you need to work with should be readily available, not stuck in drawers or buried in directories somewhere. Figure 5-1 shows how you can configure a computer desktop so that you can quickly get to what you need. As you can see, a column of icons that reflect your program and file priorities are on the left side of the screen. They represent shortcuts to the actual disk drives, folders, and programs inside the computer, out of sight. By placing these icons on the desktop, you don't have to dig from the Start menu through the hierarchies, click after click, to get to what you most often use. For example, see the desktop shortcut for a Program Compatibility application in Figure 5-1. You need only click the desktop icon to open this particular program, thus saving several steps.

 ### Watch Your Step

Keep only shortcuts — not the actual files — on the desktop. Should the desktop or Vista itself become corrupted, only the shortcuts are lost, not the program or the data.

Figure 5-1: A Windows Vista desktop.

Creating shortcuts to programs

Program shortcuts are easy to create. Just follow these instructions to make desktop shortcuts for all your favorite programs:

1. **Click the Start button.**

The Start menu appears in the bottom left of your screen.

2. **Choose All Programs.**

A list of all the programs on your computer appears in the left column. (See Figure 5-2.)

3. **Locate the item for which you wish to make a shortcut.**

You might need to filter through a couple layers of folders before you find the application you want.

Figure 5-2: The Start menu: All Programs.

4. **After you find the correct program, left-click its icon/name and drag it to a blank space on your desktop. Or, alternatively, right-click on the menu entry and choose Send To ➜ Desktop (Create Shortcut).**

This automatically creates a shortcut from the program's location to your desktop. The shortcut icon is distinguished by a curved arrow in a box, as shown in Figure 5-3.

 Information Kiosk

You can also drag and drop programs from your Recent Items list in the Start menu. This shortens the search process mentioned earlier.

To use this shortcut, simply double-click the icon that now appears on your desktop to open the application or run the program you selected.

Adding a shortcut

Figure 5-3: Windows Vista desktop with a shortcut to Internet Explorer.

Shortcuts to folders

You might also find it convenient to create shortcuts to folders where you store files that you use regularly. For example, if you were writing a book, it would be sensible to create a folder with the title of that book, put a shortcut to that folder on the desktop, and then store all the material pertaining to that book in that folder and its subfolders. You might also want to create shortcuts to your personal documents, such as pictures or music files. That way, you can easily access these materials from your desktop.

To create a shortcut to a file/folder

1. **Click the Start button.**

The Start menu appears in the bottom left of your screen.

2. **From the right side of the Start menu, choose Computer.**

This opens up the Computer window, as shown in Figure 5-4.

Figure 5-4: Locate files and folders via the Computer window.

3. **Use the Favorite Links column on the left to locate the folder for which you wish to create a shortcut.**

Clicking the Documents, Pictures, or Music folder opens up the selected folder, revealing the subfolders contained within. Select the folder you want to create a desktop shortcut for and proceed to the next step.

Note: If the file or folder you wish to add to your desktop is not saved to any of these folders, you can double-click the C: drive information to locate the file/folder you desire.

4. **Right-click the folder for which you want to create the shortcut.**

A drop-down menu appears. (See Figure 5-5.)

5. **Choose Create Shortcut.**

A shortcut copy of the selected folder is added for the folder you designated.

Again, you can determine which file is the original and which is the shortcut by the little arrow at the bottom-left corner. The icon with the arrow is the shortcut. The other icon is the original.

6. **Left-click the shortcut icon and drag it to a blank space on your desktop.**

Dragging the shortcut icon to your desktop automatically creates a link to the selected file(s)/folder(s).

Watch Your Step

Be sure to move the shortcut icon and not the original. That way, if Vista or your desktop is corrupted, your files/folders are not lost as well.

Figure 5-5: A drop-down menu appears when you right-click a drive.

Information Kiosk

If your desktop becomes too crowded, just delete unwanted or seldom used shortcuts by right-clicking a shortcut icon and choosing Delete from the pop-up menu that appears. This removes the icon from your screen.

Or, let Vista do it for you. The program keeps track of how often shortcuts are accessed and eventually asks whether it can remove unused shortcuts. Select OK when prompted by Vista's query as to whether you'd like to delete these old, outdated shortcuts. This removes them from your screen, providing you with more screen space to add more relevant shortcuts.

Using Vista's Search Features

Windows Vista by itself installs more than 36,000 separate and distinct files on your computer. The program generates a half-dozen directories with cascades of subdirectories for such things as Users; Program Files; driver files; and others, most of which are quite mysterious and need not concern the average user at all.

Very few programs these days are self-contained in a single file. Programs such as Microsoft Windows, and program suites such as Microsoft Office and Microsoft Works, comprise hundreds and even thousands of separate files that the installation utility places on your computer in the proper places.

The result is that any modern personal computer running a normal suite of programs has thousands of directories and tens of thousands of files and objects ranging from those clearly visible on the desktop to those ten levels down in a hierarchical directory. You might think that those deeply buried and mysterious files do not matter to you, but the day might come when some program you are trying to run returns an error message: `Myprogram cannot find Ineedittorun.dll. Closing.` You must then be able to find and install properly this one file — `Ineedittorun.dll` — among those tens of thousands if you want to run Myprogram.

How does Windows Vista keep track of all those files? How do you quickly find any that you need? The next section explains it all.

Basic searching in Vista

Basic searching in Vista could not be easier. Just click the Start button and then type your search term in the search box at the bottom left of the Start menu. As you type each character, the Start menu replaces the recently used items with the results of your search that contain the characters you have typed so far. (See Figure 5-6.)

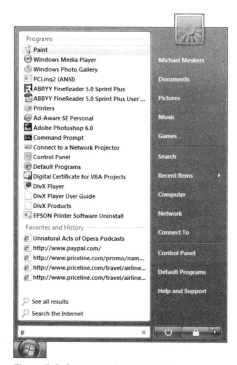

Figure 5-6: Starting an Instant Search.

Here are the results of simply typing the letter *p*. As you enter additional characters in the search box, the list changes as it zeroes in on items that match your criteria (see Figure 5-7).

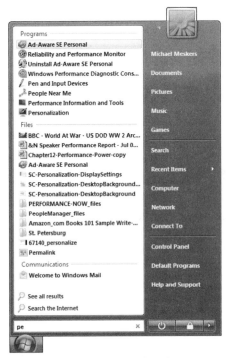

Figure 5-7: Refining an Instant Search.

Note how the addition of a single letter *(e)* greatly narrows the search. Adding more letters narrows the search still further until you either find the program or file you want or the box returns a `No items match your search` message.

If the item you want appears, just click it to open it. If it does not appear in the abbreviated results list, you can click the See All Results option at the bottom of the window to view all the potential matches located on your computer. You can also broaden your search to the Internet by using the Search the Internet option located at the bottom of the search column.

Transfer

Refer to Chapter 3 to review how to use the new IE7 Internet search capabilities.

You can also perform more detailed searches by using the Advanced Search feature located within the Start menu. Using this search tool provides you with more options to specify — and, therefore, easily pinpoint — the exact file, document, or program you are looking for.

To access this Advanced Search feature

1. Click the Start button.

The Start menu appears in the bottom left of your screen.

2. Choose Search from the right column.

This opens a blank Search Results screen.

3. Type the name of the file or program you wish to locate into the search box located in the upper right of this window.

Entering the program or file's title into the search box provided brings up a list of potential matches.

This feature works much the same way that the Instant Search box does in the Start menu. However, this feature provides you with a more extensive results list. It also allows you to narrow your search fields even further by telling Vista where you think the file you're looking for is located. For example, you can choose to search only the items stored in your documents, pictures, music, or e-mail records.

To use this feature

1. Repeat Steps 1–3 of the preceding step list.

This opens up the Search Results page.

2. Choose Organize from the main menu.

3. Choose Layout from the drop-down menu that appears.

Doing so opens the Layout submenu. (See Figure 5-8.)

Figure 5-8: Organize ➜ Layout, the Search pane.

4. Choose Search Pane.

The drop-down and Layout submenus disappear, and a new toolbar is added to your Search window. This new toolbar includes a list of categories that you can use to narrow your search range. You can choose to search all the files and programs stored on your computer, or you can select from the following categories: E-mail, Document, Picture, Music, and Other. (See Figure 5-9.)

Use this toolbar to search by category.

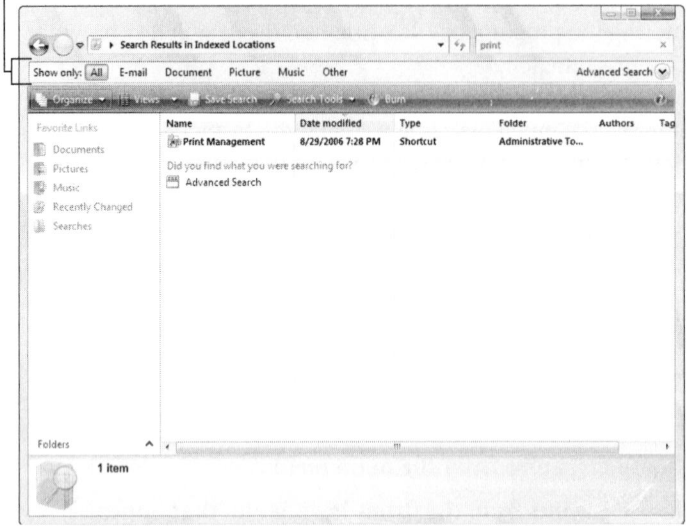

Figure 5-9: Use the Search pane to narrow the types of files that are included in your search results.

5. Click the category you want to search.

This limits your search results to only the selected types of files.

You can also expand your search capabilities by clicking the Advanced Search option at the bottom of the Results list. This tool provides you with a much wider variety of search options, as shown in Figure 5-10. For example, you can identify the files or programs you are looking for by indicating the exact location (or drive) the file is located; the date it was created; its size, author, exact filename; or the tag used to group it together with other related documents or programs. (Read more about tagging in the following section.) Use the appropriate drop-down menus to provide the Vista search engine with detailed information about the file or document you are seeking; then click the Search button. The Results list is re-created based on the new criteria you provided.

Advanced Search features

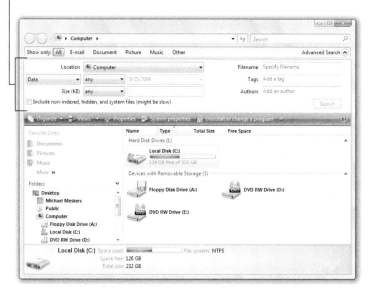

Figure 5-10: Advanced Search options.

Information Kiosk

You do not have to go to the Start menu to begin a search. Every Explorer window that you open on the desktop also includes a search box with which you can search within a document or program that you are already running or within a folder you have open. Windows Vista puts a search box in virtually every window you have open, enabling you to do a targeted search within the applications, tools, folders, and files of that window.

Step into the Real World

You can save your searches and run them again any time you like. Because it takes no little time to set up a complex search, this is a boon. Your next search might not be identical to your last, but it saves much time to be able to modify an existing search over doing the entire process all over again. After your search, just click the Save Search button in the task pane. Type a name for the search in the Save As dialog box and then click Save. Vista saves your search in the Searches folder. The next time you want to access this information, simply open your Searches folder and click the name of the search file you wish to revisit. To quickly access the Searches folder, simply open Windows Explorer, choose the More >> link on the left side and select Searches from the contextual menu that appears, as shown in Figure 5-11.

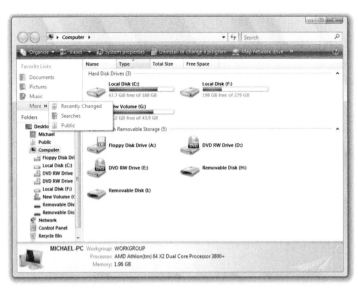

Figure 5-11: The Windows Explorer window. Select Searches to find your saved searches.

Using metadata criteria

When a single application has thousands of unique files stored in hundreds of folders and subfolders, quickly finding a single file by its location alone becomes a daunting, time-consuming task on even the fastest of computers. Fortunately, Windows Vista allows you to use a search method widely applied in the Internet world that makes use of metadata. *Metadata* — sometimes characterized as data about data — is nothing more than a group of characteristics that you can assign to any file. These criteria, which can be any number of properties that define the data rather than anything contained within the data itself, provide sorting and searching means that are independent of the file title or content. A single criterion — author name, comments, subject, tag, and so on — can be used to group many files from across drives and directories into the same group or stack or even into virtual file folders. These can be files that by type have little in common with one another (text, video, spreadsheet, images, and so on), but belong together for some user-defined reason. The metadata binds them.

To see how metadata can be helpful, look closely at Figure 5-12, which shows the contents of a single directory. In the third bar from the top, you can see the metadata criteria: Name, Date Taken, Tags, Size, and Rating.

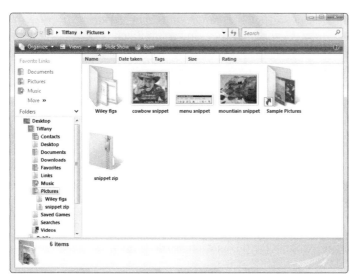

Figure 5-12: Directory window listing metadata criteria.

Of the metadata criteria shown in Figure 5-12, you can make changes to only three types of criteria:

The filename

Tags: Tags are used as personalized classification markers. For example, you can add tags to your pictures to indicate who is included in the photograph or perhaps the occasion (like a birthday or holiday).

Rating: By adding ratings to your photos, you can identify which ones you think are high quality (or print worthy) and those that might not have turned out as well. Using the ratings feature allows you to create your own personal ranking system (from one to five stars). That way, you can quickly identify and search for higher-quality items.

Both the tags and ratings criteria can be applied to several different types of files. The following section explains how to create tags for your files. These steps also work for adding ratings to your documents as well.

Information Kiosk

Not all items have a ratings metadata option. In such instances, however, you can still use the tags criteria to identify and rank your files and documents.

Tags can be anything you like, such as *What I did on my summer vacation, Trip to Italy, Wife's new clothes, Malpractice suit*, and so on. Each tag can cover all sorts of files, from photos and movies to spreadsheets in which you track expenses of the tag subject, correspondence, notes, or even special programs that are germane only to the particular tag.

To add a tag to a file or document

1. Locate the file or document for which you wish to create a tag.

Use the search methods outlined earlier to locate the specific file you wish to create a tag for.

2. Right-click the file or document name (or icon).

3. Choose Properties from the drop-down menu that appears.

The Properties window for this particular file is opened. (See Figure 5-13.)

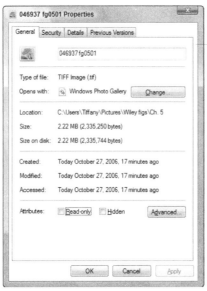

Figure 5-13: The Properties window.

4. Select the Details tab.

This tab allows you to make changes to a number of different descriptive features for your file. Some examples include the file's name, its tags, ratings (if available), comments, and so on. (See Figure 5-14.)

5. Click in the blank space under the Value column located to the right of the Tags category.

Doing so calls up a text box in which you can enter the tags you want to attach to the selected file.

Figure 5-14: Add tags to your files via the Details tab of the Properties window.

6. Enter the name of the tag(s) you would like to add to this file.

As you type, notice the option to add additional tags to this file. You may add as many tags as you like; just be sure to separate each tag with a semicolon (;).

7. Click OK.

This saves your changes and returns you to the previous screen.

If you return to the search page and look at the tag category for this item, note how the identifier you created now appears in the Tags category.

Information Kiosk

Because you can create multiple tags for each file or document, you can use this search tool to relate your files to one another in several different ways. For example, you can create a tag for each person (me, Joe, Dave, Kevin, and so on) pictured at the previous year's holiday party. You can also identify this photo by the year it was taken (2005) and the occasion (holiday). That way, when you search for any one of these tags, this picture is pulled up in the related search results.

If you refer to the earlier section, "Basic searching in Vista," you can recall how to sort and search on any or several of these criteria. Just use the Advanced Search feature to locate the files, documents, and programs associated with the tag or other metadata identifiers you created. This allows you to relate different documents to one another without having to rely on your filing system to bunch all these documents in the same folder.

To delete a file's tag, simply repeat the preceding steps and remove the identifier you no longer wish to associate with the file or document selected.

File Associations

As the previous section makes clear, Windows Vista's use of metadata tags makes it easy for you to define the properties of any file when you create it. You can also edit some properties of existing files as well as define tags to ease future sorting and searching. Going through all the many thousands of files you have on your machine would be an enormous task that few would undertake, though. Therefore, to simplify this process, use some of the file's existing characteristics (like its file extension) to help locate the item you wish to view.

File extensions are noted by the three characters — or *suffix* — appended to the period (dot) in the filename: for example, `file.ext`. These three letters define what the file does or what program created it. Microsoft Word, for example, is an executable program that has the suffix `.exe`, meaning that it runs the programs associated with Microsoft's word processing application. Files created by Word have the suffix `.doc`. Files created by Notepad have the suffix `.txt`. Linking a particular type of file to a particular application or applications (`.doc` files to Microsoft Word and `.txt` files to Notepad, for example) is *file association.*

Thus, when you click a file with a `.doc` extension, Windows runs Microsoft Word, which in turn opens the file — a document. If the extension is `.wmv`, Windows runs the Microsoft Media Player, which in turn opens the `.wmv` file, which is a movie clip.

Almost every Windows file has an extension; however, if you attempt to open a file whose extension has no association defined for it, Windows asks you what program you want to use to open the file. (See Figure 5-15.)

If the file already has an association, you can change it by right-clicking the file and then selecting Open With from the contextual menu that appears. You can go with Recommended Programs in the top pane or try another program from the bottom pane. If you expect always to open that same type of file with the same program, select the Always Use the Selected Program to Open This Type of File check box. Doing so ensures that a particular application will act as the default program for this type of file.

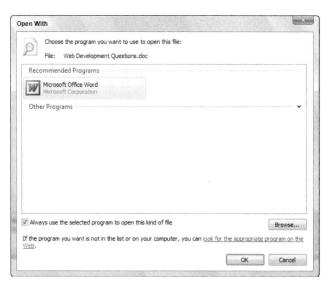

Figure 5-15: The Open With dialog box. Choose the program with which to open the file.

Information Kiosk

Some programs do the associating for you. Internet Explorer automatically anoints itself the default program for all HTML (HyperText Markup Language) and URL (Uniform Resource Locator) files. Other programs are more polite and present you with a menu of file extensions that you might or might not wish to associate with it. For example, you might favor a media player other than the Microsoft version, a different word processor than Word, or a spreadsheet other than Excel. Your choices often urge you to make them the defaults for those types of files. By selecting the default applications for specific file extensions, you eliminate the need to choose the program each time you open an item with that particular extension.

To locate a particular file using its file extension, you can enter the extension (such as .doc) into the search fields found in the Start menu, or you can open the application associated with the type of file you wish to view and then select to open an existing file within that application. For example, if you wish to view a certain Microsoft Word document, open Word and choose Open from the File menu. This provides you with a list of directories within which you can search for existing .doc files. Click the file you wish to view, and it opens in the appropriate application. Using this method of locating files is convenient if you do not remember exactly where this document is saved on your PC, but you do remember what application was used to create it.

Safeguarding your files with XPS

A paper document can be a highly secure and transportable repository of information. Affixed with appropriate seals, certifications, notarizations, and the like, a piece of paper is a virtually irrefutable bit of evidence, whether of a crime, a contract, or a historical fact. An original paper document and its certified copies are not easily altered, be they handwritten or printed. If there is doubt of a document's authenticity, it need only be compared with the original. If the original is tampered with, it is usually easily apparent. For millennia, people have carried on business and personal affairs based on durable media of one sort or another ranging from baked clay tablets, papyrus, and parchment in the ancient times to the cheap paper of modern times.

A computer-generated document, on the other hand, is infinitely malleable. Anyone can access a document on a computer and change it. The document becomes absolutely permanent only when it is printed — transferred to paper. Differences between one printout and another are apparent. However, changes to the document in the computer are not because anyone with access to that computer can change any document it contains.

Computer files can be made read-only so that unauthorized people cannot easily change them. However, the read-only attribute is a weak defense against alteration or even deletion. Internally generated *checksums,* by which some algorithm does a calculation based on factors within the document to produce a unique code that accompanies the file and can indicate that it or copies are not identical to the original, can also protect the file's integrity. The difference of a meaningless single bit between the original and a copy — or an altered original — can trigger a checksum error.

Obviously, something better is needed if computer-generated documents, especially those intended for wide distribution, are to have the same or nearly the same integrity and fidelity to an original as paper documents routinely have. That fidelity includes not only the words but also the formatting and illustration. Moreover, one should be able to read these documents without special programs and equipment much as one needs only an eye to read paper documents. The reader using a Unix-based computer should see exactly the same document as one using Windows or a Macintosh. And no reader should be able to alter the document in any way unless authorized.

Microsoft's answer to this problem is the XML (eXtensible Markup Language) Paper Specification (XPS). *XPS* is a highly complex (essentially open source) syntax that is intended to publish documents generated in any system or application and is displayable in any other system or application with near-perfect integrity. Moreover, the specification allows the author to grant or withhold rights to the document so that others may make changes at certain levels or forbid any others from altering the document at all.

Information Kiosk

The specification is essentially open source because Microsoft licenses it royalty-free to encourage other developers to include XPS viewing and publishing features into its products without cost. Microsoft intends to include the XPS feature in upcoming Office 2007 applications, which makes it easy to publish any type of Office document as an XPS file.

To call up the XPS Viewer in Windows Vista

1. **Open the document you wish to save as an XPS file.**

2. **Choose File → Print from your document's main menu.**

Doing so opens your computer's print window.

3. **Select the Microsoft XPS Document Writer as your printer and then click OK.**

Doing so opens the XPS Save the File As dialog box shown in Figure 5-16.

Figure 5-16: Save a document in the XPS format.

 Information Kiosk

If you click the Browse Folders arrow, a list of links down the left side will appear, including Recent Places, Desktop, Documents, Computer, and Network.

4. **Type the file's title into the File Name field.**

This title can be the same as the one you have used in whatever other format you originally created this file. For example, if you are saving a Word document as an XPS file, you can use the same name you've given to the Word file for your new XPS file. You can tell which one is which by its file extension, or you can choose to give it a completely different name.

5. **Ensure that XPS Document (*.xps) is selected in the Save as Type drop-down menu.**

If it is not, use the drop-down menu to select this file extension.

6. **Click Save.**

This closes the Save the Title As dialog box.

The next time you use this file, it opens in Internet Explorer. (See Figure 5-17.)

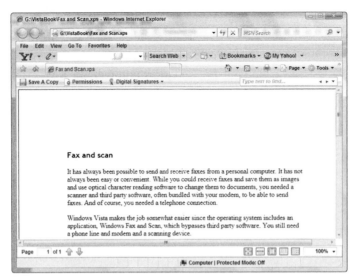

Figure 5-17: Opening XPS files in Internet Explorer.

When you open the document in Internet Explorer, you can set permissions, both for yourself as author and for others who have access to the document. However, before you set permissions for your files, you must first complete the Rights Managements Wizard. Follow these instructions to accomplish this task:

1. Open the XPS document for which you want to establish permission guidelines.

The file automatically opens Internet Explorer.

2. Choose Permissions from the IE main menu.

The Rights Management Configuration window appears. (See Figure 5-18.)

This box informs you that you must have a user account before you can create permissions for this document. This account can be the same as your network user ID (if you are using this feature at the office) or it can be your .NET Passport user account.

Figure 5-18: The Rights Management Configuration window.

Information Kiosk

The .NET passport protocol exists independently of the operating system. A .NET passport uses your e-mail address to provide you with personalized access to Passport-enabled services and Web sites. .NET Passport implements a single sign-in service that allows you to create a single username and password. After you have a .NET Passport, you will have only one name and password to remember, and you will be able to use all .NET Passport-enabled services, such as Hotmail and Microsoft Messenger (MSN). You can store information about yourself in your sign-in profile so that you will not have to retype this information when you use .NET Passport-enabled services.

3. **Click Next.**

A new dialog box appears, asking you to choose which type of user account you would like to use.

4. **Select the appropriate user account.**

If you do not have currently have a network or .NET passport account, select the .NET passport option. You can create an account later using this wizard.

5. **Click Next.**

A new window appears onscreen letting you know that your account is being activated. After the activation is complete, this window closes, and the Windows Rights Management screen appears in its place.

On this screen you are asked whether you have an existing .NET passport or whether you would like to create one now.

6. **Select the appropriate account information.**

If you already have a .NET passport, select the Yes, I Have a .NET Account option.

If you do not already have a .NET passport account, select the second option — the one that states that you do not have a .NET account but that you'd like to create one now. Then click Next. This redirects your browser to the Web site used for creating such an account.

7. **Click Next.**

Assuming that you already have .NET passport, you are prompted to enter your e-mail account and password. (See Figure 5-19.)

8. **Click Sign In.**

This opens a new window asking you to specify your e-mail address.

9. **Re-enter your e-mail address in the E-mail Address box provided and then click Next.**

The Select Certificate Type window appears. (See Figure 5-20.)

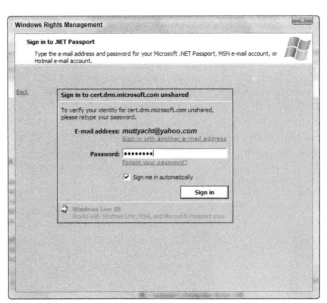

Figure 5-19: Enter your user account information.

Figure 5-20: Select an XPS certificate type.

10. **Select Standard.**

This option allows you to view and create restricted content on your computer indefinitely.

Note: If you choose the Temporary option, you will likely have to repeat the steps of this setup wizard when your temporary certificate expires.

11. **Click Next.**

Your PC downloads the appropriate certificate and produces a new window letting you know that your certificate activation is complete.

12. **Click Finish.**

This opens the Permission window, where you are finally able to set permissions for this particular file. You can choose to apply permissions, apply permissions using a template, or not apply permissions.

After you acquire the appropriate certificate, you can begin establishing permissions for your files.

To set permissions for your XPS documents

1. **Open the file for which you want to create specified permissions.**

2. **Click the Permissions button on the toolbar.**

The Permissions window appears.

3. **Choose the Apply Permissions option.**

A blue dot appears in the radio button to the left of this option, and a new Details box appears below. (See Figure 5-21.)

From this screen, you can establish what permissions users are allowed.

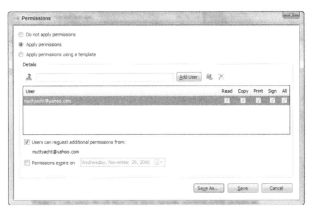

Figure 5-21: Identify which users are permitted to read, copy, print, or sign your XPS documents.

4. Type the e-mail address of the user you would like to set permissions for into the text box provided and then click the Add User button.

The user's e-mail address is moved to the User box below.

5. Click the user's account in the list below.

The user's e-mail address is highlighted in blue.

6. Use the permission boxes provided at the right to indicate which capabilities the user is permitted.

You can choose to allow the user to read, copy, print, or sign the selected document.

Information Kiosk

"Save" is not a permission. It's an option.

7. To add more users, repeat Steps 4–6 until you include all pertinent accounts.

8. Click Save.

Doing so closes the Permissions window.

Information Kiosk

You can also choose to allow everyone to have permissions for your XPS files. Simply click the icon next to the Add User button in the Permissions window. (This icon looks like two people sitting next to one another.) This creates an Everyone account in the User box. From this point, you can choose to restrict or allow permissions for this account as you would if you were doing so for any other individual user.

You can also choose to set permissions expiration dates from this screen or opt to use your e-mail account to allow other users to request permissions for this file. Both options are located at the bottom left of the Permissions screen. Simply select the appropriate check box to enable these features.

Step into the Real World

If you use the Permissions tool at your place of employment, you might also be able to take advantage of any existing company-wide XPS permissions templates. Choose the Apply Permissions Using a Template option to locate these pre-established permissions files. Use the drop-down menu to choose the template you wish to use and then select Save to apply the template to the selected file.

Partitioning Your Hard Drive

In addition to knowing how to find (and protect) some of your most important files and documents, it is important to learn how you can use your hard drive to organize and store your files and programs more efficiently.

Partitioning your hard drive allows you to control how your computer's disk space is divided. Using this feature allows you to create an environment that contains several different compartments, which can be used to store various programs or document types in separate areas on your PC's hard drive.

In simplest terms, partitioning your hard drive means dividing your existing hard drive space into separate drives (sometimes also referred to as *volumes*). It is akin to a chest of drawers that is divided up into separate drawers in which you store different types of clothing. Similarly, you can divide your hard drive into separate drives in order to have better organization of your data files. For example, you might elect to include all your media files (movies, music, pictures, and so on) in one specific drive. Or you might want to create separate drives for different user accounts. That way, all users can easily access the programs and files they have installed on the PC or downloaded from the Internet. And, of course, you could create separate drives for large-capacity projects. For example, if you have a number of large documents you are using for a research project at work, you can accumulate all the files and programs associated with this project on one individual drive.

Up until this point, most users found partitioning their hard drive somewhat complicated because previous versions of Windows did not include a straightforward process for partitioning hard drives. As a result, they usually resorted to using third-party software in order to do it. Windows Vista has adjusted this and made it a clean, just-follow-the steps method.

To partition your hard drive

1. **Click the Start button.**

   Doing so opens up the Start menu in the bottom left of your screen.

2. **From the right column of the Start menu, choose Control Panel.**

   The Control Panel window appears onscreen, as shown in Figure 5-22.

3. **Select System and Maintenance.**

   The System and Maintenance window opens, as shown in Figure 5-23.

Figure 5-22: Your computer's Control Panel.

Figure 5-23: The System and Maintenance window.

4. **Choose the Create and Format Hard Drive Partitions option from the Administrative Tools area of this window.**

You may need to scroll down to see the Administrative Tools area.

The Disk Management window appears, as shown in Figure 5-24.

In the middle of this screen, you can see your existing drives.

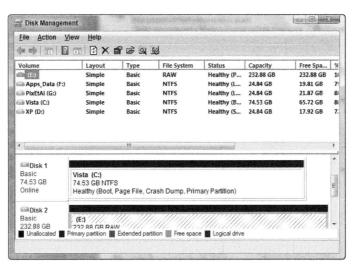

Figure 5-24: The Disk Management window.

5. Right-click the drive you wish to partition.

6. From the pop-up menu that appears (see Figure 5-25), choose Shrink Volume.

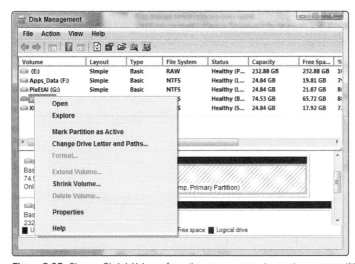

Figure 5-25: Choose Shrink Volume from the pop-up menu to create a new partition for your hard drive.

A Querying Shrink Volume box appears. After your computer assesses how much free space is available within this drive, a recommended shrink drive dialog box appears, as shown in Figure 5-26.

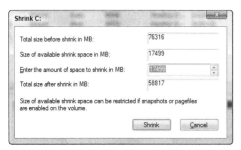

Figure 5-26: Examining your computer's disk drive partition recommendations.

7. Click Shrink to accept the default recommendation.

By clicking Shrink, you instruct your computer to divide the selected drive into two new separate drive partitions. One (the one matching the old drive letter) contains your existing files and programs. The other (new) drive is empty, containing only the free space that has been taken from the pre-existing drive.

You can also designate the exact amount of unused space you wish to use for your new partition by entering the size of the new partition into the Enter the Amount of Space to Shrink in MB field. (Refer to Figure 5-26.) If you do not specify this amount, the recommended allocation is used.

Information Kiosk

If you want to have more than one extra partition, select a smaller amount of space to shrink. Your second drive contains the amount of space you designated in Step 7, and the remainder can serve as yet another partition. Each time you wish to partition any drive that has unused space, you can run through these steps again.

After the new drive partition is created, format the unallocated space. To do so

1. Right-click the new drive partition.

2. Choose New Simple Volume from the contextual menu that appears.

The New Simple Volume Wizard opens.

3. Click Next.

The Specify Volume Size dialog box appears. (See Figure 5-27.)

4. Accept the default volume size.

You can also choose to specify a new volume size in this window. Simply enter the desired volume size into the Simple Volume Size in MB field.

5. Click Next.

The Assign Drive Letter or Path window appears. (See Figure 5-28.)

6. Use the drop-down menu provided to choose a drive letter for your partition.

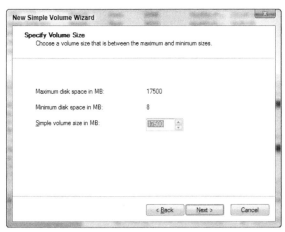

Figure 5-27: Specify the volume size of your new hard drive partition.

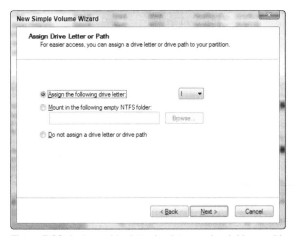

Figure 5-28: Assign a drive letter/path to your hard drive partition.

Watch Your Step

While the drop-down menu will show you only available drive letters, do be careful that you do not assign a letter belonging to removable media drives, such as DVDs and CDs. The letter you assign to your new drive/partition is arbitrary and need not be sequential to existing drive letters.

7. **Click Next.**

The Format Partition window appears. (See Figure 5-29.)

8. **Select the Format This Volume with the Following Settings option.**

This page allows you to format your new partition. You can choose to change the partitions file system and minimum allocation size; however, using the default settings is recommended to ensure that your new partition is formatted correctly, in line with the other drives that already exist on your hard drive.

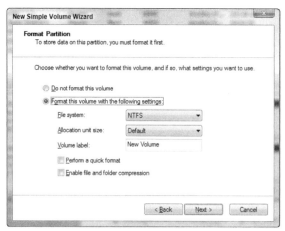

Figure 5-29: Formatting your hard drive partition.

9. **Click Next.**

This opens a summary page of all your partition selections. Be sure to review this information before proceeding to the next step.

10. **Click Finish.**

This closes the New Simple Volume Wizard. Your New Volume partition now appears in a separate row of the Disk Management screen. (See Figure 5-30.)

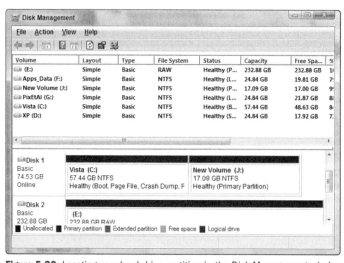

Figure 5-30: Locating your hard drive partition in the Disk Management window.

Note the new visual enhancement added to the Disk Management screen in Vista.
Underneath the drive name is a colored bar; each color has a meaning:

- **White:** The drive contains no data, no files.

- **Blue:** The drive contains files.

- **Red:** The drive has less than 15 percent of its maximum capacity available.

Dropping under the 15 percent threshold is enough to warrant a red (warning) color
because it brings with it four important consequences:

- First and foremost, you might be running out of disk space.

- If this is the drive where the Windows installation is located, your machine might
slow down when booting up or during normal usage because some of the available space in this drive is also used as a temporary memory cache for your PC.

- If you have less than 15 percent disk space available in the drive (as well as a
minimum of 300MB) where your Windows installation is located, you might
not be able to run System Restore, which allows you to retrieve files, programs,
and other data in the event that your computer is damaged. (For more on System
Restore, see Chapter 11.)

- When you have less than 15 percent disk space available in a drive, you cannot
run Disk Defragmenter. Thus, you cannot create any new partitions from this
area of your hard drive.

Windows Easy Transfer

If you have an older computer running an older version of Windows, chances are that
it contains years of data files. Perhaps even more important, it probably has many programs and applications that through long use and experience, you tailored to suit your
own wishes and needs. Now that you also have a new computer running Windows
Vista, you'd likely want to transfer not only the data from your older machine but also

the applications with their personalized settings and even the personalized settings you use with Windows itself.

 Transfer

If you have only one computer already running a Windows version and you wish to preserve the settings in that machine, merely install Windows Vista as an upgrade, as mentioned in Chapter 1.

Transferring information and applications from one computer to another used to be a tedious, lengthy, and onerous task. Admittedly, transferring data files on their own is relatively straightforward. If you have a transfer cable that directly connects the two computers or if both computers are on a network, it is a simple (although lengthy) task to simply copy the files from one machine to the other. Lacking such a connection, you can copy files to a floppy disk — or better, a CD-ROM; better still, a DVD-ROM — and then copy those files to the new computer. This takes time; if all you have is a floppy disk drive, you need a mountain of floppies.

Transferring programs and applications is not so easy. Most programs today cannot simply be copied from one computer to another. Instead, you must install them. Modern programs make entries in the Registry and store related files in many different places in addition to the main directories. It requires a special installation application that knows what files to place where so that the program runs properly. If you simply copy the program from one computer to another, it has neither the needed Registry entries nor the related system files in the Windows System directories. When you try to run the program, you get a message like `MyProgram cannot find IneedItToRun.dll`. Generally, some exceptions do exist, but in most cases, you need the original installation disc or file to place a program on a new computer.

Microsoft included the Files and Settings Transfer Wizard with Windows XP that allowed you to move all your files and settings easily. In Windows Vista, the name has been changed to Windows Easy Transfer but the function is the same. The wizard automatically moves all Windows- or Microsoft-related files, applications, and settings from your old machine to your new one and transfers anything else you ask it to. (*Note:* The program does not transfer anything from one version of Windows to another when the two are part of a dual-boot setup on one machine.)

To start the Windows Easy Transfer Wizard

1. **Click the Start button.**

The Start menu appears in the bottom left of your screen.

2. **Choose All Programs.**

A list of all the programs saved to your computer appears in the left column of the Start menu.

3. **Select Accessories from the list of programs.**

Doing so opens your Accessories folder, revealing a list of all the programs and files located in this folder.

4. **Select System Tools.**

5. **Choose Windows Easy Transfer from the System Tools folder that appears.**

This opens the Windows Easy Transfer Wizard, as shown in Figure 5-31.

Figure 5-31: The Windows Easy Transfer welcome screen; the first step of the Easy Transfer Wizard.

6. **Click Next.**

A new window opens, asking whether you want to start a new transfer or continue with one already in progress.

7. **Select the Start a New Transfer option.**

A new window appears asking you which computer you are using.

8. **Select the appropriate answer.**

Most likely, you are going to be using the new computer; however, if you're not using your new Vista PC, select the My Old Computer option.

9. **Choose which option you'd like to use to transfer your files.**

You can choose to transfer your files from one computer to another by using a transfer cable — in which case you should select the first (Yes) option — or you can explore other ways of transferring this data.

If you do not have a transfer cable, select the second (No) option. This opens a new window asking you whether the Windows Easy Transfer program is installed on your old computer. If it is not, choose to install it now. This provides you with a list of alternative transfer methods: CD, USB Flash drive, external hard drive, shared network folder, or Windows installation or Windows Easy Transfer CD.

If you have an Easy Transfer cable and select Yes, clicking this option brings up instructions (see Figure 5-32) for connecting your computers using a cable, which is basically a cord with USB drives at each end.

Windows should automatically detect this connection.

Figure 5-32: Connect your old computer to your new one with an Easy Transfer cable.

Now you can select which files you wish to transfer from your old computer to your new one. To do so

1. **From the next screen in the wizard, choose All User Accounts.**

The following directory tree window appears. (See Figure 5-33.)

2. **Select all (or handpick the specific files you wish to transfer to your new PC) by selecting the check box to the left of any folder icon (see Figure 5-33).**

3. **Click Next.**

The Easy Transfer Wizard begins to work, copying the selected files over to your new machine. *Note:* This does not remove these files from your old machine; it simply duplicates this information onto your new PC.

Your transferred files can be located in the same drive locations that they were stored in on your previous computer.

Figure 5-33: Use the directory tree provided to choose which files are to be transferred to your new PC.

file extensions: The three characters that appear after the dot (.) in a file or program name (`file.`*ext*). These letters identify what type of file/program the item is or which program was used to create it.

metadata: An assemblage of data about other data. This feature lets you assign various bits of identifying data to your files.

open source: Refers to computer source code that is accessible, readable, copyable, and modifiable.

partitions: Individual compartments located on your hard drive, which can be used for storage and file organization purposes.

ratings: A metadata resource. This tool lets you create your own ranking system (one to five stars) for various files and programs.

tags: Another metadata resource. This tool allows you to add multiple identifiers to various programs and files. You can then use this information to locate documents with a specific tag.

XML (eXtensible Markup Language): Software language used to identify different types of data.

XPS (XML Paper Specification): Microsoft's new document protection format. Using this file type enables you to create tamper-proof documents.

Last Stop

Practice Exam

1. How do you add a shortcut to your desktop?

_____

_____

_____

2. What types of items can have shortcuts? Are there any types of files that cannot have shortcuts?

_____

_____

_____

3. What is the fastest way to search your computer? Where is this feature located?

_____

_____

_____

4. What is metadata and how can you use it to associate related files to one another?

_____

_____

_____

_____

5. Should you do an Instant Search if you know where a specific folder you want to find is located? Why or why not?

_____

_____

_____

6. If you want to associate a different application with an existing file, how would you do it?

_____

_____

_____

7. What are file extensions, and what can they tell you about your documents and programs?

_____

_____

_____

8. What is XPS? What are the benefits of using this feature when creating documents?

_____

_____

_____

9. Why would you want to partition your hard drive? How is this done?

_____

_____

_____

10. Name two different types of metadata and explain how they can help you better manage your files.

_____

_____

_____

11. What is the purpose of using the Windows Easy Transfer Wizard?

_____

_____

_____

12. If you do not have an Easy Transfer cable, can you still use Windows' transfer wizard? If so, how?

_____

_____

_____

Working with Vista's Free Tools

STATIONS ALONG THE WAY

- Training Windows Vista to recognize your voice, type for you, and more
- Leaving yourself Sticky Notes
- Recording sound easily with Sound Recorder
- Taking notes and creating documents with WordPad and Notepad
- Zipping/unzipping made easy
- Cropping images with the Snipping tool
- Keeping your appointments with Windows Calendar

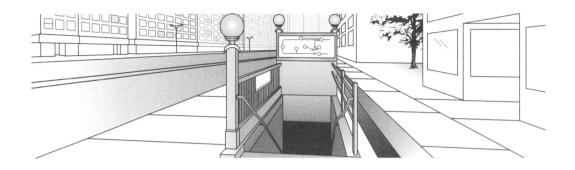

 # Enter the Station

Questions

1. How accurate is Vista's Speech Recognition feature?

2. How much effort does it take to train the computer to understand a human voice?

3. In what ways can you use your PC to create reminders for yourself?

4. What types of documents can be created with WordPad and Notepad?

5. What types of images can be cropped with the Snipping tool?

6. How are Zip files created?

7. Where are your appointments and to-do list stored?

Express Line

If you are already familiar with Vista's advanced accessories tools (including its Speech Recognition, Sticky Notes, Windows Calendar, Snipping tool, and Zip file features), skip ahead to the next chapter.

Now that you have a handle on how to manage your PC's files, you might also wish to learn more about some of Vista's advanced accessories features. The tools covered in this chapter — including Vista's Speech Recognition, Sticky Notes, the Snipping tool, and Calendar and Zip file capabilities — provide you with additional resources to help you find more sophisticated ways to use your PC. Basically, these tools are meant to turn hard-copy resources (notebooks, calendars, reminder notes, dictation devices, and so on) into electronic variations that can be stored and easily retrieved on your PC.

By using these tools, you can use your computer in a more interactive manner. For example, Vista's enhanced Speech Recognition capabilities allow you to control your computer by speaking rather than by typing or using the mouse. The Sticky Notes tool allows you to create handwritten notes for yourself that you can then export (or save) to another document; WordPad and Notepad are two word processing applications that you also use to take notes.

In addition to Vista's Speech Recognition and Sticky Notes features, you can also access a number of additional tools to enhance your general PC experience. For example, Vista's new Snipping tool allows you to crop and save various documents or online resources to your PC. The ability to *zip* (or compress) certain files allows you to reduce the combined file size for your documents, making it easier to share and store information. And lastly, the Windows Calendar provides you with a centralized location for all your important date (and time) reminders.

These Windows Vista tools have been created in hopes of simplifying your overall computing experience. These accessories are meant to provide you with advanced capabilities that allow you to increase your productivity and better manage how you use your PC.

Using Vista's Speech Recognition Feature

Windows' Speech Recognition feature is built into the Vista operating system. This tool allows you to control your PC by using voice commands rather than keyboard or mouse devices. You can also use this technology to perform a number of functions within other applications. For example, Vista's Speech Recognition capabilities also work with Microsoft Office software. This feature might also apply to some third-party programs although functionality is usually limited to simple commands such as Open, File, Save, Print, and so on.

This feature is especially helpful to people that are physically or visually impaired. Speech Recognition can also be quite useful for people who prefer to talk out their ideas or who simply do not type well. And, of course, one of the main benefits of this tool is that it frees your hands to do other things, allowing you to multitask at a much greater level than was possible with previous versions of Windows.

Setting up your microphone

The first step in using Vista's Speech Recognition feature is connecting and configuring your PC's microphone. Because this is a fairly new technology, your PC might not include a microphone as part of its standard packaging. This is an easy fix; good PC microphones are readily available at a number of retail stores. You can choose a desktop microphone that sits on your computer desk, a headset microphone, or a lavalier/tie clip type. Either type works fine; it just depends on what you prefer. However, a headset microphone is somewhat more portable. True, you do have to remain close to the PC using a headset microphone (it's plugged into your computer's console), but you can move your head without having to worry about sound distortion or too much background noise. Comparatively, if you move your head (or mouth) away from a desktop microphone, you might encounter some interpretation problems.

After you decide on a microphone, you need to connect it to your PC. Most microphone devices connect to your computer via a USB port. (Refer to Chapter 4 to learn more about USB drives.) Locate an empty USB port and connect your microphone to your computer. If your microphone does not have a USB plug, locate the appropriate input source and connect it to your computer.

After you connect your microphone, configure it before you begin using Vista's Speech Recognition tool. Follow these steps to set up your microphone:

1. **Click Start and select Control Panel from the menu that appears.**

   The Control Panel window appears onscreen. (See Figure 6-1.)

Figure 6-1: The Control Panel.

2. **Select Ease of Access.**

   The Ease of Access window opens. (See Figure 6-2.)

Figure 6-2: The Ease of Access window.

3. Select Speech Recognition Options.

The Speech Recognition Options window appears, as shown in Figure 6-3.

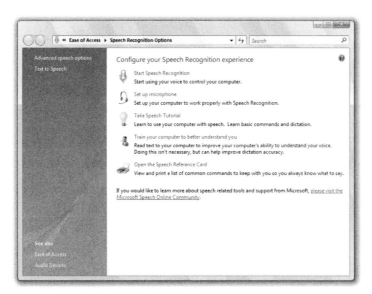

Figure 6-3: The Speech Recognition Options window.

4. Choose Set Up Microphone.

This launches the Microphone Setup Wizard. (See Figure 6-4.)

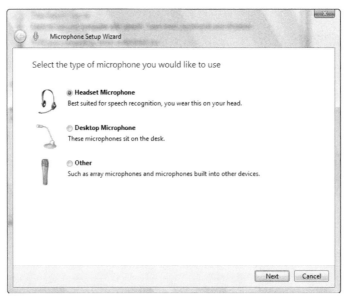

Figure 6-4: The Microphone Setup Wizard.

5. Choose your microphone type and click Next.

This brings up a new window that shows you proper placement instructions for your headset, as seen in Figure 6-5.

Figure 6-5: Reviewing proper microphone placement.

6. Read the placement guidelines and click Next.

This opens the Adjust the Microphone Volume window, as shown in Figure 6-6.

Figure 6-6: Establishing the appropriate volume for your microphone.

7. Position your microphone as explained on the previous screen and read the sentence displayed on your screen into the microphone.

This lets your computer accurately assess the correct volume level required for your microphone.

8. Click Next.

If your microphone is working properly, you see the following window (see Figure 6-7).

Figure 6-7: Your microphone is set.

If you microphone is not working properly, you are prompted to check your microphone's mute button and PC connection. You are then instructed to return to the previous screen and repeat the sentence shown on the volume page.

9. **Click Finish.**

This closes the Microphone Setup Wizard.

Working with the speech tutorial

After you have your microphone set up, you can practice using Vista's Speech Recognition tool by following these steps. These instructions direct you to the Speech Recognition tutorial. This wizard provides you with sample scenarios and examples pertaining to Vista's speech recognition commands. This tutorial affords you the opportunity to practice using this accessories tool in a controlled environment. To access this feature

1. **Open the Control Panel.**

You can access this screen by locating it in the right column of the Start menu.

2. **Select Ease of Access.**

This opens the Ease of Access window. (Refer to Figure 6-2.)

3. **Select Speech Recognition Options.**

This opens the Speech Recognition Options screen. (Refer to Figure 6-3.)

4. **Choose to Start Speech Recognition.**

This starts the Speech Recognition Wizard.

5. **Click Next.**

This reopens the Microphone Setup Wizard.

6. **Repeat Steps 6–9 of the preceding step list to confirm your microphone setup.**

7. **Click Next.**

This opens the document review window (see Figure 6-8). From here, you can choose to enable or disable Vista's Speech Recognition document review feature.

If you choose to enable this feature, Vista reviews the words and language used in your other files (Word documents, e-mail, and so on) to better understand what phrases and words you use when you speak.

If you choose to disable this feature, Vista does not review your other documents.

If you elect to enable this feature, it helps speed up the learning curve for Vista's Speech Recognition feature. In other words, this option helps the tool more quickly identify your speaking habits and preferences.

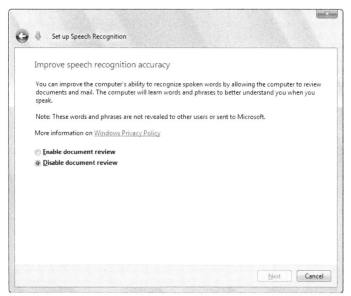

Figure 6-8: Deciding whether to use Vista's Speech Recognition document review feature.

8. **Select the radio button next to your selection and then click Next.**

This opens the Speech Reference Card page.

9. **Click the View Reference Sheet button.**

This opens the Windows Help menu. Use this screen to locate common speech recognition commands.

Note: You can print this information for future use. However, you can also obtain this information by searching Vista's Help files.

10. **Return to the Speech Recognition Wizard and then click Next.**

This opens a screen allowing you to choose whether you would like to activate Vista's Speech Recognition tool each time you start your computer.

If you would like to use this feature on a regular basis, select the check box next to this option. (See Figure 6-9.) This opens the Speech Recognition tool each time Windows is launched.

You can choose to not activate this feature every time Windows is opened, in which case the check box should be clear. If you choose this option, you can still use the Speech Recognition feature. You simply have to navigate through (or search) your PC's menus to locate and start this feature each time you want to use it.

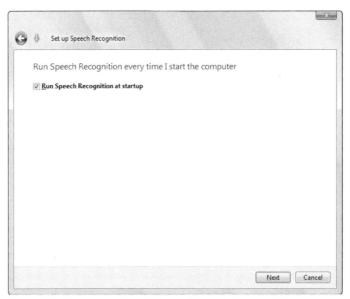

Figure 6-9: Choose to run Speech Recognition each time your PC starts.

11. **Make your selection and then click Next.**

A screen appears letting you know that you can now control your computer by voice.

12. **Click Start Tutorial.**

This begins the Speech Recognition tutorial.

Follow the instructions provided by the Speech Recognition tutorial to familiarize yourself with the voice commands available with this tool.

Information Kiosk

You can always make adjustments to your Speech Recognition properties by clicking the Advanced Speech Options link in the left column of the Speech Recognition Options window. Here, you can adjust whether you want Vista's Speech Recognition tool to start when Windows is launched and/or whether you want to allow Vista to review your other documents to improve upon its speech recognition accuracy.

Click the Advance Speech Options link, select the Speech Recognition tab, and use the check boxes provided in the User Settings section to make adjustments to your speech setting preferences. (If a check mark is present, these options are activated. If there is no check mark, these options are not enabled.)

Training the computer to understand your voice

After you complete the Speech Recognition tutorial, you might find that you'd still like some extra practice, or perhaps you would like Vista to have some extra time to familiarize itself with your voice inflection and tone. For example, perhaps you had to repeat several of the commands from the tutorial in order for the Speech Recognition tool to understand what you wanted it to do. If that's the case, you might want to spend some more time working with this feature before you actually start using it with your documents and PC commands. Fortunately, Vista has a built-in tool that allows you to do just that. To access this feature

1. Open the Control Panel.

You can access this screen by locating it in the right column of the Start menu.

2. Select Ease of Access.

This opens the Ease of Access window.

3. Select Speech Recognition Options.

This opens the Speech Recognition Options screen.

4. Choose the Train Your Computer to Better Understand You option.

This starts the Speech Recognition Voice Training Wizard.

5. Click Next.

Follow along and read the sentences that appear onscreen. This teaches your computer more about how you speak, thus improving its ability to interpret your voice specifications (inflection, tone, and volume).

Completing the Speech Recognition training sessions is recommended to greatly enhance speech recognition accuracy when you dictate to your computer. If you decide to do just one session and then use Speech Recognition immediately thereafter, you get fairly decent results. Voice recognition technology has advanced quite a bit. However, if you choose to do the second training session, your computer becomes better trained to understand your voice.

If you read at a slow to moderate pace, the two tutorials should take about 15 minutes each to complete. If you tend to speak at a quick pace, you can complete them in six to eight minutes each.

Information Kiosk

When you're training the computer to understand your voice, speak like you naturally do. This also means at the speed at which you normally speak. If you speak fast, speak quickly when doing the training modules. If you tend to you speak slowly, speak at a slower pace. This permits you to speak in your normal voice when dictating to your computer.

Reviewing spoken commands

The last link located on the Speech Recognition Options screen (refer to the preceding instructions to locate this page, if necessary) is the Open the Speech Reference Card option.

Clicking this link opens the Windows Help and Support menu articles that pertain to common Speech Recognition commands (see Figure 6-10).

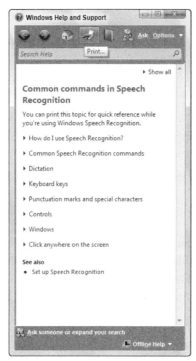

Figure 6-10: Common Speech Recognition commands.

From this screen, you can print this reference document containing the commands that you can use to control your computer. Simply click the Show All link in the upper right of this window and then click the Print icon located at the top of this page. This takes you to your Print window, where you can choose to print this information as you would any other document.

Information Kiosk

Vista's Speech Recognition feature is available in American English (US), British English (UK), French, Spanish, Japanese, and German. However, you can install an MUI (Multilingual User Interface) pack, obtainable from Microsoft, to use multiple languages with this tool.

Microsoft also anticipates providing Speech Recognition development tools for specialized fields, such as law and medicine. Such tools would concentrate on the idiomatic phrasing, grammar, and spell check features particular to those fields.

To see your Speech Recognition tool in action, connect (or turn on) your microphone and begin using the commands covered in the Help and Support menus mentioned earlier. For example, begin by saying, "Start." This opens the Start menu. Say, "All programs." This opens your All Programs menu. From here, you can choose the applications or documents you wish to open. You might even decide to open Microsoft Word and dictate a letter or memo to a friend or colleague.

Recording Sound

In addition to being able to speak directly to your operating system (and tell it what to do), you can also use Vista to record sound. Therefore, not only can Vista interpret sound waves, but it can also save this data in a format that you can easily access later. For example, you can speak directly into your microphone and record a reminder message for yourself (such as *don't forget to buy eggs*), or you can use Vista's Sound Recorder to mix, edit, and play back sounds you want to save to your PC.

To bring up the Sound Recorder

1. **Click the Start button and choose All Programs from the menu that appears.**

   The All Programs menu appears in the left column of the Start menu.

2. **Select Accessories.**

   A drop-down list of the items located in this folder appears beneath the filename.

3. **Choose Sound Recorder.**

   The Sound Recorder window appears, as shown in Figure 6-11.

Figure 6-11: Recording sound using Vista's built-in tool.

Watch Your Step

In order to record sound, you must have a working microphone and speakers attached to your computer. This allows you to input and play back the sounds you've recorded using the appropriate audio reception tools.

4. To record your sound(s), click the Start Recording button.

The red dot next to the Start Recording button turns into a blue square, letting you know that it's okay to begin your recording.

5. When finished, click Stop Recording.

The Save As dialog box appears. (See Figure 6-12.)

Figure 6-12: Save your recorded sounds.

6. Enter a name for your sound in the File Name text box and then click Save.

This closes the Save As dialog box and returns you to a new Sound Recorder session.

Note: Your sound file is saved into your Documents folder by default if you do not specify another folder in the Save As dialog box.

7. To continue recording, close the Save As dialog box and click the Resume Recording button.

This allows you to add additional sound or voice recordings to your original file. When you're satisfied with your recording, save your final sound (refer to Step 6).

To play your recording, double-click the sound file you wish to hear. This opens up the appropriate application for playing back your sound recording — most likely Windows Media Player.

Transfer

For more information about Windows Media Player, see Chapter 9.

Information Kiosk

Most sound recordings made with Vista's Sound Recorder tool are saved by default as a Windows media file (.wma), which can be played with any digital media player application, such as Windows Media Player 11 (another free application bundled with Windows Vista). Yet, if you have Windows Vista Home Basic or Windows Vista Business, your sound recordings are saved as .wav files.

Step into the Real World

There are no time restrictions for the recordings created with Vista's Sound Recorder tool. Thus, you could conceivably record various sounds for as long as you like, or at least until you fill up your hard drive. However, this wouldn't leave you much space for other files and applications. Therefore, budget the amount of time you spend recording sounds.

The size of a sound file is determined by the amount of time you spend recording. The default rate is 96 Kbps. At this rate, a ten-second recording of your speaking voice is approximately 100–150K. Consider doing a preliminary test to determine whether you need to adjust your microphone and/or check the length and file size of your recording.

Creating Sticky Notes

In Windows Vista, you can actually put your random thoughts, ideas, and ramblings onto Sticky Notes. With Sticky Notes, you can create voice and handwritten notes to serve as reminders for yourself. You can then flip through your notes at a later time; you don't even have to save them first because Vista automatically keeps a record of all the notes you create, even after you shut down your PC. You can also attach these notes to files as you would a real-world reminder note. In other words, this Windows Vista tool acts like an electronic version of a reminder note.

Information Kiosk

Sticky Notes are not the same as the Notes gadget available on the Vista Sidebar. Those notes cannot be saved to your PC or attached to another document like Sticky Notes.

Sticky Notes are easy to create, save, and use although it may take some time getting used to using your mouse as a writing utensil. Because you can't use your keyboard to type messages to yourself — instead, you use your mouse as your pen — this feature can be a bit cumbersome at first. However, it does have its benefits, such as the ability to draw freehand pictures, graphs, charts, and other visual elements that can then be attached to related files. In any event, you are free to create voice notes for yourself if you find that easier.

Information Kiosk

If you are using a Tablet PC, you can use your stylus to create Sticky Notes instead of your mouse. When you do, the Pen toolbar appears automatically, providing you with a variety of writing options.

The fastest way to bring up Sticky Notes is to do an Instant Search for this feature, but if you feel more comfortable going through the menus, then choose Start ➔ All Programs ➔ Accessories ➔ Tablet PC ➔ Sticky Notes.

 Transfer

Return to Chapter 2 to revisit how to perform an Instant Search.

After you locate and open this tool, your first (blank) Sticky Note appears, as shown in Figure 6-13.

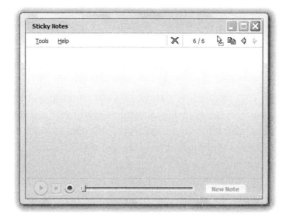

Figure 6-13: A blank Sticky Note.

Just place your mouse inside the Sticky Note and click and drag it to "write" yourself a message. (See Figure 6-14.)

 Watch Your Step

There is no Erase or Undo feature for this tool, so be careful when creating Sticky Notes. If you make a mistake, your best alternative is to delete it and start a new one.

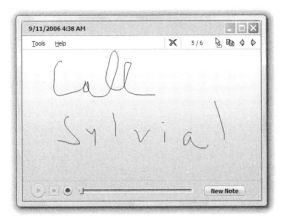

Figure 6-14: A Sticky Note in handwriting done by using the mouse.

Here are some quick-and-easy Sticky Note commands:

- **Open:** To open a new Sticky Note, click the New Note button located in the bottom-right corner of the window. This brings up a blank Sticky Note.

- **Navigate:** To navigate through your various Sticky Notes, use the back and forward arrow keys at the upper-right corner of the Sticky Notes window. These two buttons allow you to move back and forth between your existing notes.

- **Delete:** To delete a Sticky Note, click the red X button positioned in the middle of the Sticky Notes toolbar. Clicking this button brings up a dialog box asking whether you're sure you want to delete this note, which you can confirm by clicking Yes.

Information Kiosk

Sticky Notes are dated and timed, allowing you to see exactly when a Sticky Note was generated. Take a look at the date and time indicated in the title bar above the toolbar shown in Figure 6-14.

As I mention earlier, every Sticky Note you create is automatically stored as part of this Vista tool, so that the next time you open Sticky Notes, each of your messages is available to you. However, you can also choose to export these items — essentially saving your Sticky Notes to your computer as a new document file.

Watch Your Step

When you export Sticky Notes, all the notes in this application are saved to the new file, not just the currently open note. Therefore, keep your active Sticky Notes to a minimum so that you don't have to shuffle through a long list of notes each time you save (export) or open (import) these items.

To export (or save) Sticky Notes

1. Open the Sticky Notes application.

You can locate this item by doing an Instant Search for *Sticky Notes* from the Start menu.

2. Click the Sticky Notes Tools menu.

A drop-down menu appears.

3. Choose Export.

The Export dialog box comes up, as shown in Figure 6-15.

Figure 6-15: Exporting a Sticky Note.

4. Enter a name for your set of Sticky Notes in the File Name field and then click Save.

This saves your Sticky Notes collection to your Documents folder, and then returns you to your active Sticky Notes session.

Note: If you want to save this file in a different folder, be sure to select the correct folder (use the drop-down menu provided in the toolbar at the top of this window) before you click Save.

Information Kiosk

Exporting Sticky Notes is great for synchronizing your Tablet PC with a desktop computer.

To open your Sticky Notes after you have saved them to your PC:

1. **Open the Sticky Notes application.**

2. **Click the Sticky Notes Tools menu.**

A drop-down menu appears.

3. **Choose Import.**

The Import dialog box comes up, as shown in Figure 6-16.

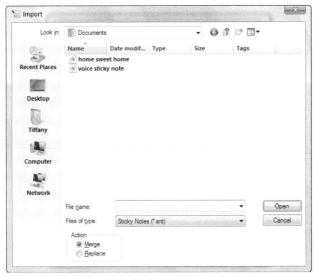

Figure 6-16: Importing (or opening) a Sticky Note.

4. **Select the file you would like to open.**

The name of the file you selected now appears in the File Name field.

5. **Click Open.**

This opens all the notes saved within this file in your existing Sticky Notes session.

Note: Your saved notes and current (or nonimported) notes are arranged according to the date and time they were created. Therefore, you might need to flip through some of your existing notes to find the saved items you are looking for.

 Information Kiosk

If you select the Replace option located at the bottom left of the Import window, you can opt to delete all your existing notes and replace them with the items stored within your saved Sticky Notes file. But be careful; if you choose this option (and confirm your decision by selecting Yes in the pop-up dialog box that appears), there is no way to retrieve this information for future use.

You can also copy and paste a Sticky Note right on top of a file in another application.

For example, try this:

1. **Open the Sticky Note you would like to attach to another file.**

2. **Select the Sticky Notes Tools menu.**

This opens the Tools drop-down menu.

3. **Choose Copy.**

This makes a copy of your open Sticky Note.

4. **Open the program or file where you would like to attach your Sticky Note.**

If you do not have a file at hand, open Notepad and type some text into it.

5. **Choose Edit → Paste within the application you opened in Step 4.**

This places a copy of the Sticky Note is the open document.

Figure 6-17 shows a Sticky Note being placed on top of an Excel spreadsheet.

Information Kiosk

You can also leave yourself a voice Sticky Note. Voice Sticky Notes follow the same principal as handwritten notes, but instead of scribbling something with your mouse, you leave yourself a reminder message with your voice. To record a voice Sticky Note, click the red (Record) button at the bottom left of a blank Sticky Note and speak into your microphone to record your message. When finished, click the Stop button. (No saving is required.)

Whenever you want to play your recorded Sticky Note, just click the Play button located at the bottom of the Sticky Note window.

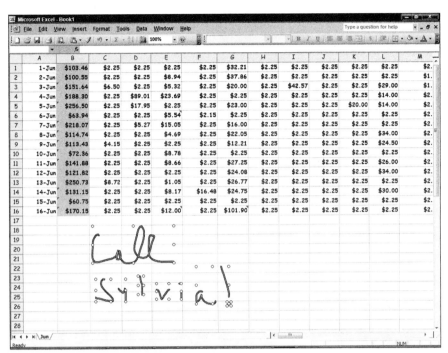

Figure 6-17: A Sticky Note pasted onto an Excel spreadsheet.

Working with WordPad/Notepad

WordPad, the free word processing program that comes with Windows Vista, is similar to Microsoft Word in that it permits you to make some formatting changes to your text. However, it does not contain the extensive word processing features of Microsoft Word. For example, WordPad does not include more advanced tools, such as a spell checker, auto-correct feature, letter wizard, mail merge, or table insertion capabilities. Yet, WordPad can still be used to produce basic letters, memos, and most text documents. You even have some customization choices. For example, you can make adjustments to your document text, such as

- Font
- Size
- Alignment
- Bullets

Here's how to work with WordPad:

1. **Click the Start button and choose All Programs → Accessories → WordPad from the menu that appears.**

WordPad opens onscreen, displaying a new blank page, as shown in Figure 6-18.

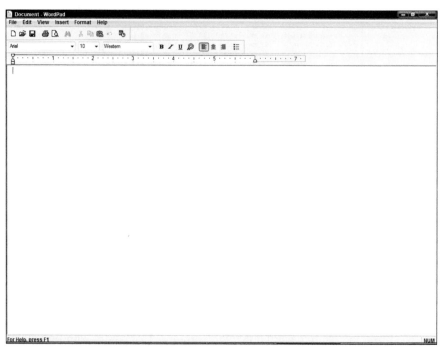

Figure 6-18: A blank WordPad document.

2. **Enter your text.**

Keep in mind that WordPad has only a limited repertoire of word processing features such as fonts, tabs, and paragraph indentation. (It does allow you to insert and paste objects, however.)

3. **When done, choose File → Save to save your document as an RTF file.**

When you save files you create in Wordpad, they are saved as an RTF file. They can be opened by any word processing application, on a PC or a Mac.

WordPad's partner program, Notepad, might not have many features, but it is free and comes in handy when generating notes you want to type and save for yourself. You can access Notepad from the same Accessories submenu you use to find WordPad. (From the Start menu, choose All Programs → Accessories → Notepad.)

By default, the Notepad program does not wrap text; when you type, the words simply go continuously across the screen, a shown in Figure 6-19. You can remedy that by choosing Format ➜ Word Wrap from the main menu. With the Word Wrap feature turned on, your text "wraps" at the end of the line so that it remains visible onscreen, as shown in Figure 6-20.

Figure 6-19: A Notepad document with a lot of typing, all on one long line.

Figure 6-20: A Notepad document with word wrap turned on.

Information Kiosk

When you save your Notepad document (using the File → Save command), you can save it as a Web page file by simply giving your file an `.htm` or `.html` extension. Many Web developers use Notepad to write the HTML code for their Web pages because it can function quite effectively as a Web page editor. (It does not insert the kind of damaging formatting tags — damaging to HTML code, at least — associated with more high-powered word processing programs.

Capturing Images with Vista's Snipping Tool

Vista's new Snipping tool greatly simplifies the cropping process for pictures, images, and screen captures. It also works on basic word processing applications, menus, toolbars, and so on. Basically, you can use the Snipping tool to capture a picture or image of something on your computer screen and save it to your computer. This feature can also be used to e-mail picture or image snippets.

Because the Snipping tool is part of your computer's operating system, you can use it no matter what program or application houses the image you wish to capture. You can crop pictures that have been saved on your hard drive, or your can snip images from the Internet. You can also use this tool to pinpoint specific parts of a Word document or online news article and cut out only the sections that interest you.

Vista's Snipping tool is a convenient and flexible tool because it permits you to crop images from any resource. And because it is included as a standard Vista accessory, you do not have to purchase separate third-party software. You also do not have to copy and paste a picture into another editing program just to use its cropping feature. This can save you time when working with cropped images.

To use the Snipping tool

1. **Locate the document/image/photo you wish to capture.**

Open this item in whatever application it exists.

2. **Keep this file or program open, click Start, and then choose All Programs → Accessories → Snipping Tool from the menu that appears.**

The Snipping Tool window, as shown in Figure 6-21, appears onscreen.

Notice how the background image fades as the Snipping Tool appears.

Figure 6-21: The Snipping tool.

3. As instructed in the Snipping Tool dialog box, use your mouse to click and drag a box around the area you wish to snip and then release the mouse.

This copies the image contained within the red lines to your Snipping Tool window. (See Figure 6-22.)

From here, you can choose to save, copy, or e-mail your image snippet.

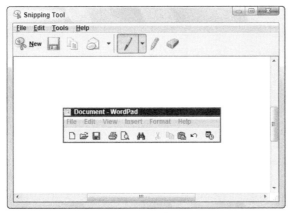

Figure 6-22: After cropping with the Snipping tool, the image is ready to be saved.

ℹ Information Kiosk

You can make notes or call attention to certain aspects of the image snippet before you save/send it by using this feature's pen and highlighter tools. (Refer to Figure 6-22.) Just click the buttons for these tools — located to the right of the Snipping Tool action items — and then use your mouse to perform the desired function. If you make a mistake, just click the Eraser icon to remove the erroneous pen and highlighter marks.

To save an image or picture with the Snipping tool

1. Choose File from the Snipping Tool menu bar.

A drop-down menu appears.

2. Choose Save As.

The Save As window appears onscreen, as shown in Figure 6-23.

Note: You can also bring up this dialog box by clicking the Save button (indicated by the computer disk icon) on the Snipping Tool toolbar.

3. Enter a name for this image into the File Name field and then click Save.

This closes the Save As dialog box and returns you to your current Snipping tool session.

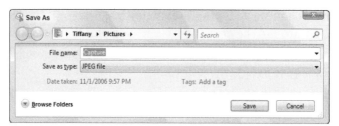

Figure 6-23: The Snipping Tool Save As dialog box.

Information Kiosk

You have the option of saving your image snips as PNG, GIF, JPEG, or HTM (HTML) files. If you do not select a different file type, your image is saved as a JPEG file by default.

If you do not indicate a different folder location, all your image snippets are automatically saved to your Pictures folder. Be sure to select a new folder in the Save As dialog box if you want to store this file in a different location.

When you reopen saved image snippets, they appear in the Windows Photo Gallery. From this screen, you can make adjustments to the image's color, fix red-eye imperfections (if you're viewing a photograph), print a copy of the image, e-mail it to family and friends (if you haven't already done so), copy it to a CD, or import it into a movie.

Transfer

Skip ahead to Chapter 9 to learn more about the Windows Photo Gallery.

Zipping/Unzipping Files

Using Microsoft's WinZip feature allows you to condense large items. This feature does not in any way corrupt your original files; rather, it uses a special file format (.zip) to compress your file's data into a more manageable size.

You can compress (or zip) a single file or a group of files. Using the Zip file format saves space on your own hard drive and is also a useful tool when sending large files via e-mail. Zipping e-mail attachments into a single condensed file makes it easier for this information to reach its recipient in a quick and an efficient manner.

Transfer

Move on to Chapter 7 to learn more about using Vista's e-mail systems.

In the past, shrinking file sizes meant having to download (and possibly even purchase) compression software. Windows Vista includes a free Zip utility, ready to use.

Compressing files

To compress multiple files into a single zipped file

1. **Select all the files that you wish to compress.**

   - *Adjacent (contiguous) files:* Click the first item in the list of files you would like to include and then hold down the Shift key while you click the last item you wish to include. This highlights all the files located in between these two items as well as the first and last items.

   - *Nonadjacent files:* Hold down the Ctrl key and use your mouse to click the individual files you would like to add to your Zip file.

2. **Right-click any one of the selected files and then choose the Send To option from the contextual menu that appears.**

   Doing so brings up another pop-up menu.

3. **Choose the Compressed (Zipped) Folder option, as shown in Figure 6-24.**

Figure 6-24: Right-click selected files and choose Send to Compressed (Zipped) Folder.

File compression begins. (See Figure 6-25.)

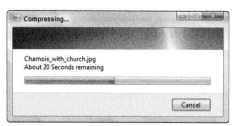

Figure 6-25: Files being compressed into a ZIP file.

4. When file compression is complete, rename the folder by right-clicking the filename, choosing Rename, and then typing in the new name, as shown in Figure 6-26.

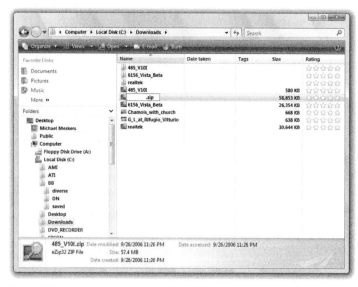

Figure 6-26: Now you can name your zipped file.

Information Kiosk

If you forget to include an item in your Zip file, you can easily add it (and additional items) to your Zip folder by simply dragging and dropping the missing information into the Zip file as you would with any other file/folder transfer.

Decompressing files

Decompressing (or unzipping) files is just as easy as compressing them. Here's how to decompress a Zip file:

1. Locate the zipped folder you wish to decompress.

2. Right-click the folder name and choose Extract All from the contextual menu that appears, as shown in Figure 6-27.

Figure 6-27: Right-click a zipped folder to rename it.

The Extract Compressed (Zipped) Folders window appears, as shown in Figure 6-28.

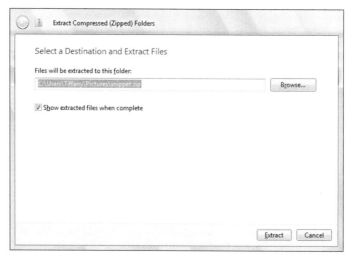

Figure 6-28: Select a destination to extract your files.

3. Use the Browse button to locate the folder where you would like to extract these items.

By default, the folder selection matches the same location as that of the Zip file.

You can choose to use the same folder for your Zip file extractions as you used for your Zip file, or you can choose to place these items in an entirely different folder.

4. Click Extract.

This creates copies of the files contained within the Zip file in the folder you specified in Step 3. Open this folder to locate the individual items previously compressed in your Zip file.

Note: Extracting documents from your Zip file does not permanently remove these items from your Zip file. You can still access all this information by opening your saved Zip file.

Information Kiosk

Although you can theoretically zip images and even videos, many images, such as GIFs and JPEGs, do not compress much at all. Therefore, you do not notice much of a reduction in their file sizes when they are compressed.

You do not have to extract all files from a zipped folder. You can also extract a select few or even just a single file. Here's how:

1. Locate the zipped folder you wish to decompress.

2. Double click on the zipped folder.

Doing so opens the folder.

3. **Simply click and drag the file (or selected files) from the compressed folder to another location.**

   The file is automatically decompressed and placed in the new location.

Windows Calendar

The Windows Calendar is a convenient time-management tool available directly through your computer's operating system. This tool allows you to keep track of your appointments, scheduled activities, and personal reminders in one centralized location. This Vista feature is a nice alternative to either hardcopy calendars or other third-party calendar programs.

Looking at Windows Calendar more closely (choose All Programs → Windows Calendar from the Start menu), you see that it offers an intuitive interface that allows the user to schedule tasks and appointments and keep track of their busy lives. In the left pane of the Calendar window (see Figure 6-29), you can select a date; in the main pane, the day is broken down hour by hour. You can type in any appointment or reminder next to any hour. There is no need to save it; if you exit the Calendar, your entries are all automatically saved.

Figure 6-29: The Windows Calendar.

Information Kiosk

To view a particular date, simply click a date in the Calendar. You can also view the current day, week, workweek (Monday–Friday), or month by selecting it from the View menu.

Setting Tasks

You can specify tasks (to-do items) in the Windows Calendar and then use the application to remind you of deadlines that need to be met or steps that need to be taken. For example, you can mark the priority level of a task so that you know which item needs to be completed first, or you can use Vista's reminder feature to send yourself an alert when you need to begin working on a particular item. To create a task

1. **With the Windows Calendar open, click the New Task button on the main toolbar.**

The New Task panel appears on the right of the Calendar display, as shown in Figure 6-30.

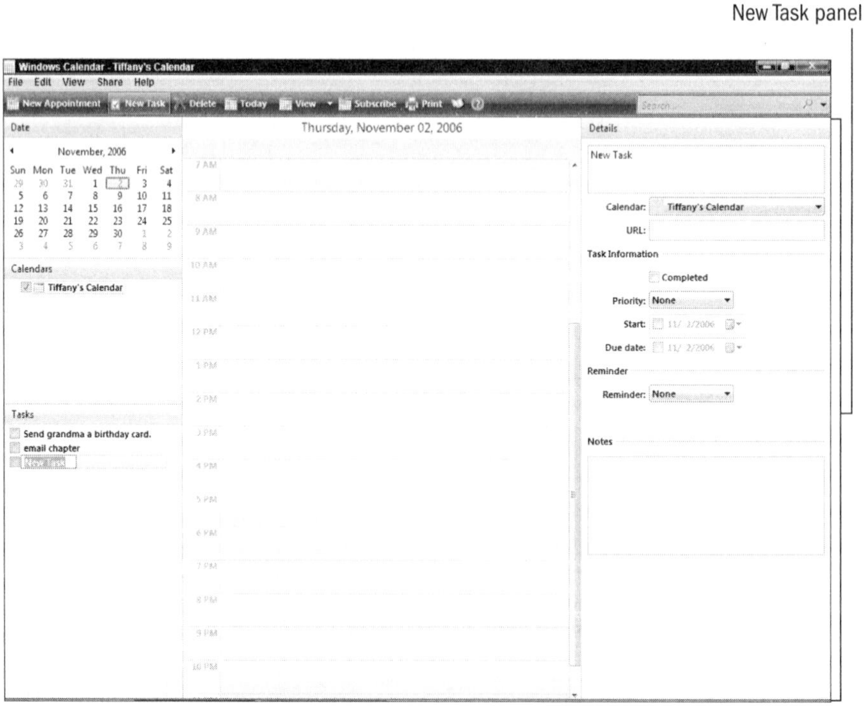

New Task panel

Figure 6-30: Setting up a new task.

2. Enter a description of your task in the Details text box.

3. Open the Priority pull-down menu to specify the importance of this task.

Your choices are None, Low, Medium, and High.

4. Enter a Start and Due date for this task in the appropriate fields of the New Task panel.

When you select the check box immediately to the left, the software lets you enter a date manually; you can also choose a date from the mini-calendar drop-down feature if you prefer.

5. Open the Reminder pull-down menu to specify whether you want Vista to remind you when this task is due.

Your options are None or On Date. If you select On Date, you can type in or select the task's reminder date in the same manner as the previous Calendar items.

When your reminder date arrives, you are prompted with a pop-up window on your computer screen, alerting you that your task deadline is approaching.

6. Enter any notes about this task that you want to make in the Notes text box.

A task with the description you've specified appears in the Tasks panel, in the left corner of the Calendar. Clicking this entry in the Tasks panel brings up all details related to this task.

After you complete your task, you can mark it off of your to-do list by marking the check box to the left of the item, or you can highlight the task and click the Delete button from the Calendar main menu to remove it from your screen.

Making appointments

In addition to creating tasks in Windows Calendar, you can also use this tool to set appointments (and reminders) for yourself. Having all your scheduled appointments in one location helps you keep track of important engagements and events. To create a new appointment

1. In Windows Calendar, click the New Appointment button on the main toolbar.

A new appointment text box appears in the middle column, while the Details panel to the right expands with criteria for the new appointment. (See Figure 6-31.)

2. With the New Appointment text highlighted in the center column, type in a brief name or description for the appointment.

The text you enter is replaced in both the center and right columns.

Choose the correct calendar here.

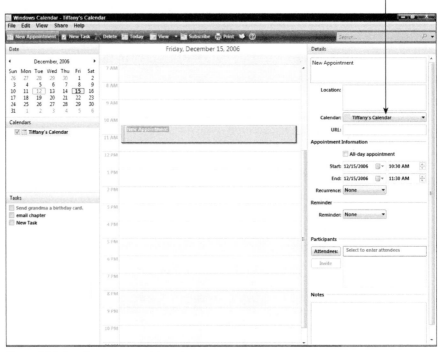

Figure 6-31: Creating a new appointment.

3. **In the Details panel, type in a location for your appointment.**

If you do not want to specify a location for your appointment, you may leave this box empty.

4. **If you have multiple calendars set up on the same computer, use the drop-down menu provided to select the appropriate calendar.**

5. **If you plan to discuss a particular Web site during the appointment or if you are meeting up with someone online, type the relevant URL or e-mail address in to the URL text box.**

6. **In the Appointment Information section of the Details panel, use the drop-down menus provided to select a start (and end) date and time.**

You can also use the Recurrence menu to specify whether this appointment is a daily, weekly, monthly, or annual event. If you select one of these labels, the appointment automatically reappears on your calendar during the appropriate time.

If you select the All-day Appointment check box you can identify the appointment as an event that takes place throughout the entire day (such as a birthday or anniversary), rather than tying it to a specific time.

7. If you would like to set a reminder for the appointment, use the Reminder drop-down menu to select when you would like to be notified of your upcoming appointment.

You can choose to be reminded a few minutes prior to the meeting or you may choose to be reminded several days (or weeks) in advance.

8. Enter any notes or reminder messages for yourself into the Notes section.

If you do not have any information you need to remember for your appointment, you might leave this box empty.

9. To exit the new appointment information, simply click on another time or date in Windows Calendar.

You may also invite others to the scheduled appointment by clicking the Attendees button in the Participants section of the Details panel. To invite other participants

1. Select the appointment you wish to invite others to and click the Attendees button in the Details panel.

Doing so opens the Windows Calendar Contacts window shown in Figure 6-32.

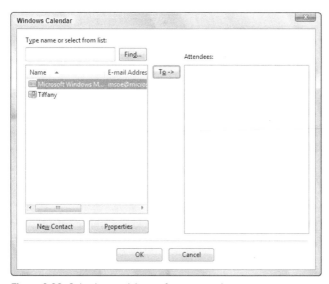

Figure 6-32: Selecting participants for your appointments.

2. Highlight the name of the person you would like to invite and click the To button in the middle of the screen.

The name you've selected now appears in the right text box as well. Repeat this step until you have selected all the participants you wish to invite.

Note: If there are people you would like to invite, but they do not appear in your Contacts list, you may use the New Contact button at the bottom left of the screen to add them to your Contacts list.

3. **When you are finished adding all your contacts to the invite list, click OK.**

This closes the Contacts window and returns you to the Windows Calendar. Notice that the names of the people you selected in the previous step now appear in the Invite text box located in the Participants section of the Details panel. (See Figure 6-33.)

Figure 6-33: Inviting others to attend your new appointment.

4. **To send invitations to these people, click the Invite button.**

This sends calendar invitations to the participants via Windows Mail.

Transfer

Refer to Chapter 7 to learn more about Windows Mail.

Subscribing to a calendar

Certain institutions — theaters, museums, sports organizations, and so on — make their calendars available to the public on a subscription basis. If you are a member of one of these organizations, you might already be aware of the group's Web site calendar. If so, you can use the Windows Calendar subscription service to automatically update your own personal calendar with the events of this group's public calendar.

To subscribe to another calendar of events

1. **Choose Subscribe from the Windows Calendar toolbar.**

The Subscribe to a Calendar window appears, as shown in Figure 6-34.

Figure 6-34: The Subscribe to a Calendar window.

2. **In the Calendar to Subscribe To field, enter the URL for the calendar you are interested in.**

Use the format suggested by the Subscribe to a Calendar window to enter your URL.

3. **Click Next.**

This opens the Calendar Subscription Settings screen, as shown in Figure 6-35.

4. **Enter a name for your calendar, select an update interval, and then click Finish.**

You can also choose to include reminders and tasks from this calendar. Just place check marks next to the items you would like to include.

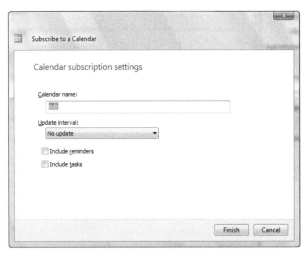

Figure 6-35: Choosing your subscription calendar settings.

Watch Your Step

Vista Calendar uses the iCalendar format. As long as the shared calendar is in this same format, you should be able to subscribe to that calendar. And the converse holds true; you should be able to share a calendar without the use of any third-party software. See the following Web site for more information: `www.microsoft.com/ windowsvista/features/forhome/calendar.mspx`.

Publishing a calendar

If you wish to share your calendar with others, you can "publish" it onto a network.

Step into the Real World

Laptops that are Windows Vista SideShow-enabled are now appearing on the market. If you own one of these laptops, you have access to one of Vista's newest time-saving tools.

The SideShow is so named because it is an illuminated display panel built into the side of a laptop that gives you immediate access to information without your having to even power-up your machine. This is especially handy when traveling.

The Windows SideShow feature does run off your laptop battery although it uses a very small amount of power. It can display the date, the time, and your appointment calendar for the day. You can also display schedules, phone numbers, and recently received e-mail messages.

Here's how:

1. From the Share menu, click Publish.

The Publish Calendar dialog box appears. (See Figure 6-36.)

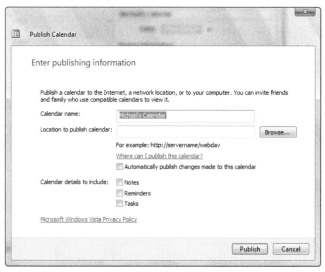

Figure 6-36: Windows Calendar: The Publish Calendar dialog box.

2. Type a name for the calendar you wish to share into the Calendar Name box.

3. Enter the location where you want your calendar to be published.

You can choose to publish your calendar to the Internet, a local network, or to your computer — in which case you can save a copy of your Windows Calendar as a document file that can later be imported into an existing calendar.

4. Click Publish.

Information Kiosk

You can publish your calendar to any Web site on the Internet that is compatible with the iCalendar format. If you are unable to publish your Windows Calendar online for others to see, check with your hosting service to see if they are able to use this file format.

The Windows Calendar publishing feature can be quite useful if you wish to share information with several people at one time. For example, you may want to publish a Little League team's practice schedule, a neighborhood-watch calendar, or your personal calendar so that your family and friends have access to your daily schedule. You can also use this feature at work to help coordinate meetings and other appointments with your co-workers.

cropping: Trim a specific area of an image or text file.

file compression: Encoding files so that they contain fewer data bits; compression also allows multiple files to be saved as a single item.

file types:

> **.wmv:** Windows Media audio/video file. Used in Windows Media Player versions 8 and later.
>
> **.wma:** Windows Media Audio file.
>
> **.wav:** Waveform (or Windows) audio file.
>
> **.png:** Portable Network Graphic file.
>
> **.gif:** Graphic Interchange Format file; used primarily for images drawn onscreen.
>
> **.jpg:** Graphic file developed by the Joint Photographic Experts Group; used primarily for digital photos.
>
> **.mht:** Multipurpose Internet HTML mail file extension used with Internet Explorer; should be scanned when received via e-mail because they can carry embedded malware.

Kbps: Kilobytes per second; represents the speed at which your PC is able to record sound.

MUI (Multilingual User Interface) Pack: Microsoft software that allows you to speak in more than one language when using Speech Recognition.

Notepad: A windows application for creating and editing text documents.

SideShow: An auxiliary display built in to some laptops allowing users to view e-mail, calendars, appointment schedules, and phone numbers without having to power up their machines.

Snipping tool: Vista's new image cropping application. This tool allows you to pinpoint and cut out the image details that interest you. You no longer have to copy the entire image into a separate editing program just to crop a picture, text document, or screen capture. This tool also permits you to save your cropped image to your computer or e-mail it to others.

Speech Recognition: The ability to convert spoken language into sound waves that can then be used to interpret command functions or dictation.

Sticky Notes: Windows Vista's new electronic version of reminder notes. These items are used to create handwritten notes and drawings, which can be saved to your computer or attached to another document.

WordPad: A windows application for simple word processing tasks. Supports limited graphic insertion and limited formatting features.

Last
Stop

Practice Exam

1. Name at least two different ways you can use Vista's Speech Recognition capabilities to interact with your PC. Provide examples of when you might want to take advantage of this feature.

_____

_____

_____

_____

2. What are the best ways to ensure high-level accuracy with Speech Recognition?

_____

_____

_____

3. Can you compress a video file? When/why might you want to do this?

_____

_____

_____

4. In what way could it be useful to publish a Windows Calendar to the Internet?

_____

_____

_____

5. What are some of the benefits of using Speech Recognition? What are some of its hindrances?

_____

_____

_____

6. When might you use Vista's Sound Recorder tool?

_____

_____

_____

7. Describe how to create a Sticky Note.

_____

_____

_____

8. When would you most likely use WordPad or Notepad?

_____

_____

9. What are the benefits of using Vista's Snipping tool?

_____

_____

10. Why would you want to compress your file(s)?

_____

_____

11. How do you decompress a Zip folder? What happens to your files when you do this?

_____

_____

Connecting to the Outside World

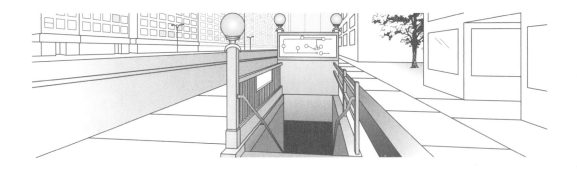

Enter the Station

Questions

1. How do you send and receive e-mail messages using Windows Mail?

2. How can rules help manage e-mail and newsgroup correspondence?

3. How could you move messages from an existing e-mail account over to Windows Mail?

4. What are the hardware requirements for using Vista's Fax and Scan program?

5. What types of files can be faxed from your computer?

6. How can you find and communicate with others in your network?

7. How does Windows Meeting Space let you collaborate with others online?

8. What kinds of networks can be set up using Vista?

9. What is a LAN, and how do you create one?

Express Line

If you are already up on the basics of how to communicate with others using Windows Vista, skip ahead to the next chapter.

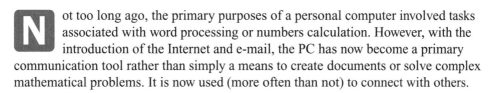 ot too long ago, the primary purposes of a personal computer involved tasks associated with word processing or numbers calculation. However, with the introduction of the Internet and e-mail, the PC has now become a primary communication tool rather than simply a means to create documents or solve complex mathematical problems. It is now used (more often than not) to connect with others.

Your connection options now are broader than ever. Not only can you use your PC to send messages to others, but you can also use it to conduct live meetings from multiple locations; Vista's Meeting Space application allows you to hold virtual meetings to collaborate with others who are in a different part of the country or even the world. In addition to being able to meet with others online, you can also use your PC to send them official documentation, via e-mail or by using your computer (and scanner) as a fax machine. You can also subscribe to newsgroup forums (online discussions, in other words) about whatever issues or topics interest you. And lastly, you can use your PC to establish your own personal computer network. This capability allows you to connect a number of computers together under one network, which comes in handy if you have several different computers you use at home or perhaps if you run a small business with multiple computers. Using either a local area network (LAN) or wireless local area network (WLAN) lets you connect a number of PCs together in a unified manner so that each PC can be used to access the same information, no matter where that particular machine is located.

Using Windows Mail

Although hardly a truly innovative piece of software, Windows Mail (formally known as Outlook Express) is a perfectly acceptable e-mail and Usenet reader that can be set up in minutes. With a very small learning curve, you can send, receive, and create e-mails; include attachments; and manage mailboxes. It also includes a junk filter, account management, and a newsgroups feature.

Setting up your Mail account

Before you can set up Windows Mail, you need to know the names of your Internet service provider (ISP) incoming and outgoing mail servers. Usually, the incoming (or POP, *Post Office Protocol*) mail server address takes the form of mail.*yourISP*.com (or POP.*yourISP*.com). The outgoing (or SMTP, Simple Mail Transfer Protocol) server address usually takes the form of smtp.*yourISP*.com. Some ISPs, like Optimum Online, use the same address for both servers. To determine the type of server used by your ISP, contact your e-mail provider.

To create a new Windows Mail account

1. Open the Start menu and click on the E-mail icon located in the top-left column.

If this item is not visible, perform an Instant Search for Windows Mail.

Clicking on the E-mail icon opens the Windows Mail Inbox, as shown in Figure 7-1.

Figure 7-1: The Windows Mail Inbox.

2. Choose Tools → Accounts from the main menu bar.

This opens the Internet Accounts window. (See Figure 7-2.)

3. Click Add.

This opens the Select Account Type window, as shown in Figure 7-3.

 Information Kiosk

The Directory Service you see listed as an account choice in Figure 7-3 refers to the online address books offered by many organizations.

Figure 7-2: The Internet Accounts window.

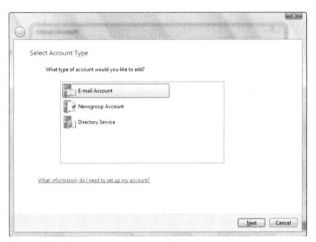

Figure 7-3: Selecting a new Windows Mail account.

4. **Select E-mail Account and then click Next.**

A new screen appears asking you to provide the name you would like to show up when you send e-mail to others.

5. **Enter a display name into the text box provided and then click Next.**

This opens the Internet E-mail Address window.

6. **Enter the e-mail address you would like to create a Windows Mail account for and then click Next.**

The e-mail server page appears (see Figure 7-4).

Note: Your ISP usually provides your e-mail address to you.

Figure 7-4: Setting up your e-mail server.

7. **Select your e-mail server type from the drop-down menu provided.**

You can choose between a POP and an IMAP server.

- POP3 (Post Office Protocol) servers are most commonly used for personal e-mail accounts. These servers hold your incoming e-mail until you check your messages, at which point your mail is transferred from the server to your PC. After you check your mail, these messages are deleted from the POP3 server.

- IMAP (Internet Message Access Protocol) servers are most commonly used for business e-mail accounts. These servers allow you to view e-mail messages without first downloading them to your computer. You can also preview, delete, and organize messages from IMAP e-mail servers.

Watch Your Step

There is a third e-mail server type — HTTP (*HyperText Transfer Protocol*) servers that are used for Web-based e-mail accounts, such as Hotmail and Yahoo! accounts. Unfortunately, Vista does not currently support this e-mail server type. Therefore, you cannot create new Windows Mail accounts for your existing Web-based e-mail accounts. You must choose another server type to proceed to the next step or simply exit the Mail Setup Wizard to abort this setup process.

8. **Enter your e-mail server's incoming and outgoing information in the text boxes provided; then click Next.**

This opens the Internet Mail Logon window. (See Figure 7-5.)

Figure 7-5: Entering your e-mail log-in information.

9. **Enter your e-mail user ID and password in the text boxes provided and then click Next.**

If you would rather not enter your password at this time, clear the Remember Password option. Removing this criterion forces you to enter your password each time you use Windows Mail. Although this might seem like somewhat of an inconvenience, it helps protect your e-mail account information. If you are comfortable with allowing your PC to save your Windows Mail password automatically, leave this option enabled.

 Transfer

Check out Chapter 4 for more information on Internet privacy and security issues.

10. **Click Finish on the final (Congratulations) screen.**

From this window, you can choose to download your existing messages at this time. To do so, place a check mark in the box to the left of this option. If you do not want to take advantage of this transfer tool, clear the check box to the left of this option.

Composing e-mail messages

After you set up your Windows Mail account, you can begin corresponding with friends, family, and colleagues through Vista's built-in e-mail system. The process for creating a Windows Mail message is similar to that of any other e-mail program.

To compose a new message using Windows Mail

1. Open Windows Mail and then click the Create Mail button.

A New Message screen opens onscreen. (See Figure 7-6.)

Note: If you click the drop-down menu to the right of the Create Mail button, you can choose from a number of existing stationery (or background) artwork for your messages.

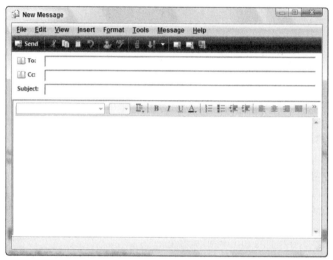

Figure 7-6: Creating a new e-mail message.

2. Enter the recipient's e-mail address in the To field.

You can add the e-mail address for your recipient in one of two ways:

- *Manually:* Physically type the e-mail address into the To field.

- *Autofill:* If the recipient's address is already part of your Contacts list, click the Address Book icon (to the left of the To field). You go to the Select Recipients panel, where you can highlight the recipient's screen name, click To, and then click OK.

The recipient's name appears in your message's To field.

For multiple e-mail addresses, separate each address with a semicolon.

 Information Kiosk

You can also send a carbon (duplicate) copy of any message by using the Cc field. To send a blind (or hidden) copy of your message, use the Bcc field in the Select Recipients panel.

3. **Enter a title for your message in the Subject field.**

The subject of your message typically summarizes the contents of the e-mail.

4. **Type your message in the box below.**

You can also choose to adjust the formatting or your message's text. Use the formatting toolbar to apply bold, italic, or underline characteristics to your text. You can also change the size of your font as well as attach files to your message. (See the upcoming instructions on how to attach a file to your e-mail message.)

5. **Click the Send button in the upper-left corner of this window.**

This sends your message to its recipients.

To attach documents, photos, or video and sound files to your e-mails

1. **Open a new Windows Mail message and choose Insert → File Attachment from the main menu — or just click the Paperclip icon in the toolbar. (See Figure 7-7.)**

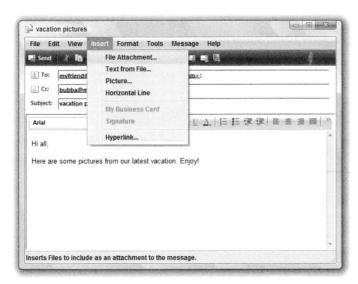

Figure 7-7: Attaching files to an e-mail message.

This brings up a file directory panel in which files are grouped by type — Documents, Pictures, Music — as well as options for Desktop, Recent Places, Computer, Recently Changed, Searches, and Public.

2. **Double-click the folder where your document is saved and then highlight the file to be attached.**

3. Click Open to attach this file to the outgoing message; or, double-click the file to add it to your e-mail message.

To attach another file, repeat Steps 1–3.

 Information Kiosk

You can also use Shift+Click and Ctrl+Click to add files in the same folder to the e-mail all at once.

When you finish attaching your documents, typing and formatting text, and addressing your e-mail, you are ready to send your message.

4. Click the Send button on the New Message toolbar to send your message to its recipient(s).

Depending on how you set up your Windows Mail, your message is either immediately sent to its recipient or is stored in the Outbox for later delivery. See the next section for more details.

 Information Kiosk

You can also use the keyboard combination Alt+S to send your e-mail messages.

Sending and receiving messages

When you click the Send button in a Windows Mail message, the message is transferred to the Outbox folder. When you next connect to the Internet, your message is then sent to its recipient(s).

If you use an always-on Internet connection, your e-mails are automatically sent to your recipient(s) because you are continuously connected to the Web. However, if you use a different type of connection, you might want to check your Windows Mail settings to ensure that you do not have to manually send the files each time you connect to the Web. To locate this feature

1. Open Windows Mail.

You can locate this application by clicking the Start button or by doing an Instant Search.

2. Choose Tools → Options from the main menu bar.

The General tab of the Options window pops up onscreen, as shown in Figure 7-8.

3. Select the Send tab.

The Send tab appears. (See Figure 7-9.)

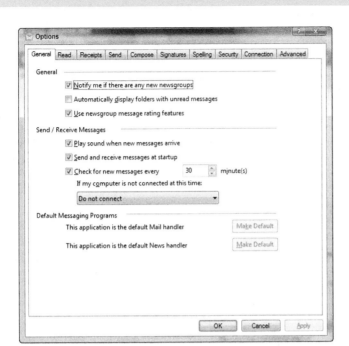

Figure 7-8: The Windows Mail Tools ➔ Options window.

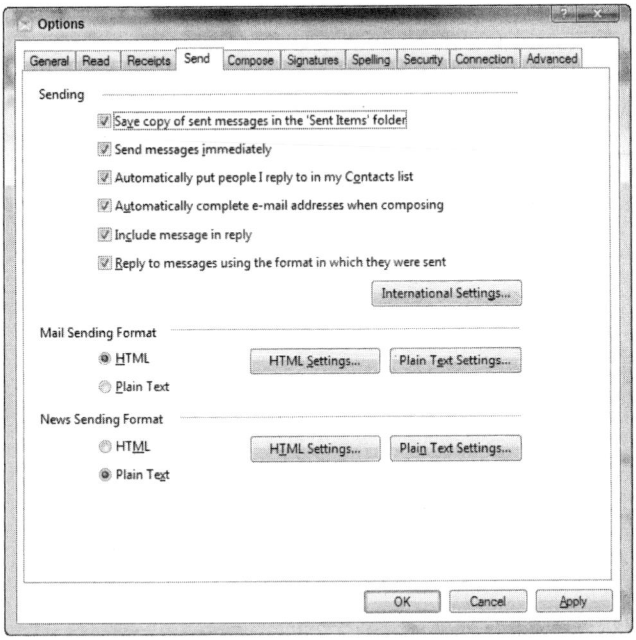

Figure 7-9: The Send tab of the Mail Options window.

4. **Select the Send Messages Immediately check box.**

That way, when you are connected to the Internet, your e-mail is immediately forwarded to your e-mail server and then to its recipient.

If this check box is left clear, all outgoing messages remain in your Outbox until you physically click the Send/Receive button on the Windows Mail toolbar (or use the keyboard shortcut Ctrl+M).

5. **Click OK.**

Doing so closes the Send tab in the Options window.

Deselecting the Send Messages Immediately check box is a carryover from the era of timed dialup accounts, when users would go online to send and receive messages while doing most of their composing of messages offline. However, even in today's broadband and wireless era, this approach can still be useful when you are working on a laptop on a train or airplane, or somewhere where wireless access is unavailable — and yet still want to keep up with your electronic correspondence.

To receive your messages, either set up Mail to automatically check for new mail at periodic intervals (via the Tools → Options → General menu, selecting the Check for New Messages Every x Minute(s) option, and specifying an interval from 1 to 480 minutes) or click the Send/Receive button.

Sorting your e-mail

When you need to refer to a particular e-mail message, you need a quick way to locate that exact message. Fortunately, Vista offers several different sorting criteria for Windows Mail. For example, you can search for a message by subject matter — in which case, your messages are placed in alphabetic order according to their Subject titles. You can also locate a message by its sender, the date it was received, whether it has an attachment, a *flag* (a reminder you can set for yourself), as well as its priority level.

 Step into the Real World

Is there any reason why you shouldn't allow Mail to automatically download new messages? Yes, there is — if you're using a server screening application like Mailwasher (available for free download at www.mailwasher.net) to preview mail remotely, and delete unwanted junk or even virus-infected messages before they have any chance to compromise your PC. When using this type of software with Windows Mail, you would only download mail after you have the chance to look through it on the server — and so the manual Send/Receive option would clearly be the better way to go.

To locate a message by using any of these criteria

1. Open Windows Mail.

2. Choose View → Sort By from the main menu bar.

A submenu appears to the right of the View menu. (See Figure 7-10.)

Figure 7-10: Sorting your e-mail messages.

3. From the Sort By submenu, select the primary criteria and order (ascending or descending) you would like to use to display your messages.

Clicking any of these categories changes the primary sorting criterion and closes the menus above.

 Information Kiosk

A faster and easier way to sort your messages is to simply click the sorting categories listed in the Windows Mail toolbar.

When you click one of these categories, your messages are arranged according to the specified criteria. If a small upward-pointing triangle appears next to the category title, your messages are ranked in ascending order. If a small downward-pointing triangle shows up next to the category title, your messages are listed in descending order.

Step into the Real World

You can also use the Windows Mail search capabilities to locate a specific e-mail. Clicking the Find button (located on the main toolbar) opens a detailed search box. Enter the criteria for your missing message and then click the Find Now button. All the messages that match your specifications appear in a list below. Simply double-click a message to open it.

Organizing Mail

When Windows Mail downloads messages, the default option is for all messages to be directed to your Inbox. However, you can set up rules to send mail to other folders.

This arrangement can be useful if, for example, you trade stocks with an online broker and receive electronic confirmations via e-mail. You could set up a folder in Mail called Confirmations; then you could set a rule to automatically send all trade confirmations to that folder. If you ever need to find an electronic confirmation, you know exactly where to look — and there is a lesser chance of an accidental deletion.

To set your own Mail rules

1. **Open Windows Mail.**

2. **Choose Tools → Select Message Rules from the main menu bar.**

A submenu appears to the right of the Tools menu.

3. **Choose Mail.**

This opens the New Mail Rule window. (See Figure 7-11.)

4. **Place a check mark by the Where the From Line Contains People option located in the Conditions section.**

This option allows you to identify messages by their senders.

5. **Select the Move It to the Specified Folder check box in the Actions section.**

The option you choose from the Actions box determines what happens to your message after it's identified.

6. **Click the blue Contains People link provided in the Rule Description box.**

This opens a new Select People window. (See Figure 7-12.)

7. **Enter the e-mail address used to identify the messages you want to be automatically sent to a new folder (other than the Inbox) in the first text box. When you're finished, click the Add button.**

After you click Add, the address information you entered is moved to the box below. You may now enter another address in the first text box if you wish. To add yet other addresses to this list, repeat this process until you add all the people you would like to include as part of this identification criteria.

Figure 7-11: Establishing a new Mail rule.

Figure 7-12: Selecting criteria for your Mail rule.

 Information Kiosk

Note that you can also click the Contacts button to bring in people who are in your Windows Mail Contacts folder.

8. Click OK.

This closes the Select People window. You should now be viewing the New Mail Rule screen.

Notice that the address(es) you entered in the Select People window are now included as part of the Rule Description details.

9. **Click the blue Specified link in the Rule Description section.**

This opens the Move window (see Figure 7-13). From this screen, you can determine where you would like your e-mails to be stored.

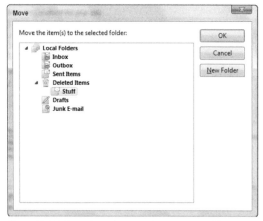

Figure 7-13: Choosing where to place your e-mails.

10. **Select the Mail folder you would like to use for the messages identified by this rule.**

You can double-click one of the folders already listed, or you can click the New Folder button to create a new folder specifically for this rule. If you choose to create a new folder, a pop-up box appears asking you to provide a name for this new folder. Enter a name for this folder and then click OK.

Note: If you choose to create a new folder, take note which existing folder is highlighted because the new folder is added as a subfolder to the currently selected folder.

11. **Click OK (if necessary).**

This closes the Move window, again returning you to the New Mail Rule window.

12. **Enter a name for your rule in the last (fourth) text box and then click OK.**

This opens the Message Rules screen. (See Figure 7-14.)

13. **Click OK.**

This closes the Message Rules page. All the messages from the people specified by this rule are now sent directly to the folder you selected earlier; these messages no longer pop up in your Inbox.

Note: The next time you attempt to create a new Mail rule, you are returned to the Message Rules page. To begin a new rule, click the New button to the right.

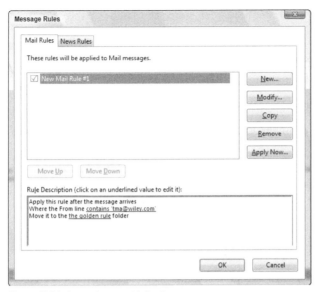

Figure 7-14: Approving your Mail rules.

As you've probably noticed, there are several different ways you can use Mail rules in addition to just sending new messages from certain people to a folder other than your Inbox. For example, you can color-code your messages by priority, delete messages that include attachments or are simply too large for your server, forward messages to a collaborative workgroup if the subject line contains certain keywords, and so on. The list is quite extensive. Feel free to play around with these options and customize your Mail system in a way that lets you work more efficiently.

Importing other e-mail accounts into Windows Mail

If you've been using a previous version of Windows, or another e-mail program, you may wish to transfer your existing e-mail messages into Vista's Mail system.

Step into the Real World

Microsoft has added a dedicated Junk E-mail module to Windows Mail. This module, which you access using the Tools ➜ Junk E-mail Options command, allows you to choose the specific level of protection that you want, from No Automatically Filtering to Safe List Only. Safe List Only tells Mail that only people or domains on your Safe Sender List (which you set on another tab in this menu) should be delivered to your Inbox. In other words, if you don't already know and trust a sender or a domain, that message is automatically treated as junk. This represents a stringent, yet secure, level of protection.

To load messages into Mail that have been stored in Outlook Express or another e-mail program:

1. Open Windows Mail.

You can find this program in the upper-left column of the Start menu.

2. Choose File → Import from the main menu.

The Import submenu appears to the right of the File menu. (See Figure 7-15.)

Figure 7-15: The Windows Mail Import submenu.

3. Choose Messages.

The Select Program window appears, as shown in Figure 7-16.

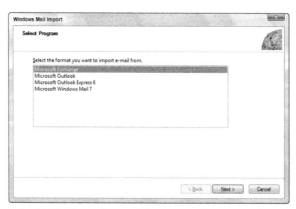

Figure 7-16: Choose the e-mail format you wish to use to import your data to Windows Mail.

Information Kiosk

To import mail from a non-Microsoft application, such as Eudora or Pegasus, you have to first export your messages from that program into one of the four Microsoft formats.

4. Select the e-mail type you wish to use to import files to Windows Mail; then click Next.

The application searches for files in the message type that you specify. If Mail automatically finds the appropriate files where it expects to find them, you are given the option to select these. If not, the wizard takes you to a Location of Messages window, where it prompts you to browse for the files. Use this screen to locate and select the appropriate folder.

5. After you identify the appropriate folder, click Next.

The Windows Mail Import Wizard asks you to specify either All Folders or Selected Folders to import.

6. Choose either the All Folders option or the Selected Folders option for importing.

If you choose the Selected Folders option, be sure to select only those folders that you want to import.

When the process is completed, the wizard brings up a screen indicating that the import process is complete.

7. Click Finish.

Your messages are imported into a Local Folders directory named Imported Folders, with the specific folders that were transferred located in a hierarchically structured subdirectory.

Accessing Newsgroups

Newsgroups are like virtual bulletin boards, which Internet users can use to post messages that others may respond to at a later point in time. The newsgroup format also acts as a large-scale discussion forum. When different users post messages about a topic and others continue the discussion on a given topic, this is a *message thread.*

Newsgroups provide people with access to other individuals who are interested in the same kinds of information. When you participate in a newsgroup, you have access to people who have knowledge — or at least an interest — in the same topics that you do. The disadvantage is that some newsgroups can seem a bit disorganized because of multiple message threads (or individual discussions) going on at the same time, in which case you might have to sift through some information that does not necessary apply to you.

Information Kiosk

Newsgroups are one of the earliest areas of the Internet to develop, even predating the Internet's becoming a publicly accessible entity. Newsgroups first started in 1979 at Duke University, as a means for those involved in technology to communicate with each other. Because a large percentage of the content of these technical discussions was about computer news, the name *newsgroups* came into use. Today, they've grown in number to more than 100,000, and you can find them in a variety of languages around the world.

Transfer

Newsgroups specifically about getting help with Windows Vista — *Microsoft communities* — are sponsored by Microsoft. For more on this topic, go to Chapter 12.

One way to find and join newsgroups is by using your Internet browser to surf the Web for topics that pique your interest. Newsgroups are also accessible via tools called *newsreader programs*. Windows Mail, conveniently enough, is a mail program and also a newsreader. In addition to using Windows Mail to manage e-mail communications, you can also use it to view newsgroup discussions.

Setting up a newsgroup account

To access newsgroups via Windows Mail, set up a newsgroup account. Here's how:

1. **Open Windows Mail and choose Tools ➜ Select Accounts from the main menu.**

The Internet Accounts window appears, as shown in Figure 7-17.

2. **Click Add.**

The Select Account Type window appears. (See Figure 7-18.)

3. **Choose Newsgroup Account and then click Next.**

A new window appears, asking you to enter a display name for your account.

4. **Enter the screen name by which you wish other newsgroup users to identify you and then click Next.**

Another window asks you to provide an e-mail address where other newsgroup members can contact you directly.

5. **Enter a return e-mail address and then click Next.**

The screen that pops up next asks you to provide information about your NNTP (Network News Transfer Protocol) server.

Figure 7-17: The Internet Accounts window.

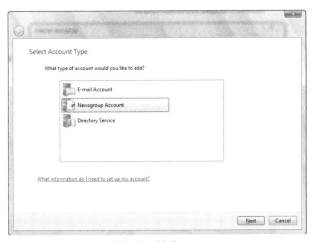

Figure 7-18: Selecting a Windows Mail account type.

 **Watch Your Step**

Many spammers collect addresses from newsgroup postings, so consider entering a slightly modified e-mail address to make their job that much more difficult. Or, you can use a dedicated e-mail address for your newsgroup subscriptions.

6. **Enter the address of your NNTP server and then click Next.**

This address is usually `news.yourISP.com`. Some servers, including all premium servers from third-party providers who specialize in newsgroup feeds at high speed, require you to log on. If your ISP requires this, be sure to select the My News Server Requires Me to Log On check box in this panel.

Selecting this option and then clicking Next brings up yet another window, where you must enter your user ID and password before you can move on to the final step.

7. **After Windows Mail processes the necessary data, you are greeted with a Congratulations page. Click the Finish button provided on this screen.**

This sends you back to the Internet Accounts page. (Notice that your new news-group account is now included on this screen.)

8. **Click Close to exit the Internet Accounts window.**

This brings up a dialog box with the message

```
You're not subscribed to any newsgroups for this
account. Would you like to view a list of available
newsgroups?
```

See Figure 7-19.

Either leave this window open on your computer as you go on to read the next section on how to subscribe to a newsgroup, or close this window to return to your current Mail session.

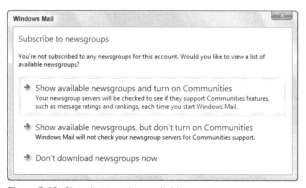

Figure 7-19: Choosing to review available newsgroups.

Subscribing to (And Reading) Specific Newsgroups

If you just created your newsgroup account in the steps listed earlier, you should still be looking at the Subscribe to Newsgroups dialog box mentioned earlier. (Refer to Figure 7-19.) From this screen you can choose to

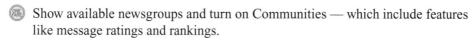

⊙ Show available newsgroups and turn on Communities — which include features like message ratings and rankings.

⊙ Show available newsgroups, but don't turn on Communities.

⊙ Don't download newsgroups now.

To view a list of available newsgroups, select either the first or second option. This opens the Newsgroup Subscriptions panel (see Figure 7-20).

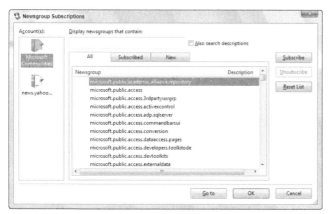

Figure 7-20: The Newsgroup Subscriptions panel.

To add a newsgroup subscription to your account

1. Open the Newsgroup Subscriptions panel.

You can also access this screen by choosing Tools ➜ Newsgroups from the main menu in Windows Mail.

2. Choose the account you wish to update from the Accounts column located on the left side of the Newsgroup Subscriptions window.

When you first open this window, the Microsoft Communities account is selected. Click the icon for the account you created to personalize your own newsgroup data.

 Information Kiosk

The three tabs in the main pane of the Newsgroup Subscription window are All, Subscribed, and New. The All tab includes a list of every newsgroup available on your server. The Subscribed tab includes only those newsgroups that you have subscribed to. And the New tab contains a listing of newsgroups that are new to the server.

The New tab can be quite useful when you revisit the newsgroup window from time to time. By letting you know what newsgroups have recently been added to the server, the New tab saves you from having to search through all the available newsgroups on your server to locate the newly added items. Select this tab to view only recently added newsgroups.

3. **Type a topic or discussion item into the search text box at the top of the main pane and then press Enter.**

This pulls up a list of newsgroups that match the topic you entered.

4. **(Optional) If nothing happens after you press Enter, click the Reset List button on the right to download a list of relevant newsgroups available on your server.**

If there are no matches for the topic you've entered, you are notified by a message in the Newsgroup description box. Try again using a different word or topic.

5. **Highlight the newsgroup you wish to subscribe to and click the Subscribe button; or just double-click the newsgroup link.**

If you look in the Subscribe tab, you can see that the newsgroup you've selected now appears in this area.

To add more newsgroups to your account, repeat Steps 3–5 until you locate all the newsgroups you wish to subscribe to.

Information Kiosk

When searching for newsgroups, if you notice a little yellow rectangular icon to the left of a newsgroup, you know it's one you've already subscribed to. Therefore, there's no need to add it to your list again.

6. **When you finish adding newsgroups, click OK.**

This closes the Newsgroup Subscriptions panel.

Mail next takes you to a panel where you can begin to read all your subscribed newsgroups. (See Figure 7-21.)

Information Kiosk

You can also access your newsgroup data by clicking the user account folders listed to the left of the main Windows Mail page. All your user accounts (and their subfolders) are located under the standard Local Folders mail files.

Figure 7-21: A listing of your subscription newsgroups.

To view the postings from your selected newsgroups, double-click a newsgroup name. A new window containing available messages appears. This window is divided in half vertically, with the top half containing the Subject line for postings and the bottom half containing a preview window featuring the text of each posting. Use your mouse to click the postings or responses you wish to read. This causes the accompanying text to appear in the preview window below.

Step into the Real World

Some newsgroups may be moderated; most, however, are not. Chances are that if you encounter a moderated site, you probably won't even know it. Some sites use a moderator to monitor the messages posted on its site. This prohibits users from posting unpleasant or incredulous messages.

Another reason to use a moderator is to ensure that the newsgroup host (usually a corporate company or organization) does not become involved in any negative or unruly discussions.

They can also help facilitate the appropriate flow and organization of the group's posted messages. For example, they can choose to place some of its most popular discussions near the top of the list so that users can easily find this information.

Information Kiosk

Double-clicking a newsgroup posting brings up the entire message as a separate window.

To join the conversation, you can either post a response to a previous message or start your own thread.

To post a response to an existing thread

1. Highlight the message that you want to respond to.

You can right-click this item and then choose Reply to Group; double-click the message; or press Ctr+G.

2. Click Reply Group on the Mail toolbar.

Note: If this is the first time you've used your account, you might be prompted by a dialog box asking you to confirm (or enter) your user information. Supply the information requested and then click OK.

This brings up a copy of the message, with the original text prefaced by > (a greater-than symbol), and a blinking cursor above the original message.

3. Type in your response. When finished, click Send.

This posts your message to the newsgroups bulletin board for everyone to read.

To reply to someone privately, bypassing the group entirely,

1. Highlight the message you wish to reply to.

You can also right-click this item and then choose Reply to Sender; double-click the message; or press Ctr+R.

2. Click Reply on the Mail toolbar.

Note: Be sure *not* to click Reply Group.

If this is the first time you've used your account, you might be prompted by a dialog box asking you to confirm (or enter) your user information. Supply the information requested and then click OK.

This brings up a copy of the message, with the original text prefaced by > (a greater-than symbol), and a blinking cursor above the original message.

3. Type in your response. When finished, click Send.

This sends an e-mail message to the person who originally posted this item.

To start your own message thread

1. Choose File ➜ New from the Windows Mail main menu.

A submenu appears to the right of the File menu. (See Figure 7-22.)

Figure 7-22: Creating an original newsgroup posting/message thread.

2. Click News Message.

This opens a new Windows Mail message already addressed to the newsgroup's Web address. (See Figure 7-23.)

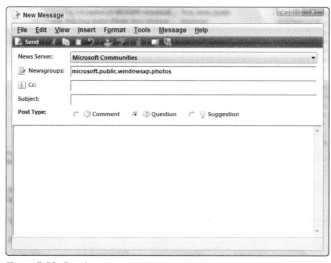

Figure 7-23: Entering a newsgroup message.

3. **Enter a Subject for your message.**

As with any e-mail message, the Subject line for your newsgroup posting should include a brief explanation or summary of the contents contained within the message itself. This lets the other newsgroup participants know whether they want to read the details of your posting.

4. **Select a Post Type category for your message.**

You can choose between Comment, Question, and Suggestion.

5. **Type your response in the text area provided. When finished, click Send.**

This posts your message to the newsgroups' bulletin board for others to read, review, and/or respond to.

To switch to another newsgroup or to return to your Inbox, click the name of the newsgroup (or Mail folder) you wish to view in the navigation pane at the left of the main Mail page.

Information Kiosk

You can use the same Windows Mail rules you used for your e-mail messages for your newsgroups. This allows you to better manage your newsgroup messages as well as your basic e-mail correspondence. To find out more about using Mail rules, review the preceding section on organizing Mail.

Watch Your Step

Like its predecessor Outlook Express, Windows Mail is at its best when used to access text-based groups. Although it can download multipart photo, video, and music files, it still lacks the appropriate binary-to-text support. (*Binary* here refers to the process whereby binary data — the 00s and 11s of computerese — is converted to text readable by humans.) The Windows Mail interface is also considered less suitable for use with binaries than its freeware and shareware competitors.

Faxing with Windows Mail

The advantage of a fax is that it instantaneously transmits an identical image, or *facsimile*, of a document (or graphic) to someone located in a different location without having to wait for a copy to be hand-delivered to them in person.

A traditional standalone fax machine performs a line-by-line scan to send or reconstruct exact replications of the documents it receives. Although you no longer need a separate fax machine when sending faxes via the computer, you do need a scanner — a dedicated scanner, or a multifunction device that has a printer and scanner in the same machine — to send faxes of existing documents.

And although it's always been possible to send and receive faxes from a personal computer, it has not always been easy or convenient. In the past, you could receive faxes and save them as images and use optical character reading software to change them to documents. However, you needed a scanner and third-party software (which often came bundled with your modem) to be able to send faxes. And of course, you needed a telephone connection.

Windows Vista makes the task somewhat easier because the operating system now includes an application — Windows Fax and Scan — which bypasses third-party software. You do, however, still need a phone line, modem, and scanning device to send faxes from your PC.

Setting up the necessary hardware

Although the Windows Fax and Scan program frees you from having to use a separate fax machine, it does require that you use a scanner if you wish to send faxes of existing documents (meaning, ones that you do not have an electronic record for on your PC) to others.

If you have a scanner (or camera) attached to your computer, chances are that Windows Vista recognizes it and automatically loads the necessary drivers to your PC. Older devices, however, might require that you use the Scanner and Camera Installation Wizard. If your devices are connected to your computer and turned on and are not automatically detected by your machine, follow the steps below to add these devices to your system.

Transfer

Check out Chapter 8 to learn more about adding additional devices to your PC.

To begin the Scanner and Camera Installation Wizard

1. **Click the Start button and choose Control Panel from the menu that appears.**

   The Control Panel opens.

2. **Choose Hardware and Sound.**

   This takes you to the Hardware and Sound window.

3. **Select Scanners and Cameras from the list of items in this window.**

   Doing so opens the Scanners and Cameras window. (See Figure 7-24.)

4. **Click the Add Device button to start the wizard.**

   The first screen you see is a welcome page explaining the purpose of this wizard — to install a digital camera, scanner, or other image device not automatically detected by your PC.

Figure 7-24: The Scanners and Cameras window.

5. Click Next.

Clicking Next opens the screen shown in Figure 7-25.

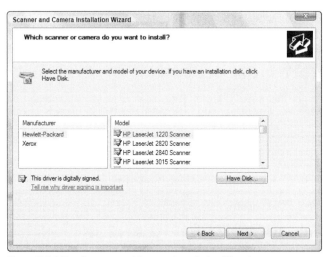

Figure 7-25: The Scanner and Camera Installation Wizard.

6. Select the manufacturer and model type for your device; then click Next.

A new screen opens, asking you to give your device a name. (See Figure 7-26.)

Figure 7-26: Naming your scanner.

Information Kiosk

Notice the Have Disk button located just below the Model choices in the Scanner and Camera Installation Wizard. If you have an installation CD for this device, click this button to manually install the software for your scanner using the CD provided with this product.

7. **Enter a name for your scanner.**

You can choose to keep the name provided by Vista, or you can type in a new name for your scanner device.

8. **Click Next.**

You are greeted with a Completing the Scanner and Camera Installation Wizard page.

9. **Click Finish to exit the wizard.**

After your computer locates your device, you are returned to the Scanners and Cameras window. Your device should now be listed in this area. If it is not, click the Refresh button to bring it up onscreen.

10. **Click Close to exit the Scanners and Cameras window.**

Running the Windows Fax and Scan program

After your PC can recognize your scanner, you can start faxing hard copy (printed) documents to others using your computer. The first step to faxing a paper document to someone using your PC is to scan it into your computer so that you have an electronic copy to work with. From here, you can use the Windows Fax and Scan feature to send this document to its recipients. You can also send faxes of documents or messages that started out as electronic files. Instructions for how to perform both of these tasks follow.

To scan a document, place it in the scanner in the manner appropriate to your machine. Then do the following:

1. **Choose Start → All Programs → Windows Fax and Scan.**

   This opens the Windows Fax and Scan program. (See Figure 7-27.)

Figure 7-27: The Windows Fax and Scan window.

2. **At the bottom of the left pane, click Scan.**

   This switches the active function of this program from Fax to Scan.

   You can tell which mode your PC is in by looking at the navigation pane located in the column at the left. If your PC is ready to fax, the Fax icon shows up. If you are ready to begin scanning, the Scan icon is present.

3. **On the main toolbar, click New Scan.**

   The New Scan screen opens, as shown in Figure 7-28.

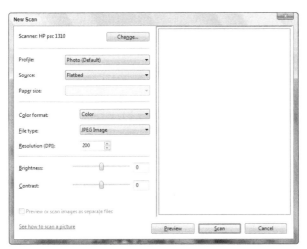

Figure 7-28: The New Scan window.

4. **Use the drop-down menus provided to select a Profile, Source, and Paper Size for your file.**

- Your *Profile selection* indicates what type of file it is that you are scanning. The majority of the time, you will choose either the Documents or Photo option. However, you do have the option to add your own profiles as well. (*Note:* The default setting for this category is Photo. Therefore, if you do not select another profile for your file, it's automatically treated as if it were a picture.)

- The *Source category* pertains to the type of scanner you're using.

  The *Paper Size category* tells your computer (and scanner) what to scan based on the measurements you give it.

Note: If any of these categories are grayed out (you cannot make a selection), don't worry. You can still scan in your documents or pictures without encountering any problems. Perhaps your scanner uses only one of the source and/or paper sizes provided. Therefore, you cannot make a selection for these categories.

5. **Use the next set of drop-down menus to select the Color Format, File Type, and Resolution for your image.**

- The *Color Format category* allows you to indicate whether you want your image scanned in black and white, grayscale, or color.

- Your selection from the *File Type menu* determines the file format used when saving the scanned image to your PC. As a general rule, JPEG images are used for scanned images. However, you can also choose to save your files as bitmap (BMP), PNG, or TIFF files. (Refer to Chapter 5 to find out more about file extensions.)

- The *Resolution* for your image determines the clarity of the item you're scanning. The higher the resolution, the clearer the picture — and the larger the file size of the finished product. This category is especially important when working with detailed pictures or photographs.

6. **After you make all the necessary selections, click Scan.**

The image is scanned into your computer. After this process is completed, the image appears as a new message in the Windows Fax and Scan window, as shown in Figure 7-29.

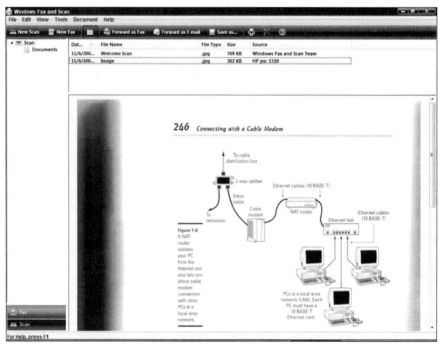

Figure 7-29: Viewing your scanned image as a new message.

After your document (or photo) has been scanned, you can begin faxing this item using the Windows Fax and Scan program.

To fax a scanned image

1. **Open the Windows Fax and Scan program and choose the Scan feature by clicking the Scan button located in the lower-left corner.**

Notice that a message containing the image you scanned earlier is now present on this page.

2. **Select the file/message you would like to fax and then click the Forward as Fax button.**

The first Fax Setup window appears, as shown in Figure 7-30.

Figure 7-30: The Fax Setup window.

![Information Kiosk icon] **Information Kiosk**

You can also choose to send your scanned images to others as e-mails rather than as faxes. Simply choose the Forward as E-mail button instead of the Forward as Fax button to create an e-mail message for your scanned images.

3. **Choose either the Fax Modem option or the Fax Server option as your fax transmission method.**

A second Fax Setup window appears asking you to enter a modem name. (See Figure 7-31.) You can either use the default fax modem or type in a new name.

Figure 7-31: Naming your fax modem.

4. **Enter a name for your fax modem and then click Next.**

This opens the third Fax Setup window, as shown in Figure 7-32.

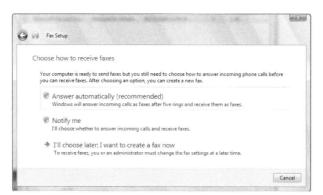

Figure 7-32: Choosing how to receive faxes.

5. **Select an option for how you would like to receive your faxes.**

You can choose to have your incoming fax messages answered automatically, to be notified of new faxes so that you can choose to answer them manually, or to make this decision later, yet proceed with sending your current fax.

After you make your selection, a New Fax window appears onscreen, as shown in Figure 7-33.

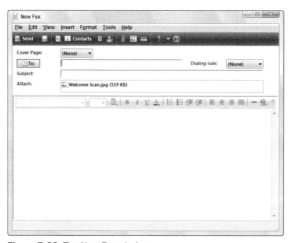

Figure 7-33: The New Fax window.

6. **(Optional) Use the drop-down menu provided to choose a cover sheet type.**

You do not have to include a cover sheet with your fax. However, if you do choose to include one, a new text box titled Cover Page Notes pops up in the New Fax window just below the Subject line. Enter any cover sheet notes or comments in this area.

7. In the To text box, enter the fax number you are sending the scanned image to.

Be sure to include the 1 + area code information when dialing long distance. Also, there is no need to separate the fax number with hyphens as you might a telephone number (for example, XXX-XXXX); instead, just type in the 11-digit number as one single string of numbers.

Enter multiple fax numbers by separating each with a semicolon.

8. Type a subject for your fax.

The Subject line for a fax serves the same purpose as the Subject line for an e-mail. Enter a title or description that provides the recipient with a clear understanding of the topic or reason for the attached message.

9. (Optional) Type in a message in the text box provided.

As with the cover sheet feature, this step is also optional. You do not have to enter anything into this area if you do not want to. It's simply there in case you need it.

10. When you're finished, click Send.

This opens the Location Information screen, as shown in Figure 7-34.

This screen asks you for information about your current country, area code, and carrier code; if you need to dial a separate number to reach an outside line; and what type of phone system (tone or pulse dialing) you are using.

Note: If you have not yet attached your PC to a phone line, you should do so now.

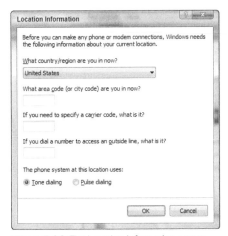

Figure 7-34: The Location Information screen.

11. Enter the information requested on this page and then click OK.

This opens the Dialing Rules screen. (See Figure 7-35.)

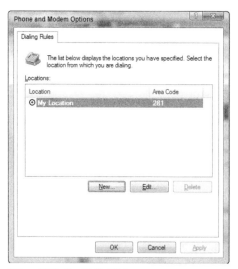

Figure 7-35: The Dialing Rules screen.

12. **Select the profile for your current location (or use the New or Edit button to alter this information) and then click OK.**

This closes the Dialing Rules window and begins the faxing process.

Notice the Windows Fax and Scan status window that appears. If you click its View Details button, you can see each step of the fax process as it is completed. This status box also lets you know when your fax has been successfully sent to its recipient(s).

You can also send a basic fax (one that does not require the use of a scanner) from your computer. In this case, click the New Fax button (in either the Scan or Fax mode) and type in your message. Then click the Send button to fax your text message to its recipient(s).

Step into the Real World

One might wonder, with dedicated fax machines and multifunction printers (which include scanning and faxing capabilities), why bother with Vista-based faxing and scanning? One answer is that the computer digitizes the documents and graphics making it simple to store, access, and manage them. A second is that the design of the Vista application closely resembles that of the Microsoft e-mail client (Microsoft Outlook) and is thus familiar to users of those programs. Eventually, these various look-alike programs might be the key to wider indexing of information within Vista.

Working with People Near Me and Windows Meeting Space

People Near Me is the new Vista technology that locates other people nearby who use a computer on the same network. When signed in to People Near Me, you can identify active users in your LAN and then invite them to participate in a live meeting using Windows Meeting Space or other programs that use peer-to-peer (P2P) technology.

Transfer

Vista's Windows Meeting Space feature is covered in more detail in the pages that follow.

A *peer-to-peer* networking platform allows multiple users working from the same subnet (or second-tier network) to communicate with one another and/or hold a live conference. You can have as few as two participants in the conference or include as many users as there are in the subnet. Without the use of an additional server, these participants can chat with one another, launch applications, work on the same documents, or play the same games. For example, strangers sitting around an airport terminal waiting for their flights could carry on a poker game, or a dozen people in the same office (but different locations) could watch a PowerPoint presentation, while two or three others chat and trade jokes.

Information Kiosk

Keep in mind that People Near Me is not a *global* peer-to-peer communications network, which requires outside servers and Internet service providers to link local computers to the world. Rather, People Near Me deals only with LANs or WLANs.

Signing in to People Near Me

To use Vista's People Near Me program, you must set up a user account and sign in. This is quick and easy to do. Follow these steps to activate the People Near Me feature:

1. **Click the Start button and choose Control Panel from the menu that appears.**

   The Control Panel window opens.

2. **Choose Networks and Internet.**

   Doing so opens the Network and Internet window. (See Figure 7-36.)

Figure 7-36: The Network and Internet window.

3. **Choose People Near Me.**

The People Near Me window opens. (See Figure 7-37.)

Figure 7-37: The People Near Me window.

4. **Click the Settings tab, if it is not already selected.**

5. **Enter a username.**

Type the name you want to appear to others in your People Near Me area.

You can also choose to include a picture of yourself in the User Information section of this tab. Place a check mark in the box provided to select this feature and then click the Change Picture button to choose an image or photograph.

6. **Use the drop-down menu in the Invitations section to identify whom you are willing to receive invitations from.**

You can choose to receive invitations from anyone, only your trusted contacts, or no one at all.

Notice the Display a Notification When an Invitation Is Received option. Place a check mark in the box provided to enable this feature.

Information Kiosk

If you wish to have Vista automatically sign you in to the People Near Me program each time you start your computer, be sure to check the box next to this feature in the Options section of the People Near Me Settings tab.

7. **Click the Sign In tab.**

The Sign In tab for your People Near Me account opens, as shown in Figure 7-38.

Figure 7-38: Signing in to the People Near Me program.

Information Kiosk

Notice the Status line located just above the Sign In/Out options. This line tells you whether you are already signed in to the People Near Me network.

8. Select the Sign In option.

A green dot appears in the radio button to the left of your selection.

9. Click OK.

If this is the first time you're using People Near Me, you are prompted with a new People Near Me confirmation page. (See Figure 7-39.)

Review and adjust the information on this page, most of which correlates to the data you previously entered on the Settings tab.

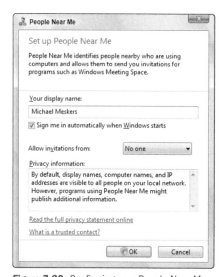

Figure 7-39: Confirming your People Near Me account information.

10. Click OK again.

This closes the People Near Me window.

Notice the icon (which looks like a person's head and shoulders) now visible in the Notification area of the taskbar. This icon indicates that People Near Me is active and that you are signed in to the program.

Sending Windows Meeting Space Invitations

Windows Meeting Space, Vista's free version of Net Meeting, allows users to meet synchronously online and collaborate with one another. Any type of electronic document can be viewed, worked on, and shared by all during these meetings.

After you sign in to People Near Me, you can begin working with Windows Meeting Space to schedule and conduct live interactive meetings. To take advantage of this collaboration feature

1. **Click the Start button and then choose All Programs → Windows Meeting Space from the menu that appears.**

   Selecting Windows Meeting Space brings up a dialog box asking whether you are ready to set up this program.

2. **Click Yes to continue.**

   This opens the Windows Meeting Space window. (See Figure 7-40.)

   If any meetings are taking place in your network, these activities can be viewed by clicking the Join a Meeting Near Me option. (This should be the default view when you open this application.)

Figure 7-40: The Windows Meeting Space window.

To start a new meeting

1. **Open Windows Meeting Space and choose the Start a New Meeting option.**

   Selecting this action item displays a series of text boxes/options on the right side of the Windows Meeting Space screen, as shown in Figure 7-41. (Note that if you were signed out of People Near Me, this step will sign you in again automatically.)

2. **Select a name for the meeting.**

   Type a title or description for the meeting in the text box provided.

3. **Enter a password for attendees (and yourself) to use to enter the meeting and then click the green arrow to the right of the password box.**

   This begins the meeting. See Figure 7-42 to view the main page of an active meeting.

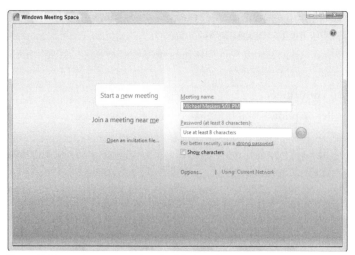

Figure 7-41: Setting up a meeting with Windows Meeting Space.

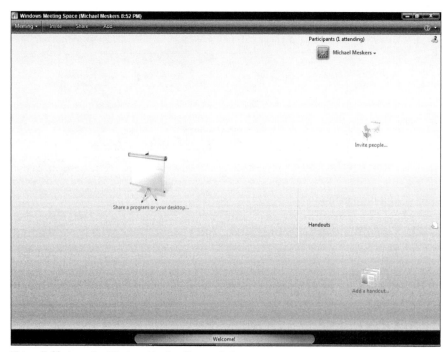

Figure 7-42: An active Windows Meeting Space window.

To invite people to attend the meeting

1. Click the Invite People icon (or the Invite button located on the main menu bar).

The Invite People window appears. If someone is signed into People Near Me and they are on the same subnet, their names will automatically appear in the Name box you see in Figure 7-43. If that is the case, then simply check the check box associated with their name and click the Send Invitations button. Otherwise, you can send them an e-mail or create an invitation to be sent out, as shown in the next steps.

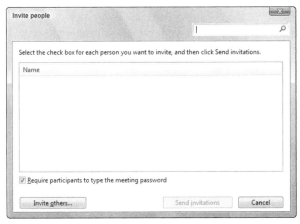

Figure 7-43: Inviting others to attend a meeting.

2. **Click the Invite Others button located in the lower-left corner.**

This opens the Windows Meeting Space window shown in Figure 7-44.

Figure 7-44: Selecting how to send meeting invitations.

3. **Choose the method you would like to use to send meeting invitations to others.**

Selecting the first option (Send an Invitation in E-mail) permits you to use your computer's installed e-mail application to send meeting invitations in the same manner that you would send any other e-mail message. If you choose to use this method, be sure to include the date and time of the meeting — as well as the password — in your message.

If you choose the second option (Create an Invitation File), a new Save As window appears asking you to enter a name for your invitation file. This file can then be attached to a standard e-mail message or sent as part of an instant message. After the recipient receives the message, he can click the attached invitation file to be taken directly to the Windows Meeting Space sign-in page. Again, be sure to include the meeting's password in your e-mail or instant message so that your attendees can sign in to the appropriate meeting.

Sharing documents (or working collaboratively) within Windows Meeting Space

The ability to have others view your documents (or desktop) in real time makes it possible to hold live interactive meetings with Windows Meeting Space. When you choose to share items with the other attendees, you allow them to view documents as you make changes to it. This way, they can make comments or address any problems as they arise rather than waiting until the document has been routed to each of them.

Sharing desktop documents

When you choose to share a document (or your desktop), Windows Meeting Space launches the appropriate program for the document that you wish all attendees to collaborate on (or it simply displays your desktop for other attendees to see). Any edits you make yourself are immediately visible to all attendees. When there is more than one attendee, an option appears onscreen allowing you to give control or take back control of the screen. When you choose the Give Control option, you can select exactly which attendee is allowed to control the screen and edit the collaboration document.

To share a document (or allow others to view your desktop)

1. Select Share from the main Windows Meeting Space menu bar.

A dialog box appears asking whether you want other people to see your desktop.

2. Click OK.

This opens the Start a Shared Session window, as shown in Figure 7-45.

The shared session window includes a list of all the documents and programs that you have open.

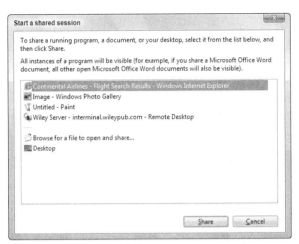

Figure 7-45: Selecting which documents you want to share.

3. **Select the item you wish to share with others or choose the Browse for a File to Open and Share option.**

You can also choose to share your entire desktop session with the other attendees by selecting the Desktop option. This feature can be quite useful if you plan to collaborate on more than one document at a time. Sharing your desktop is convenient because it prevents you from having to open and close each shared document every time you want to flip back and forth between these files.

4. **Click Share.**

This opens the shared document in the appropriate program.

In the upper-right corner of this screen is a green dot with the words `Currently Sharing` next to it. This lets you know exactly which document the attendees are viewing.

Just above the Currently Sharing indicator are three round buttons. The first has a small square inside of it; the second contains two vertical dashes; and the third includes a picture of a television set. These buttons allow you to control the status of the shared session. The first button (with the square) lets you stop the shared session. The second button (with the vertical dashes) allows you to pause the sharing session. And the last one (with the television monitor) lets you see exactly what the other attendees are viewing on their screens.

From this window, you may also choose to Give/Take Control of the shared document. Use the drop-down menu located to the right of the round control buttons to use this Windows Meeting Space feature.

Information Kiosk

If you wish any attendees to have a final version of the collaborative document, you need to send it to them after the meeting.

Adding handouts

Handouts are another way to share documents with meeting attendees. The difference between a handout and a shared document is that a shared document is housed solely on your PC. However, when you choose to add a handout, a copy of the selected file is placed on each attendee's computer. As with shared documents, only one person at a time can make changes to the collaborative file. After a change has been made, the correction automatically appears on each person's handout. Handouts can be any file you wish attendees to have a copy of. This includes PowerPoint presentations, Excel files, Word documents, and so on.

To add a handout

1. **Select Add from the main Windows Meeting Space menu bar.**

A dialog box appears letting you know that handouts are copied to each participant's computer. This window also informs you that the original file is not affected by the changes made during the meeting.

2. **Click OK.**

This opens the Select Files to Add window, as shown in Figure 7-46.

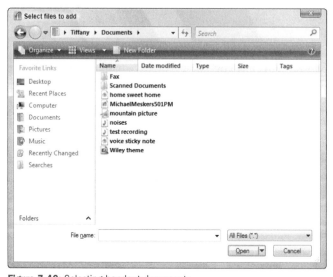

Figure 7-46: Selecting handout documents.

3. **Use your computer's file directory to select the handout item(s) you wish to share with others.**

Double-clicking a file closes the selection window and returns you to the main meeting page. Notice that the handout(s) you've selected now appear in the lower-left portion of this screen under the Handouts heading.

To add additional handouts, repeat Steps 1–3.

To end a meeting you've been chairing, choose Meeting → Exit from the main Windows Meeting Space toolbar.

Meeting attendees can leave a meeting by choosing Meeting → Leave Meeting from the same main menu.

Information Kiosk

When you exit a meeting that includes handouts, you are prompted with a dialog box asking whether you want to save changes to these files. Choose Yes to save a copy of the collaborative document to your PC.

If you choose No, the edits made to the handout during the meeting are lost because changes made as a group do not automatically show up in the original file stored on your computer.

Networking with Windows Vista

Not so long ago, networking was the arcane domain of computer science professionals and technology enthusiasts. An interface with operators was referred to as a *terminal*, and the server that managed it all was a huge mainframe computer buried deep in an air-conditioned clean room. Such systems were dedicated to the needs of the organizations that owned them and had little or no connectivity to the world outside their own walls. One company's system was generally incompatible with any other company's system performing the same type of task. And for networking beyond the confines of a single location, where the mainframe directly connected to the terminals, long distance networking generally required dedicated telephone lines or microwave transmitters and receivers.

Things became a little less arcane with the advent of minicomputers, which allowed more diversity within a company where some machines could handle terminals dedicated to one task or group and others could manage other projects with a degree of interconnectivity. But the terminal was still merely the window, and the portal to the computer still hidden away in its air-conditioned chamber. It wasn't until the Internet arrived in the late 1960s that the market for personal computers expanded, thus retiring the need for older terminals. The outdated terminals were replaced with new terminals that later became known as personal computers. Anyone with a modem-equipped PC and a phone line could link to any computer in the world, upload and download information, carry on conversations, send messages, and so on. A global network accessible to anyone was now in place. Many ISPs appeared, their purpose being to provide the connection points through which individual computers could reach other computers without the need to know the exact address of the other computer. The rise of such commercial/consumer networks as The Source, CompuServe, Delphi, Mindspring, America Online (AOL), and more, each with its own proprietary software, brought global networking to the masses.

But setting up a LAN that connected computers in a specific location or a wide area network (WAN) to connect to other computers or even networks outside the walls remained the province of the professionals and specialists. Over time, many users have learned the ins and outs of setting up a complex networking environment. However, Windows Vista now makes setting up an in-house network (which links several computers together under one networking system), as well as an Internet network connection, a simple and easy-to-understand process.

Setting up a network connection

You can run Vista without a network connection, but if you have a network card installed on your computer, Windows Vista automatically looks for available networks and pops up an icon in the taskbar that shows the state of your connection, if there is one. The networking icon — which looks like two small computer screens — tells you whether the connection is to a local network or (if the icon contains a globe) whether it is an Internet connection. If no network connections are enabled, the icon shows that, too (with a red X).

Information Kiosk

The purpose of an Internet connection is to do exactly what its name suggests: namely, to provide the user with a direct connection to the Internet. This can be achieved by several different methods. The oldest method, which is slowly being replaced by other (quicker) methods, is the dialup connection that runs through a phone line. Other (faster) methods include DSL, wireless, or cable modem connections.

The purpose of a LAN is to connect computers in a small area, whether within a home, an office, or a group of buildings. LANs are used most often because they can focus on a personalized location, have higher transmission ratings (a feature that is directly related to the smaller area of the network), and do not require leased telephone communication lines.

You may have both an Internet and a LAN connection installed on your computer at the same time.

You can also use a WLAN to access a local network or Internet connection. The functionality of this type of network is the same as a traditional connection. The only difference is that you are able to access the network through wireless (airborne) transmissions instead of a grounded landline.

To determine what type of connection you have, click the Network icon in the Notification area of the taskbar. A thumbnail window opens that describes the state of the connection and offers the options to connect to (or disconnect from) a network or to open the Network and Sharing Center. If this thumbnail window does not already indicate that you are connected to a network, click the Connect or Disconnect link. This opens a window that allows you to set up your own network connection. If you do already have an established network connection, click the Networking and Sharing Center option to view the details and sharing settings for your computer.

Clicking the Connect or Disconnect link opens the Connect to a Network window shown in Figure 7-47.

Figure 7-47: Viewing available connections.

This screen includes a listing of all the available networks in your area. Use the Connect (or Disconnect) button at the bottom right of this window to change your current network connection.

If you do not already have a network connection or if you wish to create a new one, click the Set Up a Connection or Network link located in the lower left of this screen. This opens the Choose a Connection Option window, as shown in Figure 7-48.

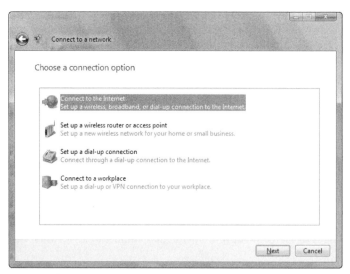

Figure 7-48: Choosing a network connection option.

This screen offers several different connection choices. For example, you can choose to set up a new Internet connection, wireless (or access point) connection, or dialup connection; or you can choose to connect to a workplace network from this screen.

- If you want to be able to connect to the Internet, choose the first (Connect to the Internet) option.

- If you want to be able to access your network without having to be physically connected to a phone line, DSL, or cable modem, choose the wireless option. (*Note:* Make sure that your PC is capable of a wireless connection — meaning that it has a wireless card installed — before selecting this option.)

- If you do not have a wireless card for your PC (or laptop) or if you do not have another connection mode — like DSL or a cable modem — choose a dialup connection. To access this network, your PC must be connected to an active phone line.

- If you wish to connect to a workplace network (either via a wireless or physical landline), choose the workplace option.

Here are instructions for how to create a new Internet connection and a computer-to-computer network.

To create a new Internet connection

1. **Click the networking icon located in the Windows taskbar.**

This dual-computer icon opens a small thumbnail image of your current network connection, if you have one.

2. **Click the Connect or Disconnect link from the thumbnail image that appears.**

This opens the Connect to a Network window. (Refer to Figure 7-47).

3. **Click the Set Up a Connection or Network link located in the lower-left corner of this screen.**

This opens the Choose a Connection Option window. (Refer to Figure 7-48.)

4. **Select the Connect to the Internet option and then click Next.**

If you are already connected to the Internet, you are prompted with a window that informs you of this fact. Choose to Set Up a New Connection anyway to proceed.

The next window that opens is the one shown in Figure 7-49.

5. **Select the method you would like to use to connect to the Internet.**

If you choose the wireless method, you are returned to the Connect to a Network window (refer to Figure 7-47) where you can choose a new network to connect to.

If you choose either the broadband or dialup connection, you are taken to a new screen asking you to provide information about your ISP.

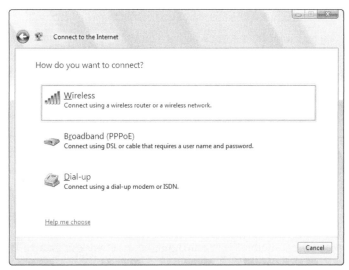

Figure 7-49: Choosing your connection options.

6. **Provide the requested information and then click Connect.**

If you do not have all the information required to complete this screen, contact your ISP provider.

To set up a computer-to-computer network in your home or small office

1. **Click the networking icon located in the Windows taskbar.**

This dual-computer icon opens a small thumbnail image of your current network connection, if you have one.

2. **Click the Connect or Disconnect link from the thumbnail image that appears.**

This opens the Connect to a Network window.

3. **Click the Set Up a Connection or Network link located in the lower-left corner of this screen.**

This opens the Choose a Connection Option window.

4. **Select the Set Up a Wireless Router or Access Point option and then click Next.**

The welcome screen for this wizard appears.

5. **Click the What Do I Need to Set Up a Network? link to determine what hardware is required to create a multicomputer network.**

6. **Click Next.**

A dialog box appears asking whether you want to make your network a private or public system.

7. **Select the No, Make the Network I'm Connected to a Private Network option.**

This ensures that others nearby cannot access the information stored on your new network.

After you make your selection, Vista searches for the necessary hardware. When it's finished, you are prompted by the window shown in Figure 7-50. This screen lets you know that the appropriate hardware has been detected but that it now needs to be configured.

8. **Choose a configuration method.**

The most direct method is to configure your network manually. However, this requires a server user ID and password. If you do not have this information or simply wish to create your network in a manner that allows you to save (and transfer) it to other machines via a USB Flash drive, select the second option — Create Wireless Network Settings and Save to USB Flash Drive.

Assuming that you opt to use the wireless USB method, you are prompted with a new window asking you to give the network a name.

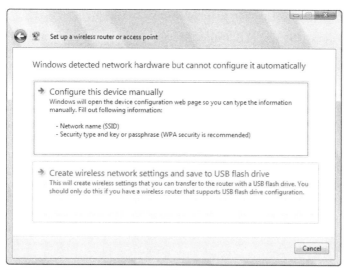

Figure 7-50: Choosing how you would like to configure your network.

9. **Enter a name for your network and then click Next.**

This opens a new window asking you to create a passphrase (or password) for your network. (See Figure 7-51.) This is yet another security measure instilled by Vista to help prevent unwanted visitors from gaining access to your private network.

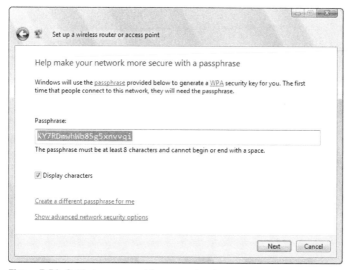

Figure 7-51: Setting a password for your network.

10. **Enter a passphrase for your network and then click Next.**

This opens the File and Printer Sharing page. From this window, you can choose to allow anyone with a valid user ID and password to access the files and printer saved to this computer, or you can choose to share the files and printer for this PC with anyone in your network. You can also opt not to share these items with anyone else.

11. **Select the sharing profile that best suits your needs and then click Next.**

The USB Flash drive window appears, as shown in Figure 7-52.

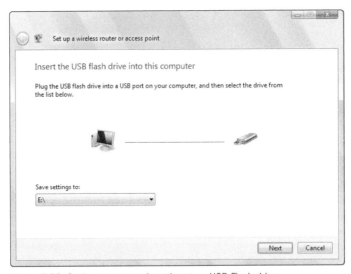

Figure 7-52: Saving your network settings to a USB Flash drive.

12. **Use the drop-down menu provided to select the correct drive for your USB connection and then click Next.**

After these files are saved to the USB Flash drive, you are shown the window pictured in Figure 7-53.

This window explains how to use the USB device to connect other computers (or devices) to your newly created network. Simply insert the USB drive into all other machines in your prospective network to transfer the necessary settings.

13. **Click Close.**

This allows you to exit the Network Setup Wizard.

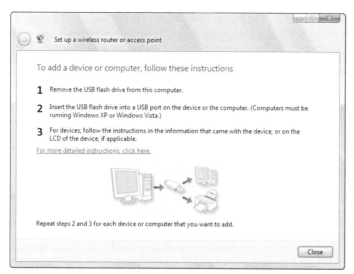

Figure 7-53: Using a USB Flash drive to access your network with other computers or printers.

Viewing networking connections

To examine the details of a network, click the Networking icon located on the Windows taskbar. Clicking this item brings up a thumbnail image of your current network connection. Select the link for the Network and Sharing Center. (See Figure 7-54.)

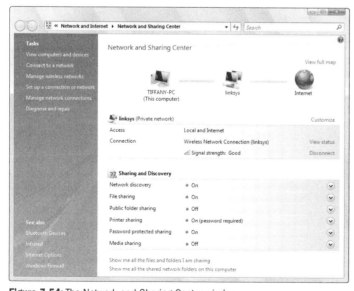

Figure 7-54: The Network and Sharing Center window.

The Network and Sharing Center window is essentially the control center for all your networking needs. The left pane shows the tasks that can be accomplished through this center, and the right pane shows the actual connections and various options for sharing files, printers, and media as well as for finding other devices on the network.

From this window, you can view and make changes to your file, printer, and other network settings. To make adjustment to these items, simply click the drop-down menu buttons located to the right of each option. Doing so reveals the details for that particular option. Select the radio button for the option you would like to enable and then click Apply.

Information Kiosk

You can also access the Network and Sharing Center through the Control Panel. Select the Network and Internet option from the Control Panel to locate the Networking and Sharing Center.

You can also monitor the various computers on your local network by using the Network feature available via the Start menu. The window that appears when you select this item (see Figure 7-55) shows all the computers in your network.

Figure 7-55: Window displaying all computers in a given network.

Click any of the computer icons listed to see what is located on that computer.

If the network is set for sharing, you can open any of the contents stored on this particular PC as if it were an extension of the computer you are working from.

local area network (LAN): Small geographical area used to create personalized networks. These networks can also be created wirelessly; wireless LANs are also know as WLANs.

newsreader: Program specifically designed to display and facilitate activity in Internet newsgroups.

NNTP (Network News Transfer Protocol): The name of the server protocol used for Internet newsgroups.

POP servers: Servers whose dedicated function is to provide incoming e-mail.

SMTP (Simple Mail Transfer Protocol): The mail server for your ISP. It delivers mail to you, which is then filtered through your designated e-mail program.

Usenet: The universally accessible, bulletin board-like series of discussion forums on the Internet, accessible via either dedicated Web sites or dedicated news-reader programs.

wide area network (WAN): Large geographical area used to connect smaller local networks. These types of networks are often used by large corporations or ISPs. The Internet is an example of a WAN.

Windows Meeting Space: The new name for what had been previously known as Net Meeting. A peer-to-peer collaborative meeting tool over the Internet. It comes bundled with Windows Vista.

Practice Exam

1. What are newsgroups, and how do you find/use them?

_____

_____

_____

2. What's the difference between a shared document and a handout in Windows Meeting Space?

_____

_____

_____

3. When you're collaborating on a document that is on your machine in Windows Meeting Space, how do you distribute copies of that file to other participants?

_____

_____

_____

4. If another participant in the Windows Meeting Space doesn't have the application that you are using during the meeting, can they still edit it with you? If so, how?

_____

_____

_____

5. If you have been using Eudora e-mail and wish to import your mail into Windows Mail, what must you do first?

_____

_____

_____

6. If you have a wireless card installed on your laptop, what is the fastest way to connect to a network?

_____

_____

_____

7. If you have a wireless card but no Internet connection, where do you go to set one up?

_____

_____

_____

8. If your scanner already came with software, why might you still want to use Windows Vista's Fax and Scanner software?

_____

_____

_____

9. What is the purpose of the People Near Me application?

_____

_____

_____

10. Name two different ways you can send scanned images to others.

_____

_____

_____

11. Describe how to use rules in Windows Mail and explain why you might want to use this feature.

_____

_____

_____

12. How do you send a Windows Meeting Space invitation? How do you begin a new Windows Meeting Space meeting?

_____

_____

_____

13. How do you set up a LAN? How do you set up an Internet connection?

_____

_____

_____

14. How do you know if you're already connected to the Internet or another local network?

_____

_____

_____

Adding (And Removing) Additional Programs and Devices with Vista

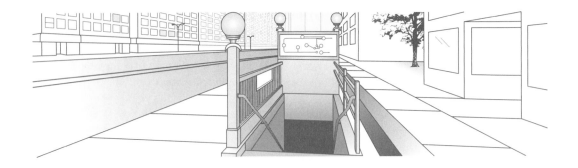

 # Enter the Station

Questions

1. How do you determine whether you have driver files for your devices in Windows Vista?

2. What are your options if devices or programs are not compatible with Windows Vista?

3. What happens when you install a device without the software that came with it?

4. How can you uninstall programs you no longer use?

5. How can you remove outdated devices from you computer?

Express Line

If you are already up on the basics of adding (and removing) programs and devices using Windows Vista, skip ahead to the next chapter.

In the days of DOS (Disk Operating System), you loaded and ran programs and applications independently of one another. Multitasking was minimal. If you tried to load two or more applications at one time, your computer usually crashed. Indeed, your application generally resided on an off-site cassette tape or a floppy disk — the big 5¼-inch kind — and had to be freshly loaded into the computer whenever you wanted to run it. Linking programs and running them simultaneously so that they could exchange data or run on the same data was simply not possible. Many, many advances in PC technology would be required before we arrived at the present, superfast multitasking environment.

Hardware and software have come a long way. The big floppy disk is a relic, and most new computers today do not even come with a drive for the smaller 3¼-inch floppy. The 650MB-capacity CD is giving way to the 4.7GB DVD-ROM. A gigabyte or more of RAM is routine, and hard drives of 80GB and more are the norm.

The World of DOS

DOS-era software was largely independent of the operating system, which, as its name implies, was largely concerned with internal housekeeping and traffic management. DOS generally kept out of the way of the programs running under its supervision. Early versions of Windows were in fact DOS-based. When you ran a third-party application, a temporary DOS-layer was placed on top of the housekeeping OS, which managed the traffic and enabled several applications to run at once. Windows and DOS would interact with each other when needed and keep out of each other's way at other times. In other words, multitasking had arrived.

Later Windows versions reduced the connection to DOS — although you could still call up DOS commands from under the Windows operating system — and increased the Windows operating system's integration with the programs running in the computer. Now, applications are *installed* — meaning that they reside permanently on a hard drive rather than being temporarily loaded into memory from some external drive. Instead of running self-contained from a single directory, Windows applications install bits and pieces of themselves in many places on the computer's hard drive, including in the Windows System directories, directories shared with other programs, and even the home directories of other programs if there is a degree of integration wanted or required. The Registry keeps track of all these bits and pieces, ensuring that each part does its job without getting in the way of other applications.

Transfer

Flip to Chapter 11 to learn about the Windows Registry.

Not surprisingly, where software developers might once have built programs that ran on their own with little regard for the operating system or other programs, the increasing sophistication and complexity of today's operating systems requires developers to pay more attention to how their programs interact with the OS and with other applications. The programs that could not keep up have died out. Of course, these requirements apply to hardware devices, too, such as printers and graphics adapters, whose drivers have to be written and rewritten to ensure that the device operates normally in any OS environment.

Ensuring Program Compatibility with Windows Vista

From the earliest versions of Windows through Windows XP, vendors have had to constantly update applications and hardware to ensure smooth running on the latest Windows version as well as backward-compatibility with earlier versions. Microsoft and vendors work closely together during this process. Microsoft has even devised a seal of approval that certifies to the computer user that a device or program can run under Windows and does not damage the system. Still, some programs run better than others, as do some hardware devices, and some do not run at all in one configuration or another. Indeed, some of Microsoft's own programs are not compatible with one another in that files generated by an earlier version might not be readable in a later version.

Because Windows Vista at its very core represents a significant departure from previous Windows versions, one would expect a greater degree of incompatibility with existing programs and devices. Recognizing that, Microsoft developed two programs that check your existing system — both hardware devices and programs — for compatibility with Windows Vista.

Using the Windows Vista Upgrade Advisor

In Chapter 1, you learned about the Windows Vista Upgrade Advisor. This program scans your entire system and tells you what works with Vista and what does not. More importantly, it tells you what level of Windows Vista your current system can support and what you need to do to support a higher level.

Here is the basic report from the Upgrade Advisor after scanning a system. (See Figure 8-1.)

The primary purpose of the Upgrade Advisor summary report is to tell you which version of Vista your computer is capable of running. This assessment is based on your PC's existing system requirements (that is, your available memory, processor speed, and graphics card capacities). Scrolling a little farther down this report, you see the system requirements details as well as sections devoted to devices and programs. These last two sections let you know whether you can expect to encounter any problems with these items while running Vista on your computer. (See Figure 8-2.)

Figure 8-1: The Windows Upgrade Advisor report (upper half).

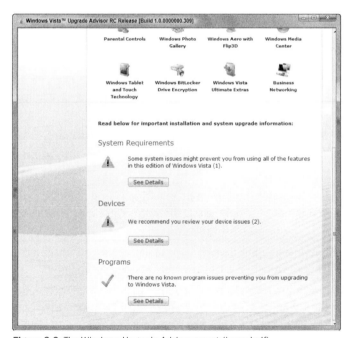

Figure 8-2: The Windows Upgrade Advisor report (lower half).

As Figure 8-2 makes clear, this particular machine has the devices needed to run Windows Vista Ultimate and has no program problems, but does suggest that some system and device issues need to be addressed.

Using Vista's Program Compatibility Wizard

The other application included with Windows Vista is the Program Compatibility Wizard, which allows you to adjust how Vista interacts with programs that might not yet work properly with Microsoft's latest operating system. When you use the Program Compatibility Wizard, you can change the display settings for these programs so that they function normally on a Vista PC. Being able to manually select a program's settings makes it possible to use programs that might otherwise be incompatible with a Vista-operated machine.

Because of the vast amount of changes made to the Windows Vista OS, Microsoft has taken the initiative to install a shortcut icon for the Program Compatibility Wizard directly on the desktop. However, if the Program Compatibility Wizard icon does not automatically appear on your Vista desktop, you can look for it by launching Help (press the F1 key) and typing `Program Compatibility Wizard` in the search field.

If you encounter any problems using the programs already installed on your PC, you can use this compatibility tool to correct the problem so that you may use the programs as you did prior to installing Vista.

To use the Windows Vista Program Compatibility Wizard

1. Double-click the Program Compatibility icon located on your desktop.

This starts the Program Compatibility Wizard. The Welcome screen for this tool opens, as shown in Figure 8-3.

2. Click Next.

This opens a screen asking you to identify where the program in question is located. (See Figure 8-4.)

You can choose to locate this program by selecting it from a list of existing programs on your computer or from the CD drive; or, you can choose to search for it manually.

If the program in question has already been installed on your machine, choose the I Want to Choose from a List of Programs option.

If you are running a program from a CD, rather than from your computer's hard drive, choose the I Want to Use the Program in the CD-ROM Drive option.

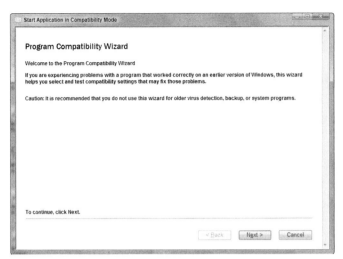

Figure 8-3: The Program Compatibility Wizard.

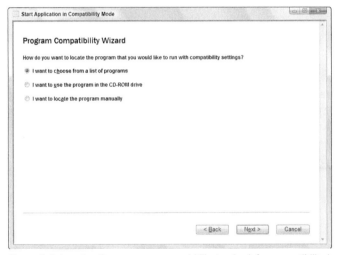

Figure 8-4: Locating the program you would like to check for compatibility issues.

If the program you are looking for is not included in the list provided by the first option and you are not running it from a CD, choose the last option (I Want to Locate the Program Manually) to search for the program on your computer.

3. Make your selection and then click Next.

4. Assuming that you have already installed the program on your machine and have chosen to select the program from a list provided by Vista, you are greeted with the following page (see Figure 8-5).

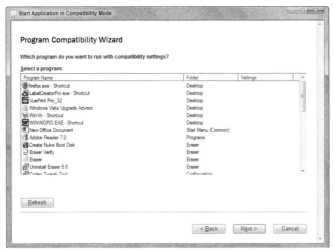

Figure 8-5: Choosing the program you need to run with compatibility settings.

5. Select the program you wish to check and then click Next.

Clicking Next opens a new window (see Figure 8-6). This screen asks you to identify the last known version of Windows capable of running the program properly.

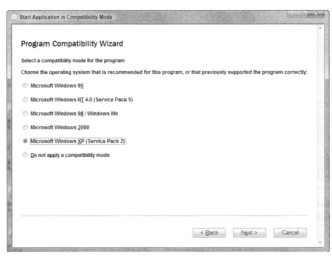

Figure 8-6: Identifying the operating system that previously supported the program.

6. **Select the appropriate Windows version and then click Next.**

Note: If you want to check the program's compatibility with Vista, select the Do Not Apply a Compatibility Mode option. This runs the program using the standard Vista settings.

Clicking Next opens the display settings window. (See Figure 8-7.) This screen allows you to choose the settings — including color, screen resolution, visual themes, desktop composition, and dpi (dots per inch) settings — applied when running the program using Vista.

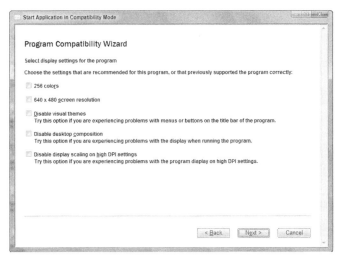

Figure 8-7: Selecting program display settings.

7. **Place check marks next to the options you would like to enable and then click Next.**

For example, if you are experiencing color or resolution problems, try adjusting these settings. If you are having trouble viewing the visual themes for your program, place a check mark in the box next to this option. And if you are having difficulties with the program's composition or dpi settings, you may disable these features as well.

However, keep in mind that you do not have to choose any of these options. In fact, if this is the first time you've used the program with Vista, you can opt to leave these options blank; this runs the programs with Vista's standard settings, which allows you to determine whether this program works properly with Vista.

Clicking Next opens a new window. (See Figure 8-8.) This screen asks whether the application requires *Administrator privileges,* meaning that it is a program that can be run only by a user who is set up as an *Administrator* (someone that has the authority to make changes to the computer's settings, programs, and so on).

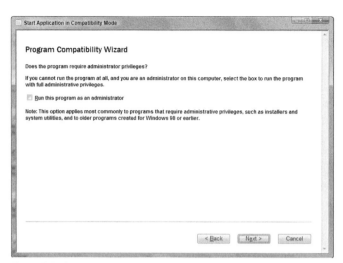

Figure 8-8: Stating whether Administrator privileges are required.

8. **Identify whether the program in question requires Administrator privileges and then click Next.**

If this program does require Administrator privileges, place a check mark in the check box provided. If the program does not require Administrator privileges, leave the check box empty.

Clicking Next takes you to a summary page, which outlines the display setting you chose in the previous screens. In this example I want Vista to mimic the settings from Windows XP, Service Pack 2, the last system to have successfully run the program in question. (See Figure 8-9).

Figure 8-9: Previewing your program's display settings.

9. **Review the display settings outlined on this screen and then click Next.**

This opens the program using the settings selected earlier.

10. **Check the functionality of the program. When you are finished, close the program.**

This returns you to the Program Compatibility Wizard. (See Figure 8-10.) This screen allows you to make further adjustments to the program's display settings or to save these settings so that the program runs in this mode each time you open it on your Vista PC.

Figure 8-10: Establishing display standards for your program.

11. **Make your selection and then click Next.**

If your program ran properly using these settings, select the Yes, Set This Program to Always Use These Compatibility Settings option. This ensures that this particular program runs correctly on your Vista machine each time you use it.

If you noticed some problems that still need to be tended to, select the No, Try Different Compatibility Settings option. This returns you to the Program Compatibility Wizard, where you can make additional changes to the program's display settings. Repeat Steps 5–11 until the desired results are achieved.

And lastly, if no special adjustments are required to run the program properly with Vista, choose the last option (No, I Am Finished Trying Compatibility Settings).

12. **Choosing the first or third option above takes you to the screen shown in Figure 8-11. This page asks whether you would like to send the program compatibility data to Microsoft. Make your selection and then click Next.**

Figure 8-11: Sending program compatibility data to Microsoft.

Choosing Yes sends the temporary files created with the Program Compatibility Wizard to Microsoft. Choosing No does not send this information to Microsoft.

Clicking Next opens the final window in the Program Compatibility Wizard. (See Figure 8-12.)

Figure 8-12: Completing the Program Compatibility Wizard.

13. **Click Finish.**

This closes the Program Compatibility Wizard.

If adjusting a program's display settings does not correct the problem, you might need to seek additional help online. If you do encounter a compatibility problem, you are presented with a screen similar to the one shown in Figure 8-13.

As you can see, this page includes a Check for Solutions Online button. Clicking this button takes you to a Web site (one provided by the program's vendor, Microsoft, or an interested third party) where you can find a solution to correct the problem. This might involve downloading a new version of the application's software or perhaps a new driver. Follow the suggestions provided to correct the program compatibility error or to contact the company that created the program to determine whether there is a way you can use this product with Windows Vista.

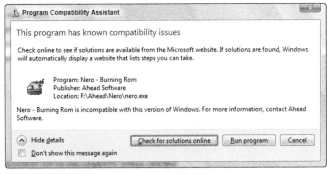

Figure 8-13: A failed program compatibility test.

Information Kiosk

Part of the problem with backward compatibility actually lies in Microsoft's drive to increase the security of Windows Vista. The essential component of the heightened security is walling off the *kernel* (central core) of Vista so that no outsiders can access it. That keeps out hackers and vandals. However, this tack also keeps out developers, whose earlier versions might have required access to the kernel.

Successfully Installing Peripheral Devices

In earlier versions of Windows, you needed to attach your peripheral devices to your PC before booting up your machine. If you didn't, your machine simply couldn't find them. It was not until Windows 95 that the plug-and-play method came along to simplify things. The original purpose of the Plug and Play feature was to permit users to add new devices to their computer without having to manually change the machine's configurations. The Windows Plug and Play feature automatically instructs the operating system to work behind the scenes to identify the new device being attached to the computer. In other words, plug-and-play capabilities are what allow you to add devices to your PC after it has been turned on.

Windows Vista continues the Windows 95 tradition; it does not matter at all if your Vista system is up and running when you attach a device. Vista usually recognizes right away that you have connected a new device and immediately looks to install it and find the right driver for it. More often than not, this occurs without a problem. This, of course, cannot be the scenario 100 percent of the time. When you first connect the device, you usually see the following notification (see Figure 8-14).

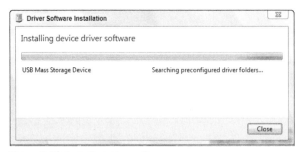

Figure 8-14: Installing driver software.

Most of the time, when the process is finished, you receive a message that reads `The device has been successfully installed.`

Not all devices install successfully. In the event of unsuccessful installation, you see the window shown in Figure 8-15.

Transfer

The Windows Update feature can provide you with a large number of additional drivers. For more on Windows Update, see Chapter 11.

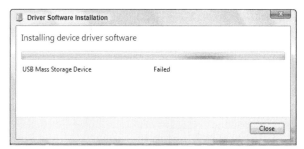

Figure 8-15: A failed driver software installation.

In order to troubleshoot a failed device installation, you need to call up the Device Manager to find, install, or reinstall a driver for the device.

Here's how the troubleshooting process is carried out:

1. **Click the Start button and choose Control Panel from the menu that appears.**

   The Control Panel window opens, as shown in Figure 8-16.

Figure 8-16: The Control Panel.

2. **In the Control Panel window, choose Hardware and Sound.**

   This opens the Hardware and Sound menu. (See Figure 8-17.)

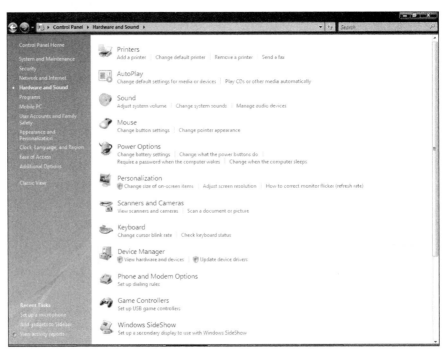

Figure 8-17: The Hardware and Sound window.

3. Choose Device Manager.

This opens the Device Manager. (See Figure 8-18.)

Figure 8-18: The Device Manager.

4. **Click the plus sign (+) next to the category of the nonfunctioning device.**

Doing so reveals the components contained within this category.

5. **Right-click the device that is not working properly.**

The nonfunctioning device can be identified by a yellow alert tag hovering over its icon.

6. **From the drop-down menu that appears, choose Properties.**

This opens the device's Properties window.

7. **Select the Driver tab and click the Update Driver button provided. (See Figure 8-19.)**

Update Driver button

Figure 8-19: The Details tab of a nonfunctioning device.

The following window appears. (See Figure 8-20.)

8. **Select the Search Automatically for Updated Driver Software option.**

Windows searches your computer and the Internet for necessary updates.

Note: If you have a software CD for the device, you should insert it into your computer's disc drive at this time. Or, if you think the software is likely to be located somewhere on your machine, you can select the Browse My Computer for Driver Software option to locate the appropriate driver software.

If no driver software updates can be located, you must contact the product's manufacturer to obtain the necessary driver software. (This information can usually be found on the manufacturer's Web site.)

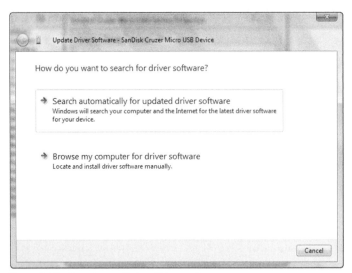

Figure 8-20: Choosing an Update Driver option.

9. After you update the driver for the malfunctioning device, you can begin using this device at your leisure.

Information Kiosk

Whenever possible, be connected to the Internet when attaching a new device so that if the operating system does not have the appropriate driver for it, you can take the option that Vista presents of looking online for the needed driver.

Watch Your Step

Most devices that you install come with their own proprietary software on a CD (or sometimes available for download from the Internet). When you do choose to install a device, have that software ready — and then when prompted, insert the CD. Here's what you need to watch out for: With many devices, as soon as you connect them to your machine, Vista immediately installs the appropriate driver. The device functions, but you might discover later that many of the options associated with the device (for printers and scanners, for example) might not be available to you. In the example of printers and scanners in particular, such devices often have control panels that monitor the printing and scanning process, as well as options associated with ink colors and paper size (printers) and file types (scanners). In order to have access to all that functionality, you need to manually install all the software that came with the device rather than letting Vista install just the necessary drivers.

Removing Inactive Programs and Devices

Removing programs or devices that you no longer need is a quick and easy process. If you have a number of old, outdated, or simply unused programs or devices on your computer, you can easily remove (or uninstall) these items from your machine. A detailed list of instructions for removing programs and devices follows.

Information Kiosk

Remove any inactive programs or devices to free more space on your hard drive for new programs and devices.

To remove an unwanted (or unused) program

1. **Open the Start menu and choose Control Panel.**

The Control Panel appears, as shown in Figure 8-21.

Figure 8-21: The Control Panel window.

2. **Click the Uninstall a Program link.**

This link can be found in the Programs section of the Control Panel. Clicking this link brings up a list of programs that are installed on your machine. (See Figure 8-22.)

3. **Select the program you would like to remove.**

The program is highlighted in blue, and a new Uninstall button appears on the toolbar just above the list of installed programs.

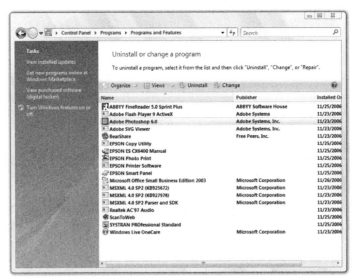

Figure 8-22: Viewing the installed programs for your PC.

4. **Click the Uninstall button.**

You are prompted with a dialog box asking whether you are sure you want to uninstall the selected program. (See Figure 8-23.)

Figure 8-23: Confirm that you want to uninstall a program.

5. **Click Yes.**

The program and its related execution files are removed from your computer.

6. **Close the Programs and Features window — refer to Figure 8-22 — by clicking the X in the upper-right corner of this screen.**

To remove an unwanted (or unused) device

1. **Open the Start menu and choose Control Panel from the list of items that appears in the right column.**

The Control Panel window opens. (Refer to Figure 8-21.)

2. **In the Control Panel window, choose Hardware and Sound.**

This opens the Hardware and Sound menu. (See Figure 8-24.)

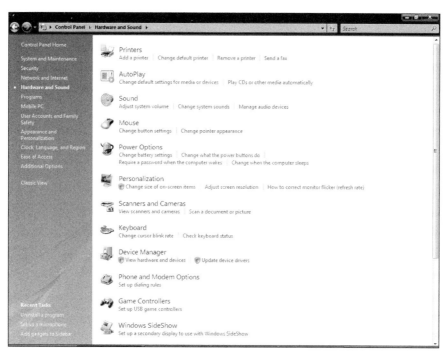

Figure 8-24: The Hardware and Sound menu.

3. Choose Device Manager.

This opens the Device Manager pictured in Figure 8-25.

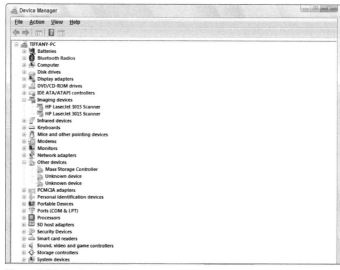

Figure 8-25: The Device Manager.

4. Click the plus sign (+) next to the category for the device you want to remove.

Doing so reveals the components contained within this category.

5. Right-click the device you wish to remove.

A drop-down menu appears.

6. From the drop-down menu that appears, choose Uninstall.

You are prompted with a dialog box warning you that you are about to uninstall the selected device. (See Figure 8-26.)

Figure 8-26: Confirm that you wish to uninstall the selected device.

7. Click OK.

The selected device is removed from your computer.

8. Close the Device Manager window by clicking the X in the upper-right corner of the screen.

You are returned to the Hardware and Sound menu.

9. Close the Hardware and Sound window by clicking the X in the upper-right corner of that screen.

Device Manager: The feature used to access and manage peripheral devices for your PC.

dpi (dots per inch): The number of dots present in each inch of your computer screen. The larger the dpi setting, the greater the number of dots and, thus, the better the screen resolution.

 *continued*

driver: Software that allows your computer to interact with its installed devices.

Plug and Play: The Windows capability that allows your PC to recognize a new device without requiring a system reboot first.

Program Compatibility Wizard: The tool used to check whether a program can run properly using the standard Vista display settings.

PS/2: A type of connector for a keyboard or mouse to a PC. (PS/2 stands for *Personal System/2*, which originated with IBM.)

USB: *Universal Serial Bus* refers to standardized connectors used to connect certain peripheral devices to personal computers.

Last
Stop

Practice Exam

1. Is it necessary to have your peripheral device connected before booting up your machine?

_____

_____

_____

2. Assume that you connected a new printer to your PC. Vista recognizes and installs it and looks for its driver, but you want to print a color document in black and white, and you can't find this option. How might you remedy this?

_____

_____

_____

3. If you install the wrong driver for a device and it does not work, where would you look to fix it?

_____

_____

_____

4. If a device functioned under your previously installed operating system but now it doesn't, what should you do?

_____

_____

_____

5. Where is the Device Manager found? What is its purpose?

_____

_____

_____

6. Name two Vista compatibility tools. What is the purpose of each?

_____

_____

_____

7. Can anyone with access to your computer remove (or uninstall) programs or devices?

_____

_____

_____

8. You connected a Windows XP scanner to your Vista machine. The manufacturer has not yet produced of Vista-capable driver for that model. What can you do to resolve this issue?

_____

_____

_____

9. The manufacturer of a device you bought and attached to your computer has gone out of business. You don't have the driver, and you can't find it with Vista. What is one source you should always check?

_____

_____

_____

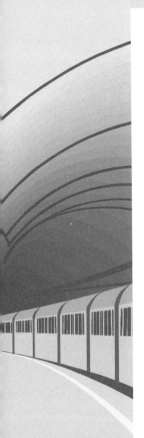

10. **The firewall program you always used under an earlier version of Windows is incompatible with Windows Vista. You need a firewall as soon as possible. What is your best option?**

_____

_____

_____

11. **Where do you go to remove devices from your PC?**

_____

_____

_____

12. **How do you uninstall programs?**

_____

_____

_____

Working with Digital Media

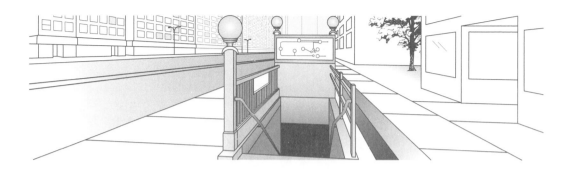

 # Enter the Station

Questions

1. What's new in Windows Media Player 11?

2. What types of files can be burned to a CD or DVD?

3. How can you create backup copies of your favorite audio, video, and digital image files?

4. What is the best way to find (and manage) your media files?

5. How does Windows Photo Gallery help you organize your digital photos?

6. What types of edits can you make to your digital images?

7. How can the Games Explorer help you discover more information about the types of games available on your Vista PC?

8. What new features and capabilities are included in Windows Media Center?

 Express Line

If you are already up on how to use and manage digital media in Windows Vista, skip ahead to the next chapter.

Multimedia, per se, is nothing new in the age of computers, but Windows Vista does bring some new things to multimedia, including better ways to organize, display, search for, and find photos and images. It brings very high-powered video — thanks to the new standards of WPF (Windows Presentation Foundation), which brings not only Aero effects but also a new video driver subsystem. The overall quality of sound in Vista is higher than in previous versions of Windows because of reengineered audio architecture as well as much more control at the user level. Finally, Vista brings a better media player, capable of handling a wider variety of video types with more controls and settings available at your fingertips.

In this chapter, you learn what's new in Windows Media Player 11, and how to rip CDs, sync your files with other media devices, locate and organize your digital photos, create CD/DVD backups of your media and data files, navigate Windows Photo Gallery, edit digital images, use the Games Explorer window, and work with Windows Media Center.

Introducing Windows Media Player 11

Media Player 11 represents a major step forward when it comes to playing your favorite media (including CDs and DVDs) as well as a wide gamut of audio and video files. It is far better at recognizing most audio and video formats than previous versions of Media Player — often, all it takes is selecting a file or inserting a disc — and it is also better at saving third-party media files to your computer and syncing your media devices (such as an MP3 player or other portable device) with the files you have stored on your PC. In this section, you find out how to play your files as well as set up playing preferences. And by the time you finish this chapter, you might very well be an expert at ripping and burning CDs as well.

You can access Media Player 11 (as with any application) by either doing an Instant Search (for Windows Media Player) or by clicking the Start button and choosing All Programs ➜ Windows Media Player from the menu that appears. Keep in mind that when you choose to play a video or an audio selection or when you insert a commercially produced CD or DVD, Windows Media Player is automatically launched.

Working with Media Player commands

Taking a look at the Windows Media Player 11 menu bar (see Figure 9-1) from left to right, you see a list of several different functions you can perform with this application. Here is a brief explanation of each of these menu items:

Now Playing: Selecting this option opens a screen that displays the current audio playlist or individual scenes from a video DVD. You can use this page to jump from one song (or scene) to another.

Library: This includes a list of all your audio, video, and digital photo files. You can use this feature to locate the files you wish to listen to, view, or save to a CD or DVD.

Rip: This option allows you to copy audio tracks to your computer from existing discs.

Burn: This is the process that actually saves your audio, video, photo, or data files to a CD or DVD.

Sync: This feature automatically syncs your portable audio or storage devices with the files on your computer.

URGE: This option provides a link to Microsoft's online music store. From the URGE Web site, you can purchase individual songs or entire albums by various artists.

Sign In: Use this button to access and sign in to the URGE Web site.

The controls beneath the main screen are the stalwart buttons you'll probably recognize from other playing devices. However, the first button (the Shuffle button) might be new to you. Clicking this button instructs the Windows Media Player to play random tracks from the media source rather than playing them in the order listed in the right panel. The button for this feature is a toggle; click it on or off to shuffle the order of the selections played.

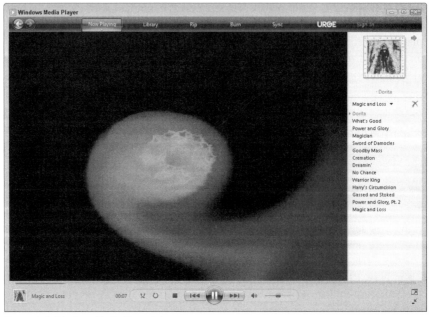

Figure 9-1: Windows Media Player 11.

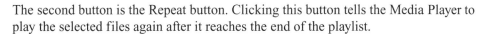

The second button is the Repeat button. Clicking this button tells the Media Player to play the selected files again after it reaches the end of the playlist.

The next four buttons are Stop, Previous, Play, and Next. These navigational tools allow you to stop, rewind, play/pause, and fast-forward (respectively) when watching movies or listening to audio tracks.

The next button to the right, which looks like a small speaker icon, is Mute. To mute the audio for your media, click this button. A small red circle with a line through it appears to indicate that the sound has been muted. Click it again to toggle the Mute feature off.

You can also use the volume bar (located to the right of the Mute button) to manually adjust the volume for your audio files. Click the circle and drag your mouse to the left or right to adjust the sound; moving your mouse to the left lowers the volume, and moving it to the right increases the volume.

Now Playing

If you select the Now Playing option, you see a list of tracks appear in a right panel of the Windows Media Player window. These tracks can be audio tracks (say, you're listening to music from a CD), or they can be individual scene tracks from a movie. If you are playing audio selections, Media Player 11 lists those tracks. If it is a video CD (VCD) or a DVD, it lists all the scene tracks it finds. If you have multiple media files on one disc — formats including AVI and MPG, and others — it not only lists those tracks but often also reads the titles of those different files and lists them as well. Simply select the track or title you want, and it plays automatically.

Perusing the Library

The Windows Media Player Library is where you go to access your audio, video, or photo files. The list of items to the left of this screen provides a number of different ways to locate your media files. You can find an item by using the Playlists or Library subcategories.

From the Playlists section, you can choose to locate your files by calling up recently viewed items. Simply click the appropriate category (Recent Music, Recent Pictures and Video, Recently Changed, or Shared By Me) to locate the files you desire. A list of all the items that belong to this category appears in the main section of the Media Player window. Double-click a single item (or song) to open it; then switch back to the Now Playing screen to view the item in question. Or, if the selected file is an audio track, you can continue working in the current screen; the audio track automatically plays from the Now Playing page. (You do not have to switch back to this page to hear the track you selected.)

You can also choose to create a new *playlist* (a specific group of songs or videos) from the Playlists menu. To do so

1. **Select Create Playlist from the Playlists menu located in the left column of the Library screen.**

The words `Create Playlist` are highlighted in blue and replaced with the words `New Playlist`.

2. Type a new title for your playlist.

A new playlist is created and saved in the Playlists category.

3. Locate a track you would like to add to your playlist and then right-click that item.

A pop-up menu appears.

4. Choose Add To.

A submenu appears to the right of the pop-up menu. (See Figure 9-2.)

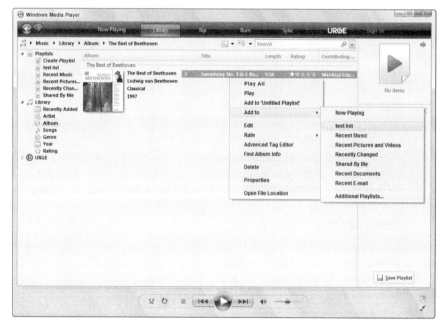

Figure 9-2: Adding tracks to existing playlists.

5. Click the title of the playlist to which you would like to add the song or video.

The media file is added to the selected playlist.

6. To add additional items, repeat Steps 3–5.

 Information Kiosk

Media files can also be added to playlists by dragging and dropping them into the appropriate list.

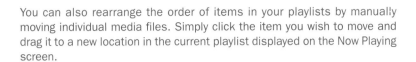

You can also rearrange the order of items in your playlists by manually moving individual media files. Simply click the item you wish to move and drag it to a new location in the current playlist displayed on the Now Playing screen.

From the Library subcategories, you can choose to locate your audio files by Artist, Album, Songs, Genre, Year, Rating, or those that have been recently added to your computer. Again, double-clicking these items opens them in the Now Playing window.

The last item in the left column of the Library screen is the URGE link. Clicking this category redirects you to the URGE Web site. From this page, you can choose to purchase individual songs or entire albums and download them to your PC.

Information Kiosk

Be connected to the Internet when you play any noncommercially produced multimedia files, especially those files downloaded from the Internet. With the variety of digital movie formats that exist, Windows might need to download additional codecs in order to be able to play certain digital media. (*Codecs* refers to the encoding or decoding of digital streams, usually to facilitate transfer over the Internet.) Windows Media Player 11 actually does this automatically. You'll see an indication in the lower-left bar of the Windows Media Player that reads `Acquiring codec`. When the player successfully acquires the codec, you see the message `codec acquired`.

Ripping CDs

If you're someone who prefers to purchase music soundtracks in a disc format (as opposed to downloading them from the Internet), you should learn to *rip* CDs, which happens when you save audio tracks to your PC from an existing CD. When you rip a CD, you convert the audio track into a digital file that Vista can read and understand when you access it via your desktop later. You can also then choose to save this file to a portable audio device so that you do not have to cart around a stack of CDs when you are on the go.

Transfer

If you are already familiar with ripping CDs, skip ahead to the next two sections to figure out how to create your own personalized music CDs or copy your saved audio files to a portable media device.

To rip a CD, simply insert the CD into your PC's CD/DVD drive. This automatically launches Windows Media Player. Select the Rip tab and then click the Start Rip button in the lower left of the screen. Vista saves the selected tracks from the CD to your PC. You can then use the Windows Media Player Library to locate your newly ripped files.

Information Kiosk

You can pick and choose which tracks are to be saved to your PC. Use the check boxes to the left of the song (or scene) titles to indicate which items to copy to your computer. When checked, that particular item will be saved to your PC. If there is no check mark, that item will not be saved to your PC.

Creating personalized audio CDs with Windows Media Player

After you accumulate a number of albums or individual music tracks, you might wish to create your own compilation CDs (or *mix tapes,* as they used to be known). Windows Media Player makes the process simple and easy to execute. All you need to do is find the tracks you wish to include on your newly burned CD and then drag and drop these items to the Burn List. Read on for more detailed instructions.

To create a *personalized* CD compilation — that is, one that includes individual tracks from multiple albums or playlists — do the following:

1. **Open Windows Media Player 11.**

   You can find this application in the All Programs section of the Start menu, or you can perform an Instant Search to locate this media tool.

2. **From the Media Player Library tab, locate the tracks you wish to include on your burned CD.**

   Use the Playlists or Library categories situated at the left of the Windows Media Player screen to find the specific tracks you want to include on your CD.

3. **Click the Burn tab.**

   The Burn tab screen opens. Notice the Burn List column located at the right of this window.

4. **Highlight the items you wish to include on your CD. Then drag and drop the selected tracks to the Burn List located in the right column of the screen, as shown in Figure 9-3.**

   You can move each item separately, or you can select a group of items and move them to the Burn List all at once.

   You can also select different tracks from various albums, artists, playlists, and so on.

5. **After you complete your Burn List, insert a blank (or rewritable) CD into your computer's disc drive and then click the Start Burn button located at the bottom of the Burn List column.**

   The Windows Media Player automatically detects the new disc and begins copying the items from the Burn List to the blank (or rewritable) CD.

Burn List

Figure 9-3: Adding a track to the Burn List.

After the burning process is complete, the Burn List shows the tracks for the Current Disc as well as the amount of time remaining on the CD.

Transfer

See the section later in this chapter on burning CDs and DVDs to learn more about making duplicate copies of entire albums or saving important data files (including pictures and videos) to a CD/DVD.

Syncing external media devices with your PC library

After you rip some of your favorite audio tracks to your PC or create personalized playlists, you might wish to save those files to a portable device so that you can have them with you when you are not at your computer. (This process can be used in lieu of creating CDs or in combination with this option. Remember to make copies of your most important — or favorite — media files in case they are lost or destroyed on your PC's hard drive.)

For audio tracks, you might use any portable audio device (a Microsoft Zune or Apple iPod, for example). For video files, you can use a Zune or iPod or any similar portable device that is intended to play videos. In either situation, the process for syncing (or copying) these files to your portable device is the same.

To sync your portable audio/video (or backup storage) device with the files you have saved on your PC

1. Open Windows Media Player 11.

This application can be found in the All Programs section of the Start menu, or you can perform an Instant Search for Windows Media Player to locate this tool.

2. Select the Sync tab and locate the media files you wish to save to your external device.

Use the Playlists and Library categories to the left of the screen to locate the files you wish to add to your portable device.

3. Click a single file (or playlist) and drag it to the Sync List section located in the panel to the far right of the screen.

The chosen file is added to the Sync List items, as shown in Figure 9-4.

4. Repeat Steps 2 and 3 until you have all the files (or playlists) assembled.

All additional files are added to the Sync List.

5. Connect your external device to your computer and then click the Start Sync button at the bottom of the Sync List column on the right side of the window.

The files in the Sync List are transferred to your external device.

Sync List

Figure 9-4: Syncing a file with your PC library.

Setting video viewing preferences in Media Player 11

Windows Media Player gives you the option of viewing a DVD or video either in a window — at its native resolution — or at full-screen. The native resolution of DVD is 720 x 480, which is considerably less than the standard screen resolution for today's LCD screens (typically 1068 x 768 for a 15" laptop or LCD monitor, 1280 x 1024 for a 17–19" model, and 1600 x 1200 for a 20–21" monitor). Also, many DVDs are now shipped in wide-screen format — 852 x 480 (like the Director's Cut version of films), which use a 16 x 9 screen ratio rather than the older NTSC (National Television Systems Committee) television standard of 4 x 3.

To display in full-screen mode, Windows Media Player 11 must interpolate from the DVD or video's native resolution. Often, some loss of quality is evident — especially if your video originally began in a low-resolution format (say, 320 x 240) and has been expanded to fit a 1280 x 1024 or 1600 x 1200 display.

If you prefer to watch your video in full-screen rather than in a window, click the full-screen icon, located in the lower right of the Media Player window. To return to the regular Media Player mode (see Figure 9-5), press Esc on your keyboard. You can also choose the size of the video by right-clicking the picture, which brings up the Video Size menu. Here, you can choose between scaling of 50%, 100%, and 200%. This menu also allows you to expand to full-screen with a mouse click.

Figure 9-5: The Windows Media Player. Note the small viewing screen, which is its original size.

When you double-click the moving image itself (or click the full-screen button at the bottom right of the screen), the playing screen enlarges to a full-screen theater effect (see Figure 9-6).

Figure 9-6: Windows Media Player, in full-screen theater mode.

Information Kiosk

If you need help with Windows Media Player, Microsoft has a site devoted to troubleshooting Windows Media Player issues. Connect to the Internet, press F1 for Help, and then type **troubleshooting Windows Media Player** in the search box. You are taken to the Troubleshooting Windows Media Player 11 site.

Listening to the (Internet) radio with Media Player 11

In addition to watching movies and playing audio CDs, Windows Media Player 11 can also be used to access and listen to music found on the Internet. For example, if you visit a Web site like www.mtv.com and you are presented with the option to play videos or soundtracks, selecting one of these links automatically opens Windows

Media Player. From the Now Playing screen, you can use the navigational buttons at the bottom of the window to play/pause, skip ahead, go back, stop, mute, or adjust the volume for the running video or music soundtrack.

Information Kiosk

Audio control in Windows Vista brings something else new to the audio environment: per-application audio control. Previously in Windows, if you adjusted the volume control in the system tray (now called the Notification area), it governed the volume of sound overall. Now, any volume control you see is application specific. The volume control in the Windows Media Player does not affect any sounds you have associated with Windows functions, nor does it affect the sounds in your Windows Mail (or any other e-mail program you might use), and so on.

Burning CDs and DVDs

Burning CDs and DVDs has become a common activity for many PC users. Not only are CDs and DVDs used to make copies of important documents and files — as opposed to using Zip drives or the old floppy disks, which many new PCs do not even have a separate drive for anymore — this technique is also being used to create spare copies of PC user's favorite audio and digital photography collections. That way, if something happens to the original — whether a copy of an important document, a photograph, or a favorite workout soundtrack — you have another copy close at hand. You can even use this feature to make multiple copies of a CD or DVD to keep in different locations. For example, you can keep a copy of a specific CD or DVD in your car, your home, or perhaps even the office. That way, you do not have to carry around the same disc from one place to the other.

Another benefit of being able to create your own CDs is that you can create personalized playlists that are specific to your own personality. For example, you can create a playlist for a special road trip or a party. You can use the burning capabilities of Windows Vista to make your own personalized soundtracks, videos, or electronic photo albums.

Transfer

Refer to the earlier "Creating personalized audio CDs with Windows Media Player" section to find out more about how to create your own music compilation CDs (or mix tapes).

You can create basically three different types of CDs and DVDs. The first is an audio CD, which I mention earlier in the Windows Media Player section. The second is a data CD or DVD; *data discs* are used to store various documents and images. And the third is a video DVD.

Transfer

Making a copy of a video DVD is best executed using Windows DVD Maker. Refer to the Windows Media Center section later in this chapter to find out more about making copies of video DVDs.

Watch Your Step

Making duplicate copies of commercial music CDs and DVD videos without permission from the original creator might be considered an infringement upon the copyright laws of that particular item. (Please note the use of the term *might* here. Many argue that "fair use" would apply to making copies for personal use, but the recording and film industries insist that the law — including laws regulating the use of so-called copy-protection technology on CDs and DVDs — is still fluid on this point.) If you are planning to make copies of multimedia for any purpose other than a personal backup copy, it is best to check with the owner of the copyright license or a proper legal authority.

The first step to burning a CD or DVD involves locating the files you wish to save to the specified disc. If you are burning an audio CD, you can usually find these files in Media Player. You might also be able to locate your recently viewed photos, videos, and documents in Windows Media Player. If the media files you are looking for cannot be found in Windows Media Player 11, use the Start menu to locate the items you seek. After you locate your media files, you can begin burning these items to disc.

Information Kiosk

To burn a disc from Windows Media Player 11, follow the instructions listed earlier for creating personalized audio CDs. Simply locate the items you wish to burn to the CD/DVD and then drag them to the Burn List. When you finish adding all the media files you wish to save to the CD, click the Start Burn button at the bottom of the Burn List column.

You can also use the traditional Windows Explorer screen (see Figure 9-7) to burn CDs and DVDs. This process is just as simple as the one that exists for the Windows Media Player.

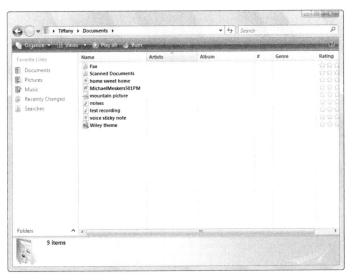

Figure 9-7: Burn CDs and DVDs from the Windows Explorer screen.

To create a CD or DVD copy of the media files saved to your PC

1. **Open the Start menu.**

   The Start menu appears in the lower left of your screen.

2. **Select the appropriate folder from the right column of the Start menu.**

   You can choose from the Documents, Pictures, or Music folders; or, you can search for an item using the Search feature located in the Start menu.

3. **Highlight the item(s) you wish to copy to the CD or DVD.**

   These items can include entire albums, playlists, digital images files, or document folders.

4. **Select the Burn button from the menu bar above.**

   You are prompted with the Burn to Disc dialog box, as shown in Figure 9-8.

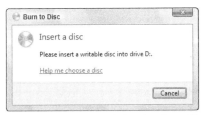

Figure 9-8: Insert a disc before burning a CD or DVD.

5. **Insert a blank (or rewritable) CD or DVD into your computer's disc drive.**

The Burn a Disc dialog box appears. (See Figure 9-9.)

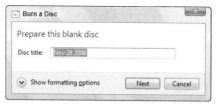

Figure 9-9: Preparing to burn a CD or DVD.

ℹ️ Information Kiosk

Should you insert a disc that already has content saved to it (such as a CD-RW), the AutoPlay window (see Figure 9-10) launches. This screen offers you two different options for burning files to a disc. Choose the Burn Files to Disc (Using Windows) option to proceed with the burning process.

Figure 9-10: The AutoPlay dialog box offers you two different burning options.

6. **Enter a name for your disc in the Disc Title field and then click Next.**

If you are prompted with a dialog box requesting permission to format your disc, click Yes. However, be aware that formatting your disc removes all existing content from the disc. Also, this process can take quite a bit of time. If you are in a hurry, you use a blank CD (or DVD) that has already been formatted to avoid this lengthy process.

After the disc is formatted, your media content is automatically saved to the CD/DVD. A new Windows Explorer screen appears, revealing the contents of the completed disc.

To view the data saved to the disc, double-click a disc item to open Windows Media Player 11 or another viewing application.

Information Kiosk

You can save media files to discs that already contain data by opening the CD's or DVD's file folders. You can view these by accessing the Computer option from the Start menu or by choosing to view files or folders from the AutoPlay window that launches when you insert the CD or DVD into your computer's disc drive and then dragging and dropping the selected files into the CD's or DVD's file folders.

Information Kiosk

When you do any CD/DVD burning, sometimes the process fails before it is finished, leaving you with an unusable CD or DVD. The most common reason why people experience CD (and especially DVD) burn-failure is insufficient available RAM (memory). You might encounter this more often while you have other tasks running. As a preventive measure, close any open applications you are not using before attempting to restart the burn process.

If your burning does fail and your machine can no longer read the DVD, do not assume that it cannot ever be used again. Try to reformat the disc. If that does not work and you receive a message that your disc is unusable, it might still work in other devices. For example, if you have a DVD recorder/player connected to your television set, the disc might actually be formattable and playable by that device.

Using the Windows Photo Gallery

Today, owning a digital camera is almost as common as owning a cell phone. The shift from using a traditional camera (with images stored on celluloid film) to using a digital camera (where the images are electronic in nature and can be downloaded to a computer and e-mailed to others) is massive in scale and has happened almost overnight. Today, digital camera sales outstrip film camera sales in the developed world by a factor of more than 4 to 1.

Now that digital cameras rule the marketplace, most people have been able to amass huge collections of photos rather easily, whether they take photos themselves, receive them via e-mail, or download them from the Internet.

Organizing these photos and then finding them when you want can be a nightmare. Windows Vista has gone a long way to making this whole process a lot easier with Windows Photo Gallery, which allows you to organize and find these photos very easily.

As a start, open Windows Photo Gallery to explore its features. Simply click the Start button and then choose All Programs → Windows Photo Gallery (see Figure 9-11).

Figure 9-11: Windows Photo Gallery.

Windows Photo Gallery displays all the pictures, images, and photos stored in your Pictures directory. To see only the digital photos saved to your PC, click the Pictures category located in the left column. To view just the videos you have stored on your computer, choose Videos from the menu in the left panel.

If the item you wish to view does not automatically appear in the Pictures or Videos section of Windows Photo Gallery, you can manually locate or search for the desired item on your hard drive. After you find the specified image, you can open this item in Windows Photo Gallery by clicking the Preview button in the Windows Explorer screen and choosing the Windows Photo Gallery option from the drop-down menu that appears. This allows you to view the selected item in Photo Gallery.

Windows Photo Gallery commands

On the menu bar located at the top of the Windows Photo Gallery page, you can find a number of functions to use with this digital media tool. A brief explanation of each of these items is listed here:

File: This menu includes options to add a folder to Photo Gallery; import images from your digital camera or scanner; delete, rename, or copy digital images; or create screen saver settings using the images located in the Photo Gallery.

Fix: Clicking this button opens the selected image in a larger editing screen, where you can choose to adjust its exposure and color, *crop* (cut out) part of the image, or fix any red-eye problems, if applicable. Note the Undo and Redo buttons at the bottom of the corrections column to the right of this screen. Use these buttons to flip back and forth between unsaved edits. (For more on the Fix command, see the "Editing Photos and Images" section later in this chapter.)

Info: Clicking this button opens a panel to the right of the main Photo Gallery viewing area. Listed within this new panel are the details for the selected image. Such image details include the image's title, date and time created, file size, resolution, rating (by five-star standards), and its related *tags* (descriptive markers).

Print: This feature allows you to either print the selected image(s) or order prints from an online vendor.

E-mail: This button lets you easily attach the selected image(s) to an e-mail message. Simply highlight the image(s) you wish to share with others, click the E-mail button, and then click the Attach button in the pop-up dialog box. This opens the Windows Mail system. From here, you can send the images to your family, friends, or colleagues.

Burn: Much like the Media Player and Windows Explorer Burn features, clicking this button allows you to save your digital images to an external media source by burning them to either a data disc (CD or DVD) or video DVD.

Make a Movie: Clicking this button opens the Windows Movie Maker application. From this screen, you can drag and drop specific images into the Storyboard scenes located at the bottom of the window. You can also use the Tasks menus (located in the column to the left) to add effects, transition elements, movie titles, and credits. You can also import media sources from this menu as well as choose to publish the final product to your computer, a DVD, a CD, e-mail, or a digital camera. To preview your movie before publishing it, use the Play button beneath the preview window to see the finished product.

Transfer

The Windows Movie Maker application is a powerful and complex program, so much so that I would not be able to do it justice within the context of a general introduction to Windows Vista. For a more thorough treatment of Windows Movie Maker, see Alan Simpson's *Windows Vista Bible,* also published by Wiley Publishing Inc.

Open: This item provides access to other image editing applications (primarily Paint) so that you can make any artistic changes to the selected image. For example, in Paint, you can add your own text as well as insert additional colors, lines, shapes, and so on.

At the bottom of the Photo Gallery screen is a toolbar that includes a number of different features that you can perform within Photo Gallery. The first item from the left is the Display Size button. Clicking this button (which looks like a magnifying glass with a plus sign inside it) brings up a sliding scale. Use this feature to adjust the size of your images as they appear on your computer screen. Moving the slider up makes the images bigger; moving it down makes them smaller.

The second button is the Thumbnail Image Reset button. If you have made adjustments to the display size of your images, you can click this button to return the images to their original (thumbnail) size.

The left- and right-pointing arrows — located on either side of the blue circular button, positioned in the middle of the toolbar — are used to move between images in the open folder. Use the left arrow to move to the image on the left, or use the right arrow to select the image to the right.

The blue circular button in the middle of the toolbar is the Slideshow button. Selecting this tool opens a new screen that shows the images from the open folder in a full-screen slide show. You can use the new toolbar at the bottom of the screen to move from one image to another or to exit the slide show. (*Note:* If you cannot view the toolbar at the bottom of the screen, simply move your mouse to the bottom-center of the screen. This brings up the aforementioned toolbar.) You can also change the themes and speed — use the gearlike button — of the slide show from this toolbar.

Back in the Photo Gallery window are two circular arrows to the right of the Slideshow button. The first one points to the left, and the second one points to the right. Clicking these buttons rotates the selected image counterclockwise (90 degrees to the left) or clockwise (90 degrees to the right), respectively.

Finally, the large red X button located at the far right of the Photo Gallery toolbar is the Delete button. Clicking this button removes the selected image from the Pictures directory or wherever it is stored on your PC.

Organizing Photos

In Chapter 5, you learned about adding metadata to files in order to make searching faster and more efficient. This, of course, carries over into managing your photos as well. *Tags* (personalized descriptive labels attached to your files) are an essential part of organizing your digital images and are prominently featured as part of the menu in the left column. When you choose Tags from that menu, you see the all the specific Tag folders where photos that have been tagged have been automatically sorted, as shown in Figure 9-12.

Step into the Real World

Using tags can make all the difference in the world when it comes to finding image files in Windows Photo Gallery. Because most people upload photos from their digital cameras, their images are typically saved with the alphanumeric names given to them during the conversion process. Additionally, subjects in photos frequently have the same names, whether they are people or objects. That adds up to quite a cumbersome naming system. In addition to naming individual photos, also consider adding tags to your images so that you can easily find them later.

Figure 9-12: Windows Photo Gallery with the Tag menus expanded.

Clicking a Tag folder displays all the images associated with that tag.

Adding a tag to your digital images is easy. Follow these instructions to begin using this feature to organize your photos.

To add a tag to a single image

1. Double-click a photo in Windows Photo Gallery.

The Details panel for that photo appears in a panel to the right of the Photo Gallery's main viewing area. (See Figure 9-13.)

Details panel

Figure 9-13: Use the Add Tags feature to organize your digital images.

ℹ️ Information Kiosk

If you want to add a tag to an image and the Details panel is not displayed to the right of the main Photo Gallery viewing area, highlight the desired image and then click the Info button on the menu bar above to access this feature.

2. **Click the Add Tags option.**

The words Add Tags disappear, leaving a blank text box for you to use to enter a new tag for the selected image. (See Figure 9-14.)

3. **Type in a new tag for your image and then press Enter.**

The new tag identifier is added to the image, appearing in the list of tags below the Add Tags option in the Details panel. (You can actually add as many tags as you want.)

Add your new tag here.

Figure 9-14: Windows Photo Gallery. Add the new tag in the blank box.

To add a tag to multiple images at the same time

1. **Open Windows Photo Gallery and then select the Create a New Tag option located in the left column.**

The words `New Tag` are highlighted in blue.

2. **Enter a new descriptive title for this tag and then press Enter.**

The new tag appears in the Tags menu listing below.

3. **Highlight the images you wish to associate with this tag.**

The items you select have a gray shaded box around them.

4. **Drag and drop this collection of images into the new Tag folder.**

Your images can now be located using the newly created tag.

Note: This does not remove the image from other Tag folders; it simply adds the new descriptive indicator to the Tag repertoire.

From the main Photo Gallery window, you can see that the new tags you created appear in the Tags menu. The Tags menu now includes the option to Create a New Tag, a category for Not Tagged items, and a separate folder for all the tags that you have created. If you click the Not Tagged category, you can see all your images that have been saved in the Pictures directory but do not yet have a tag assigned to them.

Information Kiosk

You can also add a tag to an image from the Windows Explorer screen. Open the image you wish to add a tag to and then select the Add a Tag option at the bottom of the screen. Type in the tag you would like to associate with this image and then click Save.

To delete a tag from an image

1. Double-click the desired photo in Windows Photo Gallery.

The Details panel for that photo appears to the right.

2. Right-click the tag identifier you would like to remove.

A pop-up menu appears.

3. Choose to Remove Tag.

The tag identifier is deleted for this individual image.

Information Kiosk

To remove an entire Tag folder, right-click the desired folder and choose Delete from the pop-up menu that appears. Click Yes in the pop-up confirmation box to verify this change. No actual images are deleted — only the tags associated with the images.

Editing Photos and Images

Although many of today's digital cameras include features meant to provide you with the best possible digital images available, sometimes you still need (or want) to make adjustments to your photos. With Windows Photo Gallery, you can easily adjust the brightness, contrast, and rotation of any image.

Here's how:

1. Open the Windows Photo Gallery and select the image you wish to adjust.

The image you select is highlighted in blue.

2. Choose Fix from the menu bar.

An editing panel appears on the right. (See Figure 9-15.)

Figure 9-15: Edit images from the Fix menu in Windows Photo Gallery.

From this page, you can elect to have Vista automatically adjust the image's color and exposure settings, or you can choose to make changes to these items manually by using the sliding scales that appear when you select one of these feature options. (See Figure 9-16.) You can also choose to crop, rotate the frame, and fix any red-eye problems from this screen.

Figure 9-16: Manually adjust color in a selected photo.

3. **Select the characteristic of the image that you wish to modify and then make any necessary or desired changes.**

Note that the preview screen makes immediate adjustments to the image file as you make corrections. This allows you to determine whether additional changes need to be made.

You can also use the Revert and Redo buttons at the bottom of the editing panel to flip back and forth between recent adjustments.

4. **After making final corrections to your image, save a copy of the edited version to your computer by choosing File → Make a Copy from the main menu.**

Selecting this option opens a dialog box that allows you to save your image under a new filename. This allows you to preserve the unedited version of the photo in its original state.

Information Kiosk

One fun feature contained in Windows Photo Gallery is the ability to set a photo instantly as your desktop background. When viewing the photo in the gallery, simply right-click the photo and then choose Set as Desktop Background from the menu that appears.

Gaming in Vista

As in previous versions of Windows, Vista comes with a collection of games. Games have become a whole world unto themselves in the digital era. In fact, the Entertainment Software Association estimates that 69 percent of American heads of household play computer and video games. Many computer users cite game playing as their primary computer purpose. (No surprise, then, that many businesses restrict or block access to this area of Windows.) Don't dismiss playing games in Vista entirely as trivial, though. Games can be a great way for many users to become more familiar with how their PCs function. And for children, playing games can also open a world of learning within a digital environment.

Widows Vista has greatly enhanced the audio and visual aspects in its preloaded games. You see some very nicely done 3-D effects, with a huge vocabulary of sound effects. And they are all designed such that only one player is needed.

Vista has created yet another Explorer window that encompasses them all: The Games Explorer. You can bring it up by doing an Instant Search for Games.

Opening the Games Explorer displays what you see in Figure 9-17.

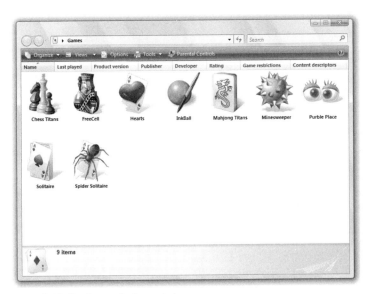

Figure 9-17: The Games Explorer window.

Click the Options menu in the Games Explorer to download from the Internet more information about the games installed on your computer. Parental Controls can be set right from the Games Explorer window toolbar as well.

Transfer

Refer to Chapter 4 for more information on setting Parental Controls.

The Games toolbar conveniently lists all properties pertinent to all Vista games. And, before you even choose to play a game, you can click any of the games listed to see a Details panel (located on the right side of the screen) that gives you information about how your computer will perform if you choose to play that particular game. (If you do not see this panel, click Organize and then Layout, making sure the Preview Pane option is selected.) Take a look at Figure 9-18 to see this information panel in action.

Games can, of course, be downloaded and installed from the Internet. However, the usual considerations should be taken into account — malware screening, your hardware capabilities to run the game, compatibility with the operating system, copyright infringement, and any needed peripheral devices (such as a joystick or touch screen).

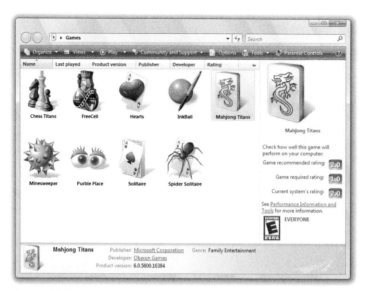

Figure 9-18: Determine how well your system is expected to perform running the selected game.

Watch Your Step

This warning applies principally to parents of children playing games. You can check ratings and games adherence to standards set by the *Entertainment Software Rating Board* (ESRB), which is a regulatory entity in charge of setting and enforcing ratings, guidelines for advertising, and privacy policies for online and offline computer and video games. A built-in feature of Games Explorer allows you to do this precursory check. You can find it in the Details panel, which appears to the right of the Games Explorer screen whenever you click a game icon. However, you first need to be connected to the Internet. After you're online, look for the ESRB logo and click it to go to the ESRB Web site, where you can find details about the game.

A Word on the Windows Media Center

In the Home Premium or Ultimate versions of Windows Vista are additional capabilities when it comes to working with media. For example, Windows Media Center lets you record TV programs to your PC, make DVD movies, listen to the radio via the Internet, and access online media as well as your own picture and music libraries. Because of the media files used with this application, it has more stringent hardware requirements, including more video RAM and a digital TV tuner. However, the capabilities are like nothing ever before experienced by a Windows user.

When you first open Windows Media Center — you can find this application in the All Programs section of your Start Menu — you are prompted with a Welcome setup page. From this screen, you can choose from three different setup options: the Express setup, Custom Setup, or Run Setup Later. The Express setup is the fastest, easiest way to set up this feature. However, if you want to create customized specifications for this application, choose the Custom setup. *Hint:* Until you use the Media Center enough to familiarize yourself with its various tools and options, you might prefer to run the setup later. The remainder of this chapter is presented under the Run Setup Later option.

After you make your setup selection, you are transported to Windows Media Center. At first, this application might seem a little foreign to experienced Windows users. Not only are the visual images somewhat different from a typical Windows application, but the menu structure/organization is quite different as well. For example, there is a clear selection box located in the center of the screen. From here, you can choose to select a new menu by using the vertical navigation buttons on your keyboard, or you can move horizontally (again, using the navigation buttons on your keyboard — this time the left and right arrows) to select another item from the menu listed above the selection box. For example, when you first open this tool, you can see that the Recorded TV option has been selected from the TV + Movies menu. If you move to the right, you can select the Play DVD option, which is also from the TV + Movies menu. (Note the category heading at the top of the selection box.) If you use the up- and down-arrow keys, you can view the Music or Online Media menus. The options for these menus are located to the left and right of the automatic selection box item.

To select a menu item, use the navigation buttons to move the desired item into the selection box and then double-click the menu item.

To go back to a viewed screen, use the back arrow in the upper left of the Media Center window. (If you do not see this button, move your mouse over the designated area, and the Back button becomes visible.)

Also, take note of the channel and performance toolbar located in the lower right of this screen. These tools allow you to change the channel and play/pause, skip forward, go backward, or mute various media devices.

To exit Windows Media Center, click the X in the upper-right corner of this application. (If you do not see this button at first, move your mouse over the designated area, and the Close button, as well as the Minimize and Maximize buttons, automatically appears.)

Recording TV to your PC

As I mention earlier, Windows Media Center allows you to record television programs to your (TV tuner-enabled) computer. To take advantage of this feature, follow these steps:

1. **Open Windows Media Center and select Guide from the TV + Movies menu.**

Doing so opens up the Television Guide screen.

2. **Use the channel plus and minus buttons (located in the lower right of the Media Center window) to find the program/channel you wish to record.**

The channel for the television program you wish to record appears onscreen.

3. **Click the Record button (represented by a small red dot) on the Media Center toolbar.**

Your show is recorded as it plays onscreen.

4. **Click the Record button again when you want to stop recording.**

After you finish recording your television program, you can find this data later by accessing the Recorded TV option in the TV + Movies menu of Media Center.

 ## Watch Your Step

If you do not have an analog or digital TV tuner installed on your PC, you cannot record (or locate) any television changes without first obtaining the required tuner hardware from Windows Marketplace. Visit www.windowsmarketplace.com to shop for various Windows hardware and software products online.

Creating DVDs in Windows Media Center

After you record a television program using your PC, you might like to make a DVD copy of the show or movie so that you have a portable edition of this media file — or you might like to take advantage of Media Center's DVD-burning tool to make copies of other media files (or discs) you already have on hand.

To make a copy of a video DVD

1. **Open Windows Media Center and choose the Burn CD/DVD option from the Tasks menu.**

A pop-up window appears telling you to insert a compatible disc.

 ## Information Kiosk

If there is already data saved to the disc you inserted, you are prompted with a dialog box asking whether to erase the files currently saved to the disc. Decide how you would like to proceed by either choosing to Erase Disc or by clicking the Cancel button.

2. **Insert a writeable DVD into your PC and then click Retry.**

The Select Disc Format window appears.

3. **Identify the type of disc you have and then click Next.**

This opens a new dialog box asking you to name your DVD.

4. **Enter a title for your DVD and then click Next.**

The Select Media screen appears.

5. **Choose the appropriate media source and then click Next.**

You can choose to burn a DVD from either the Recorded TV or Video Library files saved to your PC.

6. **Select the individual television show or video you wish to save to a disc and then click Next.**

Use the check mark options to indicate which items you would like to save to the DVD.

To add additional files, click the Add More button in the Review & Edit List window.

7. **Choose Burn DVD from the Review & Edit List screen.**

This brings up the Initiating Copy notification window.

8. **Click Yes to confirm the DVD-burning initiation process.**

The selected media files are burned to the inserted DVD. When the burning process is complete, a Completing Burn notification window appears.

From this screen, you can choose to create a duplicate copy of the burned disc (in which case you want to insert a new DVD and click Burn) or finish the burn process.

9. **Click Done when you are finished making DVDs.**

Doing so closes the Completing Burn dialog box.

Listening to the (Internet) radio

Listening to the radio via the Internet is much like locating a television channel using Windows Media Center. In either situation, you are able to use the channel buttons at the bottom right of the Media Center screen to find the station(s) you desire.

To find and listen to live radio broadcasts, follow these instructions:

1. **Open Windows Media Center and choose the Browse Categories option from the Online Media menu.**

This opens a window showcasing a variety of online channels.

2. **Click the Music & Radio option from the list of categories at the left.**

This brings up a list of the available music and radio channels.

3. **Choose the online radio station that best matches your musical interests.**

The live broadcast from this station is automatically played through your PC's speakers.

Information Kiosk

You can also access FM radio stations through Windows Media Center. To tap into FM radio broadcasts, select the Radio option from the Media Center's Music menu and then select FM Radio. You can use the channel (plus or minus) buttons on the Media Center toolbar to locate a specific station, or you can let Vista search for available stations using the Seek and Tune features.

burn: To record (data, files) onto a CD or DVD via CD or DVD burning.

codec: A term coined from *compressor-decompressor* or *coder-decoder*. This refers to the device or program that encodes or decodes a digital stream of data or signal.

File types:

    AVI: Audio Video Interleaved file format

    MPG: Video file format developed by the Moving Picture Experts Group

    MP3: Moving Picture Experts Group Layer-3 Audio file format

playlist: A list of tracks, songs, or selections (all digital) to be played by a player or software application on a computer.

Rewriteable CD: A format of an optical disc that can be written (and rewritten) upon. The most common form is CD-RW.

rip: Copying tracks (usually sound or music) from a CD onto your computer, where they can be stored as individual files.

shuffle: In the digital music world, music tracks played in a completely random order, as opposed to the order they appear in the playlist.

URGE: An online music service that offers music downloads for purchase or by subscription. It is the result of collaboration between MTV and Microsoft.

Last Stop

Practice Exam

1. How can you expand the Windows Media Player screen to full-screen size?

_____

_____

_____

2. Why is it a good idea to add tags to digital photos?

_____

_____

_____

3. What are the different ways to burn a CD or DVD in Windows Vista?

_____

_____

_____

4. If you have a file with the .avi or .mpg extension (or some even-less common video file type) that you wish to play, what can you do if the Windows Media Player can't seem to play them?

_____

_____

_____

5. If you want to burn DVDs or record TV shows on your PC, what version of Windows Vista do you need?

_____

_____

_____

6. How do you adjust the brightness, contrast, or rotation of an image?

_____

_____

_____

7. What are ESRB game ratings, and why might you want to be familiar with them?

_____

_____

_____

8. What's the fastest way to add files to a burn list?

_____

_____

_____

9. What's the leading cause for DVD burn-failure? What precautions can you take to avoid this problem?

_____

_____

_____

10. How do you remove tags you no longer need?

_____

_____

_____

EXIT

Maximizing Your Windows Power and Performance

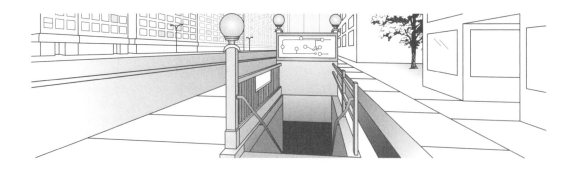

 # Enter the Station

Questions

1. Which Windows Vista power plan best suits your needs?

2. What options do you have when creating a personalized power plan?

3. How does ReadyBoost make your computer faster?

4. How can you take advantage of Vista's new (and improved) power-saving features?

5. What is Windows Reliability and Performance Monitor?

6. How do you monitor your computer's performance levels over an extended period of time?

Express Line

If you are already up on the power and performance settings of Windows Vista, skip ahead to the next chapter.

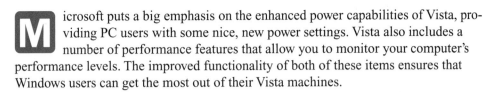

icrosoft puts a big emphasis on the enhanced power capabilities of Vista, providing PC users with some nice, new power settings. Vista also includes a number of performance features that allow you to monitor your computer's performance levels. The improved functionality of both of these items ensures that Windows users can get the most out of their Vista machines.

For example, without necessarily going out and spending lots of money on a more powerful processing chip, you can get better mileage from your Windows Vista PC processor. You can also get more life from your laptop battery as well as more memory than might normally be expected from the RAM available on your computer.

In addition to increased power options, you can also review the performance levels of your Vista computer, which allows you to monitor and make adjustments to your PC's performance settings so that your machine functions at its highest level — making your entire computer experience more efficient, productive, and enjoyable than ever before.

Power Management Options

With Windows Vista, you can easily choose a power plan that works best for you. You have three default options to choose from, or you can choose to create your own customized power plan. Whichever plan you select depends on what you deem most important — battery preservation or performance capabilities — as well as your user activities.

For example, if conserving your laptop's battery is more important to you than experiencing top-notch performance attributes, select a power plan that reflects these characteristics. If you place more importance on the performance capabilities of your PC (over saving battery power), choose a plan that takes such preferences into consideration. You can even choose a plan that provides equal distribution of both features. That way, you don't have to choose between your computer's battery or performance capabilities. And, as mentioned earlier, you can always create a modified power plan to meet your individual needs.

Working with Vista's default power plans

The first step to take full advantage of Vista's new power settings is to access Vista's default power setting by choosing Control Panel → System and Maintenance → Power Options. (You can also double-click the Power Meter icon in the system tray to bring up this screen.) The window that appears (see Figure 10-1) offers three different power plan options.

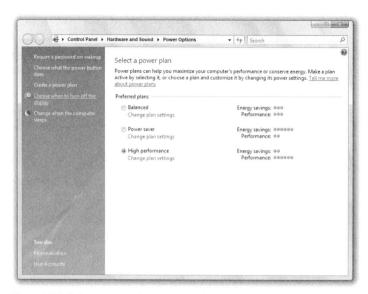

Figure 10-1: Select a power plan that works for you.

The first default power plan option is the Balanced plan. This option provides equal settings for both the battery life and performance features of your computer. The second option, the Power Saver plan, focuses more on preserving the machine's battery life than enhancing its performance. And the last option is the High Performance alternative, which is geared more toward enabling a computer's performance capabilities rather than conserving its battery life.

Choosing from the three options is simple. If you are running a desktop and always shut down the machine when it is not in use, you don't need to worry about saving power. Therefore, you should choose between the High Performance and Balanced plans.

If you are using a desktop and prefer to leave the machine turned on most of the time, you might want to consider using one of the other plans. The Balanced and Power Saver plans can provide the more effective, energy-conservation methods.

If running a laptop on battery, extending the life of your machine's battery is more likely to be a top priority. Therefore, the Power Saver plan is probably your best choice.

After you decide which plan is best for you, select its radio button and then close the Power Options window. Or, if you prefer to create your own customized power plan, move on to the next section, "Setting your own power plan," to learn more about how to adjust the power settings for your computer.

Setting your own power plan

Vista allows you to create and customize your own power plan. To do so, you must first select one of the three preset plans and then customize two additional power settings, found on the Edit Plan Settings window, which I discuss in a bit:

Turn Off the Display: The Turn Off the Display option determines when the computer screen is converted to a screen saver (or blank screen if you do not have a screen saver enabled). By setting a specific time constraint for this feature, you can control how much energy is used when the computer screen is not actively in use.

Put the Computer to Sleep: This feature works much the same way that the Turn Off the Display option works: That is, you can manually adjust the established time limit for this feature. This feature controls when the computer is placed in the Sleep mode. This feature saves energy not only by shutting down the computer screen but by putting the entire computer to sleep.

Transfer

Check out the "Powering-Off Options" section later in this chapter to learn more about your computer's Sleep mode.

To create a customized power plan

1. **Open the Start menu and choose Control Panel from the right column.**

The Control Panel window opens.

2. **Choose System and Maintenance.**

This opens the System and Maintenance menu screen.

3. **Select Power Options.**

Clicking this brings up a screen with the three default power plan options. (Refer to Figure 10-1.)

4. **Click the Create a Power Plan link in the left column of the Power Options window.**

This opens the Create a Power Plan window, as shown in Figure 10-2.

5. **Select the preset power plan you would like to customize.**

Use the radio buttons to the left of each plan to identify the plan you would like to use as the basis for your new power plan.

Figure 10-2: The Create a Power Plan window.

6. **Enter a name for your power plan in the Plan Name text box and then click Next.**

This opens the Edit Plan Settings screen. (See Figure 10-3.)

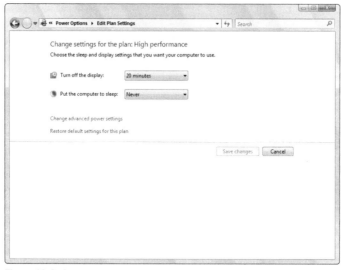

Figure 10-3: Customize your power plan settings.

Chapter 10: Maximizing Your Windows Power and Performance

From this page, you can make adjustments to both the Turn Off the Display and Put the Computer to Sleep options.

7. Use the drop-down menus provided to select new time constraints for both features.

These time limitations go into effect after the computer has been inactive for the established number of minutes indicated on this screen.

Note: If you are using a laptop, you can choose different time limitations for the computer when it runs off the machine's battery or when it is plugged into an electrical outlet source.

8. Click Save Changes.

This saves the new power plan settings to your computer and opens an updated Power Options window. Your customized plan now appears alongside the three preset options.

Information Kiosk

You can adjust your power settings without having to create a new plan. Simply select either the Choose When To Turn Off the Display or the Change When the Computer Sleeps link (located below the Create a New Plan option) in the left column of the Power Options window.

You can also use the links to make adjustments to existing power plans.

If you want to make additional adjustments to your custom power plan, you can do so via the Advanced Power Settings menu. This data can be found in the Edit Plan Settings window; refer to Figure 10-3. To locate this pane and make additional changes to your newly created power plan, follow these steps:

1. Open the Start menu and choose Control Panel from the column on the right.

The Control Panel window appears.

2. Choose System and Maintenance from the Control Panel menu.

This opens the System and Maintenance menu.

3. Select Power Options.

Clicking this item opens the Power Options window. (See Figure 10-4.)

4. Select the power plan that you would like to change and then click the Change Plan Settings link beneath the power plan title.

This opens the Edit Plan Settings screen. (Refer to Figure 10-3.)

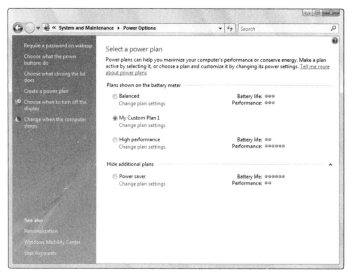

Figure 10-4: Viewing the updated Power Options window.

5. **Click the Change Advanced Power Settings link.**

This opens the Power Options window (Advanced Settings tab), as shown in Figure 10-5.

From this screen, you can choose to customize a number of different power options. For example, you can require a password entry after your computer comes out of its Sleep mode, change your machine's wireless adapter power-saving mode, determine when your computer sleeps (or hibernates), specify what action is taken when the Power button is used (or when the lid is closed on a laptop), or specify what action is taken when the battery gets low.

Figure 10-5: Taking advantage of Vista's advanced power option settings.

6. **Use the plus and minus signs to the left of the advanced power setting options to expand or contract the items contained within each category.**

If you click a plus sign, a list of items belonging to this feature is revealed below. If you click a minus sign, the detailed items pertaining to that particular feature disappear.

Information Kiosk

If you're not sure what some of the advanced power setting features do, place your cursor over the item in question. This brings up a pop-up ScreenTip that briefly explains what each feature does.

7. **Locate the items you wish to make changes to and then click the blue text to modify the existing settings.**

Clicking the blue text opens a drop-down menu for the selected item.

8. **Use the item's drop-down menu to select a new power setting option.**

Repeat Steps 6–8 until you make all the desired changes.

Information Kiosk

Just below the settings options list is the ever-present Restore Plan Default button, which you can click to restore the defaults in case you change your mind midstream.

9. **When you are finished making changes, click OK.**

This closes the Advanced Settings window and returns you to the Edit Plan Settings page.

10. **Click the red X in the upper-right of the Edit Plan Settings screen to close this window.**

ReadyBoost

As you might recall from previous chapters, one of the components that has a significant affect on how efficiently your Vista PC runs is how much RAM (random access memory) is available on your computer's hard drive. Having a sufficient level of RAM at your disposal greatly increases the functionality of your computer. Microsoft recognizes this fact and took it into consideration when crafting Vista's new ReadyBoost feature.

ReadyBoost is a Windows Vista innovation that allows you to harness memory from a source other than your own PC. This new feature allows you to add real speed to your applications by borrowing available space from an external device to gain faster processing speeds for your PC.

If you connect an external hard drive, a Flash drive, or any other storage drive (including an external memory source, such as a Secure Digital card), some of the available memory contained within those external devices can be used by Vista's ReadyBoost feature to supplement the RAM of your machine.

Information Kiosk

Recognizing that speed is always of the essence, PC users want an application to load quickly and then get to work (or even play) as soon as possible. *SuperFetch* is an innovation that helps make that happen in Windows Vista by keeping track of the programs you use most and loading them more quickly by keeping parts in memory. This feature existed in Windows XP; however, in Windows Vista, it is more sophisticated in terms of the data that is collected and put into a memory profile.

A *memory profile* is nothing that you see. Nor is there anything to set up here; it happens automatically in the background of your computer system. As mentioned earlier, Vista remembers applications you use most often and creates this profile in its memory. It is even sensitive to which days you use which applications, with the end result that they load that much faster when you need them.

When you attach such a device to your computer, you are presented with an AutoPlay dialog box, like the one shown in Figure 10-6.

Indicates your device
could provide a
ReadyBoost.

Figure 10-6: ReadyBoost is seeking to identify a device that has been attached.

When you connect a USB (Universal Serial Bus) drive to your PC, you might see the Speed Up My System option, as shown in Figure 10-6. If your USB drive is fast enough, you can use this option. (A minimum of 256MB and a maximum of 4GB of *cache space* — the amount of space allotted to temporarily storing data on the external device — can be accessed and used by ReadyBoost.)

If your USB drive (or other external device) is not fast enough, this option is not available to you, and you'll see the dialog box in Figure 10-7 when you select the Speed Up My System option.

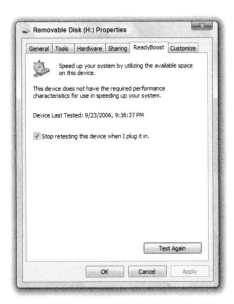

Figure 10-7: The Removable Disk Properties dialog box.

If the device itself does not meet other necessary specifications, the option does not even appear when you attach the device; see Figure 10-8.

Watch Your Step

Many devices, especially Flash drives, do not meet the Ready-Boost specifications because only a small portion of the drive is truly at "flash" speed. In actuality, the overall performance of the Flash drive is too slow. Hence, ReadyBoost cannot use any resources from that particular device.

MP3 players, while actually storage drives, cannot be used, either. However, it is not their speed that is the problem. Rather, it is their lack of available memory that prevents them from being used in conjunction with Vista's ReadyBoost feature.

Figure 10-8: The AutoPlay pop-up window, without the Speed Up My System option.

Information Kiosk

If the device is already attached, or if at any point you wish to verify whether ReadyBoost is an available option, go to Windows Explorer, select the appropriate drive, right-click, and then choose Properties from the pop-up menu. You see either a dialog box that is similar to the one in Figure 10-6 or one that is similar to Figure 10-8. If you see the one from Figure 10-6, you can probably use ReadyBoost with this device. If you are confronted with the dialog box from Figure 10-8, the device connected to your PC is incompatible with ReadyBoost.

Powering-Off Options

Contrary to popular belief, powering-off your computer is a lot less strenuous on your PC than most people believe. In fact, although powering your computer on and off does place some extra wear and tear on certain components, this process is not that hard on newer machines and creates only mild disturbances for older models. In addition, although many people believe that quite a bit of energy can be saved when the computer is shut off, the amount of energy conserved in this state is not nearly as significant as one might think.

Putting these issues aside, most users are less concerned with the wear and tear of their machine and the electrical savings but are instead much more concerned with the amount of time that the powering-off process takes.

In previous versions of Windows, users had three options for powering-off their machines. The first option involved shutting down the computer completely. This option closed all open applications and completely disabled the computer. The next option was to use the Standby feature. In essence, this alternative allowed users to place their computers in a holding pattern. And lastly, the Hibernate option, somewhat similar to the Standby option, was intended to be applied when the computer was going to be idle for extended periods of time (compared with the shortened periods of time expected during a Standby scenario).

However, despite the advantages of using the Standby and Hibernate options in previous versions of Windows, most users still chose to log off (if it was a shared computer) or to shut down their PCs when they wanted to end their Windows session. Microsoft discovered from surveys that the reason for this behavior stemmed from the fact that there was much confusion about what Hibernate and Standby actually did. As a result, most users chose neither power-saving option.

Windows Vista has since addressed these issues and has devised an improved set of power options. The first of which is Sleep, which is basically an improved version of Standby. The second is a new and improved version of Hibernate. Both powering-off methods are discussed in more detail in the following sections.

Putting your desktop PC or laptop to sleep

Sleep is the new powering-off mode for Windows Vista. This concept is actually a combination of elements from the Standby and Hibernate methods used in earlier versions of Windows. (In previous Windows editions, Standby provided a fast restart but had a significant downside in that it did not save any settings or files. And even though the Hibernate option was able to save files, it was a slow and inconvenient process.) In Vista, Sleep is the power-saving state that both saves data and allows you to boot up and get right back to work quickly. The Sleep option is definitely an improvement over the powering-off modes previously offered by Windows.

To put your computer to sleep

1. **Click the Start button.**

   The Start menu appears in the lower-left corner of your screen.

   If you look to the right of the Instant Search box, you see three buttons. The first is used to power off the machine. The second is used to lock your computer. The third button contains a small arrow.

2. **Click the button with the arrow.**

   A contextual menu appears, as shown in Figure 10-9.

3. **Choose Sleep from the contextual menu that appears.**

   When you put your machine to Sleep, all open files and documents are saved to memory, and your machine enters a low-power state.

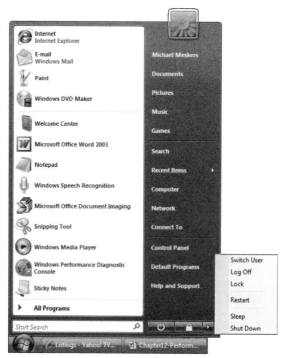

Figure 10-9: Clicking the arrow button brings up a menu that includes various power-off methods, including Sleep.

You can bring your machine back to life from the Sleep mode by any of these means:

- Press any key.
- Make a movement with your mouse.
- Tap your touch pad.
- Quickly press the Power button.

Watch Your Step

If you attempt to bring your machine back to life by holding down the Power button rather than lightly touching it, you might force your machine to turn off completely. Then you would have to boot up from scratch, thereby defeating the purpose of using Sleep in the first place.

Information Kiosk

Sleep plays out differently on laptops. Your files are saved to memory, and your machine goes to sleep. When it hits three hours of sleep, low battery, or a sudden power loss, your files are transferred from RAM to your hard drive, and then your machine completely shuts down.

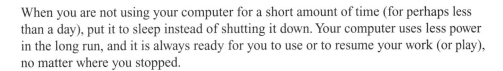

When you are not using your computer for a short amount of time (for perhaps less than a day), put it to sleep instead of shutting it down. Your computer uses less power in the long run, and it is always ready for you to use or to resume your work (or play), no matter where you stopped.

Placing your PC in Hibernate mode

If you choose to put your PC in Hibernate mode — perhaps you do not plan to use your computer again until the following day — everything that is open is saved — not to memory, but rather to the hard drive. Because it takes more time and energy to save your files and settings to the hard drive (rather than to your computer's temporary memory), it also takes slightly longer to recall a PC from a hibernation state than it does to awaken it when it is asleep.

When a computer is hibernating, it goes into an extremely minimal power-usage state. (It uses less power to hibernate than it does to sleep.) However, when you restart your computer from a hibernation state, it does takes a little longer to come back to life than if it were in Sleep mode. This difference is most noticeable between the Sleep and Hibernate methods. On the plus side, using the Hibernate mode is still much faster than starting from scratch.

Having your PC hibernate until you are ready to use it again is a much simpler process in Vista than it was in previous versions of Windows. For example, in Windows XP, you had to first enable the Hibernate support feature in the Power Options window before you could use this method. Now, it is simply a matter of a few clicks before you can use the Hibernate method.

To enable the Hibernate powering-off mode for your PC, follow the instructions provided in the preceding Sleep section — open the Start menu and use the arrow button to select a powering-off method — but instead of choosing Sleep from the contextual menu that appears, choose Hibernate.

To bring your machine out of hibernation, hold down the Power button for a moment until your screen returns to its active state.

Watch Your Step

Sleep and other power-saving states, such as Hibernate, can be turned off by default on some machines. If you encounter this problem, use the advanced power settings discussed earlier in this chapter (refer to the section, "Setting your own power plan") to activate these powering-off features.

Sleep can also be disabled if your video card is not Aero-ready. To correct this situation, you might need to update your driver or invest in a new video card.

Windows Reliability and Performance Monitor

Vista has several automatic performance monitoring and diagnostic tools as part of the Windows diagnostic infrastructure. These constantly watch your system and let you know in a timely manner when things start to go out of specification. But you can also keep an eye on things yourself with the performance diagnostic console: Windows Reliability and Performance Monitor.

If you notice that your computer is not functioning at its usual level of performance — perhaps it is running slower than normal, you can't run certain applications because of low memory, or you have trouble sending and receiving data across your network — you can use Windows Reliability and Performance Monitor to identify the cause of your problem. The visualization charts exhibited by this application are particularly helpful because they provide an overview of your computer's major resource allocations: namely, CPU, Disk, Network, and Memory. To bring up this console, run a search for either *Windows diagnostic console* or *Windows Reliability and Performance Monitor*. If you can't locate this tool via an Instant Search, you can find it by following these instructions:

1. **Open the Control Panel.**

   The Control Panel menu appears.

2. **Choose System and Maintenance.**

   Choosing this option opens the System and Maintenance window.

3. **Choose Performance Information and Tools.**

   This opens the Performance Information and Tools screen, as shown in Figure 10-10.

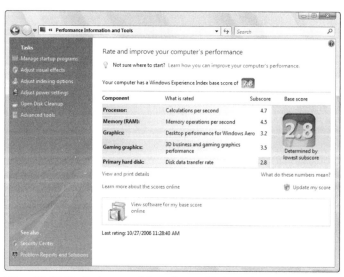

Figure 10-10: The Performance Information and Tools window.

4. Click the Advanced Tools link in the left column.

This selection produces a new menu screen. (See Figure 10-11.)

Figure 10-11: The Advanced Performance Tools menu.

5. From the menu that appears, click the Open Reliability and Performance Monitor link.

This opens the Reliability and Performance Monitor window, as shown in Figure 10-12.

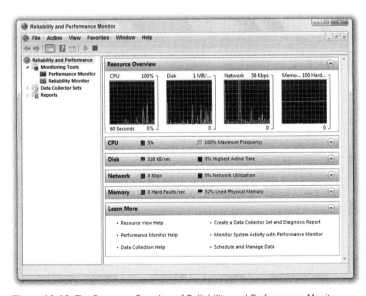

Figure 10-12: The Resource Overview of Reliability and Performance Monitor.

Information Kiosk

Windows Vista has added a new feature that allows you to see in one table a complete breakdown, by category, of all the major components that contribute to your system's performance. This performance-rating tool produces the Windows Experience Index report. To access this information, open the Control Panel, choose System and Maintenance, and then choose Performance Information and Tools from the menu screen that appears.

From this screen, you can see that your system is graded on a sliding scale ranging from 1.0 (the lowest score possible) up to a rating of 6.0. (Refer to Figure 10-10.) In addition to your machine's overall rating, there is also a separate score for your system's processor, memory, graphics (including a separate rating for gaming graphics), and hard drive.

The main viewing area includes the Resource Overview screen, which shows graphical representations of the data being accessed by your computer's CPU, disk, network, and memory arenas. To review specific details for any of these items, click the down arrow to the right of the resource's title bar. This produces a detailed list of the files and programs that are affected by this particular resource.

The **CPU section** shows the percentage of CPU resources that your total system is consuming. Clicking the downward-pointing mark at the right side expands the section and shows the percentage of resources each running process is using. (See Figure 10-13.)

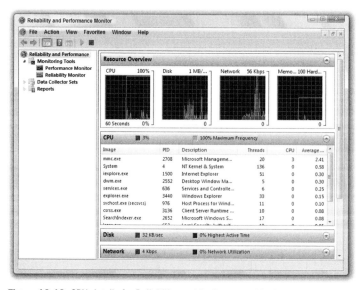

Figure 10-13: CPU details for Reliability and Performance Monitor.

If you notice any CPU ratings that seem unusually high for the type of application in question, that specific item might be the cause of your computer experiencing performance problems.

Similarly, the **Disk section** shows the total hard disk In/Out *transfer rate* (disk reads and writes in kilobytes per second). Click the down mark to see which files are using the disk.

Again, if you see any system attributes — in this case, the Read, Write or Response Time categories — that are out of the ordinary, you might be able to pinpoint which program is creating problems for your PC.

The **Network section** shows the total network data transfer rate in megabits per second. Expanding the section shows the remote computers involved in the current transfers.

If there is an individual computer that has a larger Send, Receive, or Total calculation than the other systems connected to the network, this particular machine might be responsible for generating the backlog in the network.

The **Memory section** shows the average number of hard memory faults per second and the percentage of memory in use by the total system. Expanding the section shows each process in memory as well as the hard faults and memory used by each. *Hard faults* are not memory faults per se; rather, they report only that the process had to access the hard disk to find data when it could not find them in memory.

When a program has an exceptionally high Working (or Private) rate, it is most likely the source responsible for consuming a vast amount of your computer's available memory; thus, it might potentially be causing your PC's performance problems.

The **Learn More section** provides links to Help files for each of the Reliability and Performance monitoring tools.

In the left pane of the Reliability and Performance Monitor window is a navigational tree that offers three different diagnostic methods: Monitoring Tools, Data Collector Sets, and Reports. Clicking Monitoring Tools brings up two more functions: Performance Monitor and Reliability Monitor. Both items are explained in further detail in the following sections, as are the Data Collector Sets and Reports.

Performance Monitor

Performance Monitor gives real-time information on how various systems' settings and components are performing. This feature allows you to track — by the second — dozens of processes, which you can add to or delete from a list at the bottom of the pane.

Each item, called a *counter*, is graphically displayed in its own color. Over time, running these monitors consistently can give you a feel for what is normal on your system as well as perspective when things seem abnormal. (See Figure 10-14.)

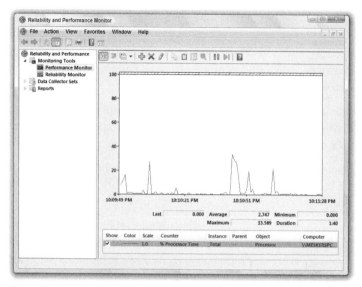

Figure 10-14: The Performance Monitor screen.

The primary advantage of Performance Monitor is that you can use it to create a personalized monitoring system. Because you can hand-select the items being tracked by Performance Monitor, you can create a customized tool for tracking the items you think are most important — as compared with the broader picture offered by Resource Overview, which provides only a summarized version of your computer's four primary resources. Performance Monitor, on the other hand, allows you to pinpoint specific items for individual tracking purposes.

To add a new counter to the Performance Monitor screen

1. **Open Performance Monitor and click the large, green plus sign on the toolbar at the top of this screen.**

   This opens the Add Counters window, as shown in Figure 10-15.

2. **Use the Available Counters box at the left to select the additional counters you would like to add to Performance Monitor.**

   Click the downward-pointing arrow to the right of each item to review the specific counters contained within each category.

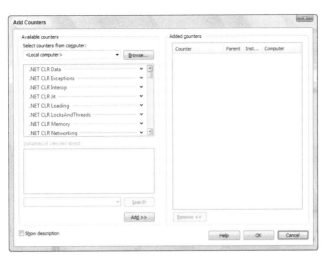

Figure 10-15: Use the Add Counters window to create new tracking lines for your Performance Monitor.

You can add all the items within a category — in which case, you click the category title itself or you can choose individual items from the counter categories.

Note: Category items are presented in blue. Specific counter items appear in black.

3. Highlight the counter item of your choice and then click the Add button at the bottom left of the screen.

This moves your selected items to the Added Counters box on the right side of the window.

4. To add additional counters, repeat Steps 2 and 3.

5. When you finish adding all the counters you desire, click OK.

This returns you to the Performance Monitor screen, where your newly added counters should now appear.

To remove a counter from Performance Monitor, highlight the counter you wish to delete in the box at the bottom of the Performance Monitor screen and then click the large red X on the toolbar above.

Reliability Monitor

Reliability Monitor keeps a running record of software installs and uninstalls and whether they are successful. It also has sections devoted to failures of all kinds: Application Failures, Hardware Failures, Windows Failures, and Miscellaneous Failures. All this information is condensed into a system stability chart with a ten-point range. (See Figure 10-16.)

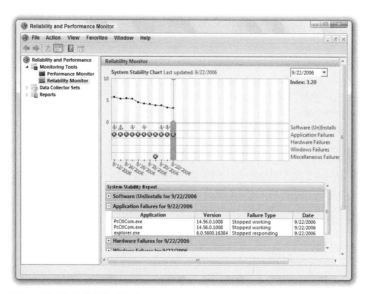

Figure 10-16: Reliability Monitor.

Reliability Monitor is useful if you need to pinpoint exactly when a problem began. For example, say you download a new version of a third-party software application that you later discover does not work properly with your operating system. You can use Reliability Monitor to find out exactly when the incompatible software was installed on your computer.

This feature can also help identify what might have caused a system or program crash. For example, if your computer encounters any type of system failure, you can turn to Reliability Monitor for more information about why this happened. If you click an instance where you have a failure scenario — indicated by a red circle with a white X inside it — and then scroll down to the failures information boxes below, you can review the failure details. The Failure Type column tells you what kind of system failure occurred and/or why it might have taken place; for example, perhaps the OS stopped responding, or there was a disruptive shutdown. Reliability Monitor can also be used to determine whether your computer has automatically installed all the most recent system updates. Click any date listed in the chart at the top of the screen and then scroll down the Software (Un)Installs information window to see the specific system and driver updates that were installed on your computer during that particular day. Having access to this information provides you with reassurance that your computer is downloading critical software updates as they become available.

Data Collector Sets and Reports

Data Collector Sets are a custom set of performance counters, event traces, and system configuration data that you define and can then run anytime you need them. The reports generated by this information can help you set up benchmarks for future performance and reliability comparisons. To create a Data Collector Set

1. **Open the Reliability and Performance Monitor window.**

Refer to the Resource Overview screen you see in Figure 10-12.

2. **Click the Data Collector Sets option in the left panel navigation tree.**

The subcategory folders for this feature appear in the main viewing window.

3. **Highlight the User Defined option and then right-click.**

Doing so produces a pop-up menu like the one shown in Figure 10-17.

Figure 10-17: The User Defined submenu.

4. **Choose New and then choose Data Collector Set from the submenu that appears to the right.**

This opens the Create New Data Collector Set Wizard. (See Figure 10-18.)

5. **Enter a name for your Data Collector Set in the text box provided.**

Remember to use a title that lets you easily identify what criteria are contained within the data set collection.

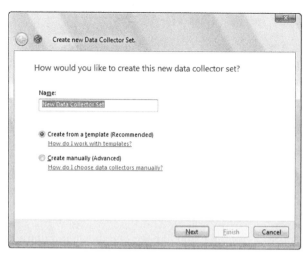

Figure 10-18: Creating a new Data Collector Set.

6. **Choose whether you would like to create the new Data Collector Set from a template (the recommended method) or manually (the more advanced option). Select the radio button to the left of your selection and then click Next.**

If you select the template method, a template selection page opens. Choose from a Basic, System Diagnostics, or System Performance template and then click Next. (*Note:* The descriptive paragraphs to the right of the selection window explain the functionality of each template type. Use this information to make an informed decision about the type of Data Collector Set you wish to create.)

If you select the manual option, a new window appears asking what type of data you want to include in your Data Collector Set. Place a check mark next to the data tags you wish to include or select the radio button next to the Performance Counter Alert option. After you make your selection(s), click Next. Use the Add buttons on the following screens to identify the criteria you wish to monitor with your Data Collector Set. Continue with this process until you reach the Root directory window.

7. **On the Root directory screen, enter a new directory file path for the location where you would like the results from your data set to be saved.**

You can use the default setting, or you can use the Browse button to locate another folder to store this data.

8. **Click Next.**

This takes you to the final Data Collector Set creation page. (See Figure 10-19.)

If you wish to permit only certain users access to this data, click the Change button. This opens a new window for you to enter a username and password.

If you wish to view the Properties details for this Data Collector Set, select the first radio button option: Open Properties for This Data Collector Set.

If you want to begin running this collection set immediately, choose the second option: Start This Data Collector Set Now.

If you are finished with the wizard and do not wish to view the Properties or the Data Collector Set results at this time, select the final option: Save and Close.

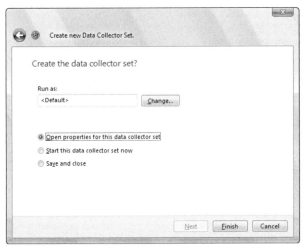

Figure 10-19: Completing the Data Collector Set creation process.

9. **Click Finish.**

This closes the Data Collector Set creation wizard.

Depending on which option you selected, you are taken to the appropriate screen. In most cases, the final selection is probably going to be the Save and Close option, in which case you are taken back to the Reliability and Performance Monitor window. From this screen, you can locate your new Data Collector Set by clicking the User Defined option in the navigation tree located in the left panel.

You can also view the reports for your Data Collector Set by selecting the Reports option in the left-panel navigation tree. The Reports section contains the data generated by each Data Collector Set. Use the navigation tree to select the desired report and bring up the requested data in the main viewing window to the right.

cache space: Memory used to temporarily store data.

Data Collector Sets: Customized performance reports that can be used to evaluate a computer's performance capabilities over an extended period of time.

Flash drive: A portable external hard drive that you attach to your computer, usually through a USB port.

hibernate: An improved power-saving mode for Windows Vista. When this powering-off method is used, files and programs are automatically saved to the computer's hard drive.

Performance Monitor: Visualization tool used to track various performance components of your computer.

ReadyBoost: The new feature in Windows Vista that harnesses extra memory from attached peripheral devices to improve a PC's processing speed.

Reliability Monitor: Tool used to record the stability of a PC. This application includes information about specific installation and failure activities.

sleep: The new powering-off method for Windows Vista. This power-saving mode combines features from the Standby and Hibernate methods used with previous Windows editions. When Sleep mode is activated, the PC saves open files and programs to its memory, allowing for quick restart capabilities.

standby: A powering-off method used in previous versions of Windows. This mode allowed for quick recall of recent Windows sessions, however, it did not possess the ability to save data like Vista's new Sleep mode.

SuperFetch: Automatically built into Vista, this feature keeps track of the programs you use most and loads them more quickly by keeping parts in memory.

Windows Registry: A centralized area within the Windows operating system serving as a depot for your system's configuration settings.

Last
Stop

Practice Exam

1. What are the principal differences between Hibernate and Sleep?

_____

_____

_____

2. What are the three default power plan settings? Briefly explain the benefits of each.

_____

_____

_____

3. How can you create a customized power plan? Why might you want to do this?

_____

_____

_____

4. Name three ways to bring your computer back from Sleep mode.

_____

_____

_____

5. What is ReadyBoost, and how can it help you work more efficiently?

_____

_____

_____

6. How can you tell whether a drive that is attached to your computer meets ReadyBoost requirements?

_____

_____

_____

7. What four areas are covered in the Windows Reliability and Performance Monitor resource overview? Please explain the significance of each.

_____

_____

_____

_____

8. In the Performance Monitor, a counter is an item used to track a computer's performance capabilities. What steps are involved when creating a new counter?

_____

_____

_____

9. How do you launch the Windows Reliability and Performance Monitor tools? What are the benefits of using these applications?

_____

_____

_____

10. What is a Data Collector Set? Why might you want to create one?

_____

_____

_____

Keeping Up, Backing Up, Disaster and Recovery

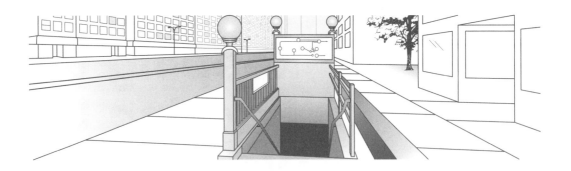

 # Enter the Station

Questions

1. How can Windows Update help keep your PC running smoothly?

2. What are the benefits of backing up your data?

3. When should you back up your entire system?

4. What is the Registry, and why might you attempt to edit it?

5. How can ScanDisk help you correct system errors?

6. What is disk defragmentation, and how can it make your computer run faster?

Express Line

If you are already up on the basics of maintaining the integrity of your system and its data, skip ahead to the next chapter.

Despite all the new security features of Windows Vista and all the safety precautions you can use during your computing activities, you might still encounter situations that require additional preemptive and post-emptive measures. For example, if you encounter a power outage before you can save an important file you have been working on diligently for the past three hours, you want to make sure that you can retrieve as much of this document as you can after your computer is up again.

You can use several methods to not only prevent such situations from occurring but to recall your files and programs in case something unavoidable does happen. An important part of prevention is to always back up your open files on a regular basis. That is not to say that you have to save your Word documents every 30 seconds. Rather, recording changes at regular intervals such as whenever you come to a good breaking point, or perhaps when you take a moment to gather your thoughts or notes — is sufficient. I also recommend backing up your documents whenever you leave the computer. For example, if you step away from your desk, for whatever reason — to answer the phone, see who is at the door, attend a meeting down the hall (if you are at work), or take a lunch break — be sure to save your documents before you leave your computer.

In addition to saving your files to your hard drive, I also recommend saving these items to an external storage device, such as a USB drive or a CD or DVD. That way, if anything happens to your computer — say, it gets stolen or is lost in a fire — you still have records of all your important documents, including your favorite pictures, music, and other files.

Too, not only your files and programs need to be safeguarded: You should also back up your entire system whenever you make any drastic changes. The System Restore section of this chapter shows you how, and the Windows Update and System Utilities portions of this chapter explain what you need to do to keep your computer running at peak performance.

Windows Update

Although Microsoft does its best to ensure that its operating systems meet the highest standards before they are released to the public, upgrades and corrections inevitably need to be made to your operating system (OS) after you install it on your computer. Often, *bugs* (processing errors), *loopholes* (missing elements that were overlooked during the final stages of creation), and new security-risk issues slip through the cracks to the final product. In such cases, Microsoft provides software updates to consumers in order to improve upon the functionality of the PC.

With most applications, you usually do not hear about all the updates, corrections, and bug fixes available unless you go to the program's manufacturer and search for those newer files. This is especially true of device drivers, which can go on working quite well long after they have technically become obsolete. Keeping all your applications, including the operating system, current with the latest revisions and security updates can be a continuing and time-consuming task. When many computers are in use, just keeping them all up to date can be a full-time job for an entire Information Technology department.

Beginning with Windows XP, Microsoft devised an online system of operating system updates, called *Windows Update.* All you had to do was click Windows Update from the Start menu, and your computer would connect to the Microsoft Update site, examine the computer to see what was current and what was not, and then download and install all sorts of updates, ranked from Critical through Important to Optional.

Information Kiosk

After Microsoft introduced its Windows Update feature, many other software vendors began emulating Microsoft's update program. By now, most vendors have similar systems that let you know when a later version of the software is available so that you can download and install it on your computer when you need it.

The new Windows Update application in Vista improves upon the one found in Windows XP. You can make it completely automatic and can carry on working while the update is being downloaded and installed. Better yet, you can now schedule updates for any time of day when the machine is otherwise idle — thus, not impinging on your work time.

Setting up Windows Update is simple. To do so, open the Start menu, choose All Programs, and then select Windows Update. (See Figure 11-1.)

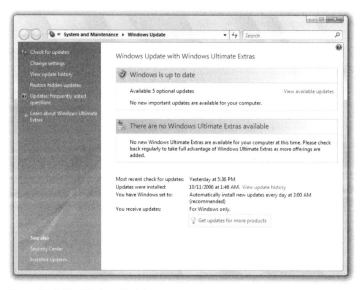

Figure 11-1: The Windows Update screen.

From this screen, you can check for new updates, change your automatic update settings, view your update history, or restore hidden updates. All these options are found in the column at the left of the Windows Update screen.

Information Kiosk

If you're running Windows Vista Ultimate on your PC, you are also eligible for additional Ultimate Extras that can be accessed via the Windows Update screen. Simply click the Learn about Windows Ultimate Extras link in the panel at the left to view the cutting-edge programs, services, and publications that are specific to Windows Vista Ultimate.

To set a specific time for your PC to seek out (and download) the latest Vista updates

1. **Open the Windows Update screen and click the Change Settings link in the column at the left.**

   This opens the Change Settings window, as shown in Figure 11-2.

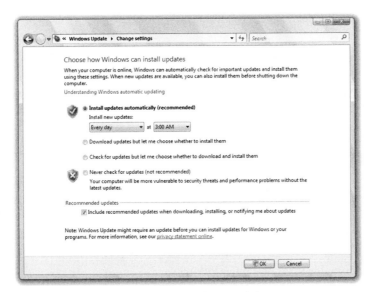

Figure 11-2: The Windows Updates Change Settings window.

2. **Select the Install Updates Automatically (Recommended) option.**

   A green dot appears in the radio button next to your selection.

   To download the updates automatically but install them manually, select the Download Updates But Let Me Choose Whether to Install Them option. This allows you to hand-select which programs/updates are saved to your computer.

To control both the downloading as well as the installation of updates, select the third option: Check for Updates But Let Me Choose Whether to Download and Install Them.

3. Use the drop-down menus provided to select the day and time during which you would like Vista to search for new updates.

You can choose to have your computer look for updates every day or just once per week, in which case you may select which day of the week this process occurs.

4. Click OK.

This closes the Change Settings window and returns you to the Windows Update screen.

 Watch Your Step

Be careful not to select the last Updates option: Never Check for Updates (Not Recommended). If you choose this alternative, you might put your PC and other personal or confidential information at risk.

The common reason you might be tempted to choose this option is that you envision situations where you might be running a process you wouldn't want interrupted by an automatic update that perhaps requires a restart of your machine. There is no need to be concerned about this. You can always choose the Check for Updates But Let Me Choose Whether to Download and Install Them option. It is located under Windows Update → Change Settings.

Although it is literally true with Windows Update that you can "set it and forget it," you still should periodically open Windows Update to see what optional updates might be available. Because only recommended (Microsoft calls them *important*) updates are automatically installed, you might miss out on occasional program or device drivers, utilities, and fonts that are also updates but entirely optional. Regularly reviewing available updates is also especially important if you select one of the alternative download/install options mentioned in Step 3 of the preceding steps.

To view available updates, do the following:

1. With the Windows Update screen open, click the Check for Updates link in the left panel. (Refer to Figure 11-1.)

If you are connected to the Internet, the window shown in Figure 11-3 appears, . indicating that Vista is searching for (and downloading) any available updates. If you are not connected to the Internet, you are prompted with a red warning message, in which case you need to connect to the Internet and click the Try Again button.

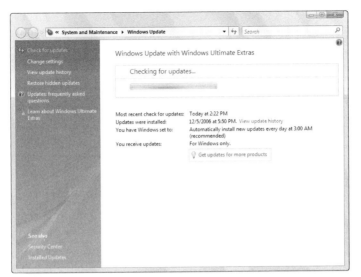

Figure 11-3: Checking for available updates.

After your computer downloads any new update files, you are returned to the newly updated Windows Update window, as shown in Figure 11-4.

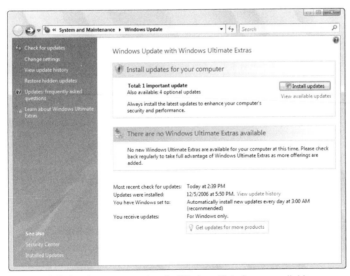

Figure 11-4: One important update for Windows Vista is now available.

2. **In the new Windows Update window, click the View Available Updates link, found directly below the Install Updates button.**

The View Available Updates screen appears, listing all available updates, as shown in Figure 11-5. Note that both Important and Optional updates are listed.

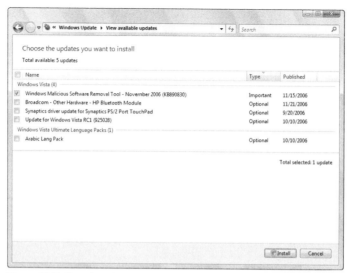

Figure 11-5: Choosing which updates to install.

3. Select the check boxes of those updates you wish to install on your machine and then click the Install button.

The selected upgrades are installed.

Information Kiosk

In addition to Windows Update, Microsoft also offers *Microsoft Update*, which provides the same sort of monitoring, downloading, and installing for other Microsoft products such as Word, Excel, PowerPoint, and more. Microsoft Update can be found on the Web at `http://update.microsoft.com/microsoftupdate`.

Windows Backup and Restore Center

In 2005, a survey by Harris Interactive, a large global marketing research firm, concluded that 35 percent of computer users never backed up their data; and, of those who did, 75 percent only did so once a month. Amazingly, small businesses fare worse: a Gartner Research (a technology research firm) report estimates that only 1 percent of small businesses back up daily.

Analysts at Gartner estimate that 15 percent of laptops purchased will break within the first year and 22 percent will falter within 4 years, compared to 5 percent and 12 percent for a desktop system. In addition, data can also rather easily be lost due to software going corrupt, computer viruses, theft, and good old human error.

Many computer users lose important data at one time or another due to the before-mentioned events. And although I doubt that there is any way to actually estimate the cost to anyone of significant data loss, if you've ever lost something on your computer, you don't need to be convinced of the importance of backing up your data.

Although the financial cost of having to restore your computer to its former state might be expensive in certain situations, it is not the most disturbing factor for many PC users. Rather, the time and energy involved when re-creating or reinstalling files and programs is so costly. And because a complete reinstallation of an OS can take hours and reinstalling programs can take days and sometimes even weeks, this can become a very time-consuming (and frustrating) process. Thus, if you take every precaution and learn important recovery strategies, you may avoid these situations.

Watch Your Step

Keep in mind that your hard drive can be damaged and rendered unusable when plugged in during inclement weather. A power surge strip usually can protect your system, although your safest bet under such circumstances would be to unplug the unit and use a backup power source unit. Forewarned is forearmed!

Fortunately, Windows Vista incorporates all these extremely important functions into one centralized location: the Windows Backup and Restore Center. You can even use this tool to restore your operating system to a state of performance from a previous date and time of your choosing.

Backing up your files

The most basic step to prevent data loss is to back up all your important files to another source, such as an external hard drive, a Flash drive, CDs or DVDs, or another storage device. By *backing up* (making duplicate copies of) these files, you can ensure that you have a spare if something ever happens to the original.

Information Kiosk

Backing up data can be done on a variety of media. For large amounts of data, you would probably be best served by using an external hard drive or a sufficient quantity of DVDs. Small amounts of data can be backed up to most available drives (given sufficient space), Flash drives, CDs, or even an MP3 player or iPod.

The first time that you decide to do a backup of files, you need to be prepared. First, be sure you have sufficient internal hard disk space, an external drive to back up to, or plenty of DVDs. (If you are backing up to DVDs and you run out of them midstream, though, you can always resume at a later point.)

How much storage would you need for a backup? The answer is — unfortunately — *very* relative. If you look in Help, Microsoft only provides a very general rule of thumb, suggesting that 200GB is a good idea. There is no precise answer because it depends on a number of factors, including

- How much data you wish to back up
- The nature of that data (is it already compressed or not?)

In backing up your data, data compression takes place (it saves on space, and speeds up the time it takes to back up data). Data already compressed, such as `.zip`, `.mpg`, `.avi`, `.jpg`, and `.gif` file formats, among many others, will not compress further, whereas `.doc, .ppt, .xls, .txt, .pdf,` and many others will.

Your safest rule is to assume that you will need the same amount of file space for already compressed files that they currently take up. And for files that can compress further, assume you need about half as much. (In actuality, it is usually much less.)

Also keep in mind that an external drive with a sizeable amount of space (250–300GB) should be more than enough. A normal, single-sided blank DVD has a maximum storage capacity of up to 4.7GB, while a blank CD has room for only 700MB.

To begin backing up your files, first open the Windows Backup and Restore Center. To locate this tool

1. **Open the Start menu and choose Control Panel from the right column.**

    The Control Panel window appears.

2. **Click the System and Maintenance link.**

    The System and Maintenance menu appears.

3. **Choose the Backup and Restore Center.**

    The Backup and Restore Center page appears, as shown in Figure 11-6.

    Note: When you open the Windows Backup and Restore Center, you see two choices in the backup section of this window: Back Up Files and Back Up Computer. The Back Up Files option lets you choose to back up only files of a certain type: all your music files, for example, or all your document files. If you choose the second option (Back Up Computer), all the files and programs on your computer are included in the backup process. Just keep in mind that if you do choose the second option, you need to be sure that you have enough space on your storage device(s). (If you attach a storage device to your PC before clicking this button, Vista displays a yellow caution icon on your screen if the selected drive does not have enough memory to save all the files and programs on your machine's hard drive.)

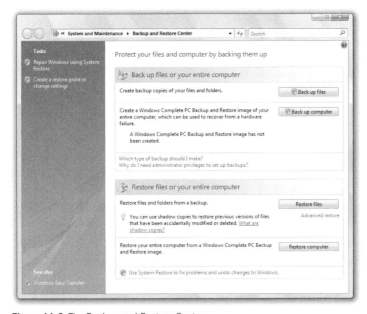

Figure 11-6: The Backup and Restore Center.

To actually back up your files, do the following:

1. **With the Windows Backup and Restore Center open, click the Back Up Files button.**

   This opens the Save Location page of the Back Up Files Wizard, as shown in Figure 11-7.

2. **In the Save Location page of the wizard, designate where you would like to save your backup files and then click Next.**

   You can choose to back up your files to an internal or external hard drive, a Flash drive, or a CD or DVD (in which case, you can use the drop-down menu provided to select which drive to use when backing up your files). Or, you can choose to back up your files to a network, in which case you either use the Browse button to locate the desired network, or type in the network's file path in the text box provided.

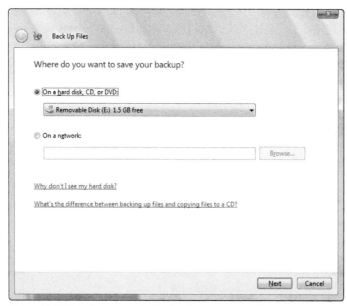

Figure 11-7: Selecting a save destination for your backup files.

3. In the new screen that appears, use the check boxes provided to select which types of files you would like to back up (see Figure 11-8). Then click Next.

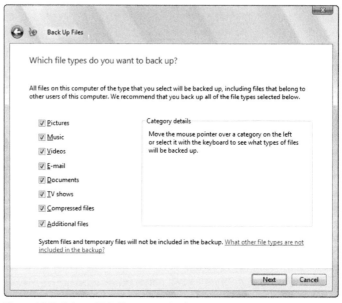

Figure 11-8: Select which file types to back up.

If a check mark is present, the files that belong to the designated category are saved during the backup process. If no check mark is present, the files in that particular category will not be saved.

4. **In the scheduling window of the wizard (see Figure 11-9), use the drop-down menus provided to establish how often (as well as what day and time) you would like the backup process to take place. Then click the Save Settings and Start Back Up button.**

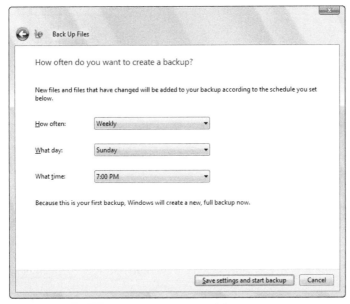

Figure 11-9: Schedule a regular backup day and time.

The backup process begins, during which the files of the type or types you selected in Step 3 are saved to the designated backup location.

Note: If you are backing up your files to CDs or DVDs, you might need to switch to a new blank disc when the current disc becomes full. Vista lets you know when it is time to insert a new disc.

Information Kiosk

You can continue to work on your computer while it is being backed up — even on files included in the backup. The last saved version of any file in the designated backup categories — even the ones in use — are saved during the backup process.

Step into the Real World

Some backup methods tend to be more involved than others. For example, if you have a lot of files or programs to back up, using discs (either CDs or DVDs) can be a much more tedious process than using an external hard drive (or a Flash drive) that has more storage space. Therefore, take into consideration how large your files are and how much space you'll need to save duplicate copies of this information before you begin the backup process. Otherwise, you might find that this procedure can be more time-consuming than you expected.

Watch Your Step

Permanent digital media does not exist! Most media can be hit with viruses. External hard drives can see their enclosures damaged and a hard drive rendered inaccessible. Hard drive failures can happen to your hard drive eventually. DVDs and CDs, even when properly stored, can deteriorate physically sometimes because of storage conditions. In addition to the obvious advice of handling equipment carefully, keep and maintain more than one backup of any important data.

Restoring data from backups

Restoring data — essentially, the exact reverse of backing up data — reloads backup files to your PC. However, because these two procedures are so closely related, Vista locates this function in the same area (the Backup and Restore Center) as the Backup feature.

To restore backup files

1. Open the Start menu and choose Control Panel from the right column.

The Control Panel appears.

2. Choose System and Maintenance.

This opens the System and Maintenance menu.

3. Choose the Backup and Restore Center.

The Backup and Restore Center appears. (Refer to Figure 11-6.)

4. Click the Restore Files button.

This opens the Restore Files window, as shown in Figure 11-10.

Note the See Recently Deleted Files link at the bottom of the screen. Clicking here allows you to back up files using items that have recently been moved to the Recycle Bin.

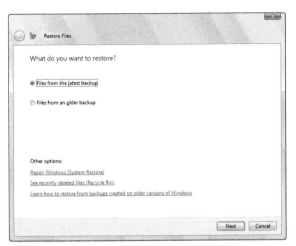

Figure 11-10: Restoring your backup files.

Information Kiosk

Click the Restore Computer button (in the lower section of the Backup and Restore Center) to restore your entire computer to a previous state saved during an earlier backup process.

The Advanced Restore option provides you with the possibility to restore files from other users, from a backup to another computer, and even from files backed up under a previous version of Windows.

5. Select which backup version you would like to revert to and then click Next.

In most instances, you want to select the Files from the Latest Backup option. However, you also have the option to restore Files from an Older Backup. This allows you to restore previous versions of a document or program that might have been corrupted during the most recent backup process.

Clicking Next opens a new window (see Figure 11-11), from which you can choose to select additional files and folders — ones that might have been created since your last restore — to include when your computer begins the restore process.

6. Click the Add Files (or Add Folders) button provided.

This opens a Windows Explorer screen. Use this window to locate and select the files or folders you want to add to the items that are to be restored to your machine.

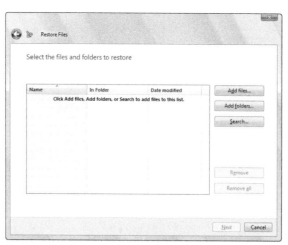

Figure 11-11: Choosing additional files and folders to restore.

7. Click Next.

The next screen that appears (see Figure 11-12) asks you to choose where you would like the restored files saved. You can choose to save them to their original location, in which case the files that exist in that particular location are deleted and replaced with the restore files. Or, you can choose to save them to a new location. If you opt to save your restored files to a new location, use the text box provided to enter a file path for these files and programs or click the Browse button to navigate to the appropriate folders.

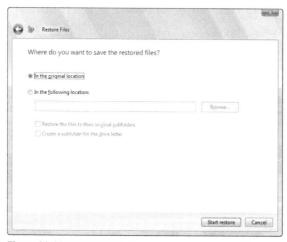

Figure 11-12: Determining where to save your restored files.

Note: If you decide to save your restored files to a new location but would still like to maintain the same organizational structure for these items, be sure to place a check mark in the Restore the Files to Their Original Subfolders check box. This ensures that all your documents are placed in the appropriate subfolders rather than being placed in one single folder.

8. Choose a location for your restore files and then click the Start Restore button.

This begins the restore process. When this process is complete, you are notified with a `Successfully Restored Files` message.

9. Click Finish.

This completes the restoration process. Your restored files can now be accessed in the location(s) specified in Step 8 of this list.

System Restore

In addition to being able to restore files, you can also restore the functionality of your computer system. *System Restore* is the tool that lets you return to a previous PC performance level. Microsoft introduced the System Restore function with its launch of Windows Me, several years ago. It was a great innovation in its time and still remains so because it allows you to turn back the clock on your system to a time when it was running more efficiently. System Restore can be a very good option when you notice problems, such as when your system runs slower when powering up or down or when errors occur after installing either a new program or new drivers for a device.

Sometimes, these problems can be solved by reinstalling a program or device (or uninstalling them). Other times, system problems can resolve themselves simply when you reboot your system. However, after you've investigated a specific problem and taken all necessary steps per whatever documentation you have on hand, System Restore can help you to restore your system to a previously workable state. And it is easy to use.

Every time you install a new program or device or update your system in any way, Windows Vista automatically creates a *restore point.* This is a point in time that you can go back to if you encounter system problems later. You can also create a restore point manually any time you choose.

Information Kiosk

System Restore is a function for which you need Administrator privileges.

The System Restore feature can be found in the Backup and Restore Center. It is the bottom-most link on the screen (refer to Figure 11-6) — Use System Restore to Fix Problems and Undo Changes to Windows. When you click this link, you see the System Restore window shown in Figure 11-13.

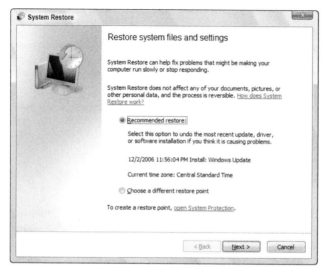

Figure 11-13: Restoring system files and settings.

After you locate the System Restore screen, do the following:

1. **Choose whether you would like to restore your system according to the data last saved on the Recommended Restore date or elect to choose a different date.**

The Recommended Restore date is usually the same as the most recent backup date. If you want to return to a specific date — perhaps one that did not include a particular software program or updated driver — select the second option: Choose a Different Restore Point.

If you opt to hand-select the restoration date, you are confronted with the screen shown in Figure 11-14.

2. **Highlight the date you wish to restore and then click Next.**

This opens a date confirmation window like the one shown in Figure 11-15.

3. **Confirm the restore point by clicking Finish.**

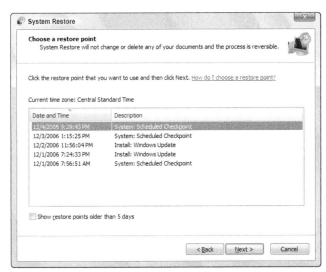

Figure 11-14: Select a specific restore point.

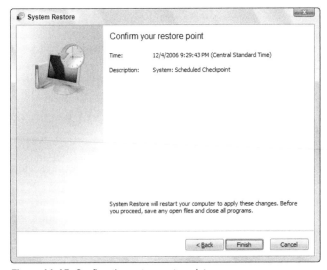

Figure 11-15: Confirm the system restore date.

System Restore starts and runs on its own until it is finished. Do not interrupt this process as it progresses. If that happens, reboot your machine and run System Restore once again. When the process is complete, your machine automatically reboots itself. After the rebooting process is finished, your system is restored and ready to work.

Information Kiosk

Creating your own restore point allows you to identify a specific date and time to which to return to if you so desire. Create a manual restore date if you are making major (or numerous) changes to your computer system. That way, if you decide that you are not particularly fond of the new changes, you can easily revert to the previous restore date.

To create a new restore point manually, open the Backup and Restore Center and click the Create a Restore Point link from the left panel. The System Properties window appears. Select the drive you wish to create a backup for — if you want to back up your hard drive, select the drive labeled (System) — and then click the Create button at the bottom of the window.

Watch Your Step

If you run System Restore after having cleaned a virus or trojan horse from your machine, System Restore can **unfortunately** restore that infected file on your machine. Most antivirus software manufacturers recommend disabling System Restore temporarily when specifically running their programs to remove malware. Each case is different, however, and you need to follow instructions explicitly for malware removal as provided by your software manufacturer. After virus removal, run an online scan of your machine to verify that your system is clean — and then create a new restore point.

Working with the Windows Registry

The *Registry* controls and directs every facet of a Windows installation, from initial boot up to shutdown, major and minor. Because the Registry plays such an important part in the overall functionality of your PC, many users (even experienced professionals) are reluctant to work with this feature. And rightly so, especially because a single incorrect digit or character in the wrong place anywhere in this multimegabyte file can cause your computer to malfunction or even refuse to boot at all.

Watch Your Step

Most of the time, don't mess with the Registry at all. When problems do arise, resolving them in some other way — such as reinstalling balky software — is often easier and safer. That can be true all the way to the drastic step of reinstalling Windows itself either as a Repair and Update or as a clean install.

Sometimes, though, a little judicious and very careful tweaking of the Registry can save much time while restoring Windows or a specific application to like-new performance, or it can have some beneficial effect such as removing an annoying pop-up window or forcing Vista to do something it is not programmed to do.

The Registry organization

Before you can edit the Registry, you have to know how it is organized.

The Registry is not one file but rather several files arranged as a hierarchical database; that is, the most important files exist at a higher level, with the less critical files cascading down. Vista holds six such files — the *hive files* — named without extensions: Components, Default, Sam, Security, Software, and System. These are stored in

`Windows\System32\Config\directory`. Another file, `NTUSER.DAT`, resides in each user's profile folder. You can open these files with a text editor, but you won't learn much about them, and you cannot edit them.

More importantly, these files are organized in logical sections that correspond to the definitions used to access them through the Vista Application Programs Interface (API). All the sections, or keys, begin with `HKEY`, which is short for *Handle to Key*.

Each key is divided into subkeys, which are further divided into more subkeys and so on *ad infinitum*. Each key can contain values, which can be

- **String values:** A list of numeric values that as a whole, represent one item
- **Binary values:** A set of 0s and 1s that instruct the computer to behave in a particular manner based upon the arrangement of these symbols
- **DWORD values:** Numbers between 0 and 2^32-1 that are used to identify types of data that are twice as long as the average storage bit
- **Multistring values:** Complex string values that include several different lines of numeric values
- **Expandable string values:** String values that fluctuate for the purpose of further defining the data contained within a string

Each key has a default value, which is essentially the same name as the key. Keys and values syntax is similar to Windows filenames, backslash and all: for example

`COMPUTER\HKEY_CURRENT_USER\ Printers\Settings\Wizard`

The major keys and their logical groupings are

- **HKEY_CLASSES_ROOT:** Stores information about registered applications, including information about file extensions and the applications associated with them
- **HKEY_CURRENT_USER:** Holds settings specific to the logged-in user
- **HKEY_LOCAL_MACHINE:** Includes settings that apply to all users on the specified computer
- **HKEY_USERS:** Contains subkeys for each user registered on the machine
- **HKEY_CURRENT_CONFIG:** Houses runtime information that is not stored permanently but regenerated at boot

Editing the Registry

Because the Registry is such a critical (and sensitive) part of your system, you are most likely not going to edit the Registry unless you have encountered a problem or learned of an improvement and someone (or some document) has told you that the way to fix the problem or make the improvement is to make changes in the Registry. That being so, you will not be instructed to try this or try that but, instead, will be given specific step-by-step instructions as to exactly what keys need to be changed or created and what values to insert in those keys. However, before you make any adjustments whatsoever to the Registry, be sure you back up your entire system — especially the Registry — before you lay a hand on it. The reason this step is so important is that if you accidentally enter the wrong value to the right key or the right value to the wrong key — or if the instructions you are following are faulty — you run the risk of rendering your computer useless.

Watch Your Step

It only takes only one bad value in one obscure subkey to make your computer behave erratically.

Information Kiosk

Only those with Administrator privileges can edit the Registry.

Starting the Registry Editor application

Although you can open the Registry files with a text editor and even make some sense out of some of the information you find there, you cannot manipulate the files with such an editor. You must use an application called Registry Editor (REGEDIT), which can also provide partial backup and restore functions to individual keys and values.

To summon the Registry Editor, click the Start button, type **regedit** into the Start Search box, and then press Enter.

Doing so brings up the Registry Editor, as shown in Figure 11-16.

The left pane, the Keys pane, is the top of the hierarchical tree. Clicking the + sign on any of the five root keys expands that key to all its first-level subkeys. Clicking a key or subkey itself displays values in the right pane, the Values pane. Clicking the + sign on each subkey opens still more subkeys, whose values can be displayed in the right pane. You can edit both the subkeys themselves and their values. But first, as mentioned before, be sure to back up your computer's Registry.

Unfortunately, a dedicated backup utility for the entire Registry does not exist in Vista as it does in earlier releases. The Windows XP System State backup, which backs up all Registry files as well as other important system level files in Windows XP, has no counterpart in Vista. Although Vista's backup system does make it easy to back up your entire computer or separately back up and restore files of a certain type (including files of a type that comprise the Registry), it does not provide a separate feature for backing up just the Registry.

Figure 11-16: The Registry Editor.

Some advanced users recognize that they need to back up the most important file directories — the six hive files: Components, Default, Sam, Security, Software, and System. Their most feasible Registry backup strategy is to simply copy the Registry to another location and then, if necessary, copy them back to their original locations in the `Windows\System32\Config\directory`. Here's an easy way to do just that:

1. **Open the Start menu and search for the Registry Editor.**

Enter **regedit** into the Start menu search box to locate this feature.

2. **With the Registry Editor open, choose the File menu.**

This opens a drop-down menu, like the one shown in Figure 11-17.

3. **From the drop-down menu that appears, choose Export.**

This opens the Export Registry File window. (See Figure 11-18.)

4. **Use the drop-down menu for the Save In field to identify where you wish to save this backup copy of your Registry files.**

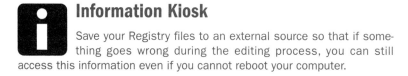

Information Kiosk

Save your Registry files to an external source so that if something goes wrong during the editing process, you can still access this information even if you cannot reboot your computer.

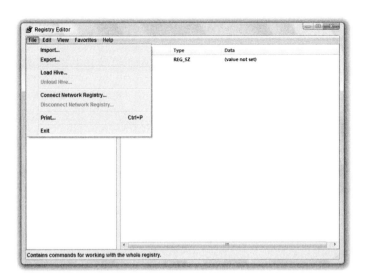

Figure 11-17: The File menu in the Registry.

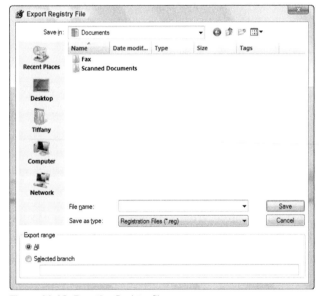

Figure 11-18: Exporting Registry files.

5. Type a name for your Registry copy in the File Name box.

Be sure to title your backup files something that you can easily remember.

6. **Use the drop-down menu for the Save as Type box to identify which files you would like to create backup files for.**

You have the option to save a copy of all Registration Files or just the Registry Hive Files. If you have enough room to save all the Registration Files, you select this option. However, if you have only enough room to save the hive files, this at least allows you to restore the most important facets of your computer if something were to go wrong during the Registry-editing process.

7. **Click Save.**

This creates a backup copy of your computer's registration files to the location designated in Step 4 of this list.

With your insurance against disaster safely stowed away, you can start working with the Registry.

Working with keys

All the keys in the Key pane, from the five root keys down, appear as folder icons. No folder icons appear in the Values pane.

Each key has a label or name, often in plain language but also in *hexadecimal* (a mathematical computing expression used to convert string values into an easily identifiable representation). Keys can be deleted, which also deletes all the keys in that particular tree. Or, new keys can be created and labeled.

When all the key file folders are closed, nothing appears in the Values pane. Click any key, though, and the folder opens with the relevant data in the Values pane, even if only to state that the values are Default or Value Not Set.

Understanding the basics of Registry editing is valuable for most computer users. This understanding can help you through some particularly challenging situations that can come up, where your only solution includes editing Registry files. For example

- Some third-party software that requires frequent updating can, at a certain point, start to produce errors.

- Certain malware (viruses and trojans) that get into your system, for which there is no corrective patch, might need to be removed from the Registry files in order to return your computer to its previous state.

- Programs that have difficulty during installation can also be corrected via Registry editing.

In these cases, if you are lucky enough to find documentation on the Web that provides solutions to these problems, you might also find that very often you are directed to edit a number of Registry files.

Step into the Real World

If you want to try your hand at editing the Registry, follow these instructions to change the Registry files so that the amount of time it takes for the Start Up menu to appear is faster than it currently is:

1. **Open the Registry Editor and select the HKEY CURRENT USER folder.**

2. **From the submenu that appears, choose Control Panel and then choose Desktop.**

3. **Double-click the MenuShowDelay entry and change the existing value from 400 to 0.**

System Utilities

System Utilities are the software programs used to help keep your computer system — especially your operating system — running properly. They are essentially the housekeeping programs that are used to clean up and help manage the data and programs stored on your PC. The two time-honored Windows utilities that have been around since Windows first appeared on the scene are Disk Defragmenter and ScanDisk.

ScanDisk (Checkdisk)

ScanDisk is a utility that is quite important to the overall health of your computer's hard disk. When you work on your computer, you access the hard drive for information or loading programs and opening files, programs, and so on. During these activities, your computer does a lot of data swapping. One result of all these operations is that some unnecessary data clutter is created. ScanDisk is the utility used to rid your computer of these impertinent files.

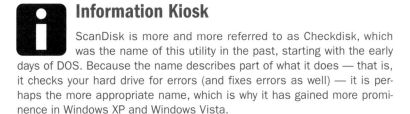

Information Kiosk

ScanDisk is more and more referred to as Checkdisk, which was the name of this utility in the past, starting with the early days of DOS. Because the name describes part of what it does — that is, it checks your hard drive for errors (and fixes errors as well) — it is perhaps the more appropriate name, which is why it has gained more prominence in Windows XP and Windows Vista.

ScanDisk, although an undeniably important utility, is almost always hidden in Windows. If you search for it under Instant Search, you cannot find it, and it is not listed under the Control Panel.

To find and run this utility

1. Open Windows Explorer.

You can either perform an Instant Search for this window or click the Computer option in the right column of the Start menu.

2. Right-click the drive you wish to scan.

A drop-down menu appears for the selected drive.

3. From the menu that appears, choose Properties.

This opens the Properties menu for the selected drive.

4. From the Properties dialog box, select the Tools tab.

The Tools tab — like the one shown in Figure 11-19 — appears.

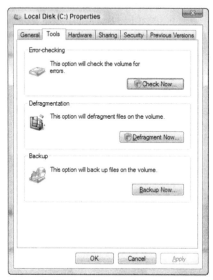

Figure 11-19: The Tools tab of the Properties window.

5. In the Error-checking section, click the Check Now button.

The Check Disk dialog box appears. (See Figure 11-20.)

Figure 11-20: The Check Disk dialog box.

6. **Place a check mark next to both the Automatically Fix File System Errors option and the Scan for and Attempt Recovery of Bad Sectors option.**

This ensures that all functionality errors and unusable sectors of the selected drive are corrected during the ScanDisk process.

7. **Click Start, located in the dialog box.**

Note: If the drive you select is the drive where Windows Vista is installed, you see a dialog box with the message `Windows Can't Check the Disk While It's in Use.`

If this is the case, select the option to check for hard disk errors the next time you start your computer by clicking the Schedule Disk Check button.

If a drive you select is any other drive, Windows Vista automatically launches the ScanDisk utility; it then runs entirely on its own.

The larger the size of your drive and the more data it contains, the longer it takes to run the ScanDisk utility program. When it finishes, you see a report describing what it found and what it fixed. Click OK to acknowledge that you reviewed these corrections. Your operating system can then resume its normal functioning.

Information Kiosk

Because ScanDisk can be run on only one drive at a time, you might need to repeat this process for each of the drives on your machine.

Disk Defragmenter

Defrag is short for Disk Defragmenter. In Chapter 5, you learned about files and folders and gained an understanding of how your computer really stores data: that is, not really by filename and directory but rather in tiny data bits that are actually scattered all over the hard drive. Over time, as you call up files, move them around, carve pieces out of some of them and insert them in others, and then resave them, the data bits already scattered all over the hard drive become even more scattered. As a result, the computer has a harder time retrieving these items. This makes your machine take longer and longer to open, save, and close your files. This is where Disk Defragmenter (Defrag) can help.

Imagine a desk at which you do your work. Over time, it becomes more and more cluttered. You might not want to throw anything away, yet you need more space. If you take your arms and push everything on top of the desk away from the middle, you clear more space by consolidating all your clutter at the outer edges. In a way, this is just what Defrag does: It consolidates your data, making the file retrieval and restoring operations much more efficient — and in the process, helps your computer do it more easily — and, therefore, faster.

Determining how often to run Disk Defragmenter depends on how often you use your computer. If a machine is in continuous operation, run it as often as once per week. If you spend an average of an hour or two a day on your machine, be sure to do it at least once per month. And it doesn't interfere with your getting your work done because you can continue to work on your computer while Disk Defragmenter runs in the background.

Disk Defragmenter is easy to find and use; this is all you need to do:

1. **Choose Start → All Programs → Accessories → System Tools → Disk Defragmenter.**

The Disk Defragmenter dialog box appears. (See Figure 11-21.)

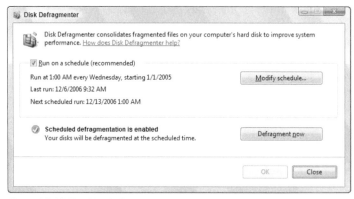

Figure 11-21: The Disk Defragmenter dialog box.

You can see that a default defragmentation schedule already exists. (By default, it's set for every Wednesday at 1 a.m.)

2. **(Optional) To change this preset schedule, click the Modify Schedule button to set a new preferred day of the week and time for this process.**

You can also adjust how often the defragmenter is run when you opt to modify the defragmenter schedule.

3. **Simply click the Defragment Now button.**

A message appears, alerting you that this process can take from a few minutes to a few hours. (See Figure 11-22.)

 Information Kiosk

You can also choose to defragment individual drives by accessing this option via the Tools tab of the Properties menu. Just follow the directions presented in the preceding section on ScanDisk, except click the Defragment Now button instead of the Check Now button in Step 5 of the list there.

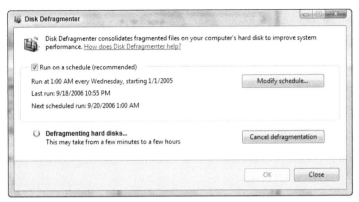

Figure 11-22: Defragmenting your hard drive can take a few minutes or up to several hours.

Disk Defragmenter runs in the background automatically, requiring no intervention on your part, but you do have to click OK when it is finished to allow your machine to resume its normal level of performance.

Information Kiosk

During disk defragmentation, you might notice that your machine's performance does slow down. This is particularly evident if you have less than 1MB of RAM.

API (Application Programming Interface): Interface used to transfer data back and forth between your computer system and active applications.

Backup and Restore Center: Location for creating backup copies of your files (or your entire computer system) and for restoring these items to your machine in case this data is lost.

disk defragmentation: The process by which existing files and programs are grouped together within a particular drive to create additional space for new data.

hive files: The six files — Components, Default, Sam, Security, Software, and System — stored in the configuration directory that do not have file extensions associated with them.

continued

HKEY: Abbreviation for *Handle to Key,* the term used to describe the main categories in the Registry.

Registry keys: Elements of the Registry that store configuration information.

ScanDisk: The system utility used to check for and correct system errors.

System Restore: The utility that allows you to restore your operating system to a previous time.

System Utilities: Software programs used to keep your operating system and other programs running smoothly. These housekeeping programs ensure that your disk space is properly allotted and that there are no corrupt files or programs on your PC.

Windows Registry: A collection (or database) of all your operating system, hardware, program, settings, and user accounts data.

Windows Update: Application used to download and install the latest Windows software corrections. Check for updates on a regular basis so that you do not miss any critical security or performance changes. This feature is accessible via Microsoft's Web site.

Practice Exam

1. What is Windows Update, and why should you use it?

_____

_____

_____

2. How can you check for new Vista updates?

_____

_____

_____

3. Where can you find the Backup and Restore Center?

_____

_____

_____

4. How can you restore your system to a previous performance level, and why might you need to do this?

_____

_____

_____

5. Why is it so important to proceed with caution when editing the Registry?

_____

_____

_____

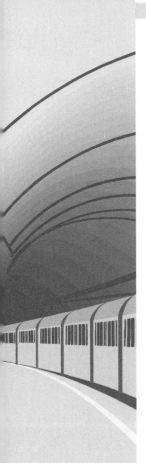

6. Name two examples when you might need to edit the Registry.

_____

_____

7. What is the primary purpose of the system utilities discussed in this chapter?

_____

_____

_____

8. Where is the ScanDisk utility located?

_____

_____

9. What are your options when defragmenting disk drives?

_____

_____

_____

10. What is the safest media to use to make a backup?

_____

_____

_____

Getting Help and Support

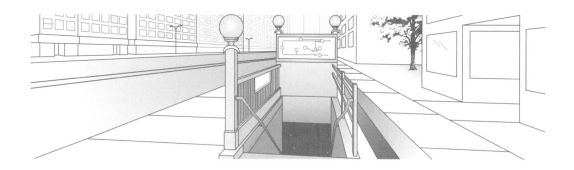

 # Enter the Station

Questions

1. What options do you have when seeking help for Vista?

2. Where can you find video tutorials to help you with step-by-step instructions?

3. What are the benefits of using Windows Remote Assistance?

4. What online Help resources are available to you?

5. How can using diagnostic tools aid in the help-seeking process?

With the ever-increasing complexity of computers (and Information Technology in general), more and more things can go wrong with your computer system. Your installed software and peripheral devices can create problems as well as affect how these items interact. And even though each of these components includes its own Help system, sometimes you need to move beyond the system-specific Help files to understand why these things don't working together like they should.

In the past, you had to spend quite a bit of time and energy trying to figure out problems on your own. Or, if you were lucky, you could call someone who could help you, such as a technically inclined family member or friend or a computer expert (who mostly likely charged you for each minute of assistance).

Fortunately, Windows Vista offers multiple sources of help when you're faced with a computer problem. You can easily access the Vista Help and Support menu with a simple click of a button, or you can reach out to Microsoft Customer Service representatives, newsgroup participants, and others. You can also use various online Help resources to answer your questions.

Using the Vista Help Tools

In Windows Vista, help is readily available everywhere you travel. In whatever screen you find yourself in, you are never more than one keystroke away from assistance.

To see what I mean, just press F1; the Windows Help and Support page appears. (See Figure 12-1.)

Figure 12-1: The Windows Help and Support window.

When this window appears, you can enter keywords into the Search Help field, or you can click one of the icons for further assistance.

Each of the six icons listed in the Windows Help and Support window specializes in its own category. Here is a brief explanation of each icon:

Windows Basics: Clicking this icon opens a list of articles that covers a broad range of Windows topics, including an introduction to your computer and its parts; an overview of the desktop; printing help; and information on using programs, working with files, exploring the Internet, using e-mail, working with digital images, and so on.

Security and Maintenance: This screen offers a security checklist for Vista users as well as a brief explanation of the new Vista safety features, including Windows Security Center, Windows Defender, User Account Controls, Backup and Restore, Parental Controls, Windows Update, and Windows Firewall. Links to more information about each of these features are also provided in this window.

Windows Online Help: Clicking this icon directs you to the Microsoft Help Web site where you can search for more information about whatever problems you encounter. This feature can be quite useful if the information included in the Help and Support screen does not quite answer your question(s).

Table of Contents: This icon provides you with a list of all the Help articles in the Vista Help and Support Center. These articles are then organized by categories. If you are seeking more information about a particular topic (rather than a specific incident), you might want to start with this outline to learn more about your options before proceeding.

Troubleshooting: This icon includes some of the most common troubleshooting questions (and answers) pertaining to Networking, Using the Web, E-mail, Hardware and Drivers, and Your Computer. If you encounter problems in any of these areas, you might check out this portion of the Help and Support menu first. Chances are that you can find exactly what you are looking for here. And if not, you can use the Search Help field to clarify your help topic.

What's New?: Clicking this icon brings up a screen that lists the new features and functionalities of a number of Vista tools. This menu is particularly helpful if you are new to Windows Vista.

Contextual help

In all Windows programs, Microsoft and non-Microsoft alike, pressing F1 brings up the Help menu. (If you happen to be connected to the Internet when you press F1, you also get the benefit of more extensive online Help resources.) There is more to the F1 key than that, though: Pressing F1 can provide you with contextual assistance. For example, press F1 when you are using Vista to get Vista-related Help; press F1 when working within a program like Word or Excel, and you call up Help for that particular program.

How the F1 key has been set up even allows you to narrow your Help search to a particular command or feature. Simply open the window or dialog box associated with that feature — be sure it's active by clicking it — and then press F1. A customized version of the Windows Help and Support window appears, highlighting help topics tailored to your featured choice. (See Figure 12-2.) And, of course, you can still enter keywords into the Search Help field.

Figure 12-2: Windows Help and Support window tailored to the Control Panel feature.

Information Kiosk

You can always access the complete Vista Help files menu (instead of just contextual Help files) by opening the Start menu and then choosing Help and Support from the column to the right.

Show Me Step-by-Step

A quick look at Figure 12-2 hints at a new Windows Vista innovation: Vista demos. You'll notice two options at the top of the Windows Help and Support window:

- **Do It Automatically:** This option allows you to sit back and watch the steps play out before your eyes.

- **Show Me Step-by-Step (Recommended):** This option refers to animated Help topics, which are, in essence, mini-videos that feature a cursor moving through all the steps needed to perform what you queried Help about. The video demo prompts you to click buttons or press keyboard keys as you go through the demo step by step.

Windows Remote Assistance

For the longest time, computer owners have found getting tech support from the outside world — especially, getting it easily — a challenging experience. In addition to that, most of the time, a cost factor is associated with tech support. In the past, tech support would generally have been free; today, free tech support is quite rare.

Windows Vista has a new option — Windows Remote Assistance — that takes advantage of either an Internet connection or a network connection to allow you to get help when otherwise it might simply have seemed out of reach.

For years, third-party software has been available that would allow you to take control of another computer from a distance. Sometimes the person taking control could be you, and sometimes it could be you allowing someone else to take control of your computer. *Windows Remote Assistance* follows in that tradition by allowing you to connect to another computer and have the person operating that computer help you by temporarily taking control of your computer. Windows Remote Assistance also works in the opposite way: That is, it can allow you to connect to another computer and help that person. This can be extremely helpful if the person assisting you with your computer problem is in a different location. It is obviously much easier to see firsthand what might be causing the problem rather than trying to have someone explain (and then identify) the conflict. For example, you could have someone remotely reconfigure your computer so that it works again rather than having to go through each Registry line verbally to identify where the problem lies.

 Transfer

Editing the Windows Registry might be necessary in order to solve certain Windows problems. To learn more about the Windows Registry see Chapter 11.

If you wish to take advantage of Windows Remote Assistance, you must first establish a Remote Assistance Connection to your computer. Here's how:

1. **Click the Start button and choose Control Panel from the menu that appears.**

   The Control Panel window opens.

2. **Click the System and Maintenance link in the Control Panel window.**

   The System and Maintenance menu appears.

3. **Click the System link.**

   This opens the System screen, as shown in Figure 12-3.

4. **From the left panel of the System window, choose Remote Settings.**

   You are now at the System Properties dialog box. (See Figure 12-4.)

5. **Select the Remote tab (if it is not already selected) and then select the Allow Remote Assistance Connections to This Computer check box.**

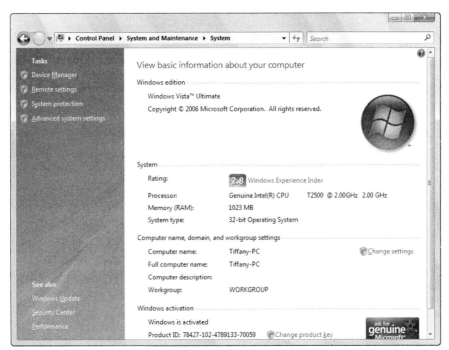

Figure 12-3: The System window.

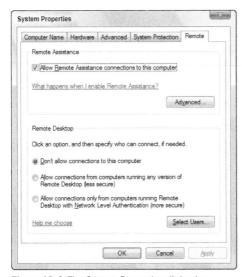

Figure 12-4: The System Properties dialog box.

6. **Click OK.**

This closes the System Properties window.

After you enable Remote Assistance, you can use it to connect to other computers or allow others to connect to yours.

The next step in connecting with others via Remote Assistance is to communicate with the party with whom you wish to collaborate and also establish when you would like to connect. This can be done by e-mail, phone, online chatting, Instant Messaging, and so on. You can then bring up Windows Remote Assistance.

Here's how:

1. **Open the Start menu and choose All Programs.**

A list of all the programs for your computer appears in the left column.

2. **Select the Maintenance folder.**

A list of items belonging to this category appears below.

3. **Choose Windows Remote Assistance.**

The following window appears. (See Figure 12-5.)

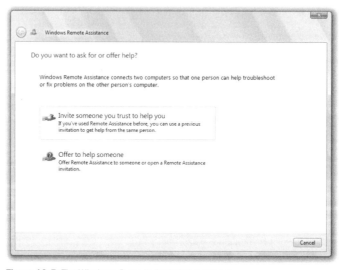

Figure 12-5: The Windows Remote Assistance screen.

By selecting the link to send an invitation, you can generate a small invitation that includes a password for the other person to use in order to gain access to your computer. (Likewise, offering to help someone else requires that he send you a password.)

To create an invitation

1. **Open the Windows Remote Assistance screen.**

A window like the one shown in Figure 12-5 appears.

2. **Select the Invite Someone You Trust To Help You option.**

A screen with the option to send an e-mail invitation or create an invitation file appears (see Figure 12-6).

3. **Select the method you would like to use to send the invitation.**

Choosing the e-mail option saves you from having to create a separate e-mail with the enclosed password. However, if you choose to save the invitation as a file, you can recover this information later if the person helping you happens to lose the invitation or you forget the password.

4. **Create a password for connecting to your computer and then click Next (or Finish, if you chose the invitation file method).**

Enter the password in the first text box. Then reenter it in the second text box to confirm that this is the correct word (and spelling).

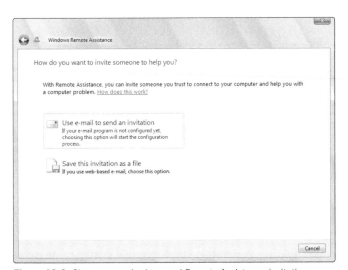

Figure 12-6: Choose a method to send Remote Assistance invitations.

Note: If you chose the invitation file method, you also need to identify where you would like to have the file saved before clicking Finish.

5. **Click Next.**

An e-mail invitation is generated.

6. **Enter the e-mail address for the other person and then send the Remote Assistance invitation.**

Doing so calls up the Windows Remote Assistance window — with toolbar — informing you that your PC is waiting for an incoming connection. (See Figure 12-7.)

Figure 12-7: A toolbar for controlling your Remote Assistance session.

After the invitation has been sent and a meeting time agreed upon, the remote assistance session can commence.

To begin the Remote Assistance session

1. **The person helping you must first open his e-mail invitation and click the link provided (or open the attached invitation file).**

Doing so opens the screen shown in Figure 12-8.

Figure 12-8: Entering the Remote Assistance password.

2. **The person helping you enters the Remote Assistance password in the text box that appears on his screen.**

This automatically generates a dialog box on your screen asking whether you would like to allow the other person to share control of your desktop.

3. **Click Yes to begin the Remote Assistance session.**

During this session, the person providing the assistance sees the screen of the person being helped. The helper has access to that person's computer and, thus, complete control of all mouse and keyboard movements. The person being assisted can see all the movements of the cursor onscreen as they take place.

When it is time to stop the Remote Assistance session, you can either click Cancel or the Stop Sharing button in the session's toolbar window — refer to Figure 12-7 — or you can press the Esc key on your keyboard. Either participant can pause or end the session.

Watch Your Step

When you receive assistance through a Windows Remote Assistance session, the person you are connected to has control and access to your computer and its data. If you do not fully trust this person, do not avail yourself of this feature with that person because it could compromise the security of your data and your computer.

Information Kiosk

Windows Remote Assistance is also compatible with Windows XP. Hence, users on these different OS versions can help each other.

Windows Communities

Newsgroups, covered back in Chapter 7, have been around as part of the Usenet area of the Internet since the Internet's earliest days. It should come as no surprise, then, that Windows Vista newsgroups exist, which focus on a variety of Windows Vista topics. Like with any other newsgroup, you can communicate with other users by posting a message as well as read ongoing discussion threads to glean helpful information.

Step into the Real World

Although a Remote Desktop Connection is quite similar to the Windows Remote Assistance feature, you don't need to give permissions, and no other person is involved. When you use Remote Desktop Connection, you log in remotely to another computer and have full access to it and all its programs and data. No invitations are required, and no communications with another user are involved.

To use this function, you need to have network access to the other computer via the Internet, and both machines need to allow Remote Desktop Access. Too, you need to have permission to connect to the remote computer. You also need to know the computer name, or its IP address, to use it remotely.

You access the newsgroups

Via Help: Go directly to the Windows Vista Newsgroups site by bringing up the Windows Help and Support window (Start ➔ Help and Support) and then clicking the Post a Question or Search for an Answer in Windows Communities link.

Via browser: Type the following URL into your Web browser:

`http://windowshelp.microsoft.com/communities/newsgroups/en-us/default.mspx`

Either way, you end up at the Windows Vista Newsgroups Web site, as shown in Figure 12-9.

From this screen, you can enter a search term into the Search For text box. Click Go, and a list of relevant newsgroup discussions pops up, as shown in Figure 12-10.

Click a newsgroup that interests you to bring up individual message postings in the box at the right. (See Figure 12-11.)

Microsoft Customer Support Online

Another help option is the Microsoft Customer Support Online tool. This resource connects to Microsoft for technical support as well as customer support. You'll find links to technical support information online as well as direct Microsoft support via different contact methods and pricing information.

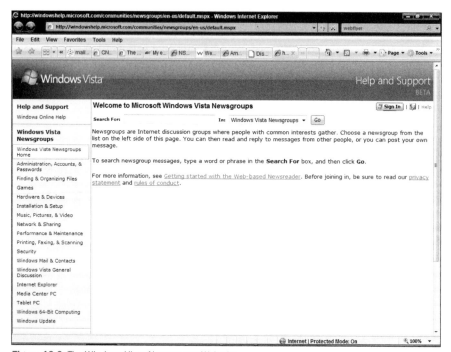

Figure 12-9: The Windows Vista Newsgroups Web site.

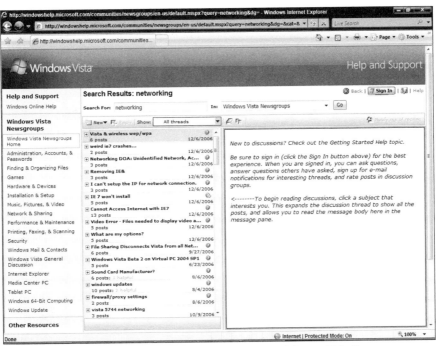

Figure 12-10: Access Vista newsgroups via the Microsoft Help and Support Web site.

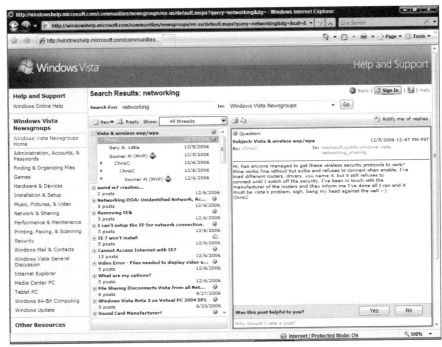

Figure 12-11: Viewing Vista newsgroup postings.

To access this Help feature, open the Windows Help and Support screen and then click the Contact Microsoft Customer Support Online link in the Ask Someone section of this window. You are taken to the screen shown in Figure 12-12.

Watch Your Step

You must first be connected to the Internet before clicking the Contact Microsoft Customer Support Online link, or you will not be able to access this Microsoft Help site.

Information Kiosk

You can also visit this Web site by entering `support.microsoft.com` into your Internet browser.

Select a product from the column at the left, or click the Select a Product button on the menu bar just above the main screen to choose an unlisted product. After making your selection, you are taken to a screen that includes help and support articles specific to the product you chose.

Figure 12-12: The Microsoft Customer Support Online Help Web site.

You can also use the Self Support Options and Microsoft Services features located at the bottom of the left column to locate the information you seek. Included in the Self Support Options are Product Solution Centers, Microsoft Technical Communities, and Support Webcasts. The Microsoft Services category includes Supporting Services, Consulting Services, and Support Lifecycle & Policies. Don't forget that Microsoft support people can now make use of Windows Remote Assistance as part of their efforts to help you.

Diagnostic tools

You can use three different Vista diagnostic tools to help identify problems on your PC:

- The **Microsoft Support Diagnostic tool** is used in conjunction with Microsoft online support to identify the cause of your PC problems. Microsoft support technicians use the information generated from this tool to offer possible solutions to your computer problems.

- The **Memory Diagnostic tool** is used to check your PC's memory to make sure it is functioning properly.

- The **DirectX Diagnostic tool** determines what incompatibilities exist between your machine and the multimedia software you are attempting to run on it.

The Microsoft Support Diagnostic tool

The Microsoft Support Diagnostic tool scans your system to determine whether any problems exist with your machine. Before using this tool, you first need to connect to Microsoft support online, as outlined in the previous section of this chapter. After contacting a Microsoft representative for additional help, you might be instructed to download and run this utility. The results of the scan are automatically sent to Microsoft if your PC is connected to the Internet; otherwise, you have to save the results of your diagnostic test to a disc or other external device (such as a Flash drive) and send it to Microsoft from a different machine. The Microsoft representative then uses the information provided by this tool to offer you possible resolution options.

Information Kiosk

Microsoft representatives know which data belongs to your computer because they assign you a specific *passkey* (or incident number) to use when running this utility.

The Memory Diagnostic tool

Comparatively, the Memory Diagnostic tool does not require Microsoft online support. Rather, it is a utility that comes installed as part of Windows Vista. To run this diagnostic tool, perform an Instant Search for "Memory Diagnostic Tool."

When the utility launches, you are presented with two choices:

- Restart Now and Check for Problems (Recommended)
- Check for Problems the Next Time I Start My Computer

The utility runs itself with no action required from you and generally finishes within 5 to 15 minutes for most computers. When it is finished, your machine automatically reboots, and you get either an alert that pops up from the taskbar informing you that you have no memory problems or a mini-report spelling out potential problems that you can e-mail to Microsoft or save for a technical support specialist to view.

The DirectX Diagnostic tool

DirectX is an Application Programming Interface (API) used with many Microsoft and other third-party, multimedia programs. If your PC encounters any DirectX compatibility issues, you might not be able to see or hear certain aspects of your multimedia files, including games, videos, and music. If you have any problems running multimedia in Windows Vista, the utility used to diagnose such problems is the DirectX Diagnostic tool. Like the Memory Diagnostic tool, it is preinstalled on your machine and ready to display the status results upon your request. To take advantage of this tool, do an Instant Search for "DirectX Diagnostic Tool." The following window appears. (See Figure 12-13.)

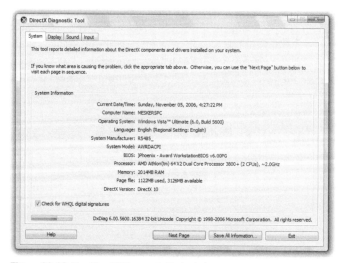

Figure 12-13: The DirectX Diagnostic Tool window.

Again, there is nothing you must run. Simply following the screens by clicking Next, and you can see the status of DirectX working with multimedia on your machine or a diagnosis of what needs to be replaced. You can save the report screens by clicking the Save All Information button. This file can then be e-mailed to the technician who has been helping you.

DirectX: An assemblage of multimedia and gaming APIs (Application Programming Interfaces) developed by Microsoft for the Windows platform to enhance the overall user experience in graphics, playback, and sound effects.

DirectX Diagnostic Tool: Diagnostic test designed to identify incompatibility issues between your Vista computer and the multimedia software used to display images on your machine.

Memory Diagnostic Tool: Utility program used to determine whether a computer's memory is functioning properly.

Microsoft Support Diagnostic Tool: Utility used to help Microsoft Help technicians identify the source of your current PC problems.

passkey: The individual incident number used to identify the specific diagnostic results for your computer.

Remote Assistance: Feature that allows another person to take control of your computer from a remote location.

Vista demos: Visual Help tutorials that provide users with step-by-step instructions for common procedures.

Last Stop

Practice Exam

1. What is the easiest and fastest way to get help in Windows Vista?

_____

_____

_____

2. How can you view Windows Vista Help demos?

_____

_____

_____

3. What happens when you press F1 while you have a particular window open?

_____

_____

_____

4. What are the advantages to being connected to the Internet when you need help?

_____

_____

_____

5. What risks do you run when using Windows Remote Assistance?

_____

_____

_____

6. How do you end a Remote Assistance session?

_____

_____

_____

7. In addition to Online Help, what are other Microsoft sources of online assistance?

_____

_____

_____

8. What are the benefits of using Windows Remote Assistance?

_____

_____

_____

9. What must you do before you can use Windows Remote Assistance?

_____

_____

_____

10. How can you get to the Windows Help and Support window?

_____

_____

_____

11. What three diagnostic tools are available with Vista? What is the purpose of each of these items?

_____

_____

_____

12. What kind of support is provided by the Microsoft Customer Support Web site?

_____

_____

_____

13. When should you not use Windows Remote Assistance?

_____

_____

_____

14. How can Microsoft support technicians differentiate between the results from your diagnostic tests and those of others?

_____

_____

_____

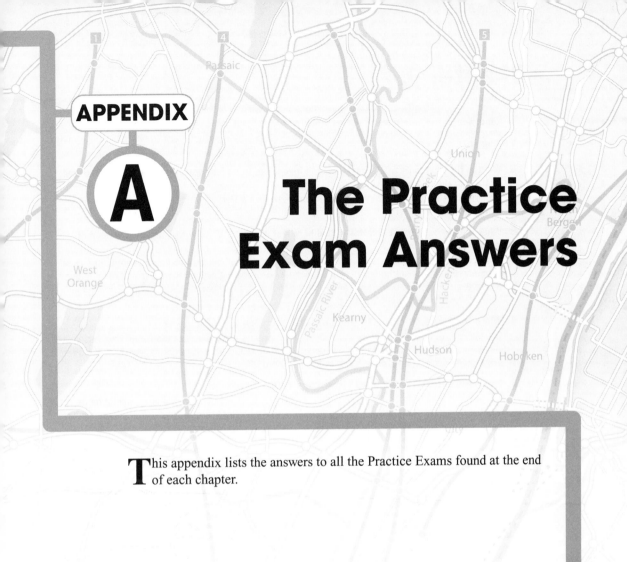

A

The Practice Exam Answers

This appendix lists the answers to all the Practice Exams found at the end of each chapter.

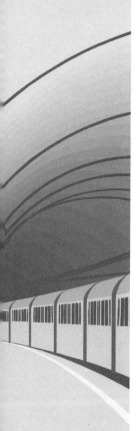

Chapter 1

1. Name the five standard versions of Windows Vista.

Windows Vista Home Basic, Windows Vista Home Premium, Windows Vista Business, Windows Vista Enterprise, and Windows Vista Ultimate. There is also a sixth edition, to be marketed primarily in the emerging market countries, known as the Windows Vista Starter Edition.

2. What is the best version of Vista to install if you plan to do only word processing, check e-mail and watch the occasional video clip?

The Windows Vista Home Basic edition is the best Vista version if you're going to concentrate on only these tasks.

3. What are the benefits of creating a dual boot installation of Vista with a previous version of Windows?

With a dual-boot installation, you can try out Vista before switching all your documents, files, programs and personal settings over to Microsoft's new operating system. Creating a dual boot also allows you to continue using programs that may not yet be compatible with Vista by running them on your previous version of Windows.

4. Why does Microsoft require 15 GB of free disk space for installing Vista?

The space provides Vista with enough room to temporarily store some of the 3,000 files associated with Windows. It also provides extra memory for Vista to use when it performs certain tasks after installation, such as displaying some of the new Aero effects.

5. Is it possible to install Windows Vista with only 256MB of RAM?

Windows Vista will run on a system with just 256 MB of RAM, but such "running" will be more like a crawl, with multitasking virtually impossible. The minimum RAM required is 512 MB; the suggested level is about twice that (1 GB of RAM).

6. If you want to install Windows Vista on a drive partition, which steps should you take to prepare the drive?

After you've run the Windows Vista Upgrade Advisor and have verified that you have the least 15 GB of hard drive space available on the drive, you should then run the DEFRAG and ScanDisk utilities on the drive partition.

7. What are the potential problems you need to be aware of when upgrading to Vista from a previous version of Windows?

If the installation process fails — and you have neglected to back up your files and programs — you run the risk of losing all these items.

If you install Vista successfully, you may run into some compatibility problems with third-party programs already installed on your PC.

If your computer does not have enough memory, or your processor is too slow, or your video card does not meet the minimum requirements for Vista, you might experience some performance problems: Large files may load slowly, and multimedia or other high-capacity programs may run slower than normal (or may not function properly).

8. What precautionary steps do you need to take before installing Vista on your current PC? What are the reasons for these actions?

First, run the Upgrade Advisor to determine whether your PC can run Vista properly. This precaution prevents you from installing Vista on a machine that does not meet system requirements.

Back up all your files and programs before attempting to install Vista. This ensures that these items are not lost forever if something goes wrong during installation.

Defragment your hard drive to reallocate available memory and hard-drive space on your PC. Doing so creates larger empty sections on your drive, allowing Vista to access related information quicker.

Run the ScanDisk utility to ensure that no existing errors corrupt (or interrupt) Vista's files.

9. What is the best version of Vista to use if you plan to play video games with enhanced graphics or engage in other home entertainment activities?

Windows Vista Ultimate is the best option in this scenario because it's better able to manage the high levels of graphics. It also includes some added multimedia features (such as the Windows Media Center) that the other editions do not.

10. How can you tell whether your current PC is capable of running Windows Vista?

You can either check your system properties manually (by going to the Control Panel and viewing the current settings) or you can run the Upgrade Advisor to determine whether your machine is Vista-capable.

11. What are the bare minimum requirements for running Vista? What are the optimal system requirements?

The bare minimum requirements are a 40GB hard drive (with at least 15 GB of free space), 512 MB of system memory, an 800MHz processor and a DirectX-9 graphics adapter. These requirements are mostly used with the Window Vista Home Basic edition.

The optimal requirements are nearly twice that of the basic requirements. They include a 80GB hard drive (with at least 15 GB of free space), 1 GB of system memory, a 2GHz processor, and a DirectX-9 graphics adapter. A machine with these properties runs better than one with less memory and/or processing speed. The Windows Vista Ultimate edition performs best under these conditions.

12. What is the difference between a Vista Capable and a Vista Premium PC?

A Vista Capable machine can run basic Vista features but may not be able to run all the new enhanced features (such as Aero effects). A Vista Premium machine can run not only the Vista basic operations, but also the more advanced features. Because Vista Premium PCs are capable of higher performance levels, their system requirements are also higher than those of Vista Capable PCs.

13. Explain why Windows Vista now comes on a DVD installation disc rather than a CD.

The DVD installation disc includes all five versions of Windows, and Vista's new, visually-enhanced applications require much more space to run and install than previous editions of Windows. Therefore, the installation disc needs more memory space (in the form of RAM, random-access memory) to load Vista's new graphics features and computing capabilities properly.

Chapter 2

1. What are the four main areas of the Windows taskbar?

They are the Start Button, the Quick Launch Area, the Windows Tabs, and the Notification Area.

2. Which option enables you to keep the taskbar off the screen until you're ready to use it again?

Right-click a blank area of the Taskbar, choose Properties, and then choose Auto-Hide the Taskbar.

3. What are the benefits of using the Aero interface in Vista?

The Aero interface in Vista allows you to apply 3-D and transparency effects so you can see elements behind other elements.

4. What are some advantages associated with using the taskbar?

Using the Taskbar provides instantaneous access to your favorite programs by creating links to frequently used programs in the Quick Launch Area. It allows you to quickly and easily move from one open program to another by using the Windows tabs in the main area of the Taskbar. It keeps you abreast of various security and software updates that need to be downloaded in the Notification Area. And lastly, the Start button menu offers you access to all the programs, documents and computer settings for your PC. In other words, the Taskbar is a convenient all-access navigational tool for your computer.

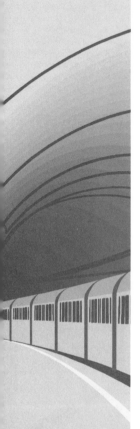

5. How do you ungroup Windows tabs?

Right-click a blank area of the Taskbar; select Properties from the context menu that appears, and then deselect the Group Similar Taskbar Buttons option.

6. If you have peripheral devices installed, where are their icons most likely to be displayed?

Most, but not all, peripheral devices display icons in the Notification Area of the Taskbar.

7. What are the different ways of moving between Windows tabs?

You can press Alt+Tab for a 2-D view, press the Windows key +Tab for 3-D view or hover your mouse over the Windows Tabs area of the Taskbar to see live Taskbar thumbnails. After you've found the correct screen, press Enter to open this window in full-screen mode.

8. What are the principal differences between the left column and the right column of the Start menu? What about the upper part of the left column and the bottom portion?

The left column of the Start menu lists programs and functional "centers" in Windows Vista. The right column is principally used to access files and devices. The upper part of the left-hand column of the menu are fixed entries "pinned" to the menu, and the bottom half consists of recently accessed entries.

9. What factors led Microsoft to create Aero?

Microsoft decided to create a user interface that was more visually stimulating because the majority of computer users are visual learners. They also wanted to make it more user-friendly; therefore, they gave the buttons a cleaner, sleeker look, while still making them easily identifiable. The redesign also reorganized some of the menu items so users don't have to navigate through so many menus to locate the items they need. This was done in order to reduce user frustration levels. And lastly, a major driving force behind Aero was that Microsoft wanted to be able to compete with the Macintosh market, which is known for its appealing GUI.

Chapter 3

1. How do you open additional browser tabs?

Press Ctrl+T or click the blank/empty tab to the right of your open tabs.

2. How do you activate the Phishing Filter?

Select the Tools menu in IE7, then select Phishing filter ➜ Phishing Filter Settings.

3. In IE7, the classic Menu toolbar is hidden by default. How do you enable this feature?

Open the Tools menu and choose Menu Bar.

4. What are RSS feeds and why would you want to subscribe to them?

RSS feeds are links to continuously updated, syndicated information. Subscribing to RSS feeds keeps you up-to-date on a variety of topics. They also allow you to view only recently posted information, which means you get to look at just the content that you haven't seen yet, rather than having to scour through an entire Web site to find new material.

5. In IE7, what are the two different ways to zoom in/out on a Web page?

You can use the Zoom feature in the Page menu or you can use the following speed keys: Ctrl+ to zoom in or Ctrl+- to zoom out.

6. How do you make IE7 open with multiple home page tabs?

From the Tools menu select Internet Options to access the General tab, then type in all the URLs of the home pages you want to have IE7 start up with.

7. How do you allow pop-ups from trusted sites?

From the Tools menu select Internet Options. In the window that appears, select the Privacy tab. Select Settings in the Pop-up Blocker section and, under Exceptions, type the URLs into the field that reads, Address of Website To Allow.

If you access a Web site and a warning bar appears that reads, "Pop-Up is blocked. To see this Pop-Up or additional options click here," you can click that bar and opt to temporarily or always allow pop-ups from that particular site.

8. What is Shrink to Fit printing?

A new Vista printing option located under the Print Preview menu, Shrink to Fit printing allows you to stretch or shrink the Web page size to fill the width of a printed page.

9. What is the purpose of the Quick Tabs feature?

The Quick Tabs feature gives you a thumbnail overview of each of your open browser tabs.

10. What are some of the add-ons available for IE7? Where are these items managed?

These additional browser tools include various forms, controls, utilities, specialized browsers and even entertainment applications. Each of these items can be found in one of the following IE7 add-on categories: Security, Time Savers, Browsers and Entertainment. To peruse these add-on categories, visit IE7's Add-ons Web page, which can be accessed by selecting the Manage Add-ons option from the Tools menu.

Chapter 4

1. If you receive a phishing e-mail, what clues should you look for to indicate that you're being directed to a spoofing site?

There is often a link embedded in the e-mail, which, when pointed at, indicates a URL different from that of the site you would expect to be going to.

2. What warning indications do you encounter when you try to change your browser's security settings to ones that are less secure?

When you're in a custom level menu (accessed by selecting Tools ➜ Internet options ➜ Security), you see next to certain selections the following: (not secure).

If you choose (not secure), the highlighting of that option changes to a beige color,

A warning bar appears with the following message: "Your current security settings put your computer at risk;"

A Web page opens with the following message on it: "Your security setting level puts your computer at risk:"

A warning dialog box appears reading, "Are you sure you want to change the settings for this zone? The current security settings will put your computer at risk."

3. If you didn't remember where the Security Center is found within Vista, what is (are) the easiest way(s) to find it?

The easiest way is always to do an Instant Search for "Security Center." Or just look under the Control Panel, where you will find a Security link.

4. Why don't icons for the Windows Firewall and Windows Defender display in the Notification Area?

Because they are always turned on by default. The Windows Vista Security icon does appear (in bright red with a yellow X on it) in the Notification Area when there is a problem that needs your attention.

5. How can you prevent search engines from storing keyword searches in their databases?

Select the Tools menu. From the drop down menu that appears, choose Internet Options, select the Internet Options window's Privacy tab and then click the Sites button. In the area of the dialog box that reads "Manage Sites," type the URL of the Web site you want to block from using cookies on your computer. Enter this information into the field labeled "Address of website."

6. **How much can you limit your children's online and general computing activities using Parental Controls?**

You can set time limits for their overall computer usage, block certain games and prohibit access to certain Web sites. You can also limit when your kids are allowed to use the computer, what types of information they are permitted to access (including which programs and peripheral devices — like Web cameras — they can use), and where they can go on the Internet.

7. **What are the benefits of using BitLocker? At what point can you decide to employ BitLocker?**

Using BitLocker protects the data stored on your computer if an unauthorized user ever gains access to your PC.

You can deploy BitLocker at any point: however, it does require the creation of a separate, clean drive partition.

8. **What are the main areas of the Windows Security Center?**

Windows Update, Windows Firewall, and Windows Defender.

9. **Is BitLocker available for all versions of Windows Vista?**

Bitlocker Drive Encryption feature is only available in the Ultimate and Enterprise editions of Windows Vista.

10. **What signs indicate that you're visiting a secure site? Where are such signs displayed onscreen?**

A secure site is indicated by a small padlock located just to the right of the address bar in IE7.

11. **When is it safe to run active content from a Web site on your machine?**

Only when you know for sure that the Web site from which you're running such content is secure.

12. **Is it better to have more than one spyware program? Why or why not?**

Many experts recommend two spyware programs. The thinking is that what one doesn't catch the other one does.

13. **If Parental Controls are not turned on, how can you determine what Web sites have been visited?**

In addition to looking at IE7's browser History files, you can see what the AutoComplete feature pulls up by typing individual letters of the alphabet one at a time in the URL field.

Chapter 5

1. **How do you add a shortcut to your desktop?**

You can either drag-and-drop program icons onto your desktop or you can right-click specific folders (or individual files) and choose the Create Shortcut option from the drop-down menu that appears.

2. **What types of items can have shortcuts? Are there any types of files that cannot have shortcuts?**

You can create shortcuts for all types of programs, folders and even individual files. There are no file types that cannot have shortcuts created for them.

3. **What is the fastest way to search your computer? Where is this feature located?**

Use the Instant Search feature located within the Start menu.

4. **What is metadata and how can you use it to associate related files to one another?**

Adding metadata in Windows Vista refers to the process of assigning keywords (called Tags) and ratings to files in order to be able to find these files more quickly and accurately.

By searching for files with specific metadata, you can pull only the files that match the aforementioned criteria, thus grouping these files together in the final search results screen.

5. Should you do an Instant Search if you know where a specific folder you want to find is located? Why or Why not?

You may want to perform an Instant Search — even if you're certain of the folder's location — if you want to find the folder quickly. An Instant Search is the fastest method for locating items. It is much quicker than having to wade through various menu options to locate the item you desire. Instead, you can let Vista do the work for you by pulling up the specific folder in the Search results screen, thus allowing you to access this folder with the click of a single button.

6. If you want to associate a different application with an existing file, how would you do it?

Right-click the file and then choose Open With... from the context menu that appears. Choose from the recommended programs listed or browse for another program and then select the Always Use the Selected Program To Open This Type of File option.

7. What are file extensions and what can they tell you about your documents and programs?

File extensions are the three letters that appear at the end of each file name. These letters tell you which application was used to create that particular file.

8. What is XPS? What are the benefits of using this feature when creating documents?

XPS is a new Vista specification that permits users to publish documents that have been created in one program in a way that people using a different program or application can view the same document without losing any of the original document's integrity.

When using the XPS syntax, you can grant viewing rights to other users, thus protecting your documents from those people you do not want to see it. You can also use this feature to block others from making changes to your XPS documents.

9. Why would you want to partition your hard drive? How is this done?

Partitioning your hard drive creates several different compartments that can be used to store various programs or document types in each section, thus, allowing you to use these areas to better organize your files and programs. You can also create separate drives for different user accounts so each person has a drive to use when saving documents or downloading program files.

To partition your hard drive, open the Control Panel and select System and Maintenance. In the Administrative Tools section of this window, choose the Create and Format Hard Drive Partitions option. In the display that appears, right-click the drive you want to partition and select Shrink Volume from its pop-up menu.

10. Name two different types of metadata and explain how they can help you better manage your files.

There are several different types of metadata. A few examples include: Name, Date Modified, Subject, Comments, Author Name, Size, Tags, Ratings, etc.

Using metadata classifications helps you better manage your files by allowing you to search for and sort these items based on the metadata criteria assigned to them.

11. What is the purpose of using the Windows Easy Transfer Wizard?

The Windows Easy Transfer Wizard allows you to transfer your data and personal settings from a previous Windows machine to a Vista PC.

12. If you do not have an Easy Transfer cable, can you still use the Windows' transfer wizard? If so, how?

Yes. By utilizing an alternative transfer method — such as using a CD, USB flash drive, external hard drive, or shared network folder to transfer data from one PC to another.

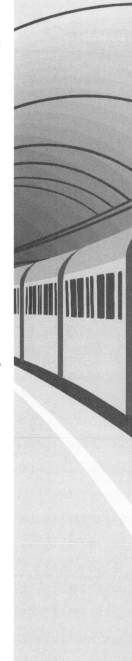

Chapter 6

1. Name at least two different ways you can use Vista's Speech Recognition capabilities to interact with your PC. Provide examples of when you might want to take advantage of this feature.

You can use Speech Recognition to instruct your PC to perform certain tasks, such as open an application program, switch to a different window, insert a word or object, scroll up/down, etc. You can also use it to leave yourself a voice recording/note or to dictate a memo.

You may want to take advantage of this feature if you're physically or visually impaired, if you want to have your hands free for multitasking purposes, or if you just prefer to speak rather than type.

2. What are the best ways to ensure high-level accuracy with Speech Recognition?

When training the computer, you should try to speak as you normally would (tone, articulation and speed). You should also do both of the Train the Computer To Understand Your Voice sessions and enable document review.

3. Can you compress a video file? When/why might you want to do this?

Technically speaking you can compress a video file; however, the end result will be a compressed file virtually identical in size to the original.

Most of the time you won't need to compress a video file. However, you might want to do so if you're sending the file to an e-mail account that doesn't accept video files but does allow attached .zip files.

4. In what way could it be useful to publish a Windows Calendar to the Internet?

You can do so for collaborative purposes with other users. In addition, institutions such as theaters or sports complexes can post their calendars to the Internet for others simply to view them.

5. What are some of the benefits of using Speech Recognition? What are some of its hindrances?

Using Speech Recognition allows you to have your hands free so you can do other things. This feature may also prove to users that can speak faster than they type. And once Vista begins picking up on some of your more common word-choice selections and overall vernacular, the entire dictation process runs fairly smoothly.

Hindrances include the fact that you must remain in close proximity to your computer microphone; this is especially true if you're using a desktop microphone. Also, until Vista familiarizes itself with your voice patterns, you may encounter some misunderstandings or interpretation problems, which can be frustrating and possibly time-consuming.

6. When might you use Vista's Sound Recorder tool?

You might you use Vista's Sound Recorder tool to leave yourself voice messages/notes or to record sounds for a later use (like creating your own music).

7. Describe how to create a Sticky Note.

Open up the Sticky Notes tool by doing an Instant Search or via the Start ➜ Accessories ➜ Tablet PC. Then use your mouse as a writing/drawing utensil to create a new Sticky Note. To open a new note, click the New Note button at the bottom of the Sticky Note window.

8. When would you most likely use WordPad or Notepad?

When you need to create a text document but you do not have another word processing application, like Microsoft Word, already installed on your PC. WordPad is typically used as an inexpensive (i.e. free) alternative to more expensive and more powerful word processing applications. Notepad can also be used as a limited word processing application; however, it is more frequently used to create HTML code files because of its ability to create text without embedded formatting features.

9. What are the benefits of using Vista's Snipping tool?

By using Vista's Snipping tool, you can cut, paste, crop and save images (or parts of an image) all in the same application. Being able to snap images from any resource — including the Web, installed programs and even individual documents — can be quite useful. You can also use the Snipping tool's Pen and Highlighter features to call attention to specific areas of the selected image.

10. **Why would you want to compress your file(s)?**

To save space on your hard drive or to create a smaller/condensed file that can be sent via e-mail.

11. **How do you decompress a Zip folder? What happens to your files when you do this?**

To decompress a zip folder, right-click the folder you want to decompress and choose Extract from the context menu that appears. You're then asked to select a place to store these files.

When you decompress a zip folder, a copy of the zip files are placed on your PC. This does not remove the files from the original zip folder.

Chapter 7

1. **What are newsgroups, and how do you find/use them?**

Newsgroups are basically online bulletin boards that you can be use to communicate with others. You can post a message (or question) or respond to someone else's posting. These postings are then visible to anyone who visits that particular newsgroup. Postings typically help answer questions or provide tips for others.

You can find these forums by searching the Web or by using Windows Mail. Click the Tools menu in Windows Mail to search for and subscribe to newsgroups that interest you.

2. **What is the difference between a shared document and a handout in Windows Meeting Space?**

A shared document is a single document housed on the meeting leader's PC. A handout is a document of which copies are distributed to all attendees in a Windows Meeting. In other words, individual copies of handouts are stored on each person's PC, while a shared document is only stored on the leader's PC.

3. **When collaborating on a document that is on your machine in Windows Meeting Space, how do you distribute copies of that file to other participants?**

Simply click the Add a Handout icon in the Windows Meeting Space screen and all attendees receive a copy of the document you designate.

4. **If another participant in the Windows Meeting Space doesn't have the application that you're using during the meeting, can they still edit it with you? If so, how?**

Yes, it is possible for such a participant to edit with you since the application, as well as the document, is actually found on your computer; they can help edit this item as a shared document.

5. **If you have been using Eudora e-mail and want to import your mail into Windows Mail, what must you do first?**

You must import your mail into one of four acceptable formats:

Microsoft Exchange

Outlook

Outlook Express 6

Windows Mail 7

6. **If you have a wireless card installed on your laptop, what is the fastest way to connect to a network?**

Click the Networking icon in the Notification Area of the Taskbar and then click the Connect or Disconnect link. Doing so opens the Connect to a Network window, which includes all available networks. Select the wireless network you want to connect to.

7. **If you have a wireless card but no Internet connection, where do you go to set one up?**

If you do not have an Internet connection or want to set up another one for, say, wireless access, click the Connect To a Network link in the Network and Sharing Center and then choose among connection options.

8. If your scanner already came with software, why might you still want to use Windows Vista's Fax and Scanner software?

The Vista Fax and Scanner software digitizes the documents and graphics making it simple to store, access and manage them. Also the design of the Vista application closely relates to that of the Microsoft e-mail client, Outlook Express and Outlook, and is thus familiar to users of those programs.

9. What is the purpose of the People Near Me application?

People Near Me is a peer-to-peer networking platform that allows many people on the same local area network or local area wireless node to communicate with one another and to hold, in effect, a conference.

10. Name two different ways you can send scanned images to others.

You can e-mail them as an attachment or you can fax them using the Windows Fax and Scanner feature.

11. Describe how to use rules in Windows Mail and explain why you might want to use this feature.

You need to open the Tools menu in Windows Mail to set up mail rules. Use the checkboxes in the dialog boxes that follow to create personalized (message or newsgroup) rules.

Using rules helps you organize your mail by allowing you to set up certain behavioral patterns — such as storing all the messages from your best friend in a particular folder or color coding messages with a higher priority. This helps keep your Inbox clean so you're not overwhelmed by new or incoming messages.

12. How do you send a Windows Meeting Space invitation? How do you begin a new Windows Meeting Space meeting?

You begin a new meeting by opening the Windows Meeting Space application and choosing the Start a New Meeting option from the list of items in the left column.

After the meeting has begun, you can invite others by clicking the Invite people... icon (or by using the Invite button on the main menu bar). You can also invite others by sending them an e-mail message with the time and password for the meeting.

13. How do you set up a LAN? How do you set up an Internet connection?

To set up an Internet or LAN connection, click the Network icon in the Notification area of the Taskbar and then click the Connect or Disconnect link. In the Connect to a Network window that appears, click the Set Up a Connection or Network link. From here you can choose what type of connection you would like to create.

14. How do you know if you're already connected to the Internet or another local network?

Check the Notification Area of the Taskbar. If you're connected to the Internet you see an image of two small icons that look like miniature computers connected to one another. If there is a red X present with this icon, you're not connected.

Chapter 8

1. Is it necessary to have your peripheral device connected before booting up your machine?

You can connect the device before, during or after the booting process.

2. Assume that you connected a new printer to your PC. Vista recognizes and installs it and looks for its driver, but you want to print a color document in black and white, and you can't find this option. How might you remedy this?

Although Vista has the drivers for most devices, you may need to install the software for that printer on your Vista machine.

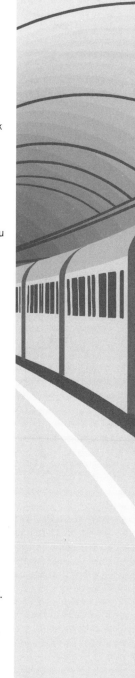

3. If you install the wrong driver for a device and it does not work, where would you look to fix it?

If the device doesn't work, and/or the driver is incorrect, you should check the Device Manager.

4. If a device functioned under your previously installed operating system but now it doesn't, what should you do?

The first step is to see whether there's an updated driver that will enable the device to function under Windows Vista. The second step would be to uninstall the device and use the Compatibility wizard to get it functioning properly.

5. Where is the Device Manager located? What is its purpose?

It is found under Hardware and Sound in the Control Panel. The purpose of this tool is to keep track of your PC's external and internal devices as well as their related drivers.

6. Name two Vista compatibility tools. What is the purpose of each?

Windows Vista Upgrade Advisor — The primary purpose of the Upgrade Advisor is to tell you which versions of Vista your computer is capable of running. It also tells you what you need to do to support a more advanced version.

The Program Compatibility Wizard — Allows you to adjust the way your operating system interacts with programs that may not yet work properly with Vista. When you use the Compatibility Wizard, you can change the display settings for these programs so they function normally on a Vista PC. Being able to manually select a program's settings makes it possible to use programs that might otherwise be incompatible with a Vista-operated machine.

7. Can anyone with access to your computer remove (or uninstall) programs or devices?

No. Only administrators can remove (or uninstall) programs and devices.

8. Assume that you have connected a Windows XP scanner to your Vista machine. The manufacturer has not yet produced a Vista-capable driver for that model. What can you do to resolve this issue?

Try reinstalling the scanner using the Compatibility wizard.

Check with the technical support department of the manufacturer to see whether a comparable driver might work.

Reinstall the scanner using a generic driver.

9. The manufacturer of a device you bought and attached to your computer has gone out of business. You don't have the driver, and you can't find it with Vista. What is one source you should always check?

Go to Windows Update and get the Optional Updates, as they usually include an extensive number of additional drivers.

10. The firewall program you always used under an earlier version of Windows is incompatible with Windows Vista. You need a firewall as soon as possible. What is your best option?

Your best option is to use the Windows Firewall that comes with Vista since it's pre-installed and there are no compatibility issues.

11. Where do you go to remove devices from your PC?

To the Device Manager, which can be found in the Hardware and Sound section of the Control Panel.

12. How do you uninstall programs?

Open the Control Panel and click the Uninstall a Program link. In the window that appears, highlight the program you want to remove and click the Uninstall button above.

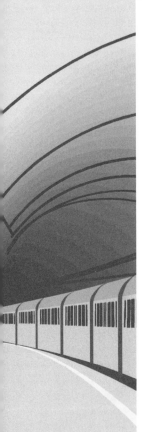

Chapter 9

1. How can you expand the Windows Media Player screen to full screen size?

You can double-click the screen, or you can click the Full Screen button.

2. Why is it a good idea to add tags to digital photos?

The naming conventions used by digital cameras are typically not very memorable; they're usually based on an obscure alphanumeric sequence. By manually adding tags, you can better organize your photos so they're easier to find later.

3. What are the different ways to burn a CD or DVD in Windows Vista?

You can use the Windows Media Player.

You can use of Windows Explorer.

You can use Windows DVD maker.

4. If you have a file with the .avi or .mpg extension (or some even-less-common video file type) you want to play, what can you do if the Windows Media Player can't seem to play it?

Be sure you're connected to the Internet to allow Windows Media Player to search for the necessary codecs to play the file. Another possibility is to click the Web Help button. If it provides you with an error code, you can search for more information at the Events and Errors Message Center online. Lastly, you can also visit the Microsoft Windows Update site.

5. If you want to burn DVDs or record TV shows on your PC, what version of Windows Vista do you need?

You need Windows Vista Home Premium or Windows Vista Ultimate.

6. How do you adjust the brightness, contrast, or rotation of a digital image?

Open the image you want to make changes to in the Windows Photo Gallery. Then select the Fix button to access the editing options for this image.

7. What are ESRB game ratings, and why might you want to be familiar with them?

ESRB stands for the *Entertainment Software Rating Board*, a regulatory entity in charge of setting and enforcing ratings, guidelines for advertising, and privacy policies for online and offline computer and video games. These ratings can be useful when you set parental controls for children playing games on computers.

8. What's the fastest way to add files to a burn list?

Drag-and-drop them from the current playlist or library files to the Burn list.

9. What's the leading cause for DVD burn-failure? What precautions can you take to avoid this problem?

Insufficient RAM (or memory) is the number one cause of burn-failure. Try shutting down any applications that you're not currently using to avoid draining your PC's available memory when attempting to burn CDs/DVDs.

10. How do you remove tags you no longer need?

Open the image you would like to remove the tag from in Windows Photo Gallery. In the Details panel, right-click the tag you want to delete and select Remove from the context menu that appears.

To remove tags from a group of images, select the appropriate tag folder and right-click. Then select Delete from the pop-up menu that appears. This removes the selected tag from each item in the tag folder. It does not, however, delete the images themselves.

Chapter 10

1. What are the principal differences between Hibernate and Sleep?

Hibernate saves everything to the hard drive before powering down completely. Sleep saves everything to RAM. Booting up from Sleep is also quicker than from Hibernate.

2. What are the three default power plan settings? Briefly explain the benefits of each.

Balanced — Administers equal parts of power to your computer's battery and performance capabilities.

Power Saver — Focuses on preserving your computer's battery power. This plan is particularly useful if you're using a laptop that is not connected to another power source.

High Performance — Gives priority to your computer's performance levels. This plan is used most often with PCs that require a large amount of graphical input or processing speed.

3. How can you create a customized power plan? Why might you want to do this?

You must first choose one of the default power plan settings. You can then adjust certain features (display turn off and sleep mode settings) of the selected plan to personalize it in your own way.

Creating your own power plan allows you to set your own power saving criteria. For example, if you choose to use the High Performance plan, but do not want to drain your computer's battery when it is not actively in use, you can decrease the amount of time that expires before the machine's display is turned off or before the computer goes to sleep — thus allowing your PC to conserve more of its battery life with the High Performance plan.

4. Name three ways to bring your computer back from Sleep mode.

Move your mouse.

Tap your touch pad.

Quickly press the Power button.

5. What is ReadyBoost, and how can it help you work more efficiently?

ReadyBoost is a feature that enhances the power and performance available when you attach certain external devices to your computer. It allows your PC to take advantage of the new device's available hard-drive space; your machine can perform faster by taking advantage of the additional memory.

6. How can you tell whether a drive that is attached to your computer meets ReadyBoost requirements ?

If the drive meets ReadyBoost requirements, then the Autoplay dialog box (which appears when you attach the drive) will offer you the option of utilizing ReadyBoost. Or, if you right-click the attached drive's icon and click the Properties tab, you can tell whether the device is capable of supporting ReadyBoost.

7. What four areas are covered in the Windows Reliability and Performance Monitor resource overview? Please explain the significance of each.

CPU: Shows the percentage of CPU (central processing unit) resources your system is consuming.

Disk: Shows the overall hard-disk in/out transfer rate (disk reads and writes) in kilobytes per second.

Network: Shows the total network data-transfer rate in megabits per second.

Memory: Shows the average number of hard memory faults per second, and the percentage of memory in use by the entire system.

8. In the Performance Monitor, a counter is an item used to track a computer's performance capabilities. What steps are involved when creating a new counter?

To create a new counter, open the Performance Monitor and click the large green plus sign on the toolbar above. From the new Add Counters window that appears, select the additional counters you would like to add to the Performance Monitor screen and click the Add button. Click OK when you're finished.

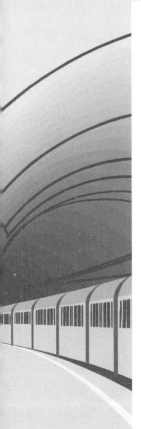

9. How do you launch the Windows Reliability and Performance Monitor tools? What are the benefits of using these applications?

Open the Control Panel and select System and Maintenance ➜ Performance Information and Tools. Click the Advanced Tools link in the left column. Then choose the Open Reliability and Performance Monitor option.

The benefits of using these tools include being able to visualize not only your system's current performance levels, but also its successful and failed activities. Accessing this data allows you to determine whether to make changes to your computer system and/or its various programs.

10. What is a Data Collector Set? Why might you want to create one?

Data Collector Sets are customized groups of performance counters. You might want to create a Data Collector Set so you can evaluate your PC's performance over time.

Chapter 11

1. What is Windows Update and why should you use it?

Windows Update is an application that automatically searches for and downloads new software updates for your computer's operating system. Using this tool ensures that your PC has the most up-to-date software and Microsoft security protection.

2. How can you check for new Vista updates?

Open the Windows Update screen and click the View Available Updates link.

3. Where can you find the Backup and Restore Center?

The Backup and Restore Center is located in the System and Maintenance section of the Control Panel menu.

4. How can you restore your system to a previous performance level, and why might you need to do this?

Utilize the Restore Computer feature — located in the Backup and Restore Center in the System and Maintenance section of the Control Panel menu — to select a specific restore point. Doing so returns your computer to the designated performance level.

You might want to take advantage of this feature if you install a program that negatively affects your computer's performance levels, or if you come into contact with a corrupt file that wreaks havoc on your PC's performance.

5. Why is it so important to proceed with caution when editing the Registry?

It is extremely important that you proceed with caution when editing the Registry because even the slightest error on your part could render your computer useless or cause it to malfunction.

6. Name two examples of when you might need to edit the Registry.

If a third-party software program begins to cause problems, you may need to correct this situation by editing the Registry. If you encounter malware — such as viruses or trojans — you may need to remove these items from the Registry if no corrective patches are available. You might also be able to overcome certain installation barriers by working within the Registry files.

7. What is the primary purpose of the system utilities discussed in this chapter?

System utilities are basically housekeeping tools for your PC. Using these applications helps keep your computer system properly organized by allocating space to the appropriate areas of your hard drive (Disk Defragmenter) and free of system errors and corrupt files (ScanDisk).

8. Where is the ScanDisk utility located?

In the Tools tab of a single drive's Properties dialog box.

9. What are your options when defragmenting disk drives?

You can adjust the preset defrag schedule, defragment individual drives (in much the same way you would run the ScanDisk application for a single drive), or run the Disk Defragmenter utility for your entire hard drive.

10. What is the safest media to use to make a backup?

No media is completely safe. All electronic media is subject to corruption, and DVDs and CDs can degrade due to storage conditions.

Chapter 12

1. What is the easiest and fastest way to get help in Windows Vista?

No matter where you're in Windows Vista, press F1. This pulls up the Windows Help and Support screen.

2. How can you view Windows Vista Help demos?

In addition to searching under Windows Vista Help Demos, visit Windows Online Help to see the complete collection of Windows Vista demos.

3. What happens when you press F1 while you have a particular window open?

The Windows Help and Support screen appears, offering articles specifically tailored to that particular program or application.

3. What are the advantages to being connected to the Internet when you need help?

In addition to being connected to Microsoft's online help — which is continuously updated — you'll also find links to Windows communities for further assistance, links to Microsoft's technical site (www.msdn.com), and sometimes links to other Web sites relating to Microsoft Vista.

4. What risks do you run when using Windows Remote Assistance?

By giving remote control of your computer to another user, you risk having your entire system, personal settings, and files altered by that user. Make sure the person you let take over your computer is someone you trust. Otherwise he or she may be able to retrieve confidential information from your computer or use it for malicious acts, such as spreading computer viruses or other forms of malware.

5. How do you end a Remote Assistance session?

There are three ways:

Click Cancel.

Press the Esc key.

Click Stop Sharing.

6. In addition to Online Help, what are other Microsoft sources of online assistance?

The Windows Vista demos site

Microsoft Communities

Microsoft technical sites

7. What are the benefits of using Windows Remote Assistance?

Vista's Remote Assistance feature allows you to help people in distant locations. Using this feature can also be much easier than trying to explain what is wrong with a PC. By seeing/using the computer firsthand, a qualified technician can determine what is actually causing the problem and then quite possibly fix it right then and there. Windows Remote Assistance also allows you to see exactly what changes the helper is making to your computer, thus providing you with information on how to correct this problem should it occur again in the future.

8. What must you do before you can use Windows Remote Assistance?

First, you must establish a Remote Assistance Connection. In other words, you must instruct your computer to permit another user to take control of your PC. Then you need to set up a time for when the Remote Assistance event will take place. After that you have to send an invitation (with a password) to the person you would like to allow access to your PC.

9. How can you get to the Windows Help and Support window?

You can find this tool in the right column of the Start menu, or you can simply press F1 from within any Vista program or application.

10. What three diagnostic tools are available with Vista? What is the purpose of each of these items?

Microsoft Support Diagnostic: This tool, which is used in connection with Microsoft's online support site, helps Microsoft technicians identify the reason behind your current PC problems.

Memory Diagnostic: The purpose of this test is to make sure your PC's memory is functioning properly.

Direct-X Diagnostic: Determines what, if any, incompatibilities exist between your PC and the multimedia software you're running on it.

11. What kind of support is provided by the Microsoft Customer Support Web site?

Both customer and technical support can be found on Microsoft's Web site. Examples include product solution centers, links to technical communities, webcasts, access to various support services, consulting services, and support life cycles, and Microsoft policy documents.

12. When should you not use Windows Remote Assistance?

You should not use Windows Remote Assistance if you do not trust the other participant. Doing so could put your computer and any confidential information stored on your PC in jeopardy.

13. How can Microsoft support technicians differentiate between the results from your diagnostic tests and those of others?

They assign a specific passkey (or incident number) to your machine when you're running a diagnostic report for your computer.

Index

Numbers

3-D Flip feature, 68–69
32-bit versus 64-bit chips, 6–7

A

accessibility tools. *See* Speech Recognition
active content, 153, 156, 190
ActiveX tool, 190
Add or Change Home Page dialog box,
    125–126
add-ons. *See also* Internet Explorer 7
    defined, 127, 131
    disabling, 129–130
    finding, 128, 129
    installing, 128–129
Advanced Performance Tools menu, 415
Aero interface. *See* desktop
antivirus software, 144, 147, 446
API (Application Programs Interface),
    448, 457, 476
Appearance and Personalization dialog box,
    75–77
Appearance Settings dialog box, 53, 54
applications. *See* programs
appointments, 267–269. *See also* Windows
    Calendar
audio. *See also* Speech Recognition
    Sound Recorder tool, 247–249
    voice Sticky Notes, 254
audio/video. *See* Media Player 11; Media
    Center; CDs/DVDs; video
AutoComplete. *See also* Internet Explorer 7
    accessing sites using, 103–104
    defined, 131
    deleting history, 104–106, 174–175
Automatic Updates. *See also* Windows
    Update
    activating, 140–141
    defined, 138–139

overview, 28
setting options, 431–432
AutoPlay dialog box, 380, 408–410
AVI (Audio Video Interleaved) format, 396

B

backgrounds, desktop, 28, 40–43
backing up before Registry edits, 449–452
Backup and Restore Center. *See also* system
    management
    backing up data, 20, 429, 435–440
    Create a Restore Point link, 446
    defined, 457
    opening, 436–437
    restoring data, 440–443
    risks of data loss, 434–435
    System Restore link, 444
Balanced power plan, 402
Bcc mail recipients, 284
binary-to-text support, 304
binary values, 448
BitLocker Drive Encryption, 166–168, 190
blocking file downloads, 183
browsers, 87, 131. *See also* Internet
    Explorer 7
bugs, 429
burning. *See* CDs/DVDs
Bush, Vannevar, 37

C

cache space, 409, 424
Calendar. *See* Windows Calendar
cameras, digital, 381
Cc mail recipients, 284
CDs/DVDs. *See also* devices
    backing up data on, 20, 429, 435–440
    burning. *See also* Media Player 11
        audio CDs, 368, 372–373
        copyright laws and, 378
        data CDs/DVDs, 378

P

padlock icons, 148
Paint program, 384
Parental Controls. *See also* securing IE7
    accessing controls, 177–179
    blocking file downloads, 183
    creating user accounts, 176–177
    defined, 175–176, 191
    game restrictions, 184–186
    program restrictions, 186–187
    time restrictions, 183–184
    viewing activity reports, 179, 187–189
    Web restrictions, 179–182
partitions/volumes. *See* hard drives
passkeys, 475, 477
passwords. *See also* securing privacy
    choosing on Vista install, 26–27
    deleting stored, 150–152
    for network connections, 331–332
    in Remote Assistance, 470
    to user accounts, 162–164
    to Windows Mail accounts, 283
PCs (personal computers). *See* computers
Pearl button, 60, 81
People Near Me feature. *See also* networks
    defined, 315
    Notification icon, 318
    opening, 315–316
    signing in, 317–318
    user account setup, 316–317
performance boosting. *See* power and
  performance options
Performance Information and Tools window, 414
peripheral devices. *See* devices
Permissions window, 219–220
Personalize Appearance and Sounds window, 41
phishing, defined, 94–95, 131
phishing e-mail, 148–150
Phishing Filter in IE7, 89, 95–97
Phone and Modem Options screen in Fax and
    Scan, 314
Photo Gallery. *See also* Media Center; photos
    burning CDs/DVDs, 383
    defined, 381–382

deleting images, 384
Details panel, 386–387
Display Size button, 384
e-mailing images, 383
File menu, 383
finding files, 382
fixing photos, 383, 388–390
Info button, 383, 386
Make a Movie button, 383
menu bar commands, 382–384
moving between open images, 384
opening, 382
opening other image editors, 384
organizing with tags. *See also* metadata
    adding to multiple images, 387–388
    adding to single images, 385–387
    adding from Windows Explorer, 388
    defined, 383, 384–385
    deleting tags, 388
    Tags menu, 388
    viewing Tag folders, 384, 385
Paint and, 384
Pictures section, 382
Print button, 383
Redo button, 383, 390
Revert button, 390
rotating images, 384
saving edited photos, 390
Slideshow button, 384
Thumbnail Image Reset button, 384
Undo button, 383
Videos section, 382
photos. *See also* video
    cropping snippets, 258–260
    digital cameras and, 381
    scanning, 308–310
    slide show screen savers, 47–49
playlists. *See* Media Player 11
Plug and Play feature, 352, 361
PNG files, 274
Pop-Up Blocker. *See also* Internet Explorer 7
    adjusting settings, 101–102
    always allow pop-ups, 101
    defined, 97, 98
    enabling/disabling, 97–99

R

radio online, 395–396
RAM (random access memory). *See also* memory
    borrowing, 407–410
    defined, 32
    requirements, 7–8
ratings criteria, metadata, 209, 231
ratings, performance, 414, 416
ReadyBoost feature, 407–410, 424
Recorder, Sound, 247–249
recording TV shows, 393–394
Redo button in Photo Gallery, 383, 390
refreshing Web pages, 108
Registry. *See* Windows Registry
Reliability and Performance Monitor. *See also*
  power and performance options; system
  management
    defined, 414, 424
    Learn More section, 417
    opening, 414–415
    Performance Monitor
        adding counters, 418–419
        defined, 417, 424
        removing counters, 419
        versus Resource Overview, 418
    Reliability Monitor, 419–420, 424
    Resource Overview
        CPU usage, 416–417
        defined, 415, 416
        disk I/O transfer, 417
        memory usage/faults, 417
        network data transfer, 417
        versus Performance Monitor, 418
Remote Assistance. *See also* help tools
    connecting computers, 466–468
    defined, 466, 477
    ending sessions, 471
    opening, 468
    security risk of, 471
    sending invitations, 469–470
    setting time limits, 468
    starting sessions, 470–471
Remote Desktop Connection, 471

Removable Disk Properties dialog box, 409
resolution, screen, 375
Restore Hidden Updates option, 28, 141
Restore, System. *See also* system management
    choosing restore points, 444–445
    creating restore points, 443, 446
    defined, 443, 458
    opening, 444
    running, 445
    viruses/malware and, 446
restoring backup data, 440–443
Revert button in Photo Gallery, 390
Rights Management Configuration Wizard,
  216–219
ripping music from CDs, 368, 371–372, 396
rotating images, 384
RSS (Really Simple Syndication) feeds. *See also*
  Favorites Center
    defined, 120, 132
    opening, 122
    removing, 122
    subscribing to, 120–121
    viewing, 122
Run dialog box, 71, 72

S

saving
    edited photos, 390
    files in XPS format, 215
    Meeting Space handout edits, 325
    Notepad files as Web pages, 258
    open Web page tabs, 114–115
    recorded sound, 248
    searches, 207–208
    snippets, 259–260
    Sticky Notes, 251–253
ScanDisk utility, 453–455, 458
scanner drivers, 356
Scanners and Cameras tool, 305–307. *See also*
  Fax and Scan tool
screen resolution, 375
screen savers. *See* desktop
search engines, default, 108

X

Z

Elevate your education.

The L Line puts learning on the express line. Each book gives you a crash course in the skills you need to master concepts and technologies that will advance your career or enhance your options. Discover how quickly you can reach your destination on The Express Line to Learning.

What you'll find on *The L Line*

- Pre-reading questions to help you identify your level of knowledge
- Real-world case studies and applications
- Complete tutorial coverage with plenty of illustrations and examples
- Easy-to-follow directions
- Practice exams that let you evaluate your progress
- Terminology overviews to clarify technical jargon
- Additional online resources

WILEY
Now you know.

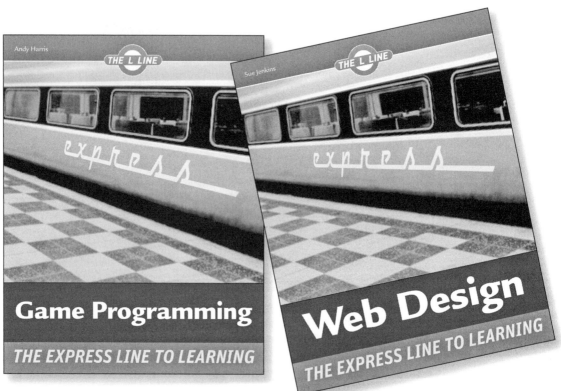

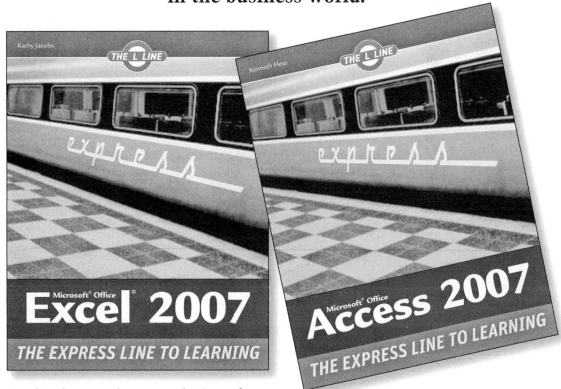

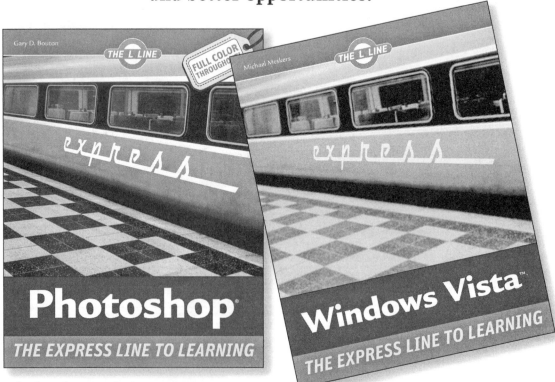